THE DEFENCE LEARNING, EDUCATION AND TRAINING HANDBOOK

D1166737

EDUCATING THE LEADER AND LEADING THE EDUCATED:

The Defence Learning, Education and Training Handbook

EDITED BY:

Colonel Bernd Horn and
Lieutenant-Colonel Jeff Stouffer

CANADIAN DEFENCE ACADEMY PRESS

Canadian Defence Academy Press
PO Box 17000 Stn Forces
Kingston, Ontario   K7K 7B4

Produced for the Canadian Defence Academy Press
by 17 Wing Winnipeg Publishing Office.
WPO30830

Photo Credit: Cpl P.R. Figiel, 17 Wing Imaging

Library and Archives Canada Cataloguing in Publication

Educating the leader and leading the educated : the defence learning, education and training handbook / edited by Bernd Horn and Jeff Stouffer.

Produced for the Canadian Defence Academy Press by 17 Wing Winnipeg Publishing Office.
Includes bibliographical references and an index.
Available also on the Internet.
Issued by: Canadian Defence Academy.
ISBN 978-1-100-21088-9
Cat. no.: D2-309/2-2012E

1. Military education--Canada. 2. Canada--Armed Forces--Officials and employees--Training.
3. Command of troops. I. Stouffer, Jeffrey M., 1962- II. Horn, Bernd, 1959- III. Canadian Defence Academy IV. Canada. Canadian Armed Forces. Wing, 17 V. Title: Defence learning, education and training handbook.

U440 E38 2013   355.50971   C2012-980217-4

Printed in Canada.
1 3 5 7 9 10 8 6 4 2

ACKNOWLEDGEMENTS

Educating the Leader and Leading the Educated: The Defence Learning, Education and Training Handbook represents a significant effort of a diverse group of researchers, educators, and military personnel dedicated to the improvement and continued development of the Canadian Forces professional development system. As such, this volume is a significant addition to the body of Canadian defence literature and will be invaluable to members of, or those who interact with, the profession of arms. To this end, we would like to thank each of the contributing authors, not only for their various chapters, but also for their willingness to voluntarily participate in the success of this publication. A special thanks is also extended to Dr. Bill Bentley, Dr. Robert Walker and Colonel Dalton Cote who helped develop and steer this project during its early stages.

We would like to express our fullest appreciation and gratitude to Melanie Denis of the Canadian Defence Academy Press for the superb production and technical support provided throughout this project. As with previous CDA publications, our appreciation is also extended to the 17 Wing Publishing Office who, without doubt, helped transform a rough manuscript into a highly professional product.

FOREWORD

Leadership in the challenging security environment of the 21st century is critically dependent on learning, education and training. The cognitive knowledge and specialized skills acquired through these processes are honed and embedded through experience tempered by professional judgement. Leaders, in turn, must ensure that the development of the next generation occurs in accordance with these closely linked activities. Although war and conflict have always been complex, unpredictable phenomena, in today's globalized world infused with rapidly advancing high technology, change is ubiquitous and new and diverse conflict scenarios constantly arise.

Furthermore, today's conflict situations invariably call for an integrated Whole of Government approach to seek viable political solutions, an assumption underlying this "Handbook". With this in mind, professional military leaders, leaders in the professional Public Service and their subordinates are well advised to understand what the noted strategic theorist and social critic Alvin Toffler meant when he observed that the illiterates of the 21st century won't be those who can't read or write. He argued, illiterates will be those who can't learn – unlearn – re-learn.[1] The DND civilian and CF Professional Development Systems will need to be constantly monitored to ensure that they reflect this essential cycle. In essence, this means that learning must be accorded at least equal weight as knowing, sense-making must precede decision-making, and emergent or systems thinking will take precedence over linear, reductionist thinking based on estimates.

Educating the Leader and Leading the Educated: The Defence Learning, Education and Training Handbook addresses these issues from a number of perspectives from the practical to the theoretical and from the tactical to the strategic levels. The chapters in the "Handbook" were written by a group of accomplished authors representing years of experience in the military, the Public Service and the professional education field more generally. All members of the Defence Team, civilian and military, are strongly encouraged to utilize the "Handbook"

---

1   Quoted in Christopher Paparone, "Where Military Professionalism Meets Complexity Science", *Armed Forces and Society*, Vol. 34, No. 3 (April 2008), 435.

FOREWORD

both for their personal edification, as well as to assist in the construction of all components of the broader professional development system for which they are responsible.

P.J. Forgues
Major-General
Commander
Canadian Defence Academy

Cynthia L. Binnington
Assistant Deputy Minister
Human Resources – Civilian

TABLE OF CONTENTS

iii

TABLE OF CONTENTS

TABLE OF CONTENTS

INTRODUCTION

"The society that separates its scholars from its warriors will have its thinking done by cowards and its fighting done by fools."
Thucydides[1]

No one likes to fail. This is not surprising, after all failure normally carries negative sanctions. But, nowhere is failure more abhorred than in the profession of arms. For in the military, failure means death and/or potentially severe national political consequence.

It is for this reason that militaries invest so much time, effort and money in training. Training defined roughly as a predictable response to a predictable situation, prepares individuals for anticipated events. It ensures as much as possible that individuals provide predictable responses (i.e. conduct the proper drills in a given situation) and achieve positive outcomes. Most, if not all military personnel understand training and its value.

The same is not true of education. Education is squishy, even ethereal in many ways. It deals with creativity, critical thinking and reasoning. It is difficult to measure how education, defined by Professor Ron Haycock as "the reasoned response to an unpredictable situation – critical thinking in the face of the unknown,"[2] actually improves performance. Unlike training where one can measure efficacy in conducting drills (i.e. show improvement with regard to less errors or faster times) or marksmanship scores, or better fitness scores, the same is not true for education.

How does one measure improvement in reasoning skills or the ability to better understand the implications of action in a socio/political context, or adapt behaviour to better turn the "hearts and minds" of a local population in a theatre of operations. Although not fully understood, education is critical to the military. After all, education, rooted in critical thinking, problem solving and analytical research, better prepares individuals to think, as well as cope with problems and situations that are unexpected. It assists individuals not only to embrace change, but adapt to and anticipate it. More importantly, education instils in people the attitude and ability to constantly learn from one's environment and to prepare, as well as react, accordingly. "Without the mature judgement which flows from

INTRODUCTION

education," observed Dr. John Cowan, a former principal of the Royal Military College of Canada, "we fall back on reflexes, which are damned fine things for handling known challenges, but which are manifestly unreliable when faced with new ones."[3]

In addition to the importance and complexity of training and education is the matter of learning and the learner. The Department of National Defence (DND) and the Canadian Forces (CF) are still largely into a "bricks and mortar" classroom paradigm of saturating students with Microsoft PowerPoint presentations. Only slowly are DND and the CF beginning to realize and adjust for the varied demographics of learners who react differently to stimuli.

But DND and the CF must adjust and move forward. They must strive to place as much emphasis on education as they do training. And, they must do so focusing specifically on the learner. This handbook is designed to assist with that continuing effort. *Educating the Leader and Leading the Educated: The Defence Learning, Education and Training Handbook* is a collection of essays on pertinent issues dealing with education and training in the military context. Essays deal specifically with key topics such as:

1. The importance of education;
2. Learning and the learner;
3. DND/ CF education and training processes and policies; and
4. Current and future concepts of education and training in DND / CF.

In essence, this volume covers a vast array of information and knowledge on topics of importance for those involved with, or simply interested in, education and training in the military context.

---

1   Cited in Joan Johnson-Freese, "Teach Tough, Think Tough: Why Military Education Must Change." AOL.Defense, <http://defense.aol.com>, accessed 4 July 2011.

2   Dr. Ronald Haycock, former Dean of Arts, Royal Military College (RMC), "Clio and Mars in Canada: The Need for Military Education," presentation to the Canadian Club, Kingston, Ontario, 11 November 1999.

3   Dr. John Scott Cowan, RMC Convocation Address, 4 October 1999, Kingston, Ontario. See also Eliot Cohen and John Gooch, *Military Misfortunes. The Anatomy of Failure in War* (New York: Vintage Books, 1991), 233-237.

PART I

HISTORY AND THEORY

CHAPTER 1

WARRIOR / SCHOLAR: A CRITICAL UNION IN THE CONTEMPORARY OPERATING ENVIRONMENT

Colonel Bernd Horn

Intuitively, virtually no-one would argue that more education is a bad thing. In fact, most would agree that, as a philosophical concept, the more education one has, the richer one is as a person. However, the moment resources or cost enter the equation, the value of education to individuals and organizations often changes. Nowhere is this more evident than in the military where fiscal pressures inevitably prompt "innovative ideas" that often revolve around cutting professional development, specifically, education. Moreover, these same pressures consistently elicit queries with regard to the value of education, specifically undergraduate and graduate degrees, to the military. Questions such as "Do all officers need degrees?" and "What is the military requirement for graduate degrees?" are frequently floated as a precursor to potential program cuts.

Although the military has historically been an anti-intellectual institution, such discourse seems incredulous considering the contemporary operating environment (COE), which, if anything, will become even more complex in the future. Globalization and persistent conflict, as well as the proliferation of cheap, accessible technology, challenge conventional understanding of conflict. Moreover, hybrid threats that include diverse combinations of irregular, terrorist, criminal, and conventional forces employed asymmetrically, all operating within populated centres in a variety of culturally diverse environments, are just some of the challenges that have added complexity to conflict. In order to be effective in this environment, military professionals must be adaptive and agile in both thought and action, as well as adept at critical thinking and sound reasoning – all benefits of education. In short, militaries require warrior/scholars who are capable of operating in the complex battlespace of today and tomorrow.

A Culture of Anti-Intellectualism?

However, this is often easier said than done. The reluctance of militaries to embrace the concept of warrior/scholar, or the importance of education for that matter, is not surprising. The conventional military mind is conservative, functional and skeptical. Above all else, it utilizes experience as the key filter to determine what is possible, what is useful and often what is considered true and real. This is not to denigrate experience, since actual observation of facts or events, as well as the knowledge and/or skill resulting from this, are powerful teachers. Moreover, experience builds confidence, as well as individual and group competence. Quite simply, experience is empirical and tangible; decisions were made, actions were taken and the results were seen if not felt. Rightfully, the military culture reveres and recognizes the experience of individuals. Campaign ribbons, qualification and specialty badges and long service medals provide an instant recognition of an individual's experience and, more often than not, bestow a degree of credibility upon the bearer.

While there is nothing inherently wrong with this approach, it can be dangerous when coupled with overt "anti-intellectualism". Experience is recognized as a critical developmental tool for officers and soldiers. In a crisis, any rational person would prefer to be led by, or teamed with, someone who has previously been tested or has faced a similar menace successfully. However, the military's traditional myopic reliance on experience as the preferred, if not exclusive, professional development tool has arguably created and perpetuated an attitude that has historically shunned intellectualism and scholarship as a useful skill set for officers and soldiers.[1] It is far from unique to state that the military is largely anti-intellectual. Former CF officer, Dr. Sandy Cotton, noted, "Having studied and written and talked to the military culture in Canada for 30-plus years, I would have to say that there is an intellectual stagnation, in some cases an anti-intellectualism."[2] In fact, there appears to be a default mechanism that rejects the concept that warriors can also be scholars.

Recent experience bears this out. The tumultuous decade of the 1990s in many respects ripped the CF asunder. The institution as a whole lost the trust of both the public and the government as a result of a series of scandals that demonstrated an apparent lack of ethical behaviour and leadership, as well as an inability to adapt to, or cope with, significant changes in society and military affairs. This appalling situation led to an in-depth examination of the CF. Tellingly, the review was not entrusted to the institution itself but rather to an external board of inquiry, as well as an array of academics and scholars. One factor that was repeatedly criticized was the absence of intellectual rigour and the lack of higher education in the officer corps.

This should not have been a big surprise. Higher education has never been an important component of officership in the CF, particularly not during the Cold War. Theoretical musings and historical studies, much less a grounding in the liberal arts, were perceived as suspect and downright unsoldierlike. Marshal of France, Herman Maurice Count de Saxe, mused, "War is a science so obscure and imperfect that custom and prejudice confirmed by ignorance are its sole foundation and support." Simply put, scholarly pursuit was anathema to the true warrior. This attitude was rooted in CF culture. To be fair it is a criticism that universally fits most militaries.

Respected British historian Sir Michael Howard reinforced the observation. "It is not surprising that there have often been a high proportion of failures among senior commanders at the beginning of any war," he asserted. Howard noted, "These unfortunate men may either take too long to adjust themselves to reality, through a lack of hard preliminary thinking about what war would really be like, or they may have had their minds so far shaped by a lifetime of pure administration that they have ceased for all practical purposes to be soldiers."[3] He argued, "Like the statesman, the soldier has to steer between the danger of repeating the errors of the past because he is ignorant that they have been made, and the danger of remaining bound by theories deduced from past history although changes in conditions have rendered these theories obsolete."[4]

Howard's observations boil down to the lack of importance the military places on education and intellectualism. Norman Dixon, in his seminal work, *On the Psychology of Military Incompetence*, wrote:

> Whether or not intellectual shortcomings lie at the heart of much military incompetence, the fact that a deliberate cult of anti-intellectualism has characterized the armed services. While its origins relate, as we shall see, to much deeper reasons for military mishaps than mere ignorance or slowness of mind, the fact remains that its effects have not been helpful. That generals and admirals between the wars denigrated progressive thinkers and poured scorn on men who wrote books which

challenged existing practices must surely have tended to stifle any exercise of intellect by those who wanted to get on, and deterred the gifted from ever seeking a military career. As Robert McNamara once remarked, "Brains are like hearts, they go where they're appreciated.[5]

Nonetheless, as already stated, anti-intellectualism was endemic to the CF. Although catastrophic events in the 1990s forced a change, arguably anti-intellectualism remains an undercurrent percolating below the surface. Dr. Cotton observed, "officers are generally quite conservative beings, and so are NCOs [non-commissioned officers]….on the social dimension they're profoundly conservative, [and] resistant to change." He insisted, "They tend to get a mindset that locks into certain ways of doing things."[6] It is widely recognized that culture is influenced by what is paid attention to, controlled and rewarded. Cultural values in turn define who we are and what is acceptable thought and behaviour. As a result, the rampant anti-intellectualism that was clearly present ensured that the divide between warrior and scholar remained a deep chasm. The former Chief of the Defence Staff (CDS), General Maurice Baril, conceded, "Our approach over the last twenty-five years has focused almost exclusively on the practical side." He stated, "In the arena of officer education for example, there was little opportunity or encouragement for officers to undertake academic study." Baril acknowledged, "It was generally accepted that to take time out for post graduate work was detrimental to your career."[7]

But once again, this admission is not a startling revelation. The attitude was prevalent and overt and could be seen and heard throughout the CF. Streamers, that is those identified with great career potential and destined to attain the highest rungs of the corporate ladder, were normally not posted to schools or required to take time out to attain bachelor, much less graduate degrees, if they were lacking. Those who showed an inclination to pursue higher education had to do so on their own and were still often seen as suspect and their loyalty questioned. Graduate training was seen as self-serving and a step towards preparing an individual for employment on the "dark side," namely, the civilian sector. Predictably, actively seeking higher education became debilitating to one's career.

Paradoxically, the few sponsored graduate education billets that were available were normally given to those on the bottom of the merit list who were nearing the end of their career.[8] Rather than use the opportunity to prepare the future corporate leadership to better command the institution, it was used as a consolation prize, a reward to some of the long serving members who failed to attain high rank. Graduate studies were viewed as an effort to allow those individuals to pad their CVs and prepare them for their second career. The only other accepted rationale for graduate education was to fill a particular requirement, normally a very technical domain such as aerospace engineering. In 1988, Lieutenant-General R.J. Evraire wrote that higher education was not conceived as a way to develop the minds of officers; rather it was a task-oriented function to acquire a skill for which there was an obvious and immediate need, mostly in technical areas.[9]

Annual Personnel Evaluation Reports (PERs) were yearly reminders of the culture's lack of respect for higher learning.[10] Education was of little consequence. It was just not seen as an important component of the military. The successful completion of a Ranger course, not to denigrate its value for tactical training or as a test of personal stamina, was of greater value to a member's future progression than was the attainment of partial or complete fulfillment of a degree. In addition, when rating personal attributes, whenever scoring limitations precluded a high grading for all attributes, intellect would often be sacrificed for categories such as loyalty and deportment, which were perceived as much more important.

Should there be any doubt of the CF's historic culture of anti-intellectualism then one need only look at the composition of its officer corps. In March of 1997, the renowned Canadian military historian, Dr. Jack Granatstein, reported to the Minister of National Defence (MND) that "the CF has a remarkably ill-educated officer corps, surely one of the worst in the Western World." He pointed out that only 53.29 percent of officers had a university degree and only an abject 6.79 percent had graduate degrees, and these primarily in technical areas.[11] Similarly, professor Albert Legault was equally scathing. "The level of education in the Armed Forces," he argued, "is particularly lacking within the framework of a democracy that thinks of itself as a model or example within the Western world."[12] Former serving officer and current military historian, Desmond Morton, another of the former MND's hand-picked consultants in 1997, asserted, "when one Canadian in five completes such a degree [bachelor degree] or its equivalent, this is no longer an elitist pre-requisite for a commission in Canada's armed forces. No self-professed profession would accept less."[13]

It was the gut wrenching analysis of the 1990s that highlighted the importance of education to the philosophical and real health of the CF. As such, a virtual phoenix arose from the ashes of the "decade of darkness" and its myriad of financial, social, operational and leadership challenges. In fact, a large a number of reforms that included: ministerial direction that all officers must hold a recognized undergraduate degree; the CDS appointment of a Special Advisor to the Office of the CDS for Professional Development; the creation of the *Canadian Military Journal* to allow a forum for professional discourse; the creation of a Canadian "war college" course; and the establishment of a Canadian Defence Academy to provide a centre of excellence for CF professional development, to name a few, were all indications that the CF apparently recognized its anti-intellectualism and failure to ensure its personnel received the required education to complement their training.

However, the long bitter war in Afghanistan has once again placed a premium on experience. Moreover, financial pressures have begun to stall, and arguably, even reverse the progress made in the realm of professional development, specifically higher learning. The CF once again seems to be slipping back to its preferred experiential paradigm, which marginalizes the importance of education.[14]

The Future Operating Environment

This apparent retrograde action is disconcerting. After all, in the complex security environment of today and tomorrow, increasingly, education is exactly what is required; education that can put training into the proper context of the particular situation that military personnel may find themselves facing. And, few would argue that we will not continue to face a complex, uncertain, at times ambiguous, but ever volatile, security environment in the future.

The need for education is virtually self-explanatory. After all, the future will remain largely unpredictable. Conflicts will invariably involve adaptive, dispersed operations against adversaries that are themselves adaptive, agile, networked and innovative. The West will face hybrid threats that will require new solutions and approaches. Geopolitical uncertainties, rapid technological developments and the proliferation of technology and weapons of mass destruction (including chemical, biological, radiological and nuclear (CBRN)) will exacerbate the complexity and threat. In addition, continued social and political instability fuelled by rampant urbanization, competition over scarce resources (e.g. water, food, fuel and other market commodities), climate change and pandemics will feed further disintegration of social order and global stability.

The consequence of that instability will lead to: illicit economic exploitation, the proliferation of weapons, the creation of terrorist training and/or staging bases, criminal activity including trade in drugs and humans, as well as the consequence of population migration and social and political instability, to name a few. The state of global affairs will also continue to invigorate international terrorism, which will continue to grow leaving no nation including Canada immune. The threat may become more potent as it becomes more and more difficult to determine who in fact we are fighting. In the future the enemy will often have no clear identity as groups such as Al-Qaeda become more of an ideology rather than a physical organization and morph into a network of networks. In addition, increasing numbers of trained and experienced veteran jihadist fighters returning to their native lands will increase the lethality and sophistication of attacks over progressively larger areas. This trend will also see the threat becoming increasingly more insidious as "home-grown" terrorists who become radicalized on the internet, or extremist institutions within Western industrialized states, lash out at their own societies.

Terrorism itself will continue to evolve as a tactic and a strategy, as well as a way of life – all at the same time. Our enemies will have both virtual (i.e. the internet) and physical (e.g. failed and failing states, rogue state sponsor) sanctuaries. These terrorist networks will behave like a virus, constantly changing and adapting. Terrorist cells will divide, proliferate and separate. Terrorist threats will emanate from individuals or cells, often with no linkage to a greater command node. In the future, our adversaries will be fluid and independent and physically disconnected (i.e. meet on the internet where they will draw motivation and inspiration.) They will employ asymmetric strategies in attacks that combine mass bloodshed and economic impact. They will continue to use the tactics of criminality, terrorism and guerrilla warfare in the pursuit of their objectives and will further refine innovative disruptive techniques as well as more traditional methodologies that include suicide bombings, improvised explosive devices and mass casualty events.

The success of the international terrorist networks will be a function of their effective exploitation of globalization (e.g. telecommunications, financing, internet interconnectivity for information operations and sharing lessons learned, techniques, tactics and procedures), as well as the proliferation of cheap technology to enhance their capacity and reach. These organizations will increasingly be networked, multi-layered and complex entities capable of detailed operational planning, synchronization and execution. They will continually learn from their collective experience and will constantly adapt and change, thus, becoming more complex, sophisticated and dangerous.

Importantly, the future threat will be increasingly irregular, if not ethereal, and adversaries will utilize asymmetric methods to conduct persistent conflict and war. We are currently, and will continue to be into the future, in a war of conflicting ideas, ideology and social values against an enemy that is capable of hiding in, and utilizing the rights, freedoms and protections of the very societies that they seek to destroy. The adversaries we face are ideologically, religiously and criminally driven as well as globally networked. Against this new and evolving threat, conventional military responses alone are challenged to bring resolution and rapid effects. In this battlespace kinetic solutions are exponentially less effective and important than non-kinetic methodologies focused on influence, deterrence, information management and exploitation, as well as intelligence.

In addition, the continuing ubiquitous presence of the global media will further challenge military personnel. Instantaneous feeds from operational areas around the globe direct into the living rooms of civilians worldwide in real time (i.e. the CNN effect) will continue to catapult seemingly innocuous tactical situations on the ground to strategic significance. The reporting of ostensibly minor events will have the potential to generate hostility around the world and create international incidents for domestic governments if the actions or words are construed as disrespectful or unnecessary (particularly if taken out of context).

In this ambiguous, complex, volatile and politically, as well as culturally, sensitive environment, traditional approaches, mindsets and responses are increasingly less effective or even acceptable. The U.S. Army has recognized that its competitive advantage is directly related to its capacity to learn faster and adapt more quickly than its adversaries. As such, it hopes to "sustain a capacity for accelerated learning that extends from organizational levels of learning to the individual soldier whose knowledge, skills, and abilities are tested in the most unforgiving environments."[15] In short, there is a recognition that everyone working in the security environment will require new competencies, but especially increased education, to remain effective.

Warrior/Scholar

So the question emerges, can, or should, a soldier also be scholar? The apparent predilection for anti-intellectualism in the military, as well as time and resource constraints aside, there is an intuitive understanding of why the military mind would focus on training and experience rather than education. After all, education is not tangible. Unlike training where quantifiable improvements in behaviour and technical prowess can be physically seen, for instance marksmanship scores or proficiency in drills, education is less evident in tangible form. It deals with creativity, critical thinking and reasoning.[16] These qualities are not always outwardly observable. Furthermore, when many in the senior leadership achieved their rank and position without graduate level university education, why should they emphasis such a requirement, a requirement that could be construed as a shortcoming in their personal circumstances and one that did not apparently prevent them from attaining success.

This attitude continues to exist as a result of a complete ignorance with regard to the importance of education to the military profession. Firstly, there still appears to be a lack of understanding of the difference between training and education. The traditional stress on training, that is "a predictable response to a predictable situation," is often confused with or considered synonymous with education, defined by Professor Ron Haycock as "the reasoned response to an unpredictable situation – critical thinking in the face of the unknown."[17] Because of the CF's excellent training regime and its current success on operations in Afghanistan, it is easy to be lulled into a perception that believes that the institution's educational needs are quite adequately looked after. What is overlooked, at great peril, is that the prescribed application of ideas and methods, as well as drills and checklists, have a purpose and functional utility, but this methodology is no longer, if in fact it ever was, enough to equip leaders to cope with and function in the complex post modern world.

Simply put, "education," according to Royal Military College of Canada (RMCC) Professor David Last, a former artillery senior officer, "is the shaping of the mind."[18] Education assists in our reasoning ability, which in turn is critical in responding to unanticipated circumstances. After all, as the adage goes, you train for certainty and educate for uncertainty. As the former Commander of the Canadian Defence Academy noted, "The method to get better at what you do is to educate yourself beyond the training you do."[19] In the end, it's about

CHAPTER 1

learning, that is, "the acquisition of new knowledge and ideas that change the way an individual perceives, understands, or acts."[20] This is crucial to soldiers and senior NCOs and particularly officers.

Equally important are the need to understand, and ability to place, the CF's ultimate purpose and its operations within the context of the larger whole and the society it serves. The French emperor Napoleon Bonaparte already recognized in the 19th century that "Tactics, evolutions, artillery and engineer sciences can be learned from a manual like geometry; but the knowledge of the higher conduct of war can only be acquired by studying the history of wars and battles of great generals and by one's own experience." He understood, "There are no terse and precise rules at all."[21] In the end, neither the CF, nor any of its components, exist in and of themselves.[22]

The requirement to comprehend "the larger picture" cannot be understated.[23] "Professional officers," asserts Professor Last, "are managers of violence." He further explains:

> Their professional education must allow them to understand it. Violence has always been a part of the interconnected human conditions that we label war, conflict, and peace. In the complex world of today and tomorrow, our understanding of these conditions needs to be more comprehensive than in the past. This is more important than technology, doctrine, and strategy, because all are subservient to purpose. There is no purpose without understanding. The officer's understanding must match that of society – otherwise he or she cannot serve it.[24]

This societal connection has another, equally important, dimension. The Canadian Military Ethos demands that the CF remain rooted in Canadian society and reflect its most important values and attitudes. In this regard it is critical to understand that, as Ambassador Paul Heinbecker points out: "we are an extensively educated people."[25] Of the thirty-three most industrialized economies surveyed by the Organization for Economic Co-operation and Development (OECD), Canada ranked second behind Russia (Japan was third and the US fourth) in the percentage of the population that has attained at least a university or college-level education. The CF must remain very reflective of this leading edge sector of Canadian society if we are to retain the trust, confidence and respect necessary to maintain the essential support of all Canadian citizens.

In addition, the importance of education to the military profession, particularly in the post modern world should be self-evident, especially in light of the series of crises that the CF endured during the cataclysmic decade of the 1990s.[26] Paradoxically, it was recognized as early as 1969, by then-CDS General Jean Victor Allard. "It matters little," he wrote, "whether the Forces have their present manpower strength and financial budget, or half of them, or double them; without a properly educated, effectively trained professional officer corps the Forces would, in the future, be doomed at best to mediocrity, and at the worst, to disaster."[27]

Intuitively, a professional soldier is better prepared to face the unknown challenges of the ambiguous, complex and uncertain battlespace by having a broad knowledge of theories that act as a guide to discretionary judgment rather than a narrow ability in only some of the practical applications of the profession of arms. As one expert concluded, "strategic effectiveness will increasingly be based on the capacity to think like a networked enemy. Therefore, the military strategist needs to understand a complex environment and a diverse range of interests, actors and issues while retaining the capacity to "simplify, focus, decide and execute."[28] Retired American Major-General Robert H. Scales underlined the need for education vice training when he commented, "This new era of war requires soldiers equipped with exceptional cultural awareness and an intuitive sense for the nature and character of war."[29]

The need for education in today's complex security environment is repeatedly stressed by practitioners who through the experience in the chaos of conflict clearly understand that education, rooted in critical thinking, problem solving and analytical research, better prepares individuals to think, as well as cope with problems and situations that are unexpected. It assists individuals to not only embrace change, but adapt to and anticipate it. More importantly, it instills in people the attitude and ability to constantly learn from one's environment and to prepare, as well as react, accordingly. Colonel John Boyd stripped it down to its simplest form. He asserted, "Machines don't fight wars. Terrain doesn't fight wars. Humans fight wars." As such he concluded, "You must get in the minds of the humans. That's where the battles are won."[30]

And, education is the domain of the human mind. Sir Michael Howard wrote:

> ...academic studies can provide the knowledge, insight, and the analytic skills which provide the necessary basis, first for reasoned

discussion, and then for action. They provide a forum, and breed the qualities, which enable the student, the teacher, the politician, the civil servant, the moral philosopher, and not least the soldier to reach a common understanding of the problems which confront them, even if inevitably there is disagreement about the solutions. This dialogue is what civilization is all about. Without it societies dissolve.[31]

Similarly, closer to home, Dr. John Cowan, a former Principal of RMCC, reinforced the necessity of education in relation to the military. "Today, when a young officer may be called upon to be a skilled leader, a technical expert, a diplomat, a warrior, and even an interpreter and an aid expert all at once," he insisted, "there is no question that good training is not enough. Skills are not enough." He added, "The job calls for judgement, that odd distillate of education, the thing which is left when the memorized facts have either fled or been smoothed into a point of view, the thing that cannot be taught directly, but which must be learned. Without the mature judgement which flows from education, we fall back on reflexes, which are damned fine things for handling known challenges, but which are manifestly unreliable when faced with new ones."[32]

Needless to say, as Cowan affirms, there will always be new challenges. This was reinforced by Lieutenant-General Andrew Leslie, a former deputy commander of the International Security Assistance Force in Afghanistan. "Individuals were sent home [from Afghanistan]," revealed Leslie, "Immaturity and the inability to actually think outside the box made them ineffective ... What they tried to do was bring their usually very limited experience from somewhere else and apply it the same way that it had been done somewhere else and that didn't work ... each mission has got its own unique drivers, cultural conditions, local nuances, relationships with your other allies or other combatants."[33]

Leslie's observation is undisputable. Up until recently the common complaint of any deploying body was that they were prepared for the last deployment not the situation that they faced. But, you don't know what you don't know. Therefore, a culture absorbed solely by experience, whether in the former decades with a reliance on the 4 Canadian Mechanized Brigade Group (CMBG) experience of preparing to beat back the Soviet hordes at the Fulda Gap in Germany; or more currently on the Afghanistan experience of fighting the elusive Taliban in Kandahar Province, is oblivious to the value, if not necessity of higher education.

However, General David Petraeus, accomplished soldier and veteran of years of combat in Iraq and former commander of North Atlantic Treaty Organization (NATO) forces in Afghanistan, supports the need for greater education, particularly graduate studies for senior officers. He affirms "that a stint at graduate school takes military officers out of their intellectual comfort zones." Petraeus believes, "Such experiences are critical to the development of the flexible, adaptable, creative thinkers who are so important to operations in places like Iraq and Afghanistan."[34] He explains that "through such schooling our officers are often surprised to discover just how diverse and divergent views can be. We only thought we knew the contours of debate on a given subject."[35] Petraeus concluded that graduate studies "provide a fair amount of general intellectual capital and often provides specific skills and knowledge on which an officer may draw during his or her career."[36] Moreover, he argued, "graduate school inevitably helps U.S. military officers improve their critical thinking skills."[37]

And so, if experience once again becomes the primary discriminator for advancement, and higher education is again deemed inconsequential, the CF will return to a system where emphasis is placed on progression in a series of key appointments and geographic postings, most notably Afghanistan. As such, successful completion of these tours then once again becomes perceived as sufficient to prepare an individual for the next higher rank and responsibilities.

Unfortunately, this type of myopic outlook and inward focused mind-set fails to see the inherent flaw of this model. Experience in itself is valuable and irreplaceable. But it is also constrained by time, geography and memory. One person's experience, particularly at a specific time and place, does not necessarily represent the knowledge or abilities that are needed for an institution to advance into the future. Moreover, the perspective from a shell-hole, turret or command post is so very limited. Service needs become defined in and of themselves without being rooted in their proper societal context. But most of all, a system that values experience as the only true arbitrator of reality suffers from human arrogance and frailty. "We see," wrote Major Seiberg in the mid-1930s, "that the Spanish Civil War has up to now demonstrated nothing really new, and also that men only regard experience as valid when it is their own experience. Otherwise it would not be possible for the same errors that led to failure in the Great War to be repeated."[38] Simply put, those who refuse to open their minds are doomed to suffer the limitations of their narrow, restricted and outdated beliefs.

The truth in this condemnation of professional development based almost exclusively on the experiential paradigm settled home in the 1990s. "Undeniably,"
wrote General Baril, "the 1990s represented the first strong test of the contemporary CF Officer Corps and we found that part of it was broken." He concluded,
"Experience in and of itself was not enough."[39] He later acknowledged that "over
the past 10 years ... we constantly found ourselves thrown into the unknown.
Complex, ambiguous and politically charged operations tested our leadership
and confronted us with ethical dilemmas." Baril further conceded, "here at home
we were slow to understand and adapt to the large-scale societal changes associated with the end of the Cold War and therefore were not prepared for these
demands."[40]

Quite simply, the warning previously given by General Allard well over two decades earlier went unheeded. As a result, his prophecy came to pass. The pre-
dicament was aptly summarized by a former Army Commander, Lieutenant-
General M.K. Jeffery. He believed, "the lack of intellectual discipline in the past
has got us where we are today [1990s]. If we don't change we will die." He added,
"the longer we resist it, the harder we make it on someone else."[41] One former
CDS insisted, "Officers need to have the right mindset to change and evolve the
profession." He added, "knowledge must be valued as a key ingredient to our
growth as individuals and as a profession."[42] After all, as American General David
Petraeus correctly identified, "The most powerful tool any soldier carries is not
his weapon but his mind."[43]

In the end, every member of the profession of arms must guard against slipping
back to old mindsets and ensure that they are ready to meet the challenges
that face them not only today but also into the future. So can a warrior also be
a scholar? The answer is definitely yes. The many tenets of scholarship, namely
precision, detailed research, communications, breadth of knowledge, placing
events in a proper economic, political and social context, drawing conclusions
and trying to discern themes therefrom, committing those to paper and then
articulating them so that others can understand the argument put forward and
learn from it, are all skills that are necessary for a soldier.

Equally important, this type of study provides vicarious experience. As already
explained, experience is seen as sacrosanct and great emphasis is rightfully
placed on it. But, due to real life limitations, experience is often constrained by
time and place. Scholarship, on the other hand, allows its virtual experience to

be timeless and cover a wider breadth of activity and circumstance. It provides soldiers with a greater repertoire of scenarios, possible solutions and context from which to draw.

The warrior scholar also contributes to the academic study by providing an intangible element to the understanding of past events. The plight of the soldier, the confusion, desperation, fatigue, fear and loneliness, in short Carl von Clausewitz's friction that is experienced at every level adds to the comprehension of past events. Those who have experienced it first hand can understand and possibly offer a more accurate interpretation of historical events by being able to draw on their own experience. Conversely, the study of the past and a scholarly analysis of why things went wrong may assist the warrior in trying to mitigate a repetition by using intellectual skill to control, correct or manage as many of those faults as possible.

Furthermore, education arms the warrior with the ability to deal with the ambiguity and complexity that our soldiers face in the battlespace of today and tomorrow. Beyond the practical there is also the intangible. That is to say, a greater breadth of knowledge, tolerance to alternate interpretations and ideas, a comfort with critical debate and discussion, the honing of analytical skills, as well as the exposure to completely new bodies of literature and thought that expand the mind just make the warrior that much more capable. General Petraeus pronounced, "The future of the U.S. military requires that we be competent warfighters, but we cannot be competent warfighters unless we are as intelligent and mentally tough as we are aggressive and physically rugged."[44] It is no different for the Canadian Forces.

So, is the warrior scholar an irreconcilable divide? Absolutely not! Unfortunately, these two entities have for too long remained divided, when in fact they should be fused to strengthen both disciplines.

---

1   Professional development is normally recognized as a combination of education, training, experience and self-development.

2   Charles "Sandy" Cotton in John Wood (ed.), *Talking Heads Talking Arms: No Life Jackets* (Toronto: Breakout Educational Network, 2003), 176. Cotton observed, "It is very, very rare for an officer with an advanced graduate degree, particularly at the doctoral level in Canada, to rise above the rank of lieutenant-colonel. Contrary to the United States for example."

3   Michael Howard, "The Use and Abuse of Military History", *The Army Doctrine and Training Bulletin* (Summer 2003), 21.

4   Ibid., 21.

5   Norman Dixon, *On the Psychology of Military Incompetence* (London: Pimlico, 1994), 161.

6   Cotton, 172.

7   General Maurice Baril, "Officership: A Personal Reflection" in Bernd Horn and Stephen Harris, eds., *Generalship and the Art of the Admiral* (St. Catharines: Vanwell Press, 2001), 139.

8   For those who served during the 1980 and 1990s this statement is not a revelation. John Fraser, the Chairman of the Minister's Monitoring Committee expressed of the period, "a lot of [senior] officers felt it wasn't important to have a degree." John Fraser, interview with Dr. Bill Bentley and Colonel Bernd Horn, 21 February 2011. Former CDS, General Ray Henault admitted, "I remember the days when a person with a Masters or PhD were not considered warriors – they were seen as having gone over to the other side." General (retired) Ray Henault, interview with Dr. Bill Bentley and Colonel Bernd Horn, 9 November 2010.

9   Lieutenant-General R.J. Evraire, *General and Senior Officers Professional Development in the Canadian Forces*, October 1988, 75. The anti-intellectual attitude was not restricted to merely higher education. Equally telling was the lack of tolerance for new ideas, criticism or self-examination. Conformity and loyalty were valued over intellect and critical thinking. Challenging the prevailing beliefs and pushing the envelope on future developments were not career enhancing. Innovation may have been applauded, but conformity was consistently rewarded.

10   The whole issue of the subjective nature of PERs can be summed up by Lord Palmerston's comment, "Merit? The opinion one man holds of another." See John A. English, *Lament for an Army* (Toronto: Irwin Publishing, 1998), 55. See also Brigadier-General Ken Hague, "Strategic Thinking General / Flag Officers: The Role of Education," in Bernd Horn and Stephen Harris, eds., *Generalship and the Art of the Admiral* (St. Catherines: Vanwell Press, 2001), 516-517.

11   Jack Granatstein, *A Paper Prepared for the Minister of National Defence by Dr. J.L. Granatstein Canadian Institute of International Affairs*, 25 March 1997, 19.

12   Albert Legault, *A Paper Prepared for the Minister of National Defence by Professor Albert Legault Laval University*, 25 March 1997, 40.

13   Desmond Morton, *A Paper Prepared for the Minister of National Defence by Desmond Morton McGill Institute for the Study of Canada*, 25 March 1997, 23-24.

14   This statement is admittedly somewhat subjective as there is no "smoking gun" directive that underscores this statement. However, one need only look at the high number of requests for equivalency for Development Period 4 (senior officer) courses; the efforts to develop easily achievable accreditation options for those senior officers lacking requisite education; the reinstitution of programs to enroll officers without degrees; the efforts of the environmental commands to repeal the need for officers to hold degrees, and the pressures to achieve savings through the elimination or curtailment of educational programs. A former CDS who served during the 1990s, upon hearing these indicators, conceded it represented a disturbing backwards trend.

15   United States of America, Department of the Army, *The Army Learning Concepts for 2015*. DRAFT. 20 April, 2010, 1.

16   "Creativity is critical requirement for adaptation. We need creativity because: When things change and new information comes into existence, it's no longer possible to solve current problems with yesterday's solutions. Over and over again, people are finding out that what worked two years ago won't work today. This gives them a choice. They can either bemoan the fact that things aren't as easy as they used to be, or they can use their creative abilities to find new answers, new solutions, and new ideas." Richard King, "How Stupid are We?", *Australian Army Journal* (Summer 2009), 186.

17   Dr. Ronald Haycock, former Dean of Arts, Royal Military College of Canada, *Clio and Mars in Canada: The Need for Military Education*, Presentation to the Canadian Club, 11 November 1999, Kingston, Ontario.

18   Major David Last, "Educating Officers: Post Modern Professionals to Control and Prevent Violence," in Lieutenant-Colonel Bernd Horn, ed., *Contemporary Issues in Officership: A Canadian Perspective* (Toronto: Canadian Institute of Strategic Studies, 2000), 26.

19   Rear-Admiral (retired) David Morse, interview with Dr. Bill Bentley and Colonel Bernd Horn, 6 October 2010.

20   This is the Canadian Treasury Board definition. See Treasury Board Secretariat, 2006. *Canada, Policy on Learning, Training and Development*, retrieved on 2 November 2010 from <http://www.tbs-sct.gc.ca/pol/doc-eng.aspx?id=12405&section=text#cha4>.

21   Quoted in Murray Simons, *Professional Military Learning. Next Generation PME in the New Zealand Defence Force* (Canberra: Air Power Development Centre, 2004), 43.

22   This is why the US military believes that "successful operational adaptability depends upon educating and developing leaders, training soldiers, and building cohesive teams who are prepared to execute decentralized operations in and among populations in coordination with Joint, Interagency, Intergovernmental, Multinational (JIIMP) partners." United States of America, Department of the Army, *The Army Learning Concepts for 2015*. DRAFT. 20 April 2010, 2.

23   Major-General Don McNamara asserted that advanced-military professional education is required "to get people to think in two ways. One, to think strategically so that they're not commanding a ship anymore, they're commanding a force, and that is a mindset that is not easy for a lot of people to change. The second thing is that they are now thinking in terms of dealing at the highest national levels and not at the level of an individual military formation. These are two major changes that are not easy for people to assume without getting some experience before they actually have to assume it." Don Macnamara in John Wood (ed.), *Talking Heads Talking Arms: No Life Jackets* (Toronto: Breakout Educational Network, 2003), 155.

24   Ibid., 9.

25   Paul Heinbecker, *Getting Back in the Game: A Foreign Policy Playbook for Canada* (Toronto: Key Porter Books, 2010), 23.

26   For details on the "decade of darkness" see Bernd Horn and Bill Bentley, "The Road to Transformation: Ascending from the Decade of Darkness," in R.W. Walker, ed., *Institutional Leadership in the Canadian Forces: Contemporary Issues* (Kingston: CDA Press, 2007), 1-25; or Bernd Horn, and Bill Bentley, "The Road to Transformation. Ascending from the Decade of Darkness", *Canadian Military Journal*, Vol. 16, No. 4 (Autumn 2007), 33-44.

27   Department of National Defence, *The Report on the Officer Development Board* (Rowley Report), Ottawa, March 1969, v.

28   Colonel Roger Noble, "'Beyond Cultural Awareness': Anthropology as an Aid to the Formulation and Execution of Military Strategy in the Twenty-First Century", *Australian Army Journal*
(Winter 2009), 67.

29   Emily Spencer, *Solving the People Puzzle: Cultural Intelligence and Special Operations
Forces* (Toronto: Dundurn Press, 2010), 115.

30   Colonel (Retired) John R. Boyd, United States Air Force, cited in Major Jason Hayes, "Preparing Our Soldiers for Operations within Complex Human Terrain Environments", *Australian Army
Journal*, (Winter 2009), 104.

31   Michael Howard, *The Causes of War* (New York: Harvard University Press, 1984), 83. Major-
General, the Honourable W.A. Griesbach stated, "Since wars cannot be arranged merely to train
officers, it follows that, after a long period of peace, the officers of an army must get their military
education from reading and study." "Military Study: Notes of a Lecture," *Canadian Defence Quarterly*, October 1931, 19.

32   Dr. John Scott Cowan, RMCC Convocation Address, 4 October 1999, Kingston, Ontario. See
also Eliot Cohen and John Gooch, *Military Misfortunes. The Anatomy of Failure in War* (New York:
Vintage Books, 1991), 233-237.

33   Spencer, 72.

34   David H. Petraeus, "To Ph.D. or Not to Ph.D…", *The American Interest* (July/August 2007), 16.

35   Ibid., 18. He further insists, "This is a very valuable experience in and of itself for those of us
in uniform who will work and live in other cultures overseas. If the range of views within our own
country is greater than we supposed, that can only help prepare officers for an even wider range
beyond our shores."

36   Ibid., 18.

37   Ibid., 19.

38   Major Sieberg, "Tank or Anti-Tank? Does the Spanish War Show Which is Superior?" Translation of an article appearing in the "Militar-Wochenblatt" of 11 February 193, National Archives, MG
31, G6, Vol 9, File: Articles, Papers, Speeches – U.

39   Baril, 140.

40   Canada, *Canadian Officership in the 21st Century (Officership 2020). Strategic Guidance
for the Canadian Forces Officer Corps and the Officer Professional Development System* (Ottawa:
DND, 2001), foreword, iii.

41   General Maurice Baril, covering letter, "Canadian Officership in the 21st Century (Officership 2020) Launch Implementation, 2 May 2001, 3.

42   Lieutenant-General M.K. Jeffery, address to the Commanding Officers Course 2001,
21 June 2001, Fort Frontenac, Kingston, Ontario.

43   Petraeus, 16.

44   Ibid., 20.

CHAPTER 2

LEADERSHIP AND THE LEARNING ORGANIZATION

Dr. Bill Bentley

The illiterates of the 21st century won't be those who cannot read and write.
Rather they will be those who cannot learn – unlearn – relearn.
Alvin Toffler[1]

A learning organization is not a building, nor is it only a disparate group of people interconnected by computers so that they can "share" or "manage" information and knowledge. Fundamentally, a learning organization is a culture. It is useful, therefore, to start thinking about a learning organization by understanding what a culture is. In this chapter a culture will be understood to be:

> A system of shared basic assumptions that a group has learned as it solved its problems of external adaptation and internal integration that has worked well enough to be considered valid and, therefore, to be taught to new members as the correct way to perceive, think and feel in relation to their problems or tasks.[2]

Such a culture is embedded in a given organization whether it is a government department, a civilian corporation, a non-governmental organization (NGO) or the Canadian Forces. Now, all these entities are more or less organized in a hierarchical fashion and tend to operate according to bureaucratic principles. The tension between such organizations and the "culture" of learning that should animate them is ubiquitous and difficult to overcome. Once overcome, the "culture" of learning must be sustained over time.

This is the function of leadership at all levels in the organization. Remember, leaders create and change cultures while bureaucrats, administrators and managers live within them. For leaders to create or move towards a learning organization they must, of course, thoroughly understand what is a learning organization.

One leading pioneer in the development of the theory of the learning organization is management scientist and senior lecturer at the Massachusetts Institute of Technology (MIT), Peter Senge, whose seminal work, *The Fifth Discipline*,
inspired extensive follow-on scholarship and endless discussion in the years
that followed.[3] Senge identified five "disciplines" which, when practiced together, create and sustain a learning organization. These disciplines are:

- Personal Mastery;
- Mental Models;
- Building Shared Vision;
- Team Learning; and
- Systems Thinking

Leaders must develop a deep understanding of each of these disciplines, put
them into practice for themselves and then infuse the members of their organization with their full meaning. A thumbnail description of the five principles
provides a fuller understanding of their importance:

Personal Mastery

Mastery might suggest gaining dominance over people or things. But mastery
can also mean a special level of proficiency. People with a high level of personal
mastery are able to consistently realize the results that really matter most deeply
to them – in effect, they approach life as an artist would approach a work of art.

Personal mastery is the discipline of continually clarifying and deepening one's
personal vision, of focusing energies, of developing patience and of seeing reality objectively. It is an essential cornerstone of a learning organization. Of course,
an organization's commitment to, and capacity for, learning can be no greater
than that of its members. Surprisingly, few organizations encourage the growth
of their people in this manner. Leaders, therefore, must ceaselessly encourage
the growth of their people around the discipline of personal mastery.

Mental Models

Mental models are deeply ingrained assumptions, generalizations, or even
pictures or images that influence how we understand the world and how we
react to it. Very often we are not consciously aware of these mental models.

Mental models of what can, or cannot, be done in different organizational settings are no less deeply entrenched. Bob Garrett, the management consultant, for example, tells us that most people so restrict their frame of reference or context (i.e., their own mental model) for the problem they are facing that little change can occur. They get into such a routine with their work that they view virtually all problems in a similar way. Consequently, when asked to change matters, they tend to operate in a confined "single loop" of learning in which they can only do "more of" or "less of" the same thing because of the given context.[4]

This issue can be particularly acute in the Department of National Defence and the Canadian Forces because both the Public Service professionals and the members of the profession of arms are embedded in a bureaucracy. It is this type of organization and work style that tends to create a particular mental model. A paradigm that deliberately creates hierarchies, stove-pipes, and greatly inhibits collaboration and team building.

The discipline of working with mental models starts with turning the mirror inwards: learning to unearth our internal pictures of the world, to bring them to the surface and hold them rigorously to scrutiny. Leaders must develop the ability to carry on "learning-ful" conversations that balance inquiry and advocacy, where people expose their own thinking effectively and make that thinking open to the influence of others. That is to say, leaders develop a process whereby they change the shared mental models of individuals regarding the "shape" of their teams and the larger organizations within which they work.

Building Shared Vision

If any one idea about leadership has inspired organizations for thousands of years it's the capacity to hold a shared picture of the future leaders seek to create. When there is a genuine vision people excel and learn, not because they are told to, but because they want to. But many leaders have personal visions that never get translated into shared visions that galvanize entire organizations. The discipline of building shared vision involves the skills of unearthing shared "pictures of the future" that foster genuine commitment and enrolment rather than compliance. This, of course, calls upon the leader's ability to communicate clearly, consistently and continuously. In this case, such communication can benefit from utilizing mental models and "rich" pictures to convey what is meant and intended. Leaders must avoid the counterproductive practice of trying to dictate a vision, no matter how heartfelt.

Team Learning

The discipline of team learning starts with "dialogue;" the capacity of members of a team to suspend assumptions and enter into a genuine "thinking together." To the Greeks "dia-logos" meant a free-flowing of meaning through a group, allowing the group to discover insights not attainable individually. Dialogue differs from the more common "discussion" which has its roots with percussion and concussion, latterly a heaving of ideas back and forth in a winner-takes-all competition. Dialogue involves learning how to recognize the patterns of interaction in teams that undermines learning. The patterns of defensiveness are often deeply ingrained in how a team operates. If unrecognized they inhibit learning. If recognized and surfaced creatively they can actually accelerate learning.

One methodology that has been specifically designed to facilitate team learning is known as Soft Systems Methodology (SSM), developed by the management scientist Peter Checkland and his colleagues at the University of Lancaster over the past 40 years.[5] SSM is defined as an organized process which articulates a social (team) learning process by structuring a dialogue concerning a problem situation, the dialogue being based on models of concepts of proposed activity (built on explicit worldviews) in order to enable action to improve to be taken. The real benefit that SSM can confer is not as much the specific outcome of a specific study; its main potential benefit is to improve the quality of the thinking capability of people in an organization.

Team learning is vital because teams, not individuals, are the fundamental learning units in modern organizations – unless teams can learn, the organization cannot learn.

Systems Thinking

Systems thinking is the fifth discipline. It is a conceptual framework, a body of knowledge and tools that has been developed over the past 50 years to make full patterns clearer and help us to see how to change them effectively. Put slightly differently, systems thinking is the practice of thinking that takes a holistic view of complex events seemingly caused by a myriad of isolated, independent, and usually unpredictable forces or factors. Systems thinking recognizes that systems (organized wholes) ranging from soap bubbles to galaxies, ant colonies to nations, can be better understood only when their wholeness (identity and structural integrity) is maintained, thus permitting the study of the whole instead of the properties of their components. Leaders who wish to move their organization or command towards a true learning organization must first and foremost, master the Fifth Discipline.

There are several models or methodologies that promote the practice of systems thinking but three of the best are undoubtedly Peter Checkland, *Systems Thinking, Systems Practice* (London: John Wiley and Sons, 1999), Charles Churchman, *The Systems Approach* (NY: Delacorte Press, 1968) and Jasmid Gharajedaghi, *A Systems Theory of Organizations* (Seaside, CA: Intersystems Publications, 1985) and his later book *Systems Thinking* (London: Elsevier, 2009).

It is vital that the five disciplines develop as an ensemble. This is challenging because it is much harder to integrate new tools than simply apply them separately. This is why systems thinking is the fifth discipline. It is the discipline that integrates all the disciplines, fusing them into a coherent body of theory and practice. Without a systemic orientation there is no motivation to look at how the disciplines interrelate. By enhancing each of the other disciplines, it continually reminds us that the whole can exceed the sum of its parts.

Another leading authority on the learning organization, Joseph Lampel, a colleague of Peter Senge at MIT, has described the learning organization in somewhat more prosaic terms. However, his approach can serve as a kind of "check-list" for leaders as they observe their organization and act to move it in the direction desired. According to Lampel there are five indicators that demonstrate whether or not an organization can be categorized as a learning organization:[6]

1. *Organizations can learn as much, if not more, from failure as from success.* Learning organizations fight the natural tendency to bury failure and forget it as soon as possible. Failure is often costly to organizations, but learning organizations realize that some of the costs can be recouped by careful consideration of the hidden shortcoming.

2. *A learning organization rejects the adage "if it ain't broke, don't fix it."* All the processes that regulate work in an organization can be improved

even when they appear efficient under superficial scrutiny. The source of the improvement is often buried deep within existing ways of doing things. A learning organization undertakes a periodic examination of systems, routines and procedures to discover whether they still perform a needed function and should be retained. New technology, new knowledge and new practices often allow organizations to redesign routines to make them more efficient and effective.

3. *Learning organizations assume that the people closest to the execution of the mission – those at the "coal-face"- often know more about important aspects of activities than their superiors.* Mobilizing this knowledge is a high priority in the learning organization. This is usually done by relying on teams where members of the organization can exchange and pool their knowledge. Sharing of knowledge is combined with an open door policy that encourages subordinates to bring problems to the attention of senior leadership. Finally, and perhaps most importantly, leaders have to learn the art of asking questions, best done at close proximity to operations. In a learning organization leaders become accustomed to walking around and interacting with their subordinates in their work setting.

4. *A learning organization actively seeks to move knowledge from part of the organization to another, to ensure that relevant knowledge finds its way to the organizational unit that needs it most.* This means breaking down "stovepipes," energetically resisting bureaucratic ideologies in favour of professional ideology[7] and encouraging both formal and informal networks.

5. *Learning organizations spend a lot of energy looking outside their own boundaries for knowledge.* Best practices and doctrine found in other security institutions and agencies are examined to determine what might benefit one's own organization. Concepts, theories and methodologies concerning learning, education and training abound in colleges, universities and even corporations that can be adapted to a defence/military environment. The learning organization concept itself, of course, is a corpus of knowledge that is slowly making it across institutional boundaries in the Department of National Defence.

Conclusion

As shown above, a learning organization may be described or defined in a number of ways. The best explanations are normally firmly anchored to Senge's five disciplines. Synthesizing the literature one can extract certain common characteristics that distinguish a learning organization which then represents yet another lens through which to view your own organization to assess how well it deserves the name "learning organization".

In summary, a learning organization:

Promotes Learning
- Values knowledge
- Values new ideas
- Values relationships
- Learning is mission critical

Learns From Experience
- Values experimentation
- Understands the importance and value of risk-taking
- Shares learning broadly

Embraces Diversity
- Promotes a culture that questions the status quo
- Creates a climate where innovation and new ideas can flourish
- Leaders at all levels are educated to deal with complexity (systems thinking)

Leads in Support of Learning
- Information is widely shared for its maximum use and benefits
- Promotes collaboration and encourages horizontal leadership
- Creates a decision-making environment that values input and explains decisions

In the end, the learning organization is inextricably tied to leadership. In essence, leadership and the creation and maintenance of a learning organization need one another. The Canadian Forces definition of leadership is, "directing, motivating and enabling others to accomplish the mission professionally, while developing or improving capabilities that contribute to mission success."[8] While there are undoubtedly times *in extremis* when leaders must be extremely directive, in the majority of cases it is through motivating and enabling that the most effective leaders get things done. And this is best accomplished in the context of a learning organization. To that specific point, the second part of the leadership definition speaks to the requirement for senior leaders especially, to create and sustain the <u>culture</u> of a learning organization. Such a culture is, in fact, a critical capability that energizes all of the other important capabilities that leads to successful institutions and militaries.

---

1   Quoted in Christopher Paparone, "Where Military Professionalism Meets Complexity Science", *Armed Forces and Society*, Vol. 24, No. 3 (April 2008), 435.

2   Edgar Schein, *Organizational Culture and Leadership* (San Francisco: Jossey-Bass, 1992), 12.

3   Peter Senge, *The Fifth Discipline* (NY: Doubleday, 1990).

4   Bob Garrett, *The Learning Organization* (London: Harper Collins, 1994), 44.

5   SSM is fully explained in Peter Checkland, *Systems Thinking, Systems Practice* (London: John Wiley and Sons, 1999).

6   Joseph Lampel, *Towards the Learning Organization* (London: John Wiley and Sons, 1995).

7   See Lieutenant-Colonel Bill Bentley, *Professional Ideology and the Profession of Arms in Canada* (Toronto: The Canadian Institute of Strategic Studies, 2005) for a detailed discussion and comparison of professional ideology vice bureaucratic ideology, also known as managerialism.

8   Department of National Defence, *Leadership in the Canadian Forces: Conceptual Foundations* (Ottawa, 2005), 30.

CHAPTER 3

THE EVOLUTION OF CANADIAN FORCES STAFF EDUCATION AND OPERATING IN A POST-COLD WAR WORLD

Dr. Howard G. Coombs[1]

At the heart of credibility is the ability to clearly demonstrate
the relevance of what we are teaching to the students.[2]
Lieutenant-Colonel Colin Magee, Director of Curriculum,
Canadian Forces College, 17 September 2008

...we have moved to a largely degreed officer corps, and have instituted
a balanced arts and sciences programme for our aspiring cadets studying
at the Royal Military Colleges. Our staff and war college curricula
is set to a graduate level, with many students taking advantage of advanced
degrees either during their professional studies or frequently
on their own time. Finally we have begun to see senior public servants
as well as civilian executives signing up for our most senior programmes
thereby bringing Whole of Government to the classroom...[3]
General Walter J. Natynczyk, Chief of the Defence Staff (CDS) Foreword to
*The Report of the Officer Development Board: Maj-Gen Roger Rowley and
the Education of the Canadian Forces,* 30 September 2009

If one wishes to understand a nation's interpretation of war and other conflict one must understand the professional military education of that nation's military, particularly that pertaining to the formation of senior staff officers. This learning shapes the activities of a nation's military through providing paradigms to interpret war and other conflict and then formulate an appropriate response. The composition and provenance of such education plays an important role in the development of specialized military competencies that permit the profession of arms to perform its primary function – the structured use of violence on behalf of the state.[4] Canada's military has adopted three discernable paradigms,

or conceptual models, in the education of its staff officers, and due to the challenges of the contemporary environment, as well as institutional change, are in
the process of implementing a fourth paradigm of professional education. These
conceptual approaches have been derived from national and international influences and experiences beginning in the late 19th century.

During the age of the Imperial Army it was the viewpoint of the British Army that
shaped the staff education of Canada's Army, the Militia.[5] While in the early 20th
century some contact occurred between the Royal Canadian Navy (RCN) and
the Royal Canadian Air Force (RCAF) with their British counterparts, it was the
Militia that seemed to have the greatest engagement.[6] Then during the Second
World War and the years immediately following, the Staff Colleges of the Canadian Army and the RCAF imbued the Canadian experience of conflict to shape
their curricula.

However, the burgeoning tensions of the Cold War combined with unification
led to the creation of a single joint staff college. This new institution implemented in its courses professional ideas of distinctly American provenance.[7] Notably
in recent years, Canada's joint staff education has adapted to changes in the contemporary environment as a result of organizational reforms originating during
the 1990s and Canada's military operations in Afghanistan. Now, Canadian staff
education is in the midst of another conceptual shift, in an attempt to meet the
demands of conflict in a post-Cold War world. As a result, it is anticipated that
Canada's senior leadership is better able to deal with the challenges of the 21st
century due to an adaptive system of professional military education.

Professional Military Education and Staff Colleges

Central to any examination of professional military education is an understanding of the knowledge that comprises the core competencies specific to the profession of arms. These proficiencies are included in the curriculums of advanced
professional military education. This material pertains to interpreting war and
other types of conflict, as well as comprehending the linkages of these military
activities to the state. In a related fashion, it is necessary to grasp the manner in
which military activities are arranged and orchestrated throughout the breadth
and depth of these forces, through plans, orders, instructions and policies to
achieve overarching goals. Also of great importance is the role of the military
as part of a multi-disciplinary national effort that would include other activities,
such as diplomacy, informational and economic initiatives.[8]

To appreciate fully the importance of how militaries fulfill national objectives, one must examine some broader considerations or perspectives pertaining to use of the profession of arms in the application of military force. For most countries, the use of force is normally a choice of last resort. The decision to use that option, at least hypothetically, is made in a deliberate and measured fashion as an *in extremis* national response when politics and diplomacy have failed. In the words of the military philosopher Carl von Clausewitz from almost two centuries past, "...war is not merely an act of policy, but a true political instrument, a continuation of political intercourse, carried on with other means."[9] The more commonly used paraphrasing of this idea is that war is an "extension of politics by other means." But Clausewitz continued with the important notion that: "The political object is the goal, war is the means of reaching it, and the means can never be considered in isolation from their purpose."[10] These ideas reflect a rational connection between policy and military activities that is generally accepted by countries like Canada, in theory, if not always in practice.[11] In this process it is important to understand the roles played by senior military commanders and their staffs, as well as the professional culture and intellectual influences that have shaped the manner in which Canada's military organizes war on behalf of its nation. Education is the manner in which these competencies are passed to practitioners.

Central to any understanding of a professional military is an awareness of the role of the staff officer in devising solutions to military problems on behalf of a nation. Staffs have existed since ancient times and assist senior commanders in carrying out national direction. In its most rudimentary form the staff can consist of personal assistants to a commander; however, in modern times, staffs have become large and highly specialized organizations. The staff forms the intellectual core of any military organization. Staffs have continually evolved since the Napoleonic Wars, when nations mobilized in order to meet the threat imposed on Europe by the armies of post-revolutionary France. Since that time the scope and complexity of conflict has expanded. Staffs have developed to deal with all aspects of military activities from operations to administration. In essence, staff officers prepare armed forces for what they have to do. The Mathematician Gerald J. Whitrow wrote, "The primary function of mental activity is to face the future and anticipate the event which is to happen."[12] In this way staff officers look ahead, attempt to foresee what is to come and organize their services for the roles that they will be assigned by government. In this fashion, they remove the burden of minutia from military commanders in order to allow those leaders to guide and manage their forces.[13] An iteration of the British Army staff manual from 1912 exhorted staff officers to act in concert with the wishes of their commander and:

> ...be unsparing in their endeavours to help the troops by every possible means in carrying out their difficult task; foreseeing and providing for obstacles and dangers that may arise; making clear what is required without ambiguity or possibility of misunderstanding; and ever careful to attend to the comfort of those under their General's command before attending to their own.[14]

This directive also made sure that staff officers understood that they had no *de jure* power outside that vested in them by the person in charge; theirs was an intellectual role:

> Staff officers, as such, have no authority over the troops or services and departments, and though they are responsible for the issue of orders, it is essential that they should remember that every order given by them is given by the authority and on the responsibility of the authorized commander.[15]

In order to become a member of a military staff, officers must demonstrate that they are proficient in their *métier*. They must also successfully complete rigorous programs of studies that provide them with specific intellectual competencies. The institutions that offer these courses of study are called "staff colleges."

It would be inaccurate to conceptualize staff colleges merely as military technical institutions. Rather, staff colleges are holistic in their curriculum and reinforce the professional aspects of the profession of arms; empiricism, administration and specialized knowledge.[16] Staff colleges also provide students the opportunity to form relationships with other military practitioners, both instructors and students. The professional relationships created in this fashion also include alliance and coalition partners who send instructors and students to each other's institutions. This transnational[17] community has bonds that facilitate the transmission of professional knowledge between connected militaries and in extreme cases sometimes has influence on armed forces greater than national authorities.

The Development of a Modern System of Senior Professional Military Education

Prior to the Second World War, a limited number of Canadian officers attended Imperial staff colleges and a larger number of Militia officers took truncated forms of staff education in Canada. In 1940, the shortage of vacancies on British courses prompted the Canadian Army to create a short wartime course to educate officers in the knowledge needed to function as staff and leaders in an expanding military organization. The first iteration was conducted in England, with the remainder of these courses being conducted in Canada, at the Royal Military College of Canada (RMCC). During the same period some officers attended British and other courses.[18] After the war, the Canadian Army Staff College (CASC) was established at Fort Frontenac in Kingston, Ontario and continues to this day as the Canadian Land Force Command and Staff College (CLFCSC). The CASC and its successor attempted to ensure that junior and mid-level officers were educated in the competencies required to command and administer army organizations, in war and peace. Prominent Canadian military historian Jack English has affirmed that this army staff college was of vital importance to the maintenance of the army's military expertise.[19]

In a similar fashion, the RCAF War Staff College commenced in September 1943.[20] In October 1945 the RCAF War Staff College was renamed the RCAF Staff College and commenced the first peacetime programs. Initially only six months in duration, this staff education was in 1948 extended to ten months.[21]

Of the three Canadian services only the Canadian Army and the RCAF had separate staff colleges. For the most part, the RCN addressed its need for staff officers by sending a small number of students to the CASC and the RCAF Staff College.[22] However, despite that cross education, unification created a need for mixed staffs of naval, army and air force officers, who all needed an understanding of integrated or joint operations.

In 1966, the Canadian Forces College (CFC) in Toronto was established as an amalgamated Canadian staff education institution. The creation of the CFC was precursor to the unification of the Canadian military in 1968 from distinct services to a single entity, the Canadian Forces. As a result, the new CFC took on custodianship of the professional education of the RCN, Canadian Army and RCAF, as well as became responsible for the education and training of future staff officers of the Canadian military.[23] This new institution subsumed the former RCAF Staff College.

In addition to these institutions, the National Defence College (NDC) was established at Fort Frontenac in 1948. It was an organization analogous to the British Imperial Defence College, created in 1927 to study the high level interface between national objectives and military policy.[24] The curriculum of the NDC was more wide ranging then that of the other Canadian senior officer education institutions and focused on not only the military, but also on the social, political, industrial, economic, and diplomatic aspects of national defence.[25] This college was closed in 1994 due to fiscal constraints.[26] However, not long after the closure of the NDC, two shorter courses were instituted at the CFC to replace the longer single course. The Advanced Military Studies Course (AMSC) commenced in 1998 and the National Security Studies Course (NSSC) was started in 1999. In 2006, these latter courses were renamed the Advanced Military Studies Program (AMSP) and the National Strategic Studies Program (NSSP). Like the NDC that they replaced, these courses aspired to teach not only the military, but also the non-military aspects of defence. As a result of the most recent bout of educational reforms, these programs were, in 2008, superseded by the National Security Program (NSP), amalgamating the AMSP and NSSP into one course of study.[27]

Consequently, the professional education of the Canadian military in the period prior to the Second World War was shaped by the British Empire. Attendance at Imperial staff colleges ensured that Canadian staff officers retained a distinctly English cast and allegiance. Many of the limited number of graduates attained high rank during their careers. However, the general reliance on the *Pax Britannica* not only imparted a distinctly British perspective to Canadian officers, but also ensured that the Canadian military was woefully unprepared for the Second World War. In an effort to remain relevant to the Empire and address domestic needs from its inception onwards, Canada's three services, with the exception of the First World War, were generally insufficiently resourced, equipped and lacked personnel. It was evident that the costly knowledge gained in the Great War concerning the demand for educated and experienced staff officers in order to conduct complex military activities was discarded in the postwar reduction of forces. Importantly, this decrease was accompanied by a return to the "arms of the Empire" for intellectual guidance regarding the conduct of complex military operations. The Canadian perspectives and ideas that had emerged from the military operations of the First World War were overshadowed by the professional knowledge provided by the British military. As a result, the Canadian services did not develop to any great extent the capacity to educate their own staff officers during the interwar years, as the paradigms used to interpret war were those provided to a limited number of officers by the Imperial staff colleges and to a larger number of Militia officers in Canada. The cost of this unprepared-ness would only become apparent with the outbreak of the Second World War.

The Canadian Army and RCAF had both expanded rapidly at the beginning of the Second World War and experienced problems related to this sudden growth. After the fact, it was evident that the general neglect of staff education during the interwar period, and concomitant lack of introspective thought on the mili-tary profession, had had an adverse influence on the Canadian services during the war. At great cost, the Canadian Army, as well as the RCAF, had come to un-derstand the need to develop and maintain their own staff education in order to produce their own educated military practitioners. As a result, the foundations of professional staff education for the Canadian military shifted from a primarily British to Canadian paradigm. This national perspective was to endure for the next two decades, until the educational reorganization precipitated by the uni-fication of the Canadian military.

In the years after the Second World War the burgeoning alliance with the United States that had been created by the necessities of that war and a post-conflict willingness to support the *Pax Americana* set the strategic context and corre-sponding tone of operations for the Canadian services in the following decades. The RCN, Canadian Army and the RCAF became closely affiliated with their American counterparts. At times, in an absence of clear policy objectives that pertained to national security the Canadian services focused on their own vi-sions of Canadian defence needs within the global environment. In some cases, this viewpoint was formed by military-to-military contacts with American ser-vices, while in other cases they were created by American perspectives provided in the milieu of alliances, like NATO, through bilateral agreements, such as North American Aerospace Defence Command (NORAD), and within multinational or-ganizations, akin to the United Nations (UN). The lack of consistent and lasting strategy, either national or otherwise, to provide a focal point to Canadian mili-tary efforts created a Cold War history of operations that were carried out in a fragmentary manner. For example, the Korean War, the use of Canadian contribu-tions to NATO and the creation of NORAD demonstrated Canada's commitment of military forces as an obligation of its alliances. This involvement occasionally took place without either a clear understanding of its ramifications or being able to provide input into how these Canadian military forces would be used.[28]

Aggravating this disconnection between national direction and military operations was the isolation of the Canadian military profession from larger society. The characteristics of the profession had come to reflect transnational military relationships formed after the Second World War. Members of the profession of arms in Canada defined themselves through their mutual interactions with the American services.

These interrelated aspects of the utilization of the Canadian military in the last half of the 20th century, along with the separation of the profession of arms from Canadian society, provide a complex and dynamic background to the increasing influence of the United States in the education of the Canadian staff officer during the Cold War.

It also must be highlighted that this use of the Canadian military and the relationship of the Canadian profession of arms to society contextualized the staff education offered after the Second World War. While the courses offered by the Canadian Army and RCAF were created using the Canadian knowledge painfully gained over years of conflict, the curricula retained some of its British heritage, as well as absorbed increasing American content. The transnational influence of the United States became especially pronounced after the restructuring of professional military education brought about by unification of the RCN, Canadian Army and RCAF into an integrated force. In the absence of Canadian joint professional military knowledge that of the United States – Canada's major Cold War partner – was used.

The new Canadian Forces staff education was built on the structure of the RCAF Staff College. However, the unification of the Canadian Forces had produced an organization that lacked an integrated doctrine. Consequently, the CFC utilized American and NATO materials to educate Canadian Forces officers. This resulted in continued ambiguity in understanding the military connections to the direction of Canada's government. This flaw was reinforced by curriculum arguing that Canada would only employ its military within an alliance or coalition.

As a result, by the 1980s the Canadian Forces had created a command and staff course that appeared to meet the needs of Canada's Cold War commitments, but lacked national perspectives on the use of military power. Officers who at-tended the CFC developed ideas concerning military operations that were not determined by Canadian military heritage, but by the alliances of the period. In the absence of introspective thought on the nature of Canada's national and international military engagement on behalf of its nation, ideas were supplied *verbatim* from the transnational community of practice established within North America. The most significant paradigm shift of the Cold War, the acceptance of the "operational level of war,"[29] was the result of this intellectual void. Adopt-ing this American change would come to shape how Canadian officers envis-aged and arranged military operations on behalf of their nation at the end of the 20th century.[30]

Post-Cold War Conflict

In the 1990s, the fragmentation of the Soviet Union, continuing globalization, perceived inequalities of resource distribution, ethnic and ideological differ-ences, amongst other factors created numerous smaller scale conflicts, both intra-national and transnational in nature. Canada's military soon found itself embroiled in peace support operations focused mainly on Eastern Europe and Africa. For the most part, the challenges of this increasingly complex and non-linear environment was met with various degrees of success by a military that had been created to deal with the relatively straightforward challenges posed by the Warsaw Pact, at sea, on land and in the air over Northern Europe.

Events such as that which occurred during Canadian deployments to Somalia in 1993 and Bacovici, in the Former Republic of Yugoslavia, during 1993-1994 created a great deal of public and private introspection regarding the nature of the profession of arms in Canada.[31] There were public boards of inquiry in addition to a number of reports, which in turn prompted governmental supervi-sion, through the Minister of National Defence, to deal with the most pertinent recommendations of these cases, particularly that arising from the Somalia In-quiry. Following on from that were projects like the *Report to the Prime Minister on the Leadership and Management of the Canadian Forces* (1997), *A Strategy for 2020* (1999) and *Officership 2020* (2001), which rejuvenated efforts to make both education and professional education relevant to Canadian military profes-sionals.[32] Also, in order to provide institutional support to these recommenda-tions the Canadian Defence Academy (CDA), was created in 2002 and in 2004 was given an official mandate "to act as the institutional champion of Canadian Forces professional development."[33]

At the same time, the demise of the National Defence College in 1994 as a result of federal budget reductions created an impetus within the Canadian Forces to address an unease regarding the lack of higher level education for senior and general officers. This concern manifested itself in the recommendations of a number of official reports starting in the 1969 *Rowley Report* through to the more recent 1995 *Report on the Officer Development Board: Part I*. All these sources indicated that a revision of senior professional military education was needed to provide educational experiences that focused on the higher level aspects of fighting wars, and on national and international studies.[34] The gap in professional military education caused by the closure of the NDC led to the approval and establishment of the AMSC and the NSSC at the CFC in 1998. The curriculum of the AMSC specifically contained competencies pertaining to the operational level of war.[35] One could argue that the trend established during the Cold War to use American professional concepts that were more suitable to the problems imposed by Westphalian notions of state-on-state conflict had endured at the dawn of the 21st century.

Modern Education Reforms

The potential impact of non-state actors with global reach increased in importance for Western nations as a result of a number of attacks on United States interests overseas in 2000. However, the bombings of the United States Embassies in Tanzania and Nairobi, as well as the *United States Ship Cole* in Yemen were by and large treated as anomalies until the destruction of the World Trade Center on 11 September 2001. This event ushered in an era of warfare in which, even for the most powerful western nations, it is obvious that some potential opponents are extremely difficult to discern, define, dislocate or destroy. These threats are asymmetric in nature requiring well-educated military leaders who use developed cognitive skills in an intellectually agile and practiced fashion to delineate the complex problems of the current security environment and apply the precepts of military doctrine to devise relevant and lasting solutions.

This is a difficult and daunting task.

A number of initiatives commenced to assist with the evolution of professional military education for senior officers. The CDA conducted an End-to-End Review of officer professional education that was completed in 2003 and noted a number of problem areas, specifically with the staff education offered to Lieutenant-Commanders/Majors – Commanders/Lieutenant-Colonels at the CFC. Following from this, in 2004 the Armed Forces Council (AFC)[36] directed an examination of this professional activity and the associated professional development of this group of officers. Consequently, as a result of this scrutiny, a number of short-comings were brought forward. Firstly, it was noted that the officers sent to the CFC for the Command and Staff Course (CSC), now known as the Joint Command and Staff Program (JCSP), frequently received this professional education too late in their career to benefit the Canadian Forces. As well, for the most part only officers that had the potential to be selected for command were being sent to the CSC leaving many other officers without the skills necessary to function in other senior officer positions. Secondly, the course functioned for the most part on professional command and staff proficiencies, but not the other skills necessary to address the institutional needs of the Canadian Forces. Lastly, it was acknowledged that the underpinnings of professional development consisted of "education, training, experience and self-development." The aspect of self-development was not seen to be adequately represented at this level of professional formation.[37]

These observations resulted in AFC direction to examine this period of a senior officer's development using a number of principles. These were: (1) a re-examination of the professional competencies required by Lieutenant-Commanders/Majors – Commanders/Lieutenant-Colonels; (2) recognize that not all officers who require this professional development will command; (3) recognize that a number of formal and informal paths could be taken to reach the same outcomes (and incidentally providing much greater flexibility for education); (4) design and put into action an educational program like the CSC for all senior officers; (5) produce a distance learning variant of the CSC; (6) examine multiple delivery methods for both distance and residential variant of the CSC; and (7) create a system to manage equivalencies, assessments of prior learning and tailored professional development proposals.[38]

Some aspects of this direction had already been implemented at the CFC and the RMCC. For example, the Master's of Defence Studies (MDS) had been finalized in 2001, along with the support of a Department of Defence Studies in teaching, research and curriculum development. Both the MDS and this faculty exist as an extension of the RMCC academic programs and provides a depth and academic rigour to what otherwise might be a narrowly focused professional program. Prior learning assessment for the MDS exists as a function of the Office of the Registrar at the RMCC.[39]

This AFC guidance was soon provided momentum. The 2005 appointment of General Rick Hillier as Chief of the Defence Staff was quickly followed by organizational turbulence in the form of Canadian Forces Transformation. This initiative created a plethora of new headquarters with a concomitant demand for staff officers. Additionally, there were increased requirements for staff officers to meet the demands of the continuing and the growing Canadian Forces engagement in Canada and abroad, in places like Afghanistan. All of this revitalized staff education and in late 2007, the AFC directed a revitalization of the professional education from Lieutenant-Commander/Major to Admiral/General. Residential and distance options for JCSP, as well as a consolidation of AMSP/NSSP into a single NSP – all which took place by September 2008.[40]

Also, during the same period, starting in the early 2000s, an evolution of the curricula of these programs took place. Increasingly, the education offered by the CFC, while informed by the practices of our American allies, has attempted to include an increasing Canadian professional content. These ongoing education revitalization initiatives have provided the Canadian Forces through CDA/CFC/RMCC the chance to offer the bulk of senior Canadian military professionals' educational activities that endeavour to reflect the demands of today's challenges in a multinational and multi-agency setting.

It would be remiss to suggest that this evolution of professional military education has not been without ongoing challenges with regards to its structure, content and delivery. There yet remains work to do in perfecting these programs.[41] Nevertheless, this revitalization is not yet finished. Both JCSP Residential and Distance continue to evolve, the NSP continues to strive for excellence in the realm of Canadian strategic thinking, while CDA examines tailored education for Admiral/General officers to match employment both actual and projected.[42]

Conclusion

Canadian military operations in the 1990s onwards have taken place in post-conflict regions or failed states. Western, including Canadian, military approaches, like that represented by the operational level of war, were originally derived from theories put forward by Clausewitz and other nineteenth-century theorists.

While still usable, these methods are more suited to application in an environment where the predominant form of conflict is between nation states. Therefore, these models are of limited utility in current times where one's opponent is often distributed internationally and robustly networked. Because the Canadian Forces are no longer dealing with the "son of Desert Storm" but rather the "stepchild of Chechnya," professional military education must be relevant and timely.[43] In order to devise feasible and suitable solutions to security problems today, the Canadian military is obliged to deal with complex and chaotic dilemmas in a fashion acceptable to a myriad of participants. Consequently, the Canadian Forces is migrating from a completely American vision of organizing military activities to perspectives shaped by the Canadian post-Cold War experience.[44] While still retaining American provenance, its Canadian usage expresses a different outlook on professional thought. The undercurrents surrounding this shifting professional knowledge are similar to those that coalesced to form the curricula of the CASC and RCAF Staff College after the Second World War, a time when Canada's staff colleges designed a new staff course that catered to their wartime experiences through education. This exemplar supplies a prism through which Canadians can interpret ongoing changes to not only the Canadian Forces and its staff education, but more importantly Canada's profession of arms, their allegiances and activities in a constantly shifting global environment.

---

1   The original version of this Chapter was presented in the *Canadian Military Journal* (see Howard G. Coombs, "In the Wake of a Paradigm Shift: The Canadian Forces College and the Operational Level of War (1987 – 1995)," *Canadian Military Journal* 10, No. 1 (Spring 2010): 19-27.

2   Canada, DND, Canadian Forces College, "5570-1(DOC) Professional Development for DOC faculty," signed by Lieutenant-Colonel C.G. Magee, dated 17 Sep 08, 5.

3   Quoted in Randall Wakelam and Howard Coombs, eds., *The Report of the Officer Development Board: Maj-Gen Roger Rowley and the Education of the Canadian Forces* (Waterloo: Laurier Centre for Military Strategic and Disarmament Studies, 2010), Foreword.

4   Lieutenant-General Sir John Winthrop Hackett, *The Profession of Arms – The Lees Knowles Lectures for 1962* (London: The Times Publishing Company Limited, 1962), 3.

5   During this period both full-time and part-time components of the Canadian Army were referred to collectively as the "Militia." The former component was known as the "Permanent Active Militia" or "Permanent Force," while the latter group, today called the Reserve, was the "Non-Permanent Active Militia." Email from Dr Steve Harris, Chief Historian, Directorate of History and Heritage, National Defence Headquarters to Author, Monday, October 22, 2007 9:33 AM.

6   See Directorate History and Heritage Archives, File 530.03 (D1), "Folder listing personnel who have attended Staff Courses, gradings obtained, files applicable to courses, received from DMT, Aug 1962."

CHAPTER 3   **39**

7   See Howard G. Coombs, "In The Wake of a Paradigm Shift: The Canadian Forces College and the Operational Level of War (1987-1995)", *Canadian Military Journal*, Vol. 10, No. 1 (Spring 2010), 19-27.

8   See Lieutenant-Colonel Bill Bentley, "Chapter 3: Professional Ideology and the Profession of Arms" in *Professional Ideology and the Profession of Arms in Canada* (Toronto: The Canadian Institute of Strategic Studies, 2005), 51-84.

9   Carl von Clausewitz, *On War*, Michael Howard and Peter Paret, eds. and trans. (Princeton: Princeton University Press, 1976; paperback edition, 1989), 87.

10   Ibid.

11   While from a Canadian perspective the clarity of the relationship between policy and military strategy has not always been well defined, the need for policy to guide military activities has been part of the legacy of the Canadian civil-military relationship. Ph.d candidate, Major-General Daniel Gosselin (former Commander of the Canadian Defence Academy) has discovered in the course of his research a continuous record of this understanding. Major-General Daniel Gosselin, "Perspectives on Civil-Military Relations, National Direction and Strategic Command", a presentation given to the Canadian Forces College, Toronto, Ontario, 11 July 2009.

12   Quoted in David Kahn, "Note: The Prehistory of the General Staff", *The Journal of Military History*, Vol. 71, No. 2 (April 2007), 500.

13   Ibid., 500-501; and for a history of military staffs see Brigadier-General (Retired) James D. Hittle, United States Marine Corps, *The Military Staff: It's History and Development*, 3rd ed. (Harrisburg, PA: The Stackpole Company, 1961).

14   United Kingdom, War Office, *Staff Manual War Provisional 1912* (London: His Majesty's Stationary Office, 1912), 7.

15   Ibid.

16   See Kahn, "Note."

17   "Transnational" is used in the sense of operating between or outside national borders.

18   John A. Macdonald, "In Search of Veritable: Training the Canadian Army Staff Officer, 1899 to 1945" (Unpublished Masters thesis. Royal Military College of Canada, March 1992), 99-112.

19   In his monograph *Lament for an Army*, John English states, "Like the British Staff College, after which it was modelled, the CASC was the nursery of the General Staff and the single most important educational institution in the army." See John A. English, *Lament for an Army: The Decline of Military Professionalism, Contemporary Affairs* No. 3 (Concord, ON: Irwin Publishing, 1998), 6.

20   William R. Shields, "Canadian Forces College History Project - Canadian Forces Command and Staff College: A History 1797-1946 – Draft (Final Edited Version)" (Toronto: CFC, 1987), 3-6/9 to 4-8/30.

21   Canada, CFC, "The History of the College" (n.d.), 3-6.

22   Canada, DND, Directorate of History and Heritage Archives, File 82/189, Memorandum from Chief of Personnel to CDS, P 4500-26 (DT) dated 16 December, 1965, "Integrated Staff Training" (Ottawa: Canadian Forces Headquarters, 11 January 1966), 1.

23   Canada, DND, Vice Chief of the Defence Staff, File F 1901-4352/8(DO), "Canadian Forces Organization Order 1.8 – Canadian Forces College, Toronto", 3 October 1966.

24   For information concerning the formation of the Imperial Defence College see Brevet-Major A.R. Godwin-Austin, *The Staff and the Staff College*, with a foreword by General Sir George F. Milne (London: Constable and Company Ltd, 1927), 285-286.

25   English, *Lament for an Army*, 82.

26   Canada, DND, *Canadian Officership in the 21ˢᵗ Century Detail Analysis and Strategy for Implementation (Officership 2020): Strategic Guidance for the Canadian Forces Officer Corps and the Officer Professional Development System* (March 2001), BN 2/15.

27   Ronald G. Haycock, "The Labors of Athena and the Muses: Historical and Contemporary Aspects of Canadian Military Education" in Gregory C. Kennedy and Keith Neilson, eds., *Military Education: Past, Present and Future* (Westport, CT: Praeger Publishers, 2002), 174-175.

28   See Howard G. Coombs with Richard Goette, "Supporting the Pax Americana: Canada's Military and the Cold War," in Colonel Bernd Horn, ed., *The Canadian Way of War: Serving the National Interest* (Toronto: Dundurn Press, 2006), 265-296.

29   The importance of this concept was that it formalized the conversion of strategic objectives into aims that could be understood and attained at the tactical level of military activity. It presupposes a linear and structured relationship of purposes from Grand or National Strategy to Military Strategy, through Operations, to Tactics. One can argue that at times this concept exists more so in theory than practice. For a Canadian perspective see Coombs with Goette, "Supporting the *Pax Americana*," and for a recent American point of view read Steven Metz, *Iraq and the Evolution of American Strategy*, with a foreword by Colin S. Gray (Washington, D.C.: Potomac Books, Inc., 2008).

30   For further information on the adoption of the operational level of war by the Canadian Forces see Coombs, "In The Wake of a Paradigm Shift," 19-27.

31   For more detail into these events see Dr. Donna Winslow, "Misplaced Loyalties: The Role of Military Culture in the Breakdown of Discipline in Two Peace Operations", *Journal of Military and Strategic Studies*, Vol. 6, No. 3 (Winter 2004), 345-367; see also, Barry Came, Luke Fisher and Mark Cardwell, "Military Investigates Misconduct", *Maclean's* (July 29, 1996).

32   Canada, Department of National Defence, *Canadian Officership in the 21ˢᵗ Century (Officership 2020): Strategic Guidance for the Canadian Forces Officer Corps and the Officer Professional Development System* (February 2001), i.

33   See Allan English, *Understanding Canadian Military Culture* (Montreal & Kingston: McGill Queen's University Press, 2004), Foreword.; and also, Canada, National Defence, Minister of National Defence, *Direction for the Establishment of the Canadian Defence Academy*, 1.

34   Lieutenant-Colonel Randy Wakelam, "Senior Professional Military Education for the Twenty-First Century" *Canadian Defence Quarterly*, Vol. 27, No. 1 (Autumn 1997), 14-15.

35   Ibid., 15-17.

36   Armed Forces Council is the senior military advisory body in the Canadian Forces.

37   Canada, National Defence, Canadian Defence Academy, "4500-1 (SSO OPD) Briefing Note for ADM HR (Mil) – The DP3 Project," prepared by LCol M.J. Goodspeed, dated 04 May 04, 2. This version should be considered a draft because it is unsigned.

38   Ibid., 3.

CHAPTER 3

39   Canada, DND, CFC, "Board of Visitors Meeting of the BoV, Toronto, 15-16 November 2004 Fourth Report to the Commandant 10 December 2004," Chair Dr. Albert Legault, This version should be considered a draft because it is unsigned.

40   Canada, DND, Armed Forces Council, "1180-1 (D NDHQ Sec) Special Commander's Council Meeting Held on 20 November 2007 – Record of Decisions," prepared by D. A. Noble, dated November 2007, 2. This version should be considered a draft because it is undated and unsigned.

41   See Canada, DND, CFC, "Board of Visitors Meeting of the BoV, Toronto, 15-16 November 2004 Fourth Report to the Commandant 10 December 2004."; Canada, DND, CFC, "Board of Visitors Meeting of the Board 25-26 April 2005 Fifth Report to the Commandant 03 May 2005," Chair Dr. Albert Legault, This version should be considered a draft because it is unsigned; and, more recent assessments are not available as the Board of Visitors, an independent body responsible for evaluating the academic and related aspects of the professional education offered by CFC, has not rendered a report since 03 May 2005. Email to Dr. Howard G. Coombs, Tuesday, 15 March 2011 20:08 PM, n.p. In possession of the author; Finally, some of the current challenges with the professional CFC programs were experienced by the author while the Program Director JCSP (DL) during 2008-2010.

42   See Canada, DND, CFC, "Program Definition – JCSP (DL) 15 Dec 07"; Canada, DND, CFC, "NSP Planning Guidance dated 13 Dec 07"; Canada, National Defence, Canadian Defence Academy, "7000-1 (SSO PD) Commander Canadian Defence Academy Guidance – Interim Professional Military Education Revitalization," signed by Brigadier-General L.E. Aitken, dated 10 March 2009; and, see also Canada, DND, CFC, Lieutenant-General (Retired) Michael Jeffery, "CF Executive Development Programme (DP5) Programme Development (December 2009)."

43   Quotes from General Charles C. Krulak, "Address to National Press Club - Three Block War: Fighting in Urban Areas 10 October 1997", Washington D.C.

44   Howard G. Coombs and General Rick Hiller, "Planning for Success: The Challenge of Applying Operational Art in Post Conflict Afghanistan", *Canadian Military Journal*, Vol. 6, No. 3 (Autumn 2005), 12-13.

CHAPTER 4

TRY AND TRY AGAIN: DEFINING AND IMPLEMENTING EFFECTIVE PROFESSIONAL EDUCATION IN THE CANADIAN FORCES

Dr. Randy Wakelam

It matters little whether the Forces have their present manpower strength and financial budget, or half of them, or double them; without a properly educated, effectively trained, professional officer corps the Forces would, in the future, be doomed to, at the best, mediocrity; at the worst, disaster.

General J.V. Allard, Chief of the Defence Staff, 1969[1]

If one were to read between the lines of General Allard's comments, then argu-ably he was saying that regardless of the challenges placed before a professional military, an inability to deal with the unanticipated can only lead to failure. For him and for the author of the report from which his foreword is taken, a properly prepared and educated officer corps was the basis on which success could be at least reasonably expected.[2]

This chapter examines the history of senior officer Professional Military Education (PME) in Canada since the end of the Second World War. Underpinning this his-tory is the premise that regardless of the type or intensity of conflict, broad edu-cation that focuses on developing the intellectual capacity to deal with complex ambiguous situations is the nexus of effective performance. Starting with PME programs during the Second World War, the chapter goes on to explore those educational concepts that were advanced during the Cold War and post-Cold War periods. The transition from the Cold War to the circumstances of the early 21st century suggests a fairly clear dichotomy between the PME required to deal with conventional operations and the shift in curriculum necessitated by current operational and strategic challenges. But this is not necessarily the case, and the professional skills and attributes that are important to institutional effectiveness are common across the spectrum of conflict.

A secondary theme also bears mention. As the reader progresses through the events of the last 70 years it will become apparent that as often as the officer corps identified what competencies were needed and how these could be educated, there have been frequent difficulties in going from espoused concept to effective program.

This chapter first provides a brief history of staff education in Canada before turning to an analysis of two major reforms to PME in Canada. The first of these was the complete reconceptualization of the profession of arms and its education needs in the late 1960s when the Canadian navy, army and air force were unified by act of Parliament.[3] The second case examines reforms to education which began in 1993 and continued to occur as much from professional introspection as from the end of the Cold War, which was itself a major catalyst for PME reform. Both periods typify the institutional challenges and paradigm shifts that the current security environment represents. Intriguingly, at the time of writing this second reformation is in many ways still in progress but there has yet to be any significant modification to the essential personal and professional competencies required of effective military professionals or of the PME needed to generate these capabilities. Finally, the chapter looks at practical questions and challenges of conducting graduate liberal arts education programs in a military institution. It exposes the tension between the policy decisions made at the highest levels of the profession and the day to day application of those policies. More particularly this last section of the chapter examines the practical application of the appropriate and necessary learning methodologies and the frictions created as the Canadian Forces College has, and continues, to transform itself from a classic staff college to a school of higher learning.

Prior to 1939, the Canadian military had sent officers to the United Kingdom for staff and defence college programs. Only a handful of officers attended each year but these were sufficient for the needs of Canada's very small permanent military. From the outbreak of hostilities until 1942, Canada continued to rely on the British services for war staff training, but in that year, steps were taken to establish Canadian Army staff courses and this was followed in late 1943 with the opening of the Royal Canadian Air Force War Staff Course in Toronto. In 1945 both programs were retained and expanded to pre-war British lengths, two years for the army and one year for the air force.[4]

The army program focused, self admittedly, on tactics up to the division level, but the context was more in keeping with what we would call the operational level and the pedagogical thrust was clearly towards developing intellectual flexibility. Describing the program, the Commandant, Brigadier-General W.A. (Bill) Milroy stated that students would graduate with a "thorough understanding of the principles and techniques" of land operations, including "specialized staff skills, a knowledge of military management, and the functions of the staff." The latter included logical and critical thinking as well as communications skills. Graduates would also gain a grasp of national security issues in their broadest sense. Finally, wrote Milroy, the course was designed to include ample opportunity for the practice of staff skills in solving "typical command and staff problems encountered in war and situations short of war throughout the world, with emphasis on the divisional level and below."[5] In sum, the Army conducted a program clearly oriented to developing staff officers for employment with large field force organizations while at the same time offering a glimpse at the geopolitical roots of defence and a grounding in critical thinking.

The air force had been on the same track even during the war. As early as August 1943, Air Commodore George Wait, the Commandant of the Royal Canadian Air Force War Staff Course in Toronto, wrote that while his curriculum focused on staff work, the program of studies also included lectures given by well-qualified visiting speakers, both officers and civilian officials, on a variety of topics, including: other services, allied and enemy forces, matters of strategic direction of the war, and war production. "Only by such a means," he noted, "can the students be given the broader and more authoritative outlook that they will require in staff positions."[6] Wait's overall philosophy was fairly clear: staff officers, although expected to produce standardized staff products, needed a healthy intellectual capacity and a breadth of knowledge which allowed them to situate their work in a broader security context in order to best develop those products. The connection to liberal education, while implicit, was apparent.

At the end of hostilities Wait proposed a much more explicit educational model.

> The [proposed] Course… is a comprehensive one, and will be *conducted on University lines*. The course is designed to make an officer *think straight* and to *get his thoughts down clearly on paper*. The amount and depth of his thinking will depend entirely upon himself. There will be little use for anyone to come on the Course expecting to do only the bare minimum of work and to get by. The candidate must want to make the Service a career; want to take the Course; *have a high level of ability*

to learn; and have a reasonable education (minimum Senior Matricula-
tion). Given student officers of this calibre, the 6 months Course should
be of great value to the R.C.A.F.[7]

This approach was still apparent a decade later as evinced in the foreword to the
1958-59 calendar that stated: "You are being given the opportunity to learn more
about the Services and their relationships to each other, and as well to read, write,
speak and think in such a manner as to improve your professional competence
and hence your usefulness to the Air Force."[8] The curriculum continued to reinforce the themes of effective thinking and communications; general knowledge
of the air force and of world affairs; an understanding of personnel matters and
of leadership; and a firm grasp of those issues involved in generating, sustaining
and employing air forces in both multi-service and international scenarios.[9] The
concluding entry in the calendar reminded students of the philosophy of the
College, one which continued to emphasize Wait's initial acceptance of education as an equal and increasingly senior partner to staff training.

The RCAF Staff College makes no attempt to graduate experts in a
particular field, nor does it expound any easy universally applicable
doctrines. Rather by providing its graduates with an *education of the
broadest scope* and by *developing habits of clear thinking*, it attempts
to provide them with the breadth of interest, *openness of mind, reasoning ability, and a broad view of their Service and profession*, which
will enable them to *master the specific tasks of any appointment and
to make sound decisions in any situation*.[10]

In passing it bears mention that the navy did not apparently see the need for a
domestic staff college and tended to focus on training of technical and tactical
competencies rather than broad education. It should also be mentioned that
at the operational-strategic level, after a brief attempt to create a joint war college which would help maintain the expertise so hard won during the war, the
government decided instead to open its own defence college – the National
Defence College – a Canadian version, more or less, of the Imperial Defence
College.

With this basic structure and educational philosophy in place, the Canadian
military entered the Cold War and at the same time embarked on a series of
significant UN peacekeeping and policing operations – what might today be

accurately described as stability operations – including Korea, Kashmir, the Suez, Congo and Cyprus to name a few during the following 20 years. During these years, Canadians played critical roles in the definition and development of the North American Air Defence Command and other NATO agencies and field formations. It was not a quiet time for the Canadian services. We might infer from the range of complex defence activities successfully undertaken during these years that the educational philosophy and curriculum in place were adequate to prepare senior officers for virtually any operational challenge.

In the mid-1960s, the government of the day decided to embark on an organizational transformation of seismic propositions. It had long been argued that there were systemic economies to be achieved by integrating certain functions of the services, particularly in the support and administrative domains, but now, the Minister of National Defence convinced his cabinet colleagues that the three services could be unified into a single service.[11] After the shock of this decision, the resided, senior leadership under General Jean Victor Allard embarked on the necessary reforms, one of which was to determine the demands that would be placed on this new institution. From these the professional attributes of the officer corps could be defined allowing the creation of the necessary PME structure to generate and develop these officers. In October 1967 that task was entrusted to Major-General Roger Rowley who, like Allard, was a combat veteran of the Second World War.

Under the mandate of the Officer Development Board, Rowley assembled a team with representatives of the three former services and set about to define the current and future security environment. Military roles in this regard fell into four broad categories: home defence including airspace and shoreline surveillance and control, as well as an ability to deal with minor lodgements; maritime defence, in particular with respect to defeating missile submarines and also in escorting expeditionary forces; meeting NATO commitments for land and air forces in Europe; and United Nations operations, normally through the provision of observers, but with the possibility of deploying peacekeepers or resorting to armed intervention.[12]

From this range of roles, Rowley defined those professional qualities that an officer would need in order to be effective in any of them:

- the soldierly virtues (classic qualities including loyalty, honour and courage; in short, a professional ethos);

- command ability (the ability to command groups of subordinates commensurate with rank);

- branch and specialty [military occupation] skill (infanteer, aerospace engineer, logistician, etc);

- list competence (the ability to employ large forces for sea, land, air or support operations; at this level, officers would not be expected to be expert in other than their own 'list') [what we would call Service or component competence];

- military expertise (knowledge of the capabilities of armed forces (both domestic and foreign) and an ability to provide strategic level military advice to government);

- intellectual capability (native intelligence for use in grasping concepts, reasoning logically and solving problems);

- executive ability (capacity to deal with problems and decisions that "defy solution"); and

- military-executive ability (the context in which the officer will apply his executive ability and military expertise and give his advice to government).[13]

He also presented these in word pictures and graphically. The latter representation took the form of a simple yet elegant graph which showed that while two of the attributes were constant (i.e., command ability and soldierly virtues), the others varied in importance with rank (and appointment). Command ability and soldierly virtues were always considered of utmost importance to the effectiveness of the officer (and arguably, to his/her organization).

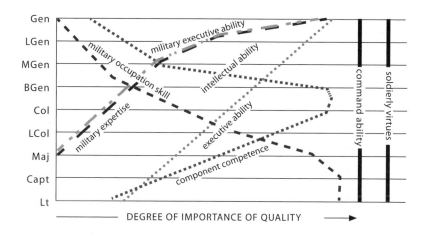

Gen

LGen

MGen

BGen

Col

LCol

Maj

Capt

Lt

military executive ability

military occupation skill

intellectual ability

military expertise

executive ability

component competence

command ability

soldierly virtues

DEGREE OF IMPORTANCE OF QUALITY ⟶

Figure 4.1: Variation in Importance of Qualities with Rank[14]

Rowley saw the other qualities as varying in importance at different points in an officer's career. For example, military occupation skills, such as commanding an infantry platoon, became less important as an officer advanced in rank, while at the same time, military-executive ability (i.e., the ability to advise government on matters of national security), would be vital for a general or admiral. Whether these qualities were unique to the Canadian military or to militaries generally, or whether they were more broadly applicable to all professions (with reference to the military replaced by other professional competencies), is an intriguing question. What appears reasonably certain is that Rowley had found a way to inclusively summarize the qualities common to all officers in the Canadian context. Having identified these officer qualities the Board was then able to derive a series of "guiding precepts" for an officer development system. Among other things, the new system must:

- prepare officers to contribute to a Canadian national strategy;

- impart the Canadian military ethic;

- remain in consonance with scientific, technological, sociological, economic, educational, military and strategic changes;

- accept the baccalaureate as the basic educational level for entry to the officer corps;

- ensure that courses taught at the military college are relevant to the technical and operational requirements of the military;

- provide the appropriate professional-development course material at the right stage to assist the officer in the orderly development of the qualities demanded of him at succeeding levels;

- encourage original research on military matters within the officer corps; and

- permit no degradation of operational effectiveness.

To attain these aims the system must, in addition, be efficiently organized, well integrated and effectively commanded.[15]

From this point the Report went on to define the structure and functions of the various schools and colleges that would make up the "Canadian Defence Education Centre," which was intended to be a single "officer factory" providing all the academic and professional education needed for the officer corps.[16] Within the Canadian Defence Education Centre (CDEC), a Canadian Defence College would offer a staff school for junior officers, absorb the existing army staff college, and create a truly joint command and staff course on the basis of the RCAF Staff College. From that point however, he proposed two new programs of study. The first he titled the Advanced Military Studies Course, defining it as a 10-month program "at the lieutenant-colonel level to broaden list competence and emphasize military expertise, particularly through the study of high-level military operations."[17] He added another new program which would replace the National Defence College. This National Security Course was intended to "develop to the fullest extent possible an awareness of the national and international environment and thus to impart military-executive ability."[18]

While these courses would impart knowledge and to some extent skills, "the policy of making the courses sufficiently demanding to help build intellectual ability and executive ability is recognized. Emphasis on the military virtues including leadership is recognized throughout."[19] In other words, the professional development process would emphasize not just skills and knowledge, but also the cultivation of logical and ethical thought. Additionally post commissioning learning, "must [include] a post-graduate program ... [fulfilling service needs for special and non-specialist officers] with a fairly extensive understanding in one or other of the many disciplines that are part of the corpus of knowledge that the military profession embraces."[20] Together the content, intellectual rigour and ethical context would contribute to the formation of military professionals.

Rowley's concept of a CDEC was not implemented for both large and small-P political reasons, nor was the AMSC. A loose confederation of pre-existing programs and agencies was instituted and the air force staff college became a joint institution – the Canadian Forces College.[21] But before moving away from Rowley, it is important to look at other recommendations that he made.

The foundation for officer professional competency and for further professional development was that officers needed not only typical training in strategy, tactics, equipment and processes, but also required a broad education which would give them the intellectual tools to deal with any situation. The fundamental building block was a university education and Rowley's recommendation was that all officers possess a Bachelor's degree from the outset of their service careers. Additionally, said Rowley, by building a degree into the recruiting criteria for new officers, the CF would have some degree of assurance that it was drawing from the best candidate pool possible.[22]

Once an officer graduated and was commissioned, the report recommended that there be access to post-graduate education, mostly for specialist officers, but also including a "sprinkling of non-specialists" who would profit from in-depth education in any one of the disciplines associated with the military profession. Finally, Rowley foresaw the possibility of aggregating the learning from the professional courses so that an officer could at some point achieve a Masters of Military Science. This was not to be a "box-top" sort of degree but one founded on legitimate learning: "co-operation between the military and academic elements will be necessary to ensure that courses that carry credit are adequately conceived and presented so that they will have academic credibility."[23]

These three elements have in fact been instituted either by or in conjunction with the Royal Military College of Canada. In fact RMCC established undergraduate degrees in the very early 1960s and while not all officers attended RMCC, this college has consistently been the source of between 20 to 30 percent of officer production.[24] Similarly, RMCC had created a graduate program in the late 1960s that directly addressed the need for graduate education (initially Masters and more recently PhDs) that are germane to the competencies required of officers. While graduate studies had been self-initiated to allow RMCC to be seen as a complete university, the War Studies and the Defence and Security Management and Policy programs have graduated hundreds of serving Regular and Reserve officers.[25] Finally as described later in this chapter RMCC, in collaboration with the Canadian Forces College, has now developed and implemented a Masters in Defence Studies which qualified students can complete in conjunction with the Command and Staff Program.

The need for developments such as these had been the subject of studies done in the late 1980s. The first of these, an National Defence Headquarters (NDHQ) initiated study called "Senior Officer Professional Development" found that the professional development activities then available for senior leaders were generally adequate but that the policy and structure lacked "purpose." As a result, the CF was failing to adequately prepare these officers for the senior appointments associated with their rank.[26] The results of this study and the fundamental soundness of the Rowley Report were commented on in an MPA thesis completed by Lieutenant-General Richard Evraire in 1988. Evraire, an infantry officer, held command appointments at the unit and brigade level as well as several demanding staff appointments including being Canada's military representative in NATO Headquarters (HQ) before retiring in 1997. Additionally he had served as commandant of the Collège militaire royal de St-Jean, the National Defence College in Kingston and the NATO Defence College in Rome. In his thesis, Evraire concluded that the professional development system for ranks up to Lieutenant-Colonel was adequate, but beyond that, it was lacking. Senior leaders did not have a systematic means of remaining current with societal or security and defence matters, the very essence of their senior appointments. He found this situation to be "unacceptable on professional and ethical grounds."[27] Evraire proposed as series of content improvements along with a suite of policy changes which would allow the senior leaders of the profession to develop and maintain the necessary competencies for strategic level appointments. Ultimately, he argued, a revitalized and refocused program would "help establish the credibility of the Officer corps as the purveyor of strategic military advice."[28]

As the next section of this chapter will demonstrate, despite the recommendations and urgings of experienced senior leaders such as Evraire, Allard and Rowley, the professional development system continued to make do, benefitting from time to time with local initiatives such as the masters programs at RMCC, but without any centrally directed and managed policy framework. As Allard had predicted, disaster was imminent.

At the strategic level, in 1987, the government released a decidedly expansionist Cold War white paper which called for unprecedented increases in both regular and reserve elements of the CF and the infusion of massive funds for equipment replacement and capability enhancements.[29] Then, in late November 1989 the Berlin Wall came down and shortly thereafter, CF personnel and equipment programs went into a relative freefall. There was of course no peace dividend as such, with 1990 marking Canada's operational involvement in the first Gulf War, while at home, extraordinary levels of aboriginal unrest led to armed standoffs and the deployment of a brigade sized task force to support civil authorities throughout southern Quebec in what came to be known as the Oka Crisis. These events quickly segued into the dissolution of the Yugoslav state and again unparalleled levels of Canadian involvement including incidents of direct combat as well as the deaths of several peacekeepers to mines, Improvised Explosive Devices (IEDs) and accidents. These operations and others, piled on top of the strategic retrenchment, might have been manageable but the profession unfortunately hit a reef of ethical crises.

In 1993, Canadian peacekeepers tortured and killed a detained Somali teenager. Subsequently the chain of command, up to the national level, tried to downplay the event and this led ultimately to a public inquiry. This inquiry found problems with decisions on how the mission had been mounted and conducted as well as the apparent refusal of several senior leaders to accept responsibility.[30] Other equally disturbing incidents followed in the former Yugoslavia. In this case there were allegations of illegal activities including black marketeering and sexual misconduct involving Canadian peacekeepers stationed at the Bakovici hospital in Bosnia. While only six soldiers were ultimately found guilty, the initial disclosure to the public was that which remained in most people's memory.[31] Meanwhile, in 1994, Lieutenant-General Roméo Dallaire found himself in charge of a seemingly hopeless task in trying to prevent the Rwandan genocide[32] and two years later a Canadian-led mission to the Congo sputtered and fizzled.

The Canadian Forces were caught in what amounted to a professional perfect storm and in the eyes of many Canadians, the vessel was foundering. By 1997, this led the Minister of National Defence to seek advice from a number of respected Canadian academics as to what should be done to fix the profession. His

"Report to the Prime Minister" detailed literally dozens of recommendations and also saw the establishment of a Minister's Monitoring Committee whose main functions were to observe and report on the restructuring of the reserve forces and reforms to officer professional education.[33]

As early as 1994, the profession itself had already embarked on a series of initiatives to set right its PME system. That year had marked the nadir of officer PME. The Federal budget, and the new Defence white paper (replacing the plan of 1987), announced the closure of two of the country's three military colleges, as well as the Staff School and the National Defence College.[34] But the same year saw the convening of a Rowley-style board to set the profession back on its feet, namely the Officer Development Review Board, under the direction of Major-General Robert S. Morton, who relied heavily on Rowley for much of his seminal thinking.[35] By early 1997, the senior leadership of the Forces had approved the creation of an Advanced Military Studies Course and a National Security Studies Course, the former for Colonels and Captains (Navy) to prepare them for operational level appointments, the latter for strategic level posts.[36] More will be said about the design development and conduct of the AMSC later in the paper.

Much more work remained to be done in reshaping the officer corps and this took place within a team, led initially by Dallaire, who had by 1998 been appointed to the *ad hoc* position of Special Advisor to the CDS for Professional Development. The series of policy statements produced under the title of *Officership 2020* laid out the context within which the CF would operate in the early 21st century and defined the salient characteristics required of the officer corps. The operating environment was characterized by an increasing "complex and ambiguous" "global security environment," a need for technical sophistication to "dominate the battle-space physically and intellectually," a complex society with stiff "competition for the best and brightest Canadian citizens," and a period demanding more "efficient and transparent resource management." To meet these challenges the officer corps would, in addition to applying military force, sound leadership and high professional standards, have to be capable of critical thinking, embracing and managing change, and creating and participating in a learning organization.[37] Once again the message to the profession was clear: change and ambiguity were constants and intellectual acuity and flexibility were essential for the health of the profession and ultimately the security of the nation.

In looking specifically at "strategic leaders," *Officership 2020* began to use the notion of competences, borrowing the concept from the Public Service of Canada. This in turn has led to the development of a Professional Development Framework (PDF) which was published in late 2006 and which in part calls for the reformulation of officer professional development.[38] This PDF (see Figure 4.2) briefly lists the challenges facing the Canadian Forces as well as the broad traits needed for effective leadership:

> ... the effect of the general renewal underway since the mid-1990's; the expanding range and increased frequency of operational missions and tasks; the presence of more military and non-military partners in peace support operations; a public more aware of and reactive to military affairs; and changes in society and the social make-up of the CF. Numerous scholars, defence analysts and defence scientists listed significant challenges for the 21st century including poor Canada-US relations, emerging technology, force restructuring, and budgeting/resourcing for military transformation. These issues all exist within the broad spectrum of new security threats, failing states, pandemics, migration, religious extremism and narco-cartels.[39]

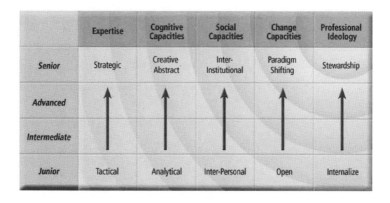

Figure 4.2: Professional Development Framework

The framework goes on to distill the necessary leadership competencies down to five streams – expertise, cognitive capacities, social capacities, change capacities and professional ideology – these having different traits over the course of an officer's career. Much like the Rowley model, none was fixed; unlike the Rowley model none tended to grow or shrink with rank and duties.[40]

CHAPTER 4

While these reforms were taking place, Canada continued to participate in a range of operations across the world and since 2002, land, maritime and air forces have been engaged in operations in South West Asia. In that theatre the CF has been involved in extensive combat operations and has suffered the first combat deaths since the Korean War. At the operational and strategic levels senior CF leaders have contributed both to the formulation of the NATO campaign plan[41] and have provided advice to the Canadian government on the most appropriate ways and means to contribute effectively to that campaign. Those ways and means have led to the definition of a Defence, Diplomacy, Development and Commerce (3D + C) strategy where all elements are seen as integrated tools in Canada's response.[42] To be clear, Canada is using a tailored and not always military response in helping resolve the problems and threats facing Afghanistan and this speaks well of the ability of senior leaders to see the bigger issues and solutions; in other words, in situations of complexity and ambiguity.

That multidisciplinary approach to campaigning had been implicit in PME programs at the Canadian Forces College for many years and by 2010 had become an explicit and growing part of the curriculum. The College's commandant from 2007 to 2009, Brigadier-General David Fraser, had commanded the Multi-National Brigade (Regional Command South) in Afghanistan, and had also served in the Bi-National Planning Group in Colorado Springs. He had a full understanding of the demands of the post-9/11 security paradigm. General Fraser indicated that one of his major concerns is that graduates of the College's programs "avoid the mental trap of being afraid to deviate from the plan. They must know how to design and use a plan as a starting point and know how to adapt it as the situation evolves…. The overall intent [of our programs] is to foster a high degree of mental agility."[43] Building and conducting courses and programs which foster the development of that ability has not always been easy and is the focus of the balance of this chapter.

The design, development and subsequent conduct of the Advanced Military Studies Course, offered from 1998 until 2008 (when it was replaced by the National Security Program), will provide the example for the challenges faced in marrying what is, for all intents, graduate level education with the prescriptive content defined by the 'needs analysis' which was conducted just over a decade ago. At that time, the normal delivery strategy of the Canadian Forces College for its Command and Staff program saw a preponderance of lectures complemented by discussions and reinforced by a limited number of case studies, individual writing projects, visits and command post exercises. While there were ample occasions for the students to express themselves, the learning environment was largely passive in nature – it was possible to pass the program without much original thinking.

Exacerbating the situation was the reliance on the use of generalist Directing Staff (DS) to work with the students in the classroom and to assess their abilities. The DS were expert in their former warfare specialties, but simply did not have the depth of expertise needed to be effective teachers and assessors across the range of topics included in the 10-month curriculum. The need for highly effective faculty had already been noted both by the RCAF War Staff Course and later by Rowley. The latter put not too fine a point on it, stating that without qualified faculty in the classroom discussions rapidly devolved to the "mutual exchange of ignorance".[44]

The design team for the AMSC saw this as a critical weakness in the College's educational philosophy, one which could not be repeated in what was to be an essential learning program for warfighting commanders. It was therefore decided that a graduate school delivery methodology would largely replace the approach used for the more junior program. The lecture discussion, a concept happily borrowed from the senior British professional development programs, was adopted as a more active way of presenting material; it had the benefit of allowing students to immediately debate impressions of a lecturer and the topic, and to then return to that lecturer with well formulated questions. The original serial of the AMSC also included seminar papers, students being required to develop two graduate quality term papers and present and defend them before their peers. The seminars and papers were assessed not by the Senior Directing Staff, but by subject matter experts, who like graduate faculty were indeed expert in the topic and guided the students along a viable path. Case studies were devised which in addition to using SMEs, provided the students with primary documentation where available; the cases were mature historical examples which ensured that adequate literature was available from which to do credible analysis. The scenarios covered a range of operations from general war to more limited campaigns and also peace support operations.

Finally, planning exercises were conducted in a practitioner-rich environment. Students were given retired operational commanders as coaches (a notion this time borrowed from the US Joint Forces Staff College at Norfolk), coaches who

were not shy about offering constructive criticism, and a range of current practitioners to represent the experts that one would normally expect to find on a
staff, or in theatre, particularly in the case of representatives from other government departments and NGOs.[45]

The overall intent of the AMSC pedagogy was to work the students such that
they first acquired a degree of mastery of the topics, working to analyze the
material provided and frequently synthesize or evaluate concepts and events.
It was expressly intended that the students would achieve levels of learning in
the upper range of Benjamin Bloom's Taxonomy of Learning[46]; that is, analysis,
synthesis and evaluation. Just knowing or doing was not sufficient for these students. While the range of material covered was defined by the complexity of
warfighting at the operational level, the key concepts were not only presented,
but they were debated and challenged as one might expect to find in a graduate setting. The concept was presented to Lieutenant-General Dallaire who was
then the senior education authority within the CF. Comparing it to his own student experiences in the UK as well as his personal experiences in Rwanda, he
was happy with the content and rigour of the syllabus.[47]

While the breadth of topics was limited, the timetable was full– the bane of
all programs at the College – and students simply did not have the amount of
time that one might expect in a graduate program. There were approximately 18
hours or more of class activities each week and students were working well into
the night, every night, to be ready to contribute in this very active curriculum.
For those who had either been away from an academic setting for some time,
did not come from a liberal arts discipline, or had no university experience, the
workload was demanding if not excessive. As a result, subsequent serials of the
course saw the reduction in the number of papers from two to one as well as a
reduction in the number of case studies.

The successes and failures of the AMSC, now almost 15 years past, have more
recently played into the development of a new activity – the National Security
Program, introduced in 2008 – which seeks to blend the content of both the
AMSC and NSSC, while at the same time in essence adopting the name from
Rowley's National Security Course. This new program was defined from the professional learning outcomes established for the pre-existing courses so that no
professional development is lost. Conversely, the delivery paradigm became fully
that of graduate education: there were three terms – one for global security

and governance issues, one for strategic leadership and resource management, and a third for command and campaigning at the operational level. Within each term, students would take core courses of 40 classroom hours. Each course would be conducted by a qualified civilian or military faculty member who had designed the course curriculum using a set of prescribed learning outcomes as the basis for content and student assessment.[48] In the initial years, military students completed all three terms, while civilian executive public servants could opt to take electives rather than the operational courses. All students were to complete electives of their choice and those seeking a Master of Arts through the Royal Military College of Canada needed to develop a major research project. As was the case with the AMSC, the intent has been to have students work to increase both their knowledge as well as their intellectual capacity to deal with complex topics.

The notion of graduate level education was not a whim. Rowley had talked about it and now the officer corps, while not embracing the concept without some grumbling, was prepared to see professional programs change their methodology so that graduate credentials could be earned. Since 2002, the Command and Staff Course has included the option for an accredited professional Master of Defence Studies for qualified students who do additional work;[49] more recently the equivalent Reserve Force program (formerly for Reserve officers only but in 2008 expanded to include both Reserve and Regular officers) has been restructured to permit the awarding of graduate credits.[50] College leadership is quick and correct to point out that the graduate degree is not the aim, rather a mature intellect, capable of dealing with the professional challenges of the post-Cold War world is still the target.

Indeed, the present day international context is not unlike the uncertainty faced by Canada's Services during the early Cold War of the 1940s and 50s and by Rowley at the end of the 1960s. Yet, there are those today who look back to those earlier years as ones of relative constancy and predictability. They were of course anything but; their ambiguities were just different than those which we face today. Regardless of the context, however, military professionals must be able to respond effectively, with logic and morality. Given these constraints, notions of education of the broadest scope, clear thinking, openness of mind, and sound (decision-making) in any situation[51] resonate as clearly today as they would have in the last half century. They add up to military effectiveness and they are priceless.

1   Randall Wakelam and Howard Coombs, eds. *The Report of the Officer Development Board: Maj-Gen Roger Rowley and the Education of the Canadian Forces* (Waterloo: Laurier Centre for Military Strategic and Disarmament Studies, 2010), 4. This edited volume contains the complete first volume of Rowley's three volume report issued in 1969. In addition there are three essays which further develop the question of senior officer education and professional thought.

2   This construct has been similarly argued by Dr. Stephen J. Harris of the Directorate of History and Heritage, DND. He argues that since a military is not often at war it must spend long periods in study in order to be prepared for any future conflicts. "The competent army is one which [is engaged in] critical study and thinking…." See: Stephen J. Harris, *Canadian Brass: the Making of a Professional Officer Corps* (Toronto: University of Toronto Press, 1986), 4.

3   Administrative functions of the three services were formally "integrated" in 1964 and subsequently the services were unified by act of parliament, becoming the Canadian Forces. See for example Jack L. Granatstein, *Canada's Army: Waging War and Keeping the Peace* (Toronto: University of Toronto Press, 2002), 352-358.

4   Harris, 192-209.

5   Brigadier-General William A. Milroy, "The Course", *Snowy Owl*, Vol. 4, No. 2 (1967-68), 2-3.

6   William R. Shields and Dace Sefers, *Canadian Forces Command and Staff College: A History 1797-1946* (Toronto: Canadian Forces College, 1987), 4-16. This document was part of a Canadian Forces College History project.

7   Shields and Sefers, 4-28. Emphasis added.

8   Department of National Defence, "Introduction", *R.C.A.F. Staff College Calendar Course 23: 1958-59*.

9   Department of National Defence, "Staff Training Studies", *R.C.A.F. Staff College Calendar Course 23: 1958-59*.

10   Department of National Defence, "Conclusion", *R.C.A.F. Staff College Calendar Course 23: 1958-59*. Emphasis added.

11   Administrative functions of the three services were formally "integrated" in 1964 and subsequently the services were unified by act of parliament, becoming the Canadian Forces. See for example Jack L, Granatstein, 352-358.

12   Wakelam and Coombs, 25-27.

13   Wakelam and Coombs, 43-44.

14   Wakelam and Coombs, 45.

15   Wakelam and Coombs, 49.

16   Wakelam and Coombs, 86.

17   Ibid.

18   Ibid.

19   Ibid.

20   Wakelam and Coombs, 87.

21   The plan was attacked by proponents of the Royal Military College, Canada's original cadet college as the latter would have closed its doors under the ODB construct. There was also limited support from the Minister who reminded Rowley's successor that the desire of the times was to reduce the military presence in the national capital rather than increase it as the CDEC would have done. See: Randall Wakelam "Officer Professional Education in the Canadian Forces and the Rowley Report, 1969", *Historical Studies in Education/Revue d'histoire de l'éducation*, Vol. 16, No. 2 (Fall 2004), 287-314.

22   Wakelam and Coombs, 38-39.

23   Wakelam and Coombs, 87.

24   Royal Military College of Canada Calendar 1959-60.

25   Royal Military College of Canada Calendar 1967-68, 222-225, See also Richard A. Preston, *To Serve Canada: A History of the Royal Military College Since the Second World War* (Ottawa: University of Ottawa Press, 1991), Appendix P.

26   Richard J. Evraire, *General and Senior Officer Professional Development in the Canadian Forces*, unpublished MPA thesis, (Kingston: Queen's University, 1988), 11. The study cited by Evraire was subsequently renamed "The General and Senior Officer Professional Development Study" or informally the "Lightburn Study" after its principal author.

27   Evraire, 11-12.

28   Ibid., 103.

29   Department of National Defence, *Challenge and Commitment: A Defence Policy for Canada* (Ottawa: 1987).

30   These events contributed to the replacement of two Chiefs of Defence Staff and the protracted embarrassment of the profession during the extensive board of inquiry. See: Commission of Inquiry into the Deployment of Canadian Forces to Somalia, *Dishonoured Legacy: The Lessons of the Somalia Affair, Report of the Commission of Inquiry into the Deployment of Canadian Forces to Somalia*, (Ottawa: Public Works and Government Services Canada, 1997).

31   See: The Canadian Encyclopedia. *Military Investigates Misconduct*, retrieved on 31 October 2011 at <http://www.thecanadianencyclopedia.com/index.cfm?PgNm=TCE&Params=M1AR TM0010961>; Raymond Belanger, "Bakovici scandal ... the beat goes on", *Esprit de Corps* (1 June 1998), retrieved on 31 October 2011 from *The Free Library by Farlex* at <http://www.thefreelibrary.com/ Bakovici+scandal+...+the+beat+goes+on.-a030527627>.

32   His personal experience has since been captured in Roméo Dallaire, with Brent Beardsley, *Shake Hands with the Devil: the Failure of Humanity in Rwanda* (Toronto: Random House, 2003). A feature film of the same name was released in 2007.

33   Hon. Douglas M. Young, *Report to the Prime Minister on the Leadership and Management of the Canadian Forces* (Ottawa: Department of National Defence, 1997).

34   Department of National Defence, *National Defence Budget Impact 1994* (Ottawa: 1994), 7-9.

35   Department of National Defence, *Report of the Officer Development Review Board* (Ottawa: 1995).

CHAPTER 4

36   The author was one of three designers for these two courses and subsequently led the development team which fleshed out the curriculum for the first AMSC. See: Randall Wakelam "Senior Professional Military Education for the Twenty-First Century", *Canadian Defence Quarterly*, Vol. 27, No. 1 (Autumn, 1997), 14-18.

37   These themes were repeated in many Officership 2020 publications. See for example, Canada Department of National Defence, *Canadian Officership in the 21st Century: Detailed Analysis and Strategy for Launching Implementation* (Officership 2020) (Ottawa: 2001).

38   Robert W. Walker, *The Professional Development Framework: Generating Effectiveness in Canadian Forces Leadership*. (Kingston, ON: Canadian Forces Leadership Institute, Technical Report, 2006).

39   Walker, 9. Walker drew these notions from a range studies done by Karol J. Wenek, a researcher for CFLI and long time military psychologist and Human Resources Specialist. Among these were *Institutional Challenge and Change in the 21st Century: The Road Ahead for Canadian Forces Leadership*, presentation at Armed Forces and Society (IUS) Conference, Kingston, Canada, October 2002.

40   Walker, 31. The figure depicts the four leader levels in the vertical and the five leader elements horizontally.

41   See for example General Rick Hiller and Howard Coombs, "Planning For Success: The Challenge of Applying Operational Art in Post-Conflict Afghanistan", *Canadian Military Journal*, Vol. 6, No. 3 (Autumn 2005).

42   See: Department of Foreign Affairs and International Trade, *Canada's International Policy Statement: A Role of Pride and Influence in the World* (Ottawa: 2005). The document is divided into four sections: Defence, Diplomacy, Development and Commerce, retrieved on 7 December 2011 from <http://merln.ndu.edu/whitepapers/Canada_2005.pdf>.

43   Comments by Brigadier-General David A. Fraser to faculty at Canadian Forces College Toronto, Sep 2007.

44   Wakelam and Coombs, 215.

45   Department of National Defence, *CFC 203 Advanced Military Studies Course Syllabus Course 1*, (Toronto: 1998).

46   In the 1950s Benjamin Bloom, an American psychologist, developed a framework, or taxonomy, to describe the various forms of learning. See for example: J.S. Atherton, "Learning and Teaching; Bloom's Taxonomy", *Learning*, retrieved 31 October 2011 from <http://www.learningandteaching.info/learning/bloomtax.htm>.

47   The author was the lead developer for the original AMSC and participated in the briefing to Lieutenant-General Dallaire in the fall of 1996.

48   This is not to suggest that these courses would slavishly follow a "training" plan fixed set of lessons, but that the faculty member, normally holding a relevant advanced degree and or significant experience in the discipline, would design the course so that the student met certain expectations.

49   The program is described on both the College website and the Royal Military College website. RMCC is the actual degree granting body, <http://www.rmcc.forces.gc.ca/aca/ac-pe/gsc-adc/au-ua/fa/ds-ed-eng.asp>, accessed 7 December 2011.

50   At the time of writing this "trial" program may or may not survive funding cuts that are likely to be applied across National Defence in 2011.

51   Royal Canadian Air Force , "Conclusion.", *R.C.A.F. Staff College Calendar Course 23: 1958-59* Toronto, 1958.

CHAPTER 5

ENCOUNTERING AND COPING WITH COMPLEXITY: SYSTEMS THINKING AND METHODOLOGIES

Dr. Bill Bentley

Introduction

National security professionals, both those in uniform and civilian officials, constantly deal with complex problems. These occur on and off the battlefield, especially at the operational and strategic levels of war and conflict. These problems are more than complicated – much more. Complex problems exhibit properties and behaviours not found in complicated problems, no matter how difficult. Complex problems can only be fully understood through the lens of complexity science, and the main cognitive tool required to cope with this complexity is systems thinking. National security professionals, therefore, must be educated in the disciplines of complexity theory and general systems theory.

This chapter will distinguish between analytical, linear thinking suitable for analysis and decision-making in the realm of complicated problems, and systems thinking necessary to deal with complex problems. The essential elements of complexity theory will be discussed as they apply to the General System of War and Conflict. The chapter concludes with an explanation of one powerful systems thinking methodology suitable for inclusion in all advanced professional development curricula.

Linearity and Analysis

Most readers will have been carefully and successfully educated in a mode of thinking profoundly shaped by Newtonian science. This cognitive orientation is referred to as analytical thinking, a phrase derived from the fact that it is based on analysis; that is, the breaking down of a problem into its component parts to identify what is broken or wrong. Once this issue is rectified the parts are reassembled to form a working whole. In effect, the whole is equal to the sum of the parts.

This approach to decision-making and problem solving has been enormously successful when dealing with linear systems, no matter how complicated. For a system to be linear it has to meet two simple conditions. The first is proportionality indicating that changes in system outputs are proportional to systems inputs. Thus, for example, the speed of your car is directly proportional to the degree of compression on the car's accelerator pedal. Such systems display what in economics is called "constant returns to scale," implying that small causes produce small effects and large causes generate large effects.

The second condition of linearity, called additivity, underlies the process of analysis of such systems, as described in the first paragraph above. The central concept, as already mentioned, is that the whole is equal to the sum of the parts. This allows the problem to be broken into smaller pieces that, once solved, can be added back together to obtain the solution to the original problem.

Complexity

There are, however, many problems that disobey both proportionality and additivity. That is to say, they are non-linear and are referred to as complex problems. These types of problems or systems are described and explained by complexity theory.[1] Several variants of this theory found their way into the social sciences soon after their development in the natural sciences. Between the 1930s and 1950s scientists (especially physicists, mathematicians and ecologists) built a significant case against the dominant Enlightenment (Newtonian) paradigm. Premised on the belief in human rationality and fundamental physical order, this paradigm promulgated linear patterns for demonstrating high levels of order and predictability by using reductionist methods that postulated that all physical phenomena will change in a gradual manner and following foreseeable trajectories. The subsequent Industrial Revolution seemed to confirm the ability of human beings not only to comprehend but also to manipulate and control the natural world. In this respect, the framework of instrumental-rational action has become the standard against which alternate claims are justified. However, during the 20th century development of the theory of relativity and quantum mechanics initially probed and then pushed the limits of the linear Enlightenment paradigm. Out of this arose complexity theory that demonstrated that while some phenomena are orderly, others are apparently disorderly and non-linear but highly interactive.[2]

Interactive complexity is based on the behaviour of the parts and the result-ing interactions among them. The greater freedom of action of each individual part and the more linkages among the components the greater is the system's interactive complexity. Interactively complex systems are also highly sensitive to inputs; immeasurably small inputs can generate disproportionately large effects. Equally important with interactive complexity, it is often impossible to isolate individual causes and their effects since all the parts are connected in a complex web. Interactive complexity produces fundamentally unpredictable and even counter-intuitive behaviour. Such systems must be viewed holistically – the whole is greater than the sum of the parts. They cannot be properly investigated using analytical techniques; rather, they require systems thinking to achieve a full understanding of their dynamics and behaviour.

Complex adaptive systems (CAS) constitute a special case of complex systems. They are capable of changing and learning from experience. Complexity theo-rist John Holland defines a CAS in a social, political or organizational context as a dynamic network of many agents acting in parallel, constantly acting and reacting to what the other agents are doing.[3] Such systems exhibit coherence under change via conditional action and anticipation, and they do so without central direction. Since the control of a CAS tends to be highly disbursed and decentralized, any coherent behaviour in the system arises from the competition and cooperation among the agents themselves. It is the accumulation of all the individual decisions taken by the multitude of agents that produces the overall behaviour of the system.

The concept of a CAS is actually a very broad meta-concept, but at its core is a single image – the concept of an adaptive whole – a system that will contain sub-systems, while itself being capable of acting as a sub-system of yet a wider system. Such an adaptive whole may be able to survive in a changing environ-ment which is delivering shocks to it, if it has available both processes of com-munication and a repertoire of responses which can enable it to adapt to its changing circumstances. The general model of this kind of organized complex-ity is that there exists a hierarchy of levels of organization each more complex than the one below. The higher level is characterized by emergent properties that do not exist at the lower level. Indeed, more than the fact that they do not exist at the lower level, emergent properties are meaningless in the language appropriate at the lower level. Emergence, therefore, is a function of conjunc-tion whereby systems characteristics do not result from superposition (additive effects of system components-additivity) but instead from interactions among components.[4]

In such a model we can now see that elements of such a system, particularly at lower levels in the hierarchy, may be more or less linear and, therefore, amenable to analytical thinking. That is to say that analysis has not been discarded but rather is subsumed in the broader cognitive orientation of systems thinking.[5]

In response to the phenomena of hierarchy and emergence a specialized theory – hierarchy theory – has been developed. It is the discipline concerned with the fundamental differences between one level of complexity and another in a given system. Its ultimate aim is to provide both an account of the relationship between different levels and an account of how observed hierarchies come to be formed, what generates the levels and how emergence occurs. These hierarchies are characterized by processes of control operating at the interface between levels. In a hierarchy of systems, maintenance of the hierarchy will entail a set of processes in which there is a flow of information for purposes of regulation and/or control.

One leading systems theorist, Jamshid Gharajedaghi identifies five principles that, acting together as an interactive whole, define a CAS:[6]

Openness. Openness means that the behaviour of a CAS can be understood only in the context of its environment. The system's boundary thus becomes an arbitrary, subjective construct defined by the interest and level of ability and/or authority of the participating agents.

Purposefulness. A purposeful system is one that can produce not only the same outcomes in different ways in the same environment but different outcomes in both the same and different environments.

Multi-dimensionality. The ability to see complementary relations in opposing tendencies and to create feasible wholes with unfeasible parts.

Emergent Properties. Emergent properties are the properties of the whole, not the property of the parts, and cannot be deduced from the properties of the parts. However, they are the property of the interactions, not the sum of the actions of the parts and, therefore, have to be understood on their own terms.

Relying exclusively on an analytical approach fails to produce an understanding about emergent properties. The use of systems thinking is required to produce this understanding.

Counter-intuitiveness. This means that actions intended to produce a desired outcome may, in fact, but not necessarily, generate opposite results. Again, this phenomenon stands on a level of complexity that is also beyond the reach of the analytical approach.

War as a Complex Adaptive System

Before turning to the nature of systems thinking and systems methodologies that help in coping with Complex Adaptive Systems, it is important to see how war and conflict comprise such a system. As such, the General System of War and Conflict can only be fully comprehended through systems thinking. Perhaps the greatest military theorist of all time, General Carl von Clausewitz, understood this almost intuitively when he was working on his treatise – On War – during the years 1818-1830. American historian Allan Beyerchen explains in a seminal article published in the journal International Security titled, "Clausewitz, Non-Linearity and the Unpredictability of War" that Clausewitz had developed his theory of war as a response to the existing paradigm of Newtonian physics and the rationalistic tendencies of the Enlightenment. In reaction to the Positivistic approaches of Jomini and von Bulow, Clausewitz replied that war was not susceptible to linear thinking. On the contrary, Clausewitz's On War is suffused with the understanding that every war is an inherently complex, non-linear phenomenon. In a profoundly unconfused way Clausewitz understood that seeking exact, analytical solutions does not fit the reality of the problems posed by war.[7]

According to Clausewitz:[8]

> In war everything is uncertain and calculations have to be made with variable quantities. Other theorists direct their inquiry exclusively towards physical quantities, whereas, all military action is intertwined with psychological forces and effects. They consider only unilateral action, whereas, war consists of a continuous interaction of opposites.

He goes on to emphasize this, insisting upon the importance of interactivity's role in properly defining war:[9]

War belongs to the province of social life. War is not an activity of the will exerted upon inanimate matter as in mechanics, or upon a living but passive, yielding subject like the fine arts, but against an active and reacting force. Strictly speaking war is neither an art nor a science, rather it is part of man's social existence.

This insight was extended by Clausewitz to address the concept of non-proportionality, another characteristic of complex systems. Here cause and effect are not necessarily predictable – small causes can produce disproportionately large outcomes and vice versa. Thus, Clausewitz points out that in war:[10]

Success is not due simply to general causes. Particular factors can often be decisive – details known only to those who are on the spot. Issues can be decided by chances and incidents so minute as to figure in histories simply as footnotes.

In essence, the General System of War and Conflict is a meta-system comprising a hierarchy of sub-systems ascending from the tactical sub-system to the operational sub-system to the strategic sub-system and ultimately to the policy, or political, system as depicted below in Figure 5.1.

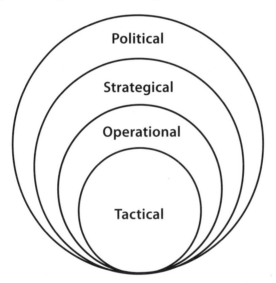

Figure 5.1: The General System of War and Conflict

There are numerous actors interacting at every level in the hierarchy of the over-all system and the number of major actors and other important factors increases as one moves up the system. At the same time each sub-system interacts with the others, directly or indirectly, thus increasing complexity even further. As one rises through the system, emergent properties are identified; such as, for example, the emergence of manoeuvre in the operational sub-system being that of a function of mass and mobility as opposed to fire and movement in the tactical sub-system.

An explicit recognition of the complex nature of war and conflict has recently been articulated very well by a leading US military theorist, Brigadier-General (ret'd) Huba Wass de Czega:

> Recent missions and their contexts have exceeded in novelty and complexity any that the US Armed Forces have experienced. Their novelty makes experience-gained intuition and published doctrine less reliable. Their complexity is not the more familiar kind, the complicated detail or structure such as those encountered in such operations as D-Day or Operation Desert Shield and Desert Storm but of a more difficult variety – the complexity that arises out of the interactions between the various elements of a problem over time and due to subtle relationships between cause and effect. It would be a mistake to suggest that this kind of complexity is only a property of irregular warfare or insurgency. This is a general condition.[11]

Systems Thinking

As discussed above, reductionism and analysis are not useful with interactively complex systems because they lose sight of the dynamics among components. The study of interactively complex systems must be systemic rather than reductionist and qualitative rather than quantitative and needs to use different heuristic approaches (modelling-design) rather than analytical problem solving.

The analytical approach has remained essentially intact for nearly four hundred years but systems thinking has already undergone three generations of change. The first generation of systems thinking (operations research) dealt with the challenges of interdependency in the context of mechanical (deterministic) systems. The second generation of systems thinking (cybernetics and open systems) dealt with the dual challenges of interdependency and self-organization (neg-entropy) in the context of living systems (ecology, for example).

CHAPTER 5   **71**

The third generation of systems thinking (modelling-design) responds to the triple challenges of interdependency, self-organization and choice in the context of socio-cultural systems (war, for example).

Systems thinking is the practice of thinking that takes a holistic view of complex events or phenomena seemingly caused by a myriad of isolated, independent and usually unpredictable forces or factors. Systems thinking views all events and phenomena as "wholes" interacting according to systems principles as described by Gharajedaghi. These principles underpin vastly different events and phenomena. Systems thinking recognizes that systems (organized wholes) ranging from soap bubbles to galaxies, ant colonies to nations can be better understood only when their wholeness (identity and structure) is maintained, thus permitting the study of the whole instead of the properties of their components. As a modelling language, systems thinking illustrates cause and effect relationships that cannot be adequately explained by the subject-verb-object constructions of natural languages like English.

In other words, the art of systems thinking lies in being able to recognize increasingly dynamically complex and subtle structures amid the wealth of details, pressures and cross-currents that attend all real settings. In fact, the essence of mastering systems thinking as a discipline lies in seeing patterns where others see only events and forces.

As with the concept of a CAS, systems thinking is a meta-subject. It is employed using specific systems thinking methodologies such as those advocated by a number of well known systems theorists such as Barry Richmond, Russell Ackoff and the aforementioned Jashmid Garajedaghi.[12] A particularly useful methodology is Soft Systems Methodology developed by Peter Checkland and his colleagues at the University of Lancaster in the UK. In fact, Checkland's book *Systems Thinking, Systems Practice* (London: John Wiley, 1999) is an excellent account of the whole systems movement and a complete history and description of SSM.[13]

Soft Systems Methodology

SSM is a learning system, a systemic method of inquiry. It makes use of models of purposeful human activity to explore complex adaptive systems. Comparing models with the perceived real world structures a discourse between conflicting interests which enable decisions to be made to improve the situation.

SSM is, in the language of social theory, a shift from one philosophy and sociology to a different philosophy and sociology. It is a move from Positivism and Functionalism to Phenomenology and Interpretive Sociology. The nature of this shift is one away from a static view of social reality as "something out there" which can be studied objectively by an outside observer as if social reality were similar to natural phenomena, to a process view which sees social reality as something being continuously constructed and reconstructed by human beings.[14] SSM is, thus, an advanced third generation version of systems thinking that recognizes that learning and acting in socio-cultural contexts (like war) requires that the process be fully informed by the major human sciences and their philosophical underpinnings.

SSM is conducted in basically three stages. The first stage is referred to simply as "Finding Out" about the complex problem, also called the ill-structured or "wicked" problem. The process is structured around three analyses. The first is a "stakeholder" analysis which identifies all the major actors in the situation and their relationship to one another. The second is a "social" analysis that establishes an understanding of the values, norms and roles at play in the situation. The third is a "political" analysis, in the sense of finding out where power lies in the system – which individuals, groups or communities. A key component of this overall analysis is clearly a sound understanding of the strategic culture at play.

An important technique employed in SSM in this stage is the creation of "rich pictures" of the situation as it emerges from the three analyses. The rationale for this is that the complexity of a human situation is always one of multiple interacting relationships. Finding out about a complex situation involves more than an explanation of objects within it. In complex problems, the relationships between objects in the system are also of the utmost importance. To meet this end a picture is a preferred method for demonstrating relationships; in fact, it is a much better medium for that purpose than linear prose. Hence, as knowledge of a situation is assembled it is recommended that the SSM practitioner begin to draw simple pictures of a situation. These invariably become "richer" (more sophisticated) as the inquiry proceeds and so such pictures are never finished in any ultimate way. In making a rich picture the aim is to capture, informally, the main entities, structures and viewpoints in the situation, the processes evolving, the current recognized problems and any potential ones.[15]

The second stage in the SSM process is to develop an agreed upon starting hypothesis of the structure of the problem – a hypothesis that will be revisited as learning takes place. This is called a theory of action, a simple and suggestive insight about how to solve the problem. It is a creative spark that inspires the modelling team and provides focus to maintain the coherence of the modelling effort. The method employed in SSM is to develop an agreed Root Definition (RD). This is a hypothesis about purposeful action that describes what might be done to intervene and improve a "messy" situation. It is called a root definition because it is rooted in an agreed, explicitly stated worldview. In SSM an RD always takes the basic form: do what (P)? how (Q)? why (R)?

Frequently the PQR formula will be sufficient to craft a workable RD, however, PQR can be enriched by considering six other important elements that can be included in the RD. These are represented by the mnemonic CATWOE. "C" is the client or group for which the action is to be taken either as beneficiaries or victims. "A" represents the individuals or groups who will carry out the action, or are otherwise involved. "T" is the transformation intended by the action to be taken. For example, transform a dangerous insecure environment to one in which the population is safe and development can take place. "W" is the worldview that underpins, justifies or rationalizes the action being taken. "O" represents the owner(s) of the action who wield control over the transformational process, or, in other words could stop it if they so chose. Finally, "E" is the overall extended environment in which the "system" will operate. This frequently represents various constraints that could affect the action.

Using CATWOE to fully develop the RD, the final result is usually stated as: "A system, owned by some entity, to achieve what, using which resources for what purpose." At this stage in SSM it is useful to look forward to the modelling phase and ask – what would be the measures of performance by which the operation of the system would be judged? Thinking out what these criteria would be really sharpens up the thinking about the purposeful activity being modelled. Three criteria are relevant in every case and should always be named. These are:

- Criteria to tell whether the transformation (T) is working, in the sense of producing its intended outcome; i.e., criteria for efficacy;

- Criteria to tell whether the transformation is being achieved with optimal use of resources; i.e., criteria for efficiency; and

- Criteria to tell whether this transformation is helping to achieve some higher level or long-term aim; i.e., criteria for effectiveness.

These three criteria will always be relevant in developing any model, but in particular circumstances other criteria might also apply, such as elegance or ethicality.

The third phase of the SSM process is known as model building and is described as putting together the activities needed to describe the transforming process; in other words, linking the activities needed to achieve the transforming process. Given the guidelines provided by PQR, CATWOE and the three Es (Effectiveness, Efficiency, Efficacy) this task is not difficult. The main skills called for are logical thinking and imagination. The most common error at this stage is to take your eyes off the conceptually based root definition and start modelling some real world version of the purposeful activity being modelled.

It is the dialogue/discourse that takes place among the participants in the modelling process that real learning takes place. Various activities are discussed and selected and their importance and interrelationships are teased out. Once the model has reached a level of maturity that a reasoned decision can be made the participants turn their attention to the real world "wicked" problem that generated the whole SSM process in order to take the necessary action to improve the situation.

Summary

Complexity, ill-structured problems and "wicked" problems abound in the security arena and in defence and military organizations everywhere. As stated at the beginning of this chapter the majority of actors, especially senior actors, operating in these environments are well educated to deal with the complicated elements contained within the wider complexity but not the whole system(s) itself. In the Department of National Defence and the Canadian Forces more emphasis needs to be placed on developing systems thinkers through inclusion of this subject in a range of curricula in the military and the Public Service. In addition, there are several short courses available here in Canada, as well as in the US and the UK. Finally, leaders throughout the system should allocate some professional development time to the subject in the form of Professional Development (PD) events such as short seminars and working groups.

The significant problems we have cannot be solved at the same level of thinking with which we created them.

Albert Einstein

1   See Jamshid Garajedaghi, *Systems Thinking: Managing Chaos and Complexity* (NY: Elsevier, 2006).

2   Emilian Kavalski, "The Fifth Debate and the Emergence of Complex International Relations Theory", *Cambridge Review of International Affairs*, Vol. 20, No. 3, (September, 2007), 435-454.

3   John Holland, *Hidden Order: How Adaptation Builds Complexity* (Reading, Mass.: Addison-Wesley Publishing, 1995), 145.

4   Jeffery Goldstein, "Emergence as a Construct: History and Issues", *Emergence, Complexity and Organization*, Vol. 1, No.1 (1999).

5   John Barton and Tim Haslett, "Analysis, Synthesis, Systems Thinking and the Scientific Method: Rediscovering the Importance of Open Systems", *Open Systems in InterScience*, Issue 24 (2007), 143-155.

6   Gharajedaghi, 12.

7   Allan Beyerchen, "Clausewitz, Non-Linearity and the Unpredictability of War" in *International Security*, Vol. 17, No. 3 (Winter, 1992), 82.

8   Carl von Clausewitz, *On War*, translated by Michael Howard and Peter Paret (Princeton: Princeton University Press, 1976), 135.

9   Ibid., 169.

10   Ibid., 595.

11   Huba Wass de Czega, *Refining the Art of Command for the 21st Century*, retrieved on 15 October 2011 from <http://www.operationaldesign.com/RESTRICTED/coursebook.htm/02/04/09>.

12   See especially, Barry Richmond, *An Introduction to Systems Thinking* (ithink software: High Performance Systems Incorporated, 2001); Russell Ackoff, *The Art of Problem Solving* (NY: John Wiley, 1978).; Peter Checkland, *Systems Thinking, Systems Practice* (London: John Wiley, 1999).

13   Peter Checkland, *Systems Thinking, Systems Practice* (London: John Wiley, 1999).

14   Phenomenology is the study of the nature of the phenomenon of meaning. Interpretive sociology is a school of sociology pioneered by Max Weber. Weber believed that man is a social animal suspended in webs of significance he himself has spun. Culture is these webs and the study of it, therefore is not an experimental science in search of laws but an interpretive one in search of meaning.

15   Peter Checkland, *Learning for Action* (Chichester: John Wiley, 2006), 2.

CHAPTER 6

THE SENIOR NON-COMMISSIONED OFFICER CORPS: BEYOND THE TRAINER / DISCIPLINARIAN PARADIGM

Colonel Bernd Horn

Renown Canadian military historian Desmond Morton noted "Non-commissioned officers [NCOs], promoted from the ranks, enforced discipline, managed routine administration, and socialized recruits – and sometimes their commissioned superiors – in military ways. By common consent, they formed the backbone of their unit."[1] In essence, his description of the senior NCO in the First World War seems timeless and his description was as accurate in the 20th century as it is largely today. Few would argue that one of the fundamental hallmarks of a modern military is the existence of a professional senior NCO corps. After all, it is the senior NCOs that are instrumental in ensuring that the day to day affairs of the military are executed – whether for training, discipline or the conduct of operations. They concentrate on force preparation, specifically training individuals and small teams to ensure that they are motivated, well-trained (i.e., meet the standards of performance for a given trade, skill or function) and ready to carry out their mission. They are also instrumental in the professional development of young soldiers and junior NCOs. On operations, they ensure those attributes and skills learned in training are put into practice. In short, senior NCOs get the day to day jobs of the military done.

Although senior NCOs have always been the backbone of any military, their importance has grown even greater in the modern battlespace. Operations in the chaotic and complex security environment of today necessitate more than ever the presence of a strong, professional senior NCO corps. Their roles as trainers and disciplinarians has evolved to also include that of educator. The safe, templated and well known Cold War paradigm disappeared almost overnight. Moreover, the new security environment was marked by complexity, ambiguity, and an ever present media, as well as nefarious enemies and threats that were embedded in the context of failed and failing states. This reality thrust additional responsibilities, namely that of educators, on the Senior NCO corps.

In the post-Cold War era the sanctity and security of the old conventional wisdom that held true for almost half a century was shattered. The carefully prepared plans for the defence of Germany became irrelevant. Gone was the familiar and carefully templated Soviet enemy.[2] Military leaders, both officers and senior NCOs, whose entire careers were rooted in, and defined by, the comfortable predictability of the Cold War were faced by a brave new world. Conflict had become exponentially more complex and unpredictable. "Today's world is without precedent," cautioned French military analyst Phillippe Delmas, "it is as different from the Cold War as it is from the Middle Ages so the past offers no basis for comparison."[3]

As such, the transition from Cold War, to post-Cold War, to the post-9/11 era greatly impacted the senior NCO corps. During the Cold War, senior NCOs were an integral element in the army that emphasized large mechanized formations that would fight an attritional symmetrical battle on the central European front. Although integral to the day to day training and discipline of the military, operationally they were but a microcosm of a bigger whole. Battle was waged in large mechanized formations, supported by distant weapon systems, air armadas and fleets at sea.

Then suddenly things changed. In the post-Cold War era, the allure of a peace "dividend" and a promise of a revolution in military affairs generated beliefs that the necessity of large ground forces would wane. Moreover, the trend towards a more technologically reliant and functional military institution fuelled talk of possibly downsizing, re-rolling and transforming the senior NCO corps. The new era of peace support operations occurred in such volatile areas as the Former Yugoslavia, Somalia and Haiti, where the world grappled with chaos and violence of failed and failing states thereby re-emphasizing the role of small unit leadership at the sub-unit and platoon levels.

More cataclysmic yet was the aftermath of the terrorist attack on the Twin Towers of the World Trade Center on 11 September 2001 (9/11). As the Americans launched their global war on terror, enemies of the US and their allies adopted asymmetric means to combat the militarily and technologically superior military forces arrayed against them. Doctrinally, an asymmetric threat is a concept "used to describe attempts to circumvent or undermine an opponent's strengths while exploiting his weaknesses, using methods that differ significantly from the opponent's usual mode of operations."[4]

In short, the enemy adopted fourth generation warfare (4GW), a concept that refers to a nonlinear, asymmetric approach to war in which agility, decentralization and initiative are instrumental to success. According to Colonel Thomas X. Hammes, one of the key advocates of the concept, "[4GW] uses all available networks – political, economic, social, and military – to convince the enemy's political decision makers that their strategic goals are either unachievable or too costly for the perceived benefit." He explains, 4GW "is an evolved form of insurgency."[5] It is nonlinear, widely dispersed and undefined. The distinction between "civilian" and "military" also often disappears as civilians become viable targets. After all, 4GW is designed to attack political will. As witnessed in Iraq and Afghanistan, the militant forces combating allied coalition forces utilize every advantage possible, such as targeting civilians, using religious or medical sites as sanctuary, staging areas, logistical centres or actual locations to launch attacks, as well as using improvised explosive devices (IEDs) and suicide bombers.

Herein lies the difficulty for the practitioner. Military leaders are required to operate in, and be comfortable with, ambiguous and uncertain surroundings. Their options for the type of, if not the use of, force is often restricted. In addition, born of necessity, they require the capability of adapting physically and theoretically to changes not only in their immediate operational area but also in the larger international security environment. The new defence environment also demands that individuals, units and formations be agile, flexible and capable of responding to the unforeseen and unexpected. It becomes a constant battle – the person on the ground interfacing with the population – making decisions, often life or death decisions, on a constant daily basis. It becomes, once again, a senior NCO's war.

It is for this reason that the current security situation necessitates that all military institutions have a professional senior NCO Corps that can function beyond the traditional role as trainers and disciplinarians. They must also be educators. After all, they represent the cerebral cortex of a unit and have always been, and will continue to be, essential to the effectiveness of the military, specifically because of their traditional roles and responsibilities. The current struggle in both Iraq and Afghanistan demonstrate that regardless of the ascendancy of technology, the senior NCO Corps will always be required to satisfy a function that is indispensable to the viability of a military institution. Technology changes the tools with which militaries fight, but it does not change the reality of man's role in conflict. War will never be clean or sterile. Clinical strikes by stand-off, long range precision guided missiles, designed to limit collateral damage and minimize friendly casualties, are only effective if the damage wrought is of significance to the recipient. As US Marine Corps Lieutenant-General Paul van Riper has postulated, what if the enemy simply ignores the attack?[6]

Although technological and scientific breakthroughs cannot be ignored, the technological edge that is potentially provided can be of limited utility in situations such as are presently being experienced in South East Asia and those that were experienced in Rwanda, Somalia and Haiti. "The warrior's trade," argues George Friedman, chairman of Strategic Forecasting in Baton Rouge, "will remain one of courage, dedication and suffering." He adds, "Precision-guided munitions will not render war antiseptic any more than did the tank or crossbow or bronze armor. Technology changes how men fight and die, but it does not change the horror and glory of battle, nor does it change the reality of death."[7]

Similarly, Dr. Williamson Murray, a retired army officer commented, "What makes this techno-craze so dangerous is that it flies in the face of 2,500 years of history, not to mention modern science. Friction, ambiguity, chance and uncertainty are not merely manifestations of inadequate communications and technology that U.S. military organizations in the next century may overcome, but rather manifestations of the fundamental nature of the world, where if something can go wrong, it will."[8] Van Riper argues that "Real war is an inherently uncertain enterprise in which chance, friction and the limitations of the human mind under stress profoundly limit our ability to predict outcomes; in which defeat to have any meaning must be inflicted above all in the minds of the defeated..."[9] Quite simply, technology can assist and enhance the capabilities of fighting soldiers, but in the end it will never be able to totally replace them. War will always remain a truly human endeavour.

It is within this context, namely the ugly reality of conflict, complete with its ambiguity, fear, friction and uncertainty, that the prodigious importance of the senior NCO emerges. In spite of the changing nature of conflict, society or technology – there are a number of core responsibilities of the senior NCO corps that cannot change without imperiling the effectiveness of a nation's military. This is plainly visible when the actual functions of the senior NCO are examined. First, they provide the critical link between the soldiers and the officer corps and vice versa. In this vein, the senior NCO often fulfils a role similar to that of an ombudsman for the rank and file. Furthermore, the senior NCO is an administrator, trainer, mentor and at times parent figure to those entrusted to their charge. In addition, he/she is also a motivator and disciplinarian, as well as a combat leader and tactician.

It is clearly evident from this superficial summary that the senior NCO corps is the moral cement – the glue – that holds an army together. "The choice of non-commissioned officers," insisted Baron Frederick von Steuben, "is an object of the greatest importance." He explained, "The order and discipline of a regiment depends so much upon their behaviour, that too much care cannot be taken in preferring none to that trust but those who by their merit and good conduct are entitled to it." He added, "Honesty, sobriety, and a remarkable attention to every point of duty, with a neatness in their dress, are indispensable requisites."[10] This reality changed little in a century and half. In 1942, General Bernard Law Montgomery echoed Steuben's sentiments when described non-commissioned officers as the backbone of any unit.[11]

Needless to say, Steuben and Montgomery were neither the first nor last commanders to make such a resolute assertion in regards to the senior NCO cadre. The reason for these accolades merits closer scrutiny. After all, to fully understand the importance of the senior NCO Corps, one must have a full and comprehensive understanding of their traditional roles and responsibilities.

Land Force Command, in its seminal doctrinal publication *Canada's Army*, states that senior NCOs "...are the link connecting soldiers to their officers and officers to their soldiers. Their role is to translate the intentions of commanders into action."[12] This interpretation is rooted in law. The *Queen's Regulations and Orders* specify the general responsibilities of all non-commissioned officers. These include the observance and enforcement of various regulations, rules, orders and instructions; promoting good discipline, welfare and efficiency of all who are subordinate to the member; and reporting to the proper authority and infringement of the pertinent statutes, regulations, rules, orders and instructions governing the conduct of any person to the Code of Service Discipline.[13]

Simply put, senior NCOs conducts the daily business of an army. They are expected to carry out instructions to achieve the institutional aim, as well as ensure the well-being of the soldiers. Senior NCOs are also trusted to pass on the ethos and traditions of the military in general and the respective regiment in particular. Furthermore, they are required to pass on and explain directives from their superiors to their subordinates, as well as ensure that all direction is efficiently and effectively executed.

In addition, there is a justified expectation by officers that their senior NCO has a more up to date, as well as more accurate, insight into the general feeling and morale of the rank and file and that potential problems or discontent are passed up the chain of command. This sentiment was clearly articulated in 1880, by then Colonel William Otter, in his *Guide: A Manual for the Canadian Militia*. Otter explained that it was essential that NCOs know intimately all of the characters and capabilities of their men. In regard to the Sergeant-Major, he insisted that he must be an advisor to the unit Adjutant and in general must act as "the eyes, ears and conscience of the battalion." For this reason, Otter stated, that a Sergeant-Major had to be a "man of sound sense and judgment, of good temper and kind but firm in execution of his duty."[14]

It is in this knowledge of, and closeness to, the troops that the senior NCO proves his/her greatest strength. For only with a complete and proper understanding of an individual can you truly elicit their greatest potential. Moreover, the NCOs' full comprehension of their subordinates, as well as their pivotal role as the link between the soldiers and the officers, positions them to act as an ombudsman for their personnel. Discontent and morale problems can often be avoided or quickly resolved by timely intervention or advice. In this vein, senior NCOs provide clarity and context to transgressions in behaviour and perceived affronts or injustices. In addition, they provide voice for aggrieved, intimidated and/or overanxious subordinates, particularly young soldiers.[15] In essence, their maturity, experience and knowledge provide a steadying influence in an institution that is steeped in human endeavor with all the confusion and frailty that inherently accompanies such enterprise.

Notwithstanding the importance of the aforementioned roles, instrumental to the vitality of any army is the quality and capability of its fighting forces. Here lies a fundamental and all important role of the senior NCO – that of the trainer. Training is of immense importance in influencing behaviour. It is also critical in imparting those abilities and skills that will determine the survival of individuals in combat and the success of an army on the battlefield. Although seldom articulated in this manner, the performance of an army rests largely on the skill and professionalism of its senior NCO corps. "The NCO is expected to provide advice on everything," stated Chief Warrant Officer (CWO) Randy Northrup. He asserted,

"NCOs share knowledge experience, honesty, loyalty and support."[16] Similarly, "it is the NCO," explained Command Sergeant Major Wilbur V. Adams, Jr., "who directs individual training, builds physical readiness, and teaches core values of leadership and moral courage."[17]

Young recruits are introduced and taught the basics of soldiering and military life. Upon joining their unit, soldiers continue to learn basic and advanced skills necessary to fulfill their role as combat troops. The proficiency of the individuals creates the foundation upon which collective training can be conducted. "We had exceptionally good sergeants," recalled Corporal Denis Flynn, of the 1st Canadian Parachute Battalion in the Second World War. "They knew how to organize and prepare soldiers," he explained, "That was their key function – teaching soldiers how to do their job and survive."[18] His simple recollection underlines a salient point. If the senior NCO corps is deficient, the foundation of a unit, and the army in general, will be weak and, thus, condemn the entire structure to collapse. It is not surprising that Colonel Otter believed that the fundamental success of a unit was "in a great measure dependent on the alertness and skill of the NCOs."[19] He believed that NCOs "are the very 'stuff' of the army."[20] CWO Greg Lacroix, a former Canadian Forces CWO stated, "I have been saying for some time now that these operations [war in Afghanistan] are riding on the backs of the NCOs. Unfortunately they come home and we burden them with more demands for training our men and women."[21]

What must be remembered is that the NCOs' skill, used to train unit personnel, is not limited exclusively to soldiers. It is commonly recognized as an age-old truth, by military personnel worldwide, that there is nothing more dangerous than a second lieutenant. This threat is mitigated to a large extent by the senior NCO corps. Notwithstanding the fact that a young officer of this rank is in a superior position of authority to senior NCOs, in reality their education and training, in regards to unit and military life, is actually shaped to a great degree by their NCO subordinates. *Canada's Army* institutionalizes this concept. It articulates that senior NCOs "... have an important responsibility in teaching newly joined officers hands on skills in the mechanics of soldiering and leadership. This includes offering advice, helping solve problems, and providing feedback and information."[22] Similarly, American First Sergeant Jeffrey J. Mellinger in an open letter to his NCO corps explained, "Training your platoon leader is not only your job but your responsibility. If he fails, the platoon fails, and so do you." He added, "As the senior and most experienced NCO [platoon sergeant] in the platoon, you must pass on the benefit of that wisdom and experience to your platoon leader as well as to the soldiers."[23]

The importance of the NCO's role as a trainer was clearly recognized by the German military. For example, in the interwar years, NCOs were career professionals who were carefully selected and enjoyed considerable prestige in society. Upon completing his military career, the German NCO was guaranteed a pension of 1,500 marks, as well as preferential hiring in the civil service, railroads, and the postal system.[24] Tom Clancy, a recognized expert on military affairs, and American General Fredrick M. Franks, a former commander of Training and Doctrine Command (TRADOC) and the Commander of VII Corps during the Gulf War in 1990-91, provide a more contemporary view of the importance of the senior NCO corps as trainers. They wrote:

> The years of fighting in Vietnam had drawn Europe-based forces down to unacceptable strengths. Worse, the insatiable appetite for personnel had stripped our forces of officer leadership, and almost destroyed the Army's professional noncommissioned corps, long the backbone of the Army. A series of hasty training programs to fill depleted ranks had left the Army with NCOs who all too often were poorly trained in basic leadership techniques. Because the NCO is the first-line leader in the Army, the one person primarily responsible for the basic individual soldier skills on which every successful operation depends, training and discipline suffered. In some cases, it went to hell.[25]

Lockstep with the requirement to train individuals is the imposition and enforcement of discipline. Once again, the senior NCO has always been the linchpin. As already stated, universally, the NCO is the crucible of success in any army. He/she inculcates discipline through personal example and training. By his/her words and actions he/she defines to the soldiers what is acceptable behaviour and what is not. It is the senior NCO that often, most effectively promulgates, explains and enforces directives, orders and policies. This should not be surprising. This is the result of the close, direct and daily contact between a senior NCO and his/her men. "From the perspective of a line company enlisted man," explained one Second World War veteran, "our day to day lives were impacted intensely by NCOs. They were the flesh and blood leaders we knew."[26] This is why historically senior NCOs have been an invaluable resource to the military and often the difference between success and failure on operations.

An example of the catastrophic results of a failure in discipline was clearly evident in the Canadian Airborne Regiment during its deployment to Somalia in 1992-93. Years of poor manning practices, a large number of weak NCOs (as well as officers) and a failure to maintain discipline within the unit, led directly to the torture killing of a Somali youth. Incredibly, although evidence has shown that both NCOs and officers were aware, and/or should have been aware that the beating of a detainee was transpiring, nothing was done to stop the killing in time. This transgression became cataclysmic, and combined with other events, eventually led to the disbandment of the unit; the first in Canadian history to be done so as a result of perceived disciplinary problems.[27]

The importance of discipline in the military to ensure the subjugation of personal will to that of the institution, as well as the NCO's role in achieving this, is unquestioned. But the true value of the senior NCO cannot be really appreciated by simply detailing individual responsibilities. This is to miss their historical contribution to the army. In totality, beyond administrator and trainer, the senior NCO is a mentor, motivator and often parent figure to his/her soldiers. His/her actions instill trust, loyalty and ensure performance in the most trying conditions. During the Second World War, "mother" became German slang among the field soldiers to denote the senior sergeant in a company. The rationale behind this is not difficult to comprehend. For instance, Karl Fuchs, who served in such a position, wrote home to his father during the war, "I've become such an integral part of my company that I couldn't leave it ever again."[28] Similarly, Hans Werner Woltersdorf asserted, "my unit was my home, my family, which I had to protect."[29]

Dr. John McManus's study of the American combat soldier in the Second World War replicated the German experience. He found that in most cases the natural leaders in combat were the NCOs. One veteran's account was typical of his finding:

> ...[The platoon sergeant] was caring and wanted to make sure his men had what they needed. He boosted morale. He checked weapons every day, made sure the men had dry socks. He hovered over us like a mother hen.[30]

As already alluded to in the anecdotes, nowhere is the senior NCO's importance easier to ascertain than during combat or operations in general. It is here that the senior NCO proves his/her undisputed title as the backbone of the military. He/she becomes the key to operational success, turning commander's intent into action. It is in operations that the sum of all responsibilities and tasks of the senior NCO are welded together – where he/she acts as technician, tactician and leader.

The senior NCOs' role as technicians is clearly evident. Their comprehensive knowledge of weapons and equipment as a result of their technical training and the instruction of others make them an invaluable advisor to officers and instructor/supervisor to soldiers. Their ability to ensure the care, maintenance and first line repair of various unit material is instrumental to unit effectiveness, particularly during the immediacy and stresses of operations.

But of equal importance to the success of a unit is the senior NCO's role as tactician and combat leader. Many may argue the sobriquet of tactician. After all, he/she simply carries out orders. During the First World War, the German NCO, similar to that of most other nations, "primarily served his men as a model of military toughness, a disciplinarian and enforcer of military regulations and 'discourager' to the 'Drueckeberger' (slacker) in combat, but not as a model battlefield tactician."[31] But this soon changed with the evolution of mechanized warfare. In the Second World War, the concept of the senior NCO as a tactician was simply unavoidable. If for no other reason, casualties forced them to take on this responsibility. "As a Platoon Sergeant, 4 Platoon, 'B' Company, [1st Canadian Parachute Battalion]," recalled Sergeant R.F. Anderson, "there were many times in the field when I had no Officer by reason of casualty or illness. This meant a delay in getting a replacement which had to come from England, so in many cases companies were led by senior NCOs..."[32] Fellow paratrooper Corporal Dan Hartigan agreed. "We lost over 50 percent of our officers on D-Day," he explained, "15 of the 27 I believe."[33] He added, "the fighting in the weeks that followed turned from an officer's war to a senior NCO's war." McManus' study supports this anecdotal evidence. "With surprising frequency," he concluded, "combat soldiers looked to their sergeants for leadership day in and day out in combat. A major reason for that was the turnover in officers."[34]

But the claim of tactician is not built exclusively on the senior NCO's ability to become a battlefield replacement for officer casualties. The nature of his/her position within the military, not to mention the established doctrine, necessitates this. One of Israeli's outstanding field commanders, Yigal Allon, proclaimed that the great battles of the 1948-49 War, the Sinai Campaign in 1956, and the Six Day War in 1967, were "won in the NCO's courses of the *Haganah* and the *Palmach*." He explained:

> The most brilliant plan devised by the most capable general depends
> for its tactical execution on the section-leaders. Poor section-leaders
> may ruin the best-laid plans; first-rate section-leaders will often save
> badly devised plans. This for one simple reason: the section-leader is
> the sole level of command that maintains constant and direct contact
> with the men who bear the brunt of the actual fighting. It follows, then,
> that the section-leader is to be trained as a tactical commander and as
> an educator of his men. [In the Israeli Defence Force] section-leaders
> are trained to command independently in the field in every instance
> in which they are required to operate alone with their units. In regular
> combat, moreover, when the section-leader acts within the framework
> of his platoon and under orders from his superior officer, he still requires
> a high standard of knowledge and an ability to sum up the situation.[35]

In the current ambiguous, complex and volatile security environment, the senior
NCO plays an ever increasingly vital role. In an environment where winning the
hearts and minds of the local population is in direct competition with an enemy
who will exploit any advantage and any perceived weakness, the example, guidance and direction of the senior NCO on the ground represents the difference
between life and death, for both civilians and military members on a daily basis.

Whether the designation of tactician is accepted or not, in the end, the NCO's
primary function in combat is still one of leading his/her men against an enemy
as far as possible, undiminished in strength to achieve a military objective. To
accomplish this, he/she must provide leadership, direction and guidance. Moreover, he/she must render psychological, as well as physical, support by furnish-
ing an example of courage, as well as a sense of calm and a presence of mind regardless of surrounding turmoil. Additionally, throughout, the senior NCO must
remain with the element that is closest to the enemy and, thus, danger.

This reality is the ultimate proof of the NCO's undeniable importance to the
efficiency of the army. It is generally accepted that leaderless groups usually
become inactive. The provision of this leadership, often in the face of chaos,
routinely falls to the senior NCO. This is only natural, after all, in relation to their
troops they represent the first level of command. To the NCO cascades the easily quoted, yet more difficult to execute, task of "closing with and engaging the
enemy."

In this endeavour, the NCO's presence becomes all important. Of a group of combat veterans surveyed, 89 per cent emphasized the importance of getting frequent instructions from leaders when in a tight spot. They felt that coolness in combat was contagious. In fact, 94 per cent of the respondents believed that "men feel they fought better after observing other men behaving calmly in a dangerous situation."[36] Quite simply, "men like to follow an experienced man.... [an] experienced man knows how to accomplish objectives with a minimum of risk. He sets an example of coolness and efficiency which impels similar behaviour in others."[37] For this reason it is not surprising that studies of Second World War combat veterans indicated that in respect to courage, 42 per cent expected it of their NCOs, who they most closely related to and relied on, while only 30 per cent expected it of their officers.[38]

Anecdotal evidence provides some graphic examples. "I was getting jittery," confessed Private Alexandre Huton, "but the sergeant was steady as a rock. What a soldier!" He further elaborated:

> We moved again, this time over a cratered field, the sergeant always moving in front of us. Twice he stopped and dug his toes in the dirt, then he lead [sic] us around a mine. That was typical of the sergeant, he tried everything himself first before he would allow the rest to follow. When we came to wide dikes the sergeant swam across first to see if we could make it across. We moved up on the made road again, the sergeant stopping to cut the Jerry telephone wires with his bayonet and again we had to fall flat while Jerry field guns rolled past us. The sarge was always taking note of their equipment and direction. He didn't miss a trick...I'd lost track of where we were going but the sarge was leading us and we took his word for it.[39]

Similarly, the actions of another NCO, Company Sergeant-Major (CSM) John Kemp, reinforce the above image. One official report recorded, "CSM Kemp who had assisted in organizing the men for the attack, with complete disregard for his own safety, led his men against the farm house in spite of the heavy fire. By his personal example, he enabled the small force to overrun the enemy defences and capture the position."[40] In another example, Private Bill Gates of the Royal Marines recalled, "I rushed on behind one of our Sergeants, a great big bloke who seemed afraid of nothing, and I felt so long as I stayed behind him I'd be OK."[41]

In a similar vein, assessments of combat soldiers provide a clear idea of not only the expectations of the men but also the importance of the NCO. For example, CSM Charlie Martin of the Queen's Own Rifles was described by his men as a Riflemen's dream sergeant. He was by all accounts "an outstanding soldier," who could always be found up front "even if there was only a small patrol action." To those who knew him, he "was a 'come on' not a 'go on' leader."[42]

Indisputably, the senior NCO's responsibilities as administrator, trainer, disciplinarian, mentor, leader and tactician are pivotal to the efficacy of an military. Their example, close proximity and relationship to their soldiers enable them to motivate individuals in the face of fear and danger and accomplish tasks. Studies from Korea and Israel reveal that unit NCOs provide the emotional support for the squad and manage this by a mixture of modeling, sustaining and teaching.[43] Quite simply, they are the glue that holds an military together. Thus, regardless of technological and scientific developments, as long as human conflict exists, the requirement for men and women to go in harm's way will remain.

Indisputably, these key roles and responsibilities are critical to the success of a modern armed forces. However, arguably, they are no longer enough. The new complexity in conflict discussed earlier, combined with the CNN effect, often couched in terms of the "strategic soldier," and exacerbated by societal expectations, necessitate that a greater emphasis be placed on the education of non-commissioned members (NCMs) instead of the long-standing exclusive focus on training. In turn, the senior NCO must use this knowledge and become an educator, passing on important knowledge to his/her subordinates. After all, "the large formation, closely controlled and highly supervised troops in the warfare models of the cold war era have given way to scattered small units in distant countries," argues Colonel Paul Maillet, the Department of National Defence director of Defence Ethics, "who have reduced support readily available in ambiguous and high intensity ethical situations." He adds, "A wrong decision in the glare of the media can have far reaching consequences that can affect peacekeeping mandates and strategic and national policies and aims."[44]

Herein lays the paradox: this realization underlines the need for both the retention of the traditional roles and responsibilities of the senior NCO corps, as well as the requirement to change the manner in which the individual NCO is prepared to fulfill his/her function. The traditional stress on training, that is "a predictable response to a predictable situation," must be better balanced with education, defined by Professor Ron Haycock as "the reasoned response to an unpredictable situation – critical thinking in the face of the unknown."[45] Simply put, the prescribed application of ideas and methods, as well as drills and check-lists, have a purpose and functional utility, but this methodology is no longer enough to equip leaders to cope with and function in the complex post mod-ern world. "There are no standard 'drills,'" remarked Art Eggleton, the Minister of National Defence, "for the many complex challenges that our troops confront in places like Bosnia."[46] This reality has become even more paramount in Afghani-stan where much of the counter-insurgency and the battle for the hearts and minds of an alien xenophobic culture lies in the hands of senior NCOs and their subordinates.

Undeniably, senior NCOs, in the same manner as officers, must be taught how to think and use abstract concepts to assist in the resolution of practical problems that they may face. They must expand their knowledge and acquire a broader outlook, as well as develop greater socio-political skills. They must understand and apply cultural intelligence so that they can interact and influence host-nation populations. Furthermore, they must become comfortable with ambigu-ity and change. Critical thinking and innovation must become their guiding light instead of the traditional heavy reliance on written procedures given in technical publications and uni-dimensional experience. To achieve this, education must be aggressively pursued. And, in turn, importantly, they must be capable of shar-ing that knowledge with their subordinates; in essence, becoming educators.

The requirement for greater education is also rooted in the necessity of dealing with today's soldiers. Pierre de Reil, French Minister of War in 1793, wrote "as long as the soldier believes himself equal in intelligence and knowledge to his com-manders, he will not obey."[47] With the average recruit entering the CF increas-ingly with a minimum of a high school education or better, the senior NCO is required to continually advance his/her own base of knowledge so that he/she can not only deal with the ambiguity and complexity of operations, but also so that he/she can teach, train, motivate and lead progressively more sophisticated subordinates.[48] The old days of drill sergeants castigating recruits or soldiers with derogatory, expletive filled expressions, or taking a "problem individual" out be-hind the woodshed to "sort him out" are not only inappropriate but are also no longer effective. Senior NCOs must understand and be capable of motivating their new charges, despite generational differences and new societal expecta-tions, norms and values. Once again, education is the key.

The challenge before the CF is a daunting one – how to retain the timeless strength of the senior NCO corps that has made it the crucible to success of the military, yet ensure its evolution to keep it a viable and relevant force in the future. The key to success lays in understanding the role and responsibilities of the senior NCO corps and ensuring that they are given the educational foundation to provide them with the necessary knowledge, as well as thinking strategies, to deal with ambiguity and change. In addition, it is also important to recognize that as long as there is human conflict, regardless of technological and scientific breakthroughs, their ability to train, educate and lead well-trained soldiers into chaos, danger and turmoil will remain the definitive test of a military's efficacy.

---

1   Desmond Morton, *When Your Number's Up* (Toronto: Random House of Canada, 1993), 95.

2   In 1987, Georgi Arbatov, advisor to Mikhail Gorbachev, announced to the West, "We are going to do to you the worst thing imaginable – We are going to deprive you of your enemy." Pascal Boniface, *The Will to Powerlessness. Reflections on Our Global Age* (Kingston: Queen's Quarterly, 1999), 37.

3   Phillippe Delmas, *The Rosy Future of War* (New York: Free Press, 1995), 213.

4   Colonel W.J. Fulton, DNBCD, "Capabilities Required of DND, Asymmetric Threats and Weapons of Mass Destruction", Fourth Draft, 18 March 01, 2/22.

5   Colonel Thomas X Hammes, *The Sling and the Stone* (Minneapolis, MN: Zenith Press, 2006), 2.

6   Paul van Riper and Robert H. Scales, "Preparing for War in the 21st Century, *Parameters* (Autumn 1997), 11. See also Charles J. Dunlap, "21st Century Land Warfare: Four Dangerous Myths," *Parameters*, (Autumn 1997), 27-37. The four myths are: 1- Our most likely future adversaries will be like us. 2- We can safely downsize our military in favor of smaller, highly trained forces equipped with high-technology weapons. 3- We can achieve information superiority and even dominance in future conflicts. 4- Modern technology will make future war more humane if not bloodless.

7   George and Meredith Friedman, *The Future of War* (New York: St Martin's Griffin, 1998), xi.

8   Williamson Murray, "Does Military Culture Matter?", *Orbis* (Winter 1999), 37-38.

9   Van Riper and Scales, 5.

10   Major-General M.K. Jeffery, "The Non-Commissioned Officer of the Future Army: Introduction", in Douglas L. Bland, ed., *Backbone of the Army. Non-Commissioned Officers in the Future Army* (Kingston: McGill-Queen's University Press, 2001), 2.

11   John A. English, *Failure in High Command* (Ottawa: The Golden Dog Press, 1995), 318.

12   Land Force Command, *Canada's Army* (Ottawa: DND, 1998), 52.

13   *Queen's Orders and Regulations*, Article 5.01.

14   Major-General Sir William Dillon Otter, *The Guide: A Manual for the Canadian Militia*, 9th ed. (Toronto: Copp, Clark Company, 1914), 21-22. See also Ronald G. Haycock, "The Stuff of Armies: The NCO Throughout History", in Douglas L. Bland, ed., *Backbone of the Army. Non-Commissioned Officers in the Future Army* (Kingston: McGill-Queen's University Press, 2001), 9-23.

15   An interesting anecdote provides some clarity. During the WWII a promising young sergeant was asked to take his commission. He refused. "You see," he said, "what I am really interested in is the personal contacts with the men and I know that if I become an officer I should not have the same chance of helping them as I have now." Lieutenant R. Bernays, "Man-Officer Relationships", *The Army Quarterly*, Vol. XLVI, No. 2 (August 1943), 253.

16   Interview with Chief Warrant Officer Randy Northrup, 22 January 2007.

17   Wilbur V. Adams, Jr., "The Non-Commissioned Officer in the United States Army: Leading by Example", in Douglas L. Bland, ed., *Backbone of the Army. Non-Commissioned Officers in the Future Army* (Kingston: McGill-Queen's University Press, 2001), 87.

18   Corporal Denis Flynn, interview with author 18 April 2001.

19   Colonel Otter, as quoted in Haycock, 18.

20   Haycock, "'The Stuff of Armies'", 19.

21   Chief Warrant Officer Greg Lacroix, Canadian Forces CWO. E-mail to author 10 September 2007.

22   *Canada's Army*, 52-53.

23   First Sergeant Jeffrey J. Mellinger, "Open Letter to Three NCOs," *Infantry*, May-June 1989, 20. This aspect of a Senior NCO's responsibility is universal. The famous British Lieutenant-Colonel Colin Michel (of the Argylls) wrote, "My platoon sergeant, a tough little man called Dempsey was obviously just the professional I needed to nurse me into my new job." Colin Mitchell, *Having Been a Soldier* (London: Mayflower Books), 41.

24   James S. Corum, *The Roots of Blitzkrieg* (Kansas: University of Kansas, 1992), 11.

25   Tom Clancy with General Fred Franks, Jr. (ret.), *Into the Storm* (New York: Berkley Books, 1998), 85.

26   John C. McManus, *The deadly brotherhood. The American combat soldier in World War II* (Novato: Presidio, 1998), 219.

27   See Report of the Commission of Inquiry into the Deployment of Canadian Forces to Somalia, *Dishonoured Legacy. The Lessons of the Somalia Affair* (Ottawa: Canadian Government Publishing, 1997), Vol. 1, 244-247& 324; and Vol. 2, 429-470. See also Bernd Horn, *Bastard Sons - A Critical Examination of the Canadian Airborne Experience*, 1942-1995 (St. Catharines: Vanwell Publishing, 2001).

28   Stephen G. Fritz, *Frontsoldaten. The German Soldier in World War II* (Lexington: University of Kentucky Press), 18-19.

29   Ibid., 19.

30   McManus, 218-220.

31   Karl H. Theile, *Beyond Monsters and Clowns. The Combat SS* (New York: University Press of America, 1997), 99.

32   Sergeant R.F. Anderson, letter to author, 19 December 2000.

33   Corporal Dan Hartigan, interview with author, 30 October 2000.

34   McManus, 202.

35   John A. English, *On Infantry* (New York: Praeger, 1984), 191.

36   John Dollard, *Fear in Battle* (Westport, Connecticut: Greenwood Press, Publishers, 1944), 28. See also Elmar Dinter, Hero or Coward (London: Frank Cass, 1985), and Stanley J. Rachman, Fear and Courage (San Francisco: W.H. Freeman and Company, 1978).

37   Dollard, 44. It is generally accepted that "the presence of careful and thoughtful leadership builds up a force which helps resist fear."

38   Elmar Dinter, *Hero or Coward* (London: Frank Cass, 1985), 53.

39   Lionel S.B. Shapiro, "I Dropped Alone," *MacLean's*, Vol. 1 (August 1944), 5-6.

40   Jean E. Portugal, *We Were There. The Army. A Record for Canada*, Vol 2 of 7 (Toronto: The Royal Canadian Military Institute, 1998), 968.

41   Edmund Blandford, *Two Sides of the Beach. The Invasion and Defense of Europe in 1944* (Edison, NJ: Castle Books, 2001), 222.

42   Ibid., 706.

43   Colonel Ian Palmer, "The Emotion That Dare Not Speak Its Name?", *The British Army Review*, No. 132 (Summer 2003), 36.

44   Colonel J.P.M. Maillet, "Defence Ethics Program Ethics and Operations Project", memorandum dated 20 January 2000.

45   Dr. Ronald Haycock, former Dean of Arts, Royal Military College, "Clio and Mars in Canada: The Need for Military Education", presentation to the Canadian Club, Kingston, Ontario, 11 November 1999.

46   Speaking Notes for the Honourable Art Eggleton, Minister of National Defence, Canadian Forces College, 19 June 2000, 10.

47   John A. Lynn, *Bayonets of the Republic* (Chicago: University of Illinois Press, 1984), 89.

48   More and more one hears of the "corporal with a Masters Degree" as the way of the future. Although there are several cases such as this in the CF, largely in the Reserves, a few do not make a trend. The argument that soon there will be no marked difference between the NCO cadre and the officer corps may be considerably premature. These apocalyptic warnings are not new. "The results of popular education have borne fruit," wrote Major R.A.C. Radcliffe in 1943, "and there are to-day a considerable number of men in the ranks who have learnt to think and reason for themselves." He went on to state that the improved education of the men in the ranks made them "more critical of their officers in every way." Major R.A.C. Radcliffe, "Officer-Man Relationships", *The Army Quarterly*, Vol. XLVI, No. 1 (May 1943), 114-116. In a similar vein, another account from 1943 revealed, "In the old Army there was a blind obedience, the result of strict discipline, which was often confused with loyalty to one's officer's and to the Army. To-day there is a much more questioning quality ... the N.C.O.s and men nowadays are not blindly loyal to their senior officers just because the latter happen to hold the King's commission. They first wish to satisfy themselves that their officers are thoroughly capable, and, as intelligent men, they take mental

note of every action, look and word of their seniors...." C.W. Valentine, "Army Morale and its Relation to Discipline and Efficiency", *The Fighting Forces*, Vol. XX, No. 1 (April 1943), 24. Although the need for education will become increasingly important at all levels in DND and the CF, it will remain as the predominant difference between non-commissioned members and the officer corps.

CHAPTER 6

PART II

LEARNING

CHAPTER 7

THE CF LEARNER OF
TODAY AND TOMORROW

Lieutenant-Commander (Ret) Randy Purse

Introduction

The Canadian Forces Training and Education (T&E) community invests significantly in instructional systems, processes, and structures. Historically, the drivers to change have been new technology, efficiencies, or organizational re-structuring. Recently, scholars have suggested that the evolving learner is in fact, becoming a driver for change within CF T&E. One need only look at Canadian society and global population shifts to realize that learner demographics are changing. Within the larger Canadian learning community, the extent of change has been most evident in the mass of literature on the needs of unique cohorts defined by age, life stage, cultural background, or technological competence. The CF has not yet seen the full weight of this demographic change. While there are some isolated attempts to respond to the changes in learners, there will be systemic implications that will likely impact on the CF's learning frame of reference.

The CF T&E community writ large is effectively responsible for ensuring that CF learners are trained and educated to the level required to meet the CF mission. Once the performance requirements are identified, CF professional development institutions place considerable emphasis on identifying learner entry level and determining how to develop learners with the required competencies needed to meet learning outcomes that will support effective job performance. Accordingly, the T&E community must work from a valid set of assumptions about the CF learner.

For decades, the CF Training and Education community has relied upon the basic, relatively static perception of a homogeneous learning audience that is predominantly white males from low to middle socio-economic standing. There has been some progress in the past twenty years, predominated with greater emphasis on gender integration and increasing levels of diversity, but that has done little to change the global view of learners. It is important to note that the rate of demographic change in Canadian society is already impacting on composition of CF learner populations within recruit and initial occupation training and education as well as the military colleges. The CF learner is clearly evolving beyond the typically held stereotype. It is therefore timely to reflect on the CF learner of today and the future to provide a more accurate baseline for CF T&E. This chapter will provide a general description of the CF learners, draw broad conclusions about the CF learning audience, and then discuss the implications for CF T&E.

Who are the CF Learners?

Popular learning literature of late has been dominated by discussion of "new" learners. Characterizations such as Millenials, Twitch Learners, Generation Y, Net Geners, and Digital Natives have driven learning experts within academia, industry and public sector to reflect on their learning audiences and have even caused some to significantly change the way they design and deliver instruction.

The CF should not be excluded from such discussions as these learners are represented in our recruiting and initial occupation training populations. Few would argue that these particular learners are the same as those of two or three decades ago. However, as with any generalization, T&E managers and practitioners should be cautious about applying these characterisations across the CF learning population. Rather, the CF should provide measured responses based upon an accurate depiction of the CF learner. So, if the CF learners are not those characterized in popular literature, who are they?

CF Learners are Increasingly Culturally Diverse

The Canadian population is experiencing decreasing natural growth and increasing immigration growth. For example, over the past year, immigration represented roughly 70 percent of all current growth and such increases will be likely for the foreseeable future. Moreover, as the natural population ages and fertility rates decline, the majority of Canada's youth are becoming first and second generation immigrants. According to an April 2008 Statistics Canada report, one in six Canadians now identify themselves as visible minorities, with over half coming from South Asia and China.[1]

The Department of National Defence is reflecting this demographic change where 20.6 percent of the civilian population identify themselves as immigrants and 17.1 percent as a visible minority.[2] Park reported that civilian representation differed from military significantly in nearly every demographic characteristic.[3] In fact, the CF has considerably less diversity within its ranks. Only 5.9 percent of the military population identifies itself as an immigrant and 6.4 percent as a visible minority. This should not be all that surprising. As reported by Jung[4] and Wait[5], the recruitment pool for the CF traditionally has been fit, young, white males between the ages of 17 and 24, coming from rural areas or from urban areas with a population of less than 100,000. This recruiting legacy has continued to influence CF demographics. However, recent changes to recruiting policies and practices have stressed the need to attract a broader range of recruits to better meet demographic[6] and operational[7] imperatives. As a consequence, the CF's overall demographic composition is reflecting greater cultural diversity with increasing representation from urbanized, multi-cultural and mixed gender populations.[8]

Another component of the cultural diversity is the linguistic composition. Within Canada, 58 percent declare English while 26 percent declare French as their first official language.[9] Within the public service, of which DND is representative, 70.9 percent declare English and 29.1 percent declare French as their first official language.[10] The growing immigrant population is resulting in a new linguistic demographic, the allophone.[11] According to Statistics Canada, the proportion of allophones increased substantially to 20 percent (from 13 percent in 1981) and it is estimated that 80 percent of all immigrants come from countries where neither French nor English is the first language.[12] Given recent CF recruiting efforts in urban populations where immigrants tend to reside, the CF is seeing a consequent increase in allophones. Clearly, the CF learner population is becoming more culturally diverse and, also, linguistically diverse.

CF Learners are Multi-Generational

Cultural diversity is one aspect of are CF learning population. Within Canada, we are also experiencing a dramatically aging population. Canada's population continues to age with the mean age in 2009 at 39.2 and fertility rates persistently below generation replacement level while we are seeing increased life expectancy. Most recent projections indicate that the mean age could be 44 by 2030[13] and within the same period it is anticipated that almost all population growth will be from immigration.[14]

The DND and CF are experiencing similar dynamics. As of 2009, the average age of the public service employee was 43.9 years old, up about 5 years since 1983.[15] The average age of the CF member is younger at 35, but has also been increasing over the past decade. Table 7.1 below shows the percentages of respective age groups of the Department of National Defence civilian population and military population.

Age Group	Military	Civilian
15-24	19.3	19.3
25-39	51.8	33.3
40-54	28.3	36.6
55-64	0.6	10.7

Table 7.1: Military and DND Civilian Ages by Percentage[16]

Not surprisingly, the military population is less distributed and tends to be younger than the civilian population due to the military emphasis on youth and earlier retirement age.

Within the military, another indicator of the CF learner diversity is years of service. The highest percentage of CF personnel has between 10-24 years of service (Table 7.2). The CF promotes continuous learning and provides ongoing professional development as well as frequent occupational and operational training opportunities. Consequently, the CF learning population is not comprised of a single age group. Rather, CF learners are multi-generational representing a broad range of ages of personnel in various stages of life.

Years of Service	All
Less than 10	34.2
10-24	53.3
25 or more	12.5

Table 7.2: CF Personnel and Years of Service[17]

CF Learners are Increasingly More Educated

In general terms, education levels in Canada are increasing where there has been a full percentage point increase in the proportion of men and women who had a university certificate, diploma or degree at the bachelor's level or above between 2001 and 2006.[18] The following table identifies education levels for military and DND civilian population by percentage.

Education	Military	Civilian
Less than High School	6.5	13.3
High School diploma	28	19.5
Some post-secondary	12.7	6.6
Post-secondary degree/diploma	52.6	59.6

Table 7.3: Education Level as a Percentage of the Military and DND Civilian Population[19]

Further, rates of degree attainment increase with city size indicating that the urban areas are the greatest sources of educated human capital. So, given hiring and recruiting practices, this trend should extend to the DND/CF population. Additionally, based on recent analysis, more CF members are taking advantage of educational support programs. Therefore, increasing education levels are likely to continue.

CF Learners are Becoming Digitally Literate

Digital literacy is used in contrast to the more generic 1989 term "information literacy" which is "the ability to recognize when information is needed and have the ability to locate, evaluate and use effectively the needed information."[20] Digital literacy is described as:

[A] person's ability to perform tasks effectively in a digital environment, with "digital" meaning information represented in numeric form and primarily for use by a computer. Literacy includes the ability to read and interpret media (text, sound, images), to reproduce data and images through digital manipulation, and to evaluate and apply new knowledge gained from digital environments...[21]

The difference is in the source of the information. Information literacy implies the use of a breadth of technologies, while digital literacy is exclusive to digital based technologies, primarily the computer. The distinction is how information is now being retrieved compared to the past.

The perception that only the younger population is digitally literate is false and has grown out of popular literature. The ubiquitous nature of information

technology has resulted in people from all walks of life and all age groups becoming more digitally literate. Many CF members have grown up in a digital era
with readily available technologies and are quite comfortable in a digital learning environment. Further, the job demands can also play a role in increasing
technological competence beyond the norm for any given age group. These
dynamics are clearly evident within the CF population and as such, CF learners
are becoming more digitally literate.[22]

General Conclusions about CF Learners

My own view…is that either (a) most universals are so general as to be
without intellectual force or interest, are large banalities lacking either
circumstantiality or surprise, precision or revelation, and thus are of
precious little use; or (b) if universals do have some degree of non-
triviality, circumstantiality, and originality, if they actually assert
something interesting enough to be wrong, they are ill-based.

Clifford Geertz[23]

Recent discussions about CF learners have included characterisations from popular literature such as Millenials, Twitch Learners, Generation Y, Net Geners, and
Digital Natives. Within the broader learning community, these characterizations
may have an element of truth particularly within post-secondary learning institutions. As such, the CF should reflect on what has been validly concluded about
such learners and consider applying it to those specific populations. However,
there is little evidence to suggest that the characteristics apply to the greater CF
learning audience. Rather there are four meaningful generalizations that can be
applied now and in the future to the larger CF learning audience based upon the
data available and CF norms. CF learners will:

- increasingly reflect the cultural and linguistic diversity of the larger
  Canadian population;

- reflect multiple generations;

- arrive with higher levels of education than in the past; and

- be increasingly digitally literate.

In general terms, the CF learner is evolving from the image that is traditionally
held (Table 7.4).

Characteristic	Traditional Stereotype	Emerging Learner
Cohort age	Similarly aged cohorts advancing at a like pace with common learning needs.	Multiple-generation cohorts with a broad range of learning preferences/needs and various appreciations of learning, and differing levels of ascription to technology.
Cultural, socio-economic demographic	Homogeneous, largely Caucasian, lower-middle class Franco/Anglo male with high-school or lower education.	Culturally and socio-economically diverse with increasing incidence of post-secondary education.

Table 7.4: The Evolving CF Learner

Stemming from these generalizations, there are two valuable conclusions that provide a clearer context for CF T&E. First, the CF learning audience has evolved from the traditional homogeneous audience upon which many of our current instructional practices are based. Moreover, it will continue to evolve and this should drive changes to how we view learners and learning. The second is that generalizations that apply to the CF learning audience in the broadest sense suggest only that there is no "one size fits all" approach that will address the needs of all learners. Instead, there should be a concerted effort to gain a current and valid picture of each learning audience within each learning context.

The Implications

In the broadest sense, understanding that CF learners are evolving and becoming increasingly diverse should drive T&E practitioners to reflect on systems, procedures and practices that are influenced by learner dynamics. More specifically, this chapter highlights implications for:

- The general approach to learners and learning;

- Learner analysis;

- Instructional design; and

- Facilitation of learning.

There are Implications to the General Approach
to Learners and Learning

Even if it has not been formally acknowledged, the CF is predisposed to legacy thinking on learners and learning. T&E staff at all levels struggle with biases developed from their pasts as students and in their roles as teachers, instructors, or professors. The organizational demands on learning, advances in cognitive science and learning, and, of course, the growing diversity of the learning audience have significantly changed the learning landscape

In the face of the evolving learner, legacy thinking can seriously undermine development of *learner relevant* T&E strategies. T&E staff should therefore reassess their assumptions about learners and reflect on their personal philosophy about learning. Learning programs, professional networks, information sessions, guidance and feedback are some of the mechanisms that can help ensure that the perspectives of those working within the T&E community keep pace with both the evolving learner and the learning discipline.

There are Implications for Learner Analysis

Whether through the Canadian Forces Individual Training and Education System (CFITES) or some other form of instructional or curriculum design, all CF T&E is designed to meet defined learning outcomes.[24] This is crucial to ensuring that personnel are sufficiently trained and educated to accomplish the CF mission. Where large numbers are required to be trained in common skills and knowledge, responsible authorities leverage efficiencies of systematically designed learning programs to ensure that all learners have the same opportunity to achieve the desired outcomes. In such cases, it is more expedient to view learners as a group and the learner analysis tends towards capturing the representative norm.[25]

This norm establishes a set of common learner characteristics which influences all of the downstream instructional design decisions. If the analysis either includes inaccurate assumptions about learners or excludes members of the learning group, there is risk that the design and subsequent conduct will negatively impact on at least some of the learners. As an example, the discussion above on increasing education levels may suggest that all of those entering the CF are effective learners. It should not be assumed that education alone indicates success in learning competence.[26] Rather, where practicable, the learner analysis should include indicators that highlight the learners "ability to learn" so that any potential challenges can be addressed.

The evolving learning audience speaks to the need to broaden our learner analysis. The systemic default towards the representative norm should be expanded to attend to the diversity of the learning audience (Figure 7.1). This slight shift in perspective comes at only a minor cost in time and effort, but, can significantly enhance the understanding of the learning needs of all learners. This would better inform designers and instructors of the types of methods, media and learning environment that will enable learning success including the chance of success for atypical learners.

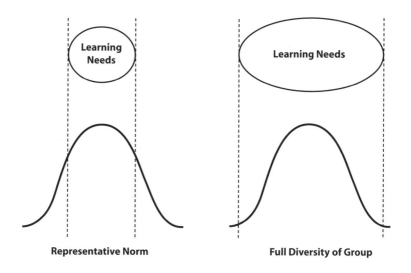

Figure 7.1: Representative Learner Analysis

There are Implications for Instructional Design

With the CF, the performance objectives (or educational objectives) drive the learning requirement or *what is to be learned*. The instructional design focuses on *how it is to be learned*. Even with an accurate learner analysis, there are times when expediency wins out over quality and the traditional instructor-led, classroom-based approach wins out over more thoughtful instructional design. Certainly, organizational expediency and efficiency are desirable qualities for T&E, but this does not dictate the methods or means for learning. Instructional designers should keep in mind that learners are important clients subordinate only to the ultimate employer. Accordingly, while organizational demands may be constraining, where possible, they should be balanced with the needs of the learners.

That said, a competent instructional designer can readily address a more diverse learning audience even under the typical CF T&E constraints. Attending to the needs of a diverse learning audience may only involve subtle changes to delivery modes or media. In other cases, it may involve selection or design of more dynamic learning activities that consider the breadth of the learning audience. In unique circumstances, it may be beneficial to plan for additional support to help atypical learners overcome distinct challenges. In all cases, the learning should also be supported by bias free and objective assessment. As a point of perspective, instead of viewing diversity as a challenge, it can and should be seen as an enabler to enhance learning. So, the self-imposed question for designers should be "How can I leverage the learner diversity within my instructional design?"

There are Implications for How Learning is Facilitated

Instructors are on the frontlines of formal learning and they are impacted by the quality of the instructional design. If there is an effective instructional design, this can greatly enhance their ability to facilitate the required learning – provided they have the necessary skills and tools to do so. If the instructional design is poor, they need to be able to overcome the design flaws.

Instructors know when they are not hitting the mark with learners. However, they sometimes lack the authority, confidence, or abilities to make the required changes to improve the learning experience. One significant issue is how instructors view themselves within the learning environment. While there are still those who support the traditional "teacher" role, there is greater pressure for instructors to take on a broader role as "facilitators of learning". This shift in perspective requires the instructor to evaluate the learner, the content to be learned and the resources at their disposal and then define how to influence the learning to achieve the desired outcomes. Different competencies are required than in the past and also a larger tool box that provides instructors with a variety of methods and techniques to address a wide-range of learning issues that may not have been considered in the original design. There are numerous initiatives out there to help guide and educate CF instructors in adopting this different perspective on learning and instruction and it is hoped that some of these become systemic.

Summary

The traditional perspective of learners as a relatively homogeneous group is no longer accurate. Instead the CF is experiencing an evolving learner that is diverse in terms of age and cultural background while also reflecting greater levels of education and digital literacy. Looking at the larger CF population, there are a number of implications. The CF T&E community should look towards a "new norm" in how it views learners and also what it should to do in order to respond to their needs. This is not to say that existing processes do not work, just that there should be more insight and depth of learner analysis which will better inform instructional design and conduct.

Certainly, the CF learning audience is dynamic and will continue to evolve as it reflects more and more the changes in Canadian society. It will be important for the CF T&E community to stay engaged and discuss the implications and best practices within learning. This will help ensure that all learners are provided the best possible opportunities to learn and develop thereby contributing to overall CF effectiveness.

---

1   Canadian Broadcasting Corporation (2008), CBC News Wednesday, April 2, "1 in 6 Canadians are a visible minority: StatsCan." This is referencing Statistics Canada "The Daily" 2 April 2008 highlighting Census 2006: Ethnic origin, visible minorities, place of work and mode of transportation.

2   Jungwee Park, "A Profile of the Canadian Forces - Statistics Canada Catalogue no. 75-001-X", Perspectives (July 2008), 18. Also retrieved on 27 Sep 2010 from <http://www.statcan.gc.ca/pub/75-001-x/2008107/pdf/10657-eng.pdf>.

3   Jungwee Park, 18.

4   Hans Jung, "Can the Canadian Forces Reflect Canadian Society?", *Canadian Military Journal*, Vol. 8, No. 3 (Autumn 2007), 27-36.

5   Tracy Wait, *DSHRC Research Note 2/02* (Ottawa : Department of National Defence, 2002).

6   The CF put into place new recruiting practices and employment policies specifically aimed at ensuring that women, as well as Aboriginals and Visible Minorities, are accorded an equitable opportunity to join the CF and advance within their chosen career.

7   Within the Canada First Defence Strategy, the CF will expand to 100,000 personnel (70,000 Regular Force and 30,000 Primary Reserve) by fiscal year 2027-28. See Canada First Defence Strategy accessed 15 November 2011 from <http://www.forces.gc.ca/site/pri/1/recruitm-recrutem-eng.asp>.

8   Tracy Wait.

9   Statistics Canada (2009), *Canada Year Book Overview 2009 – Languages* , accessed 10 December 2010 from <http://www41.statcan.gc.ca/2009/50000/cybac50000_000-eng.htm>.

10   Wayne G. Wouters, (2010), *Seventeenth Annual Report to the Prime Minister on the Public Service of Canada*, 17 accessed 24 November 2010 from <http://www.clerk.gc.ca/local_grfx/docs/reports/17rpt-eng.pdf >.

11   An Allophone is a Canadian term for an immigrant who first language is neither French nor English. (See : Oxford Corpus, in Catherine Soanes and Angus Stevenson, eds., *Concise Oxford English Dictionary: 11th edition revised 2008*, (New York : Oxford University Press, 2008).)

12   Statistics Canada, *Canada Year Book Overview 2009 – Languages.*

13   Statistics Canada, Social Fact Sheet, retrieved on 10 Dec 2010 from <http://www.statcan.gc.ca/pub/11-008-x/2010001/article/11132-eng.htm>.

14   Statistics Canada, *Canadian Demographics at a Glance Catalogue no. 91-003-X*, retrieved on 10 Dec 2010 from <http://www.statcan.gc.ca/pub/91-003-x/91-003-x2007001-eng.htm>.

15   Wouters, 17

16   Jungwee Park, 18.

17   Ibid., 19.

18   Statistics Canada, *Social Fact Sheet.*

19   Jungwee Park, 18.

20   American Library Association, *Presidential Committee on Information Literacy. Final Report* (Chicago: American Library Association, 1989), retrieved on 10 Oct 2010 from <http://www.ala.org/ala/mgrps/divs/acrl/publications/whitepapers/presidential.cfm>. Note that this definition is also endorsed by the Association of College and Research Libraries.

21   Barbara R. Jones-Kavalier and Suzanne L. Flannigan, "Connecting the Digital Dots: Literacy in the 21st Century", *Educause Quarterly*, Vol. 29, No. 2 (2006), retrieved on 10 Oct 2010 from <http://www.educause.edu/EDUCAUSE+Quarterly/EDUCAUSEQuarterlyMagazineVolum/ConnectingtheDigitalDotsLitera/157395>.

22   This is not synonymous with being "digital natives" who are a specific demographic segment of the Millennial population. In short, there is no scientifically based evidence that suggests that "digital natives" *learn* differently, but rather the media they *prefer* to use for learning may be different. (See : Marc Prensky, "Digital Natives, Digital Immigrants", *On the Horizon- MCB University Press*, Vol. 9, No. 5 (2001), retrieved on 10 Oct 2010 from <http://www.marcprensky.com/writing/Prensky%20-%20Digital%20Natives,%20Digital%20Immigrants%20-%20Part1.pdf>; Thomas C. Reeves, "Do Generational Differences Matter in Instructional Design?", *The Instructional Technology Forum*, retrieved on 10 Oct 2010 from <http://it.coe.uga.edu/itforum/Paper104/ReevesITForumJan08.pdf>.

23   Clifford Geertz, *Available Light: Anthropological Reflections on Philosophical Topics* (Princeton: Princeton University Press, 2000), 134.

24   Whether the requirements are defined by legislation, a job specification, or an accredited university curriculum, the point is that the learning is not arbitrary and the learners will not

typically be afforded the opportunity to contribute to the learning objectives driven by these requirements.

25   Canada, *Canadian Forces Manual of Individual Training and Education Vol 4 – Design of Instructional Programs*, (Department of National Defence, Director General Public Affairs, 1999), 3.

26   William J. Rothwell and Hercules C. Kazanas, *Mastering the Instructional Design Process: A Systematic Approach* (San Fransico: Jossey-Bass Inc, 1998), 91.

CHAPTER 8

INFORMAL LEARNING –
AN ENABLER TO SUCCESS

Wendy H. Appelbaum

Informal Learning

In these complex times, creating an environment where employees not only cope but thrive in acquiring the critical knowledge, skills and abilities required to succeed is contingent on a multitude of factors. What is becoming evident is that learning and development activities have taken centre stage as the mechanism with which to address the business needs of an organization, forcing the organization to raise the profile to a more strategic level. How an organization proactively addresses its mandate has evolved from the implementation of traditional formal mechanisms (in-class, online learning, performance support tools) to the informal, which are expanding at a rapid rate. As informal approaches are structured much more loosely, they present a challenge when it comes time to assess their value and/or evaluate their impact.

Much has been written about informal learning, with many schools of thought with respect to what is viewed as "formal" and "informal". Informal learning has often been attributed to learning that happens in the workplace and through collaborative processes. The concept of unstructured activities often found in the workplace has been used to describe informal learning practices. The *2009 Learning and Development Outlook* report expands on this theme:

> Learning that takes place in the workplace through mentoring, peer-coaching, and "shoulder-to-shoulder" learning that does not involve formal instruction in a classroom, online, or through other structured formats.[1]

Informal learning has also been described as a natural participation process where, as a result of sharing, information becomes useful and relevant.[2] In contrast, the formal aspects of learning "…can be likened to riding a bus, as the route is preplanned and the same for everyone" where informal learning is more akin to "riding a bike in that the individual determines the route, pace, etc."[3] and that it can be "incidental and integrated into daily activity."[4] In this regard, the learner is in control of his or her own learning. Informal learning can be unplanned but still valued and recognized by the learner. It has also been noted that these activities are "easier to observe, describe and research than those that are unintentional and more integrated into other tasks"[5] but also that "these activities only make up a small proportion of what is really taking place."[6] Malcolm and others argue that "[a]ttributes of formality and informality are present in the majority of learning situations, but that the inter-relationships between such informal and formal attributes vary from situation to situation."[7]

In trying to define these two approaches it is fair to say that both formal and informal learning are interconnected and can include elements of both.[8] One of the most comprehensive informal learning studies was carried out in 2001 by Graham Cheethan, a Senior Policy Advisor with the Department for Education and Employment in the United Kingdom and Geoff Chivers, a professor at the Business School in Loughborough University, also in the UK. These researchers created a taxonomy of informal professional methods, learning experiences and events as follows:[9]

- Practice and repetition (e.g., simulation, preparation before event, drill/practice);

- Reflection (e.g., self-analysis, group/collective reflection, debriefing, mental re-running);

- Observation and copying (e.g., shadowing, positive/negative role modelling, structured/informal/critical observation);

- Feedback (e.g., appraisal/performance reviews, 360 feedback, evaluation exercises, effective listening);

- Extra-occupational Transfer (e.g., pre-entry experiences, out of work learning, theory into practice, transfer of experience);

- Stretching activities (e.g., challenging/pioneering activities, broad-based holistic experiences, demanding/complex tasks/problems);

- Perspective Changing/Switching (e.g., role transfer, job exchanges, mental perspective switching);

- Mentor/Coach Interaction (e.g., advice, counselling, instruction/demonstration, sounding board activities);

- Unconscious absorption or osmosis (e.g., networking, working with role models/colleagues, apprenticeship);

- Use of psychological devices/mental tricks (e.g., mental/cognitive models, graphical representations, visualization, mental preparation, whole-brain learning techniques);

- Articulation (e.g., teaching/tutoring, speaking at conferences, development of learning materials); and

- Collaboration (e.g., working in multi-disciplinary teams, team building/working, learning from professionals, presenting).

Given the varying perspectives on what unite and differentiate informal and formal learning, the emphasis needs to be placed on what the learner is gaining from these methods, and how this gain is occurring.

Surrounding Circumstances

In a world impacted by demographic shifts, a more diversified population, an ever increasing need for "knowledge workers", the rapid pace of evolving technology, the impacts (and benefits) of globalization and the results of a shifting economy, achieving success in such a complex environment will require versatile and robust models to address the ongoing needs of organizations. Saba's white paper *Learning 2.0: Using Web 2.0 to Create Effective Informal Learning* further expands on this: "[t]he combination of a changing global economic landscape and evolution of new communication technologies clearly demonstrates the organizational demand for new learning paradigms to support this new economic world in which we live."[10]

The impending retirement of the Baby Boomers highlight the importance of ensuring that critical knowledge is transferred to the next generation of leaders.

In order to maintain the quality and efficiency of services, employees will need to be up and running quickly with the critical knowledge and skills required to be effective in meeting the business priorities. This is of particular importance with respect to the new generation of employees entering the workforce, commonly referred to as "digital natives," the generation of young people born since 1980 who have an innate confidence in using new technologies such as the internet, videogames, mobile telephony and "all the other toys and tools of the digital age."[11]

The collaborative and often participatory nature of how information is transforming the learning field is impacting development, delivery and communication. Additional challenges are resulting from the competition for skilled workers, and the ability to harness the benefits of an increasingly diverse population. For organizations to be successful, they will need to be much more strategic in addressing a diverse workforce and ensure that the appropriate learning is delivered and in a manner that is relevant to each individual.

The rate with which technology continues to evolve has been a key contributor towards the shift in the learning landscape. Access to critical information, when and where needed, the ability to connect with anyone (i.e. the social aspect) at anytime and most importantly the advent of mobile devices has resulted in more of a "self-serve, social and mobile" approach.[12] Technology has altered the way we communicate, how we engage in business, how we socialize, and it is ultimately driving the nature of the work environment. The ability to adapt quickly to not only the changing work environment but in the way we perform will determine the level of success an organization achieves.

Recent events bear this out. The recession of 2008 forced organizations to make difficult choices with respect to how business priorities could be met; for some, this resulted in cutting initiatives in the areas of Human Resources, while others focused on using the time to ramp up their employees and prepare for an economic recovery. Globalization is continuing to impact how each organization manages its business, with the ongoing pressure of a competitive labour market and an increasing need for innovative solutions and increased productivity. These pressures are creating a demand for highly qualified and highly educated workers, hence the term, "knowledge workers."

Given the fact that we have had one of the strongest labour markets in the last 30 years, remaining competitive in this new economy will demand that we are sufficiently equipped to address these ongoing challenges. This can only be accomplished if people are equipped with the appropriate knowledge, skills and abilities to make the critical decisions and engage in viable solutions. The current economic downturn is only increasing these pressures.

Indicators of the New Reality

If we are to measure the value that is placed on learning, traditionally, the biggest indicator would be the allocation provided to each employee to pursue "formal learning activities". The 2009 Learning and Development Outlook report provides a picture of the current state:

> Canadian organizations spent an average of $787 per employee, or 1.5 per cent of their payroll, on training, learning, and development. This level of expenditure has decreased in real terms by over 40 percent in the past decade and a half. In 2008, the amount of training each employee received annually was 20 hours, down 30 per cent from just four years ago.[13]

As a result of the decrease, it is difficult to assess whether employees are receiving fewer opportunities with respect to learning, training and development as there appears to be a rise of informal learning activities. In fact, it is estimated that "56 percent of all learning occurs informally, up significantly from 2004."[14] One of the key challenges in assessing how much learning is actually occurring is due to the fact that the "intangible nature of informal learning renders the measurement of its inputs, let alone outcomes, challenging."[15]

Irrespective of this, informal learning does not appear to be a trend that will disappear anytime soon. This is particularly timely given the economic trends with respect to fiscal restraint. Researchers in 1999 hypothesized that this could have an impact on hiring practices, particularly with respect to the selection of those that require less formal training.[16] Despite the lack of concrete data in tracking the amount and impact, there appears to be an enthusiasm with respect to embracing informal learning and an understanding of its value as a mechanism used to fill knowledge gaps during an economic downturn. Saba's report on *Learning 2.0* further expands on this idea:

> ....the learning organization is no longer the sole provider of learning as the structured "publishing" model is usurped on a daily basis by

individuals, peers or teams collaborating horizontally across the enterprise in an increasingly unstructured, impromptu and as needed manner.[17]

The way that governments have transformed how they carry out their operations through the use of informal and collaborative mechanisms is another clear indicator of this shift. The many challenges that we are faced with are driving the need for governments to be more effective; leveraging informal collaborative models are a mechanism used to achieve this. In order for governments to be more responsive in addressing these challenges, they are looking at how policies are developed with respect to how information is shared and delivered in the overall management of government operations. Informal learning mechanisms in the form of social media (Web 2.0) technologies are providing the appropriate infrastructure to build a collaborative government capability in the management and delivery of information. The *2009 Deloitte Research Report on Collaborative Government and Web 2.0* described the benefits of this model:

> Government 2.0 is more than simply adopting Web 2.0 tools for government. It is about recognizing that conventional governments are unable to address society's challenges alone. It is also a philosophy and culture that reflects society's radically new way of interacting and communicating, which governments must accept if they hope to maintain pace.[18]

There is great potential for government to continue working towards these outcomes in supporting collaborative tools and practices pertaining to information sharing; this will result in improved policy outcomes and more effective management of information. The integration of Web 2.0 technologies have the power to transform government into an institution that ensures that its citizens are better informed, that services are provided to them in the most efficient manner and are driven by democratic principles.

In their 2009 report, *Change your World and your World will Change You: The Future of Collaborative Government and Web 2.0*, Deloitte Research focuses on the collaborative possibilities afforded by these tools that have the potential to not only achieve this vision, but also ensure that the basic principles of government (i.e. transparency, accountability and quality of responsiveness) are adhered to. They highlight key Government 2.0 initiatives in New Zealand and Canada: for example, New Zealand put in place a wiki initiative that enables ordinary citizens to contribute (through a blog) to the reform of their Police Act to better serve its citizens.

Natural Resources Canada is noted as one of the leaders in the early adoption of 2.0 technologies and is particularly noted for their North Star Project; this initiative was focused on building a comprehensive Natural Resources Policy Framework, which further evolved into a 2.0 strategy to address collaboration and knowledge management needs. Other successful Government 2.0 initiatives have included the Departments of Defence of Australia and the United States. For instance, the Australian government initiated a formal taskforce to integrate government 2.0 into all aspects of government with a focus on service delivery and innovation. This resulted in identifying the needs for more improved support services, accessible and reusable information, clarification with respect to how government records are defined, and most importantly a desire for more coordinated leadership and guidance from the government. The Business Transformation Agency, as part of the United States Department of Defense, initiated the modernization of business operations with a key focus on transforming the areas of learning, recruitment and knowledge management.

Mitigation Strategies to Ensure Success

In order for informal learning strategies to create maximum impact, there are some fundamental principles that need to be in place to ensure successful implementation. The following provides some of the key principles.

Linkages to Business Priorities

Given the workload pressures sustained by employees, the links to business priorities must be clearly articulated, the informal delivery mechanisms supported by management and the benefits clearly identified to all levels of employees. The message that needs to be communicated is how these tools will support the overarching business priorities.

Incorporation of Learning Theory and Principles

Much in the same way "formal learning" products are developed with the intent for successful knowledge transfer, "informal products" must adhere to the same principles. Understanding the roots of informal learning is crucial with respect to not only the development of future tools and applications but in providing a credible platform with which to "sell the benefits". Informal learning finds its roots in traditional learning theory as follows:[19]

- Behaviourism with its emphasis on feedback, repetition and reinforcement (as it pertains to instruction);

- Cognitive psychology, with respect to assimilation of information and the use of mental processes in the formation of mental models (this is further expanded on by the Gestalt approach in the use of mental images to support perception and memory);

- Piaget's theories on the evolutionary process of development (using what has been developed to date);

- Vygotsky's focus on the linkages between language and thought through various points in development;

- Bandura's social learning theory, where learning is viewed as continuous and dynamic and with an equal emphasis on the learning environment;

- Gagne and Briggs combination of both behaviourism and cognitive principles in the development of task analysis;

- Cybernetics through the systems approach to training; elements of constructivism and discovery learning;

- The contributions of Malcolm Knowles' work on andragogy; and

- David Kolb's learning cycle with respect to experiential learning.

To further understand these linkages, it is important to explore some concrete examples of informal learning. The cycle of coaching contains elements of expert modelling, with feedback provided by a coach; this leads to a reduction of support as the learner gains confidence and where the goal for the learner is to be able to describe the processes used in addressing issues and reflection and finally, the gradual move towards exploration.[20] Observation and Role

Modelling can be dissected to highlight elements of attention, retention, production and motivation with the oversight of the expert.[21] Mentoring, though at times formal, can also be informal where the mentor can provide functions related to coaching, counselling, role modelling, advisor, confident, but in general adhere to three main roles: "educative, supportive and managerial."[22] Simulation and transfer activities contain links to assessment and to the gradual transfer of learning outside the work environment.[23] Collaborative learning is directly linked to social development theory and the "zone of proximal development" with the emphasis on the level of mental development that can be achieved as a result of collaboration. Work-based learning (with all its challenges in categorization) is highlighted by elements of pro-activity, critical reflection and creativity that need to be present.[24] Work in the area of social development is probably one of the more closely linked areas with respect to social learning and Web 2.0 (3.0) applications. It is at this juncture that the construction of knowledge can be derived from multiple influences in one's own environment combined with the integration of one's own personal experiences. An added benefit resulting from this collaborative focus has been identified around the idea that the group or organization becomes more knowledge as the individuals that form this group become more knowledgeable.[25]

Learner Styles and Preferences

Given what we know about how individuals learn, particularly educational theorist David Kolb's work with the experiential learning inventory,[26] those developing training and learning solutions are well aware of the need to ensure that the design of a learning activity address varied learning styles. In implementing informal learning solutions, as with formal learning approaches, understanding the various learning styles and preferences of those targeted is a key enabler of success. Understanding the demographic profiles and characteristic traits that exist within the workforce, specifically the Baby Boomer generation (as well as pre-boomers in some cases), Generation X (born between 1961-1981) and, more recently, the Generation Y/Millennials,[27] will require varied and flexible instructional approaches. For example, due to an increase in working-memory capacity, instructional approaches should be designed differently for those that are older than for a younger generation.[28]

As for younger generations, though not empirically proven, they are noted as being more intuitive with respect to technology, are more hands-on, have a preference for visual learning and are better able to multi-task. As part of their *Lifelong Learning Book Series*, the Open University of the Netherlands argues that the necessity in adapting instructional approaches is based not only on the requirements but on the learner's individual level of achievement "Style-by-strategy and achievement-by-strategy interactions complement each other and should not be considered separately" in addition one should ensure that "expertise be a distinguishing factor when employing instructional methods."[29]

Though there are specific characteristic traits that can be attributed to each of these generational groups, it has been suggested that another way to address the varied audiences is to group users into those that are creators of information, those that provide feedback, those that benefit from information and those that support the development of applications to support these informal learning mechanisms.[30]

Implications to Design

The shift from formal to informal will require us to look at the design from a different perspective. Significant differences will focus on the transition from clear-cut problem solving approaches to those that require a multi-perspective approach, a more domain-general approach where the best use of knowledge, skills and abilities is put to use, a focus on more self-management/autonomy in self-reflection with respect to problem-solving, with a significant shift to more of an expert-expert model (as opposed to expert-novice),[31] to an increased emphasis on real-life reference situations where learners must "apply their acquired knowledge, skills, and attitudes to perform authentic tasks, thus promoting far transfer."[32] In 2001, Graham Cheetham and Geoff Chivers emphasized the approach that needs to occur:

> In looking at design, we also have to consider the links between formal and informal and the emphasis on imparting core knowledge and basic professional skills and, very importantly, on developing a range of learning skills, especially those linked to informal learning.[33]

Informal learning needs to be structured in such a way where meeting the desired competencies is attainable and through a combination of collaborative and sound instructional approaches and through effective delivery mediums where critical information can be accessed in a timely manner.

Performance Measurement/Evaluation Activities

Despite the critical role that evaluation plays, the amount of time dedicated to evaluation activities is decreasing.[34] This is further challenged by the fact that developing measures and indicators is not only difficult to define but close to impossible to properly evaluate, due to the ability to isolate the specific variables that influence "impact" and the allocation of time required to measure the change. Given this context, it is not surprising to find that "only 10 per cent of organizations evaluated the effects of informal learning in their workplace, and they did so by investigating learners' reactions (Level 1)."[35]

In spite of these challenges, this should not inhibit an organization in looking at the value of these informal mechanisms as part of the overall strategy in supporting employees in their performance and career progression. What these outcomes *can look like* will be directly linked to the processes involved in addressing business requirements. For example, informal learning activities can be integrated into formal learning activities and evaluated "as a whole" (i.e., how knowledge, skills and abilities come together), while other informal activities can be evaluated as part of a larger plan in addressing core competencies.

Specific examples of this could involve measuring the knowledge gain and impact resulting from updating/accessing information from a wiki (as part of a larger learning requirement), to the transfer of knowledge to the job resulting from attending a conference, to measuring the impact of a job shadowing assignment on a specific work task. Irrespective of the approach, what needs to be kept at the forefront is to ensure that the measures and indicators associated with each of the informal learning mechanisms are linked to the performance objectives required for meeting the business priorities.

Impact on Learning

Given the decreased spending on formal training, informal learning approaches are now being used to fill the critical skill shortage gaps. The impact is tremendous due to technology's ability to enable individuals to learn at anytime, anywhere and address the need for varied learning preferences and styles through multiple informal delivery mediums. Societal pressures forcing individuals to update knowledge and skills on a regular basis are quickly becoming part of the norm as the ability to consult with experts and collaborate is readily available. In 2008, Jeroen van Merrienboer and Slavi Stoyanov, professors at the Open University of the Netherlands described the driving force behind this need. They reported: "Learning is becoming a constant attribute of personal human life, not only for adapting but also for pleasure, satisfying curiosity, and in terms of Maslow, self-actualization and self-fulfillment."[36]

This is having an impact on the knowledge, skills and abilities required to be a lifelong learner, how applications and tools will support this in the context of learning, the type of instructional approaches that can support lifelong learners, and the type of support needed to be provided to sustain this over the long-run. In supporting these learners, the question to ask is *how are organizations addressing these needs to ensure that they achieve value?* What it means to be a learner is changing as the shift from the classroom or online environment is transitioning to various communities of practice, where learners "participate in more than one learning network, and the composition of those networks continuously changes"[37] Learners are now exposed to a variety of cultures, backgrounds, areas of expertise and roles taken on within networks and communities.

In addition to the changing roles of learners, how knowledge is imparted is also undergoing transformation. Traditional instructional design models will need to expand to address the capabilities and intended objectives of these informal learning tools. Van Merrianboer and Stoyanov (2008) argue that "traditional instructional design models focus on one particular domain of learning such as procedural, declarative or attitudinal learning (compartmentalization);"[38] they cannot adequately address the rapid changes resulting from this evolution. They conclude this point by stating that "new models are needed, which use real-life learning tasks as the driving force for learning."[39]

One of these approaches is the ability to address large groups; this is resulting in what is being referred to as the "mass customization" of learning which is comprised of "personalized media that provide adaptive online learning, that is information and support that is tailored to the particular needs and preferences of individual users and learners".[40] The focus should not be on creating a generational divide and categorizing learners but on ensuring that these informal mechanisms take into account the characteristic traits and preferences of learners, where the tasks related to these objectives are clearly communicated and where the autonomy of the learner drives the process with respect to which strategies are applied in meeting these tasks.

A key success factor will be attributed to the reflection that needs to occur in addressing these tasks as this often results in knowledge transfer. The impact that informal learning is having on the learning field in general is demonstrated by the fact that information can be retrieved anytime, anywhere, through a variety of mechanisms and most notably, its ability to be gathered and shared by multiple people. In Brandon Hall's 2010 white paper on *Understanding Social Learning in Organizational Settings*, they highlight the most significant benefit of all: "When this collaboration results in increased knowledge that is then accessible to others, the amount of collective intelligence in an organization or in the world in general rises (example: Wikipedia)."[41] The white paper also highlights the benefits of networking, communicating, interacting with learning applications, experts and peers which results in the ability to dialogue, engage in instantaneous peer reviews, and to work in a parallel, sequential and synergistic fashion.[42] The establishment of community networks and social networking tools and applications can be "an effective instructional approach in the development of a collaborative learning community."[43]

With respect to the technologies developed for gaming, simulations and the creation of virtual worlds where key skill sets pertaining to coordination, multitasking and problem-solving are addressed, in 2005, Eric Klopfler, an Associate Professor and Director of the MIT Teacher Education Program, noted that "… many games draw heavily upon important 21st century skills such as problem-solving, collaboration and communication."[44] Brandon Hall further adds to this point by stating that it is for these reasons that "it is thought by some that the new generation of employees will eventually make great leaders."[45] In looking at the overarching impact of informal learning, it is important to highlight some of the issues that have been identified with respect to some of these trends, specifically the challenges in assessing the overarching impact of these informal learning tools, the nature of how this learning is transferred and the isolating effects that can occur through the diminishing physical contact.

Summary

The ongoing pressures facing our society in the form of demographic shifts, fiscal restraint, an increasingly diverse population, a knowledge-based economy and the competitive nature of a global workforce, are forcing organizations to look at new and innovative ways to address business requirements. Despite the challenges associated with ensuring that critical knowledge, skills and abilities are addressed through formal learning mechanisms, it is clear that organizations are taking informal learning seriously and harnessing the power of these tools and applications to fill the gaps. As we transition into a new learning landscape and seek to address our requirements through a variety of tools and applications, it is more important than ever that we ensure that these informal learning strategies are grounded in clearly communicated learning objectives.

The emphasis should remain on the requirements that are driving the informal solution with the informal method chosen as an optimal method of delivering this requirement. In looking at improving the performance of an organization through the use of informal learning, we need to have a clear understanding of the linkages between these tools and the desired competencies to be gained in support of the overall mandate. The creation of an enabling environment where employees can move through this "system" and participate in a manner that is conducive to their learning preferences in accessing critical information requires a solid infrastructure.

As outlined in this chapter, building this infrastructure is well worth its time when assessed in terms of the gains realized by an organization. When employees receive the support they need to not only do their jobs effectively, but understand the individual value they bring to the "success", everyone benefits. It is here where the buy-in and ultimate support of the organization will be gained, which will ultimately lead to future support for other initiatives of this nature.

---

1   The Conference Board of Canada Outlook, *Learning and Development Outlook 2009: Learning in Tough Times* (Ottawa, ON: The Conference Board of Canada, 2009), 30.

2   SABA, *Learning 2.0: Using Web 2.0 to Create Effective Informal Learning – How Organizations are Harnessing the Collective Intelligence of Their Employees to Improve Effectiveness* (Redwood Shores, CA: 2007), 2.

3   Jay Cross, *Informal Learning: Rediscovering the Natural Pathways that Inspire Innovation and Performance* (San Francisco, CA: Pfeiffer, 2007), in Shelly A. Berg and Seung Youn, "Factors that Influence Informal Learning in the Workplace", *Journal of Workplace Learning*, Vol. 20, No. 4 (2008), 230.

4   Phil Hodkinson, Helen Colley and Janice Malcolm, "The Interrelationships between Informal and Formal Learning", *Journal of Workplace Learning*, Vol. 15, No. 7/8 (2003), 313-18; Victoria J. Marsick and Marie Volpe, "The Nature and Need for Informal Learning", *Advances in Developing Human Resources*, Vol. 1 (1999), 1-9, as quoted in Shelley A. Berg and Seung Youn, "Factors that Influence Informal Learning in the Workplace", *Journal of Workplace Learning*, Vol. 20, No. 4 (2008), 230.

5   Shelly A. Berg and Seung Youn Chyung, "Factors that Influence Informal Learning in the Workplace", *Journal of Workplace Learning*, Vol. 20, No. 4 (2008), 230.

6   Victoria J. Marsick and Marie Volpe, "The Nature and Need for Informal Learning", *Advances in Developing Human Resource*, Vol. 1 (1999), 1-9, as quoted in Shelley A. Berg and Seung Youn, "Factors that Influence Informal Learning in the Workplace", *Journal of Workplace Learning*, Vol. 20, No. 4 (2008), 2.

7   Phil Hodkinson, Helen Colley and Janice Malcolm, "The Interrelationships between Informal and Formal Learning", *Journal of Workplace Learning*, Vol. 15, No.7/8 (2003), 315.

8   Don Clark, "Formal and Informal Learning", retrieved on 20 October 2010 from <http://www.knowledgejump.com/learning/informal.html>.

9   Graham Cheetham and Geoff Chivers, "How Professionals Learn in Practice: An Investigation of Informal Learning Amongst People Working in Professions", *Journal of European Industrial Training*, Vol. 25, No. 5 (2001), 44-46.

10   Cross, 230.

11   Neil Selywn, "The Digital Native – Myth and Reality", *Aslib Proceedings: New Informal Perspectives*, Vol. 61 (2009), 365.

12   Brandon Hall, *Understanding Social Learning in Organizational Settings* (Sunnyvale, CA, 2010), 9.

13   The Conference Board of Canada Outlook, *Learning and Development Outlook 2009: Learning in Tough Times* (Ottawa: The Conference Board of Canada, 2009), i.

14   Ibid., 1.

15   Ibid., 4.

16   Stephen Gorard, Ralph Fevre and Gareth Rees, "The apparent decline of informal learning", *Oxford Review of Education*, Vol. 25 (1999), 437-456, quoted in Thomas J. Conlon, "A Review of Informal Learning Literature, Theory and Implications for Practice in Developing Global Professional Competence", *Journal of European Industrial Training*, Vol. 28, No.2/3/4 (2004), 7.

17   Cross, 230.

18   William Eggers, *Government 2.0: Using Technology to Improve Education* (Maryland: Rowman & Littlefield, 2007), as quoted in Deloitte Research, *Change Your World and the World will Change You: The Future of Collaborative Government and Web 2.0* (Quebec, QC, 2009), 1.

19   Graham Cheetham and Geoff Chivers, "How Professionals Learn in Practice: An Investigation of Informal Learning Amongst People Working in Professions", *Journal of European Industrial Training*, Vol. 25, No. 5 (2001), 252-256.

20   Ibid., 257.

21   Albert Bandura, *Social Foundations of Thought and Action: A Social Cognitive Theory* (Englewood Cliffs, NJ: Prentice-Hall, 1986), as quoted in Graham Cheetham and Geoff Chivers, "How Professionals Learn in Practice: An Investigation of Informal Learning Amongst People Working in Professions", *Journal of European Industrial Training*, Vol. 25, No. 5 (2001), 259.

22   Peter Hawkins and Robin Shohet, *Supervising in the Helping Professions* (Milton Keynes: Open University Press, 1989), as quoted in Graham Cheetham and Geoff Chivers, "How

Professionals Learn in Practice: An Investigation of Informal Learning Amongst People Working in Professions", *Journal of European Industrial Training*, Vol. 25, No. 5 (2001), 259.

23   Graham Cheetham and Geoff Chivers, "How Professionals Learn in Practice: An Investigation of Informal Learning Amongst People Working in Professions", *Journal of European Industrial Training*, Vol. 25, No. 5 (2001), 261.

24   Ibid., 267.

25   Brandon Hall, *Understanding Social Learning in Organizational Settings* (Sunnyvale, CA, 2010), 20.

26   Don Clark, "Kolb's Learning Styles and Experiential Learning Model", *Big Dog and Little Dog's Performance Juxtaposition*, retrieved on 13 October 2011 from <http://www.nwlink.com/~donclark/hrd/styles/kolb.html>.

27   Wikipedia, *Generation Y*, retrieved on 12 November 2010 from <http://en.wikipedia.org/wiki/Generation_Y>.

28   Jeroen J.G. Van Merrienboer and Slavi Stoyanov, "Learners in a Changing Learning Landscape: Reflections from an Instructional Design Perspective" in Jan Visser and Muriel Visser-Valfrey, eds., *Lifelong Learning Book Series* (Netherlands: Educational Technology Expertise Center, 2008), 82.

29   Ibid.

30   David Osimo, *Web 2.0 in Government: Why and How* (Luxembourg: Joint Research Center 2008), 18-19.

31   Van Merrianboer and Stoyanov, 70.

32   Ibid.

33   Graham Cheetham and Geoff Chivers, "How Professionals Learn in Practice: An Investigation of Informal Learning Amongst People Working in Professions", *Journal of European Industrial Training*, Vol. 25, No. 5 (2001), 285-286.

34   The Conference Board of Canada Outlook, *Learning and Development Outlook 2009: Learning in Tough Times* (Ottawa, ON: The Conference Board of Canada, 2009), 48.

35   Ibid.

36   Van Merrienboer and Stoyanov, 76.

37   Ibid., 76-77.

38   Ibid., 84-85.

39   Ibid.

40   Ibid., 76.

41   Brandon Hall, *Understanding Social Learning in Organizational Settings* (Sunnyvale, CA, 2010), 20.

42   Ibid., 23.

43   Ibid., 22.

44   Eric Klopfer, "Playing to Learn", A Cable in the Classroom Production July/August (2005), re-trieved on 21 Oct 2010 from <http://educationarcade.org/files/articles/Cable_in_the_classroom.pdf>.

45   Brandon Hall, *Understanding Social Learning in Organizational Settings* (Sunnyvale, CA, 2010), 26.

CHAPTER 9

THE IMPACT OF GENERATIONAL LEARNING ON TRAINING AND EDUCATION IN THE CANADIAN FORCES

Dr. Norman D. Vaughan

A recent study of the Canadian Forces population[1] indicated that there are significant generational differences emerging in its workforce. Many of the senior staff fall into an age group between 40-54, while new recruits and future leaders are drawn from a younger cohort (18-39). Furthermore, research has indicated that there are significant differences in the learning styles and expectations between these two diverse groups.[2] This emerging area of research has been called "generational research" and the results of this work have significant implications for the way Individual Training and Education (IT&E) is planned, designed and conducted in the CF. Therefore, the objective of this chapter is to review the literature on generational learning and to provide the reader with an overview of the expectations, preferred learning styles and technological capabilities of potential applicants. The goal is to enable a more precise application of alternate training strategies, technology and instructional methodologies within the CF IT&E. Specifically, this chapter examines three fundamental questions:

1. Are there common learning profiles used by 18-39 year olds?

2. How do 18-39 years olds learn, and does this learning style differ from that used by older learners?

3. What impact does the learning style of CF applicants have on IT&E?

The term "generational cohort" is used throughout the chapter to describe groups of individuals who were born during the same time period and who experienced similar events during their formative years. These common life experiences create cohesiveness in values, attitudes, and beliefs that result in a social character distinct to each generational cohort that are formed through socialization and remain relatively stable throughout the cohort's lifetime. Generational learning research focuses on the environmental forces that shape learners' interactions in their academic, workplace, and personal lives.[3] It also provides an understanding about how these forces impact learners' reactions and communications with training staff and each other.

This research suggests that people born within an approximately 20 year period share a common set of characteristics based on the historical experiences, economic and social conditions, and technological advances that they have experienced.[4] The term first came into popularity in the 1960s when it was used to distinguish the rebellious Baby Boomer generation from their parents. This notion of generational differences has been widely discussed in the popular press as well as in a few scholarly publications. Sociologists have speculated that the various generations of students enrolled in today's higher education institutions as well as the different generations of employees in the workplace require a different approach to education and training. Extensions of this speculation are that CF Training Establishments should take generational differences into account when developing and delivering instruction.

Defining the Generations

The terms used to label various generations are not standardized because the different researchers and consultants who are exploring and writing about generational differences have come up with a variety of different names to label each of the generations. In addition, there is significant disagreement among the various authors about which span of years should be included within any one generation. Table 9.1 presents a comparison of the different labels given to various generations as well as the different chronological schemes used to assign people born in any given year to one of the generations defined by the sources listed in the first column.

Source	Labels				
Howe & Strauss, 2000	Silent Generation (1925–1943)	Boom Generation (1943–1960)	13th Generation (1961–1981)	Millennial Generation (1982–2000)	
Lancaster & Stillman, 2002	Traditionalists (1900–1945)	Baby Boomers (1946–1964)	Generation Xers (1965–1980)	Millennial Generation; Echo Boomer; Generation Y; Baby Busters; Generation Next (1981–1999)	
Martin & Tulgan, 2006	Silent Generation (1925–1942)	Baby Boomers (1946–1960)	Generation X (1965–1977)	Millennials (1978–2000)	
Oblinger & Oblinger, 2005	Matures (<1946)	Baby Boomers (1947–1964)	Gen-Xers (1965–1980)	Gen-Y; NetGen; Millennials (1981–1995)	Post-Millennials (1995–present)
Tapscott, 1998		Baby Boom Generation (1946–1964)	Generation X (1965–1975)	Digital Generation (1976–2000)	
Zemke, Raines & Filipczak, 1999	Veterans (1922–1943)	Baby Boomers (1943–1960)	Gen-Xers (1960–1980)	Nexters (1980–1999)	

Table 9.1: Generational Labels and Dates Reported from Key Sources[5]

For the purpose of this chapter, the generations have been labeled and delineated using the most common terms found in the literature. These generational labels and dates are illustrated in Table 9.2.

Label:	Mature Generation	Baby Boomers	Generation X	Millennials	Generation Z
Date:	<1946	1946–1964	1965–1980	1981–2000	2001-present

Table 9.2: Generational Labels and Dates

A number of researchers stress that the birth year is only one factor to consider in distinguishing among generations.[6] They suggest that generations are shaped much more by history than by chronological dates. For example, researchers have indicated that the following three attributes more clearly identify the nature of a generation than just years of birth:[7]

- *Perceived membership* – The self-perception of membership within a generation that begins during adolescence and coalesces during young adulthood.

- *Common beliefs and behaviours* – The attitudes (toward family, career, personal life, politics, religion, etc.) and behaviours (choices made in regard to jobs, marriage, children, health, crime, sex, drugs, etc.) that characterize a generation.

- *Common location in history* – The turning point in historical trends (e.g., from liberal to conservative politics) and significant events (e.g., the Vietnam War) that occur during a generation's formative years (adolescence and young adulthood).

In addition, Jean M. Twenge, Professor of Psychology, states "the society that molds you when you are young stays with you the rest of your life."[8] She further emphasizes that when you were born has more influence than the family who raised you. To reinforce this idea, Twenge quotes an Arab proverb, "Men resemble the times, more than they resemble their fathers."[9]

A synthesis of the literature indicates that there are currently four generational cohorts present in the Canadian workforce; Matures, Baby Boomers, Generation X, and the Millennials. In terms of the Canadian Forces, a recent Statistics Canada report[10] indicates that 71 percent of the CF population is currently in the Gen X and Millennial age brackets (Figure 9.1).

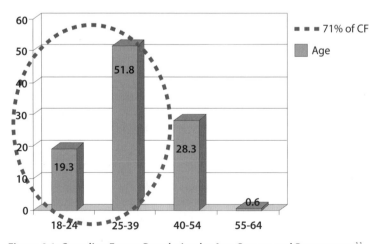

Figure 9.1: Canadian Forces Population by Age Groups and Percentages[11]

A brief overview is provided for each of the four generational cohorts.

Matures

The Mature generation was born prior to 1946 and represents a very small percentage of the Canadian workforce and they are probably non-existent in the Canadian Forces (since the vast majority have retired). This generation was born too late to participate in the Second World War and too early to become full-blown flower children. They have always been one step out of sync with the times. The Matures were young adults when it was hip to be a teenager.[12] They have adopted their elders' values of loyalty, dedication, and commitment to command/control leadership within hierarchical organizations. Their outer-focused "we" attitude helped to rebuild the North American economy in the 1950s and they looked forward to the ultimate rewards such as the status of owning their own home and lifetime employment in a solid organization. The two key technology developments for this generation were the widespread adoption of the radio and the telephone, which helped connect urban and rural communities throughout Canada. The radio and telephone were also used to support early forms of distance education and training such as the broadcast of lectures (e.g., Alice Springs School of the Air[13]) and teleconferencing, which are still widely used today.

Baby Boomers

The common consensus is that the Baby Boomer generation was born between 1946 and 1964. Many members of this generation are now retiring from the Canadian Forces.[14] This generation has had a tremendous impact on Canadian society, changing our economy in profound ways. The Baby Boomers grew up in a period of rapid and sustained economic growth.[15] This economic sense of security allowed Boomers to enjoy a comfortable lifestyle. They moved to the suburbs, discovered credit spending, and had no problem with debt service. Boomers have an *optimistic* outlook on life and they have always thought that anything is within their grasp, even as they experienced increased divorce rates, brink of nuclear war, the Cuban missile crisis, and the Vietnam War.[16] This generation is nostalgic for their youth as exemplified by the number of "golden oldies" radio stations that are now available. The single most important technological development during the Boomer's adolescence was the television, which permitted them to experience real time world events. Television was also used to broadcast educational and training material that could be used to support instruction in the classroom and at a distance (e.g., home or a remote site).

Generation X

Members of Generation X were born from 1965 to 1980. This generation has experienced the overwhelming impact of technology and media in their lives.[17] They were born in the chaotic time of Watergate, the Jonestown massacre, corporate downsizing, AIDS, the Challenger explosion, and the Exxon Valdez oil spill. As a result of these events in their adolescence, Gen Xers are skeptics about education, government, and industry.[18] They were the first "latch-key kids", who spent part of their day at home unsupervised because both parents worked, an experience that taught them resourcefulness. Gen Xers have never experienced a world without TV, MTV, CNN, and cable channels, and they expect to be entertained.[19] Members of this generation live in the present and focus on their personal well-being. Frequent job changes are commonplace and money is only a part of their larger perspective about life. This generation "works to live instead of living to work."[20] Members of the Mature and Baby Boomer generations often view Gen Xers as disrespectful because they are outspoken[21]. A recent Statistics Canada report[22] indicates that the majority of the Canadian Forces personnel are Gen Xers (currently between 30 and 45 years of age). Postman suggests that Gen Xers are "amusing themselves to death" through this expectation of being "entertained" during educational and training events.[23] He also indicates that this focus on "edutainment" leads to a superficial rather than a deep approach to learning.

Millennials

The Millennial generation was born between 1981 and 2000.[24] They have more technology experience than any other generation, including the majority of their trainers and commanding officers who are probably Gen Xers and Baby Boomers. The Millennials also live in the present and expect immediacy of technology. They respond well to group activity, relate to their parents' values, showcase their abilities, and participate in service activities.[25] They have well developed visual-spatial skills acquired by electronic game use.[26] Today's media bombards them with messages that tell them what to think, buy, wear, and eat. Millennials readily acknowledge that the internet is their first source of information. Howe & Strauss assert that they are the most diverse generation in history and are much more capable intellectually than those cohorts that preceded them.[27] In contrast, Twenge refers to the Millennials as Generation Me.[28] She argues that for this generation, the individual has always come first, and feeling good about yourself has always been a primary virtue. Twenge adds that:

> Generation Me's expectations are highly optimistic: they expect to go to college, to make lots of money, and perhaps even to be famous. Yet this generation enters a world in which college admissions are increasingly competitive, good jobs are hard to find and harder to keep, and basic necessities like housing and health care have skyrocketed in price. This is a time of soaring expectations and crushing realities.[29]

This Millennial generation represents the new and future recruits of the Canadian Forces and Statistics Canada data[30] indicates that they are coming with higher levels of education as illustrated in Figure 9.2.

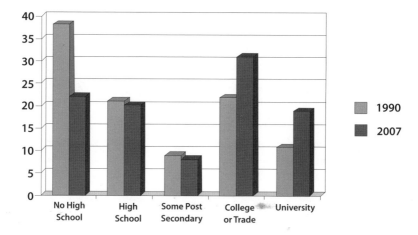

Figure 9.2: Canadian Forces Education Levels by Percentage[31]

In terms of implications for training and education, the literature suggests that the Millennials have a strong preference for the use of technology and appreciate the mentorship of older generations, such as the Baby Boomers.[32]

Generational Learning Characteristics and Associated Use of Technology

The consensus of scholarship and popular opinion is that there are generational differences that are worth taking into consideration for workplace and training contexts.[33] For example, there are differences with respect to attitudes, work habits, and motivators that anyone managing cross-generational training should understand. Table 9.3 adapted from Lancaster and Stillman's[34] book *When Generations Collide. Who They Are. Why They Clash. How to Solve the Generational Puzzle at Work* highlights these differences for the three generations that currently exist in the Canadian Forces.

Factor	Baby Boomers (46 to 64 years old)	Gen X (30 to 45 years old)	Millennials (10 to 29 years old)
Attitude	Optimistic	Skeptical	Realistic
Overview	They believe in possibilities, and often idealistically strive to make a positive difference in the world. They are also competitive and seek ways to change the system to get ahead.	The most misunderstood generation, they are very resourceful and independent and do not depend on others to help them out.	They appreciate diversity, prefer to collaborate instead of being ordered, and are very pragmatic when solving problems.
Work habits	• They have an optimistic outlook. • They are hard workers who want personal gratification from the work they do. • They believe in self-improvement and growth.	• They are aware of diversity and think globally. • They want to balance work with other parts of life. • They tend to be informal. • They rely on themselves. • They are practical in their approach to work. • They want to have fun at work. • They like to work with the latest technology.	• They have an optimistic outlook. • They are self-assured and achievement focused. • They believe in strong morals and serving the community. • They are aware of diversity.

Table 9.3: Generational Differences[35]

The information presented in Table 9.3 suggests that both the Baby Boomer and Millennial generations are generally optimistic in their outlooks and that Millennials often look to the Boomers for mentorship and guidance in the workplace. Conversely, they indicate that Gen Xers have a more skeptical outlook on life, prefer to work independently, and want to balance work with other parts of their lives. Carolyn Martin, Master Trainer for Rainmaking Thinking, and Bruce Tulgan,

Founder of Rainmaking Training, state that workplace "clashes" frequently take place between Boomers and Gen Xers because of their different outlooks on life and work habits (e.g., Boomers often being workaholics while Gen Xers prefer to have more balance to their lives).[36]

Robert Debard, Professor at Bowling Green University, also believes that the values of Boomers, Gen Xers, and Millennials have implications for managers and trainers in the workplace.[37] Table 9.4 outlines the perspectives that these three generational cohorts have towards twelve value-based criteria.

Views Toward:	Baby Boomers	Gen X	Millennials
Level of trust	Confident of self, not authority	Low toward authority	High toward authority
Loyalty to institutions	Cynical	Considered naive	Committed
Most admire	Taking charge	Creating enterprise	Following a hero of integrity
Career goals	Build a stellar career	Build a portable career	Build parallel careers
Rewards	Title and corner office	Freedom not to do	Meaningful work
Parent–child involvement	Receding	Distant	Intruding
Having children	Controlled	Doubtful	Definite
Family life	Indulged as children	Alienated as children	Protected as children
Education	Freedom of expression	Pragmatic	Structure of account-ability
Evaluation	Once a year with documentation	"Sorry, but how am I doing?"	Feedback whenever I want it
Political orientation	Attack oppression	Apathetic, individual	Crave community
The big question	What does it mean?	Does it work?	How do we build it?

Table 9.4: Generational Differences on Twelve Criteria[38]

Table 9.4 again indicates that the Millennials have a stronger connection with the Boomers than Gen X. The Millennials have a higher trust in authority, are more committed to an institution, prefer a structure of accountability, and crave community. Conversely, Gen Xers have low trust in authority, are less committed to an institution, are pragmatic in their approach to individual training and education (IT&E), and prefer to work alone.

In terms of specific IT&E characteristics for each of the generational cohorts, there have been a number of recent articles that focus on the Millennials but not as many that document and compare the other generations. The one exception to this trend has been in the field of nursing education, which has a series of reports on this topic. Two articles that have been frequently cited are "Teaching Learners from Varied Generations"[39] and "Generational Diversity Teaching and Learning Approaches."[40] Table 9.5 summarizes the learning characteristics and preferences for feedback that these researchers have identified for the three generational cohorts that exist in the Canadian Forces.

	Baby Boomers	Generation X	Millennials
Learning Characteristics	• Accustomed to being dependent on educator • Want to have a say in own learning • Want a caring environment • Respond to positive feedback, desire to do well • Connect learning to outcomes • Want to feel connected to others in the learning environment	• Are comfortable with technology • Self-directed learners • Want clear information of practical value • Use fun and humour; games and activities are appropriate • Can manage delayed gratification	• Grew up experiencing digital media and internet access • Use mobile devices to access and process information • Technology is expected • Prefer to work in groups and teams • "Always on" connectivity blurs work time and learning • Want "augmented reality" – real work environments similar to the work setting such as simulations and virtual reality. • Active learners; seek innovations; want immediate response to learning needs and questions • Have difficulty focusing on one thing; prefer to multitask • Have difficulty honing skills of critical analysis necessary to read between the lines due to volume of available information. • Use "hyper-learning" models as opposed to linear acquisition of information; want to construct information on their own • Enjoy being mentored by older generations
Feedback Preference	• Once a year - with lots of documentation	• Sorry to interrupt but how am I doing?	• Whenever I want it at the touch of a button

Table 9.5: Learning Characteristics of the Generations[41]

This summary of generational learning characteristics suggests that Gen Xers and especially the Millennials expect digital technologies, simulations, and virtual reality environments to be part of their training experience in the Canadian Forces.

Technology Skills and Information Literacy

There has been considerable debate about how widespread access to computers and internet connectivity have affected the Gen X and particularly the Millennial generation, who are the first people to have grown up in a world where access to these technologies are as commonplace as the telephone and the television were for earlier generations.[42] It has become almost commonplace to assume that the Millennials have sophisticated technology skills, simply because they are the first generation to grow up with computers and widespread, if not ubiquitous, internet access. Prensky has described the Millennials as the first "digital natives" of the Information Age.[43]

While it is clear that middle and upper class Millennials are more likely to possess and use the latest high tech gear such as iPods, smartphones, and game consoles, there is also evidence that their information literacy, especially with respect to judging the quality of information obtained on the internet through search engines such as Google, is unacceptably weak:

> Having grown up with widespread access to technology, the New Gen is able to intuitively use a variety of IT devices and navigate the internet. Although they are comfortable using technology without an instruction manual, their understanding of the technology or source quality may be shallow.[44]

Despite these shortcomings, there are those who believe the Millennials are fundamentally different from previous generations in ways that require new approaches to training and those who believe that how people learn is not fundamentally affected by generational membership. On one side of the debate are people like Marc Prensky, an internationally acclaimed speaker on education and learning, who stated that:

> Our students have changed radically. Today's students are no longer the people our educational system was designed to teach. Today's

students have not just changed incrementally from those of the past, nor simply changed their slang, clothes, body adornments, or styles, as has happened between generations previously. A really big discontinuity has taken place. One might even call it a "singularity" – an event which changes things so fundamentally that there is absolutely no going back. This so-called "singularity" is the arrival and rapid dissemination of digital technology in the last decades of the 20th century.[45]

Others take issue with Prensky's optimistic interpretations of the findings of recent brain science research. For example, Mark Owen argues that setting up dichotomies such as digital natives and digital immigrants may lead to poor decisions about the design of new training environments.[46] Owen cites Brown and Duguid's book on *The Social Life of Information*:

Brown and Duguid's central theme is that access to information does not equate to knowledge. Brown and Duguid note, much of what we recognize as learning comes from informal social interactions between learners and mentors. These social interactions are difficult to achieve in mediated instruction. They recognize that technology can enhance instruction in remarkable ways; however, it cannot replace the insights that students receive by struggling to make sense of information with both peers and mentors. They contend that the gung-ho tunnel vision of commentators like Prensky – seeing only one way ahead (if all you have is a hammer, everything looks like a nail), has lead to erroneously simplified and unrealistic expectations of what our future in the information age will be like.[47]

Even Prensky tempers his enthusiasm when it comes to considering the learning results that teachers are reporting concerning their digital native Millennial students:

Still we often hear from teachers about increasing problems their students have with reading and thinking. What about this? Has anything been lost in the Digital Natives' "reprogramming" process? One key area that appears to have been affected is reflection. Reflection is what enables us, according to many theorists, to generalize, as we create "mental models" from our experience. It is, in many ways, the process of "learning from experience". In our twitch-speed world, there is less and less time and opportunity for reflection, and this development concerns many people. One of the most interesting challenges and opportunities in teaching Digital Natives is to figure out and invent ways to include reflection and critical thinking in the learning (either built into the instruction or through a process of instructor-led debriefing) but still do it in the Digital Natives language. We can and must do more in this area.[48]

And, Healy,[49] a teacher and educational psychologist, argues in her *Failure to Connect: How Computers Affect Our Children's Minds – For Better or Worse* that the development of abstract reasoning ability requires the physical experience of action, the kind of experience that is decreased when children are placed in passive modes for many hours by television.

Will members of the Millennial generation enter the Canadian Forces with advanced technology skills and strong information literacy as some have predicted? Or are their technology skills shallow and superficial? Is their information literacy limited in fundamental ways that actually limits their powers to reflect, reason, and make decisions? At this point in time, the research literature in this area provides no clear answers, and thus the debate continues. On the one hand, some researchers and pundits suggest that the information literacy of the Millennials (digital natives) far exceeds that of earlier generations (digital immigrants), and that this has profound implications for how the Millennials should be educated and trained. On the other hand, some argue that the media-saturated environment in which today's youth have grown up has actually stifled some of the fundamental thinking and social interaction skills that derive from human-to-human interaction, including a decline in the capacity to reason, engage in critical reflection, and exhibit intellectual curiousity.[50] For example, a recent study about the use of Facebook at Ohio State University demonstrated that students who are frequent users of this social network website spend less time studying and have lower grade point averages than those students who are not Facebook members.[51]

Without better research, the debate will continue about the impact of the Information Age on the learning needs, preferences, and potential of the Millennial generation. Recently, there has been much discussion about how extensive use of digital technologies impacts the human brain. Prensky[52] illustrates how rodents in enriched environments develop positive brain change in as little as two weeks over their kin in impoverished environments leading to the conclusion that Millennials who have grown up as digital natives have brains that are "wired" differently than their Gen X parents and Baby Boomer grandparents. This is a popular notion that currently lacks solid scientific support but this may change with continuing advances in brain tomography, which involves examining image slices of the brain achieved through MRI (magnetic resonance imaging) and SPECT/PET (single photon/positron emission computed tomography).

Video Games, Simulations, and Virtual Reality Environments

Some have tried to make the case that Gen X and even more so the Millennials, have been positively affected by the sophisticated interactive games and simulations they have spent so much of their youth playing.[53] Whether playing interactive video games has bad or good effects is the subject of much speculation, but relatively little robust research.[54] In terms of negative side effects, several prominent psychologists[55] have presented research that indicates some popular video games such as *Doom*, *Grand Theft Auto*, and *Tomb Raider* encourage antisocial and even violent behavior. Healey has also expressed concern about the lack of language stimulation and the accompanying decline in linguistic capabilities that stem from over-exposure to video games.[56]

In addition, several research studies have begun to link intensive video game use to childhood obesity and a decline in physical fitness.[57] Recent Statistics Canada reports on the fitness of Canadian children, youth, and adults indicate that since 1981 childhood obesity has been rising along with corresponding physical inactivity levels for all age groups of the population, which has led to a decline in aerobic fitness, flexibility, muscular strength, and endurance for all Canadians.[58] These studies do not make any direct correlations between video game use and levels of physical fitness but recent research at the Harvard Medical School clearly demonstrates how important regular exercise is for improving the function and performance of the brain, specifically in regards to happiness, stress management, intelligence, aggression control, and memory.[59]

Despite the negative issues associated with video game use, several gaming scholars have concluded that video games may actually have some positive effects on the young people who play them. James Paul Gee, an expert on literacy studies, has concluded that playing contemporary video games has positive outcomes with respect to many cognitive skills.[60] In his book, *What Video Games Have to Teach Us About Learning and Literacy*, Gee identifies 36 important learning principles that are inherent in good video games.[61] These include enhancing the ability to detect patterns in seemingly chaotic events and learning to think like a scientist. The notion that video games may do more good than harm, a seemingly implausible idea just a few years ago, is beginning to enter the public's consciousness as evidenced by recent books such as *Playing the Future: What We Can Learn From Digital Kids*,[62] *Everything Bad is Good For You*,[63] *Why Video Games are Good for your Soul*,[64] and *Don't Bother Me Mom – I'm Learning*.[65]

These authors and other researchers have stated that interactive video games can also help develop decision-making, teamwork, leadership, and risk taking skills, which are critical for the 21st century workplace. For example, Steven Johnson states that playing interactive games yields "collateral learning" related to decision-making:

> Start with the basics: far more than books or movies or music, games force you to make decisions. Novels may activate our imagination, and music may conjure up powerful emotions, but games force you to decide, to choose, to prioritize. All of the intellectual benefits of gaming derive from this fundamental virtue, because learning how to think is ultimately about learning how to make the right decision: weighing evidence, analyzing situations, consulting your long-term goals, and then deciding.[66]

Stephanie VanDenventer, Director of Paradox Learning Systems, and James White report that children teaching adults how to play video games exhibit expert behaviours such as:

> . . . actively seeks new information; incorporates new information; assesses situations using multiple pieces of data; organizes, classifies, and categorizes information; consistently applies successful behaviours; is confident about one's own knowledge; is willing to take risks; employs corrective action when needed; can consider input from multiple sources; recognizes patterns; uses holistic thinking; is able to integrate information with behaviors; uses inductive thinking; strategizes; thinks critically; and recognizes constraints and misinformation.[67]

And, John Beck and Mitchell Wade, authors of the book *Got Game: How the Gamer Generation is Reshaping Business Forever,* write:

> How hard this new cohort works, how they try to compete, how they fit into teams. How they take risks – all are different in statistically verifiable ways. And those differences are driven by one central factor: growing up with video games.[68]

They also maintain that gamers prefer to learn through trial and error and like to play to win. Using the results of a survey of 2,500 people in the United States, they argue that gamers possess the types of 21st century skills that the workplace demands today, such as the capacity to multitask, take risks, and exhibit leadership. To take advantage of these skills, Beck and Wade recommend that businesses present their workers with challenges and acknowledge success or failure in meeting the challenges in public ways.[69]

In addition, Alice Mitchell and Carol Savill-Smith's review of the literature on gaming has led them to the conclusion that well-designed interactive games have the potential to:[70]

- Engage unmotivated learners;

- Engage learners who lack confidence in ability to learn;

- Develop skills in literacy;

- Develop mathematical skills;

- Develop skills in visualization;

- Develop capacity for strategic and tactical decision-making; and

- Develop critical thinking and problem solving skills.

It is important to keep in mind that research focused on the impact of video games on cognitive skills is subject to the same problems that undermine confidence in all forms of educational research.[71] Generally, the measures used to assess aptitude, attitudes, outcomes, and other variables are much less reliable and valid than those employed in the "harder sciences." Despite the weaknesses of the research, there is growing consensus among educational and psychological researchers that the positive cognitive effects of playing video games may outweigh the negative, and even more importantly, that those who play video games may be developing skills and expectations that can be leveraged to their advantage in some learning situations and environments.[72] It is also clear that members of the Millennial generation spend more time playing games than Gen Xers and that Gen Xers in turn play more than Baby Boomers.[73] Another obvious trend is that the interactive games that each successive generation has played have become increasingly sophisticated. Today, members of the Millennial generation seem especially susceptible to becoming "addicted" to massive multiplayer online games such as *Call of Duty: Modern Warfare 2*. Some argue that the increased fidelity of contemporary video games decreases the likelihood that the Millennials will be satisfied with the relatively dull screen layout and limited interactions of most training games and simulations.[74]

In any case, with new evidence suggesting that playing video games does more good than bad and with the Canadian Forces increasingly composed of recruits who have spent large amounts of their free time playing these games, standards and instructional staff are advised to explore the real and potential effectiveness of training games and simulations.

Impact and Recommendations for CF Training & Education

There is an abundance of advice from generational learning consultants and "gurus" about how to train members of the Millennial generation who will be the new and future recruits of the Canadian Forces. This section attempts to synthesize this advice and provide recommendations on how generational learning styles and digital technologies can be used to support the management and conduct of CF Individual Training and Education.

Performance Orientation

CF Doctrine dictates that all IT&E must be performance oriented and directly linked to CF job requirements. Thus, tasks to be achieved in training must match operational performance requirements. The literature provides a number of generic recommendations for improving performance through workplace training. For example, Eric Chester, founder and president of Generation Why, in his book *Getting Them To Give A Damn* provides the following workplace training guidelines:[75]

- Begin with an orientation, not skills training;

- Assess what they know;

- Continually reinvent your training;

- Communicate where to turn for answers;

- Don't just train the what, train the why; and

- Keep training fun, interactive, and engaging.

Lynne Lancaster and David Stillman in the "Training the Generations" chapter of their *When Generations Collide. Who They Are. Why They Clash. How to Solve the Generational Puzzle at Work* suggest that standards and instructional staff should focus on the "three Ss" of a training event:[76]

- **Setting** – Make sure the setting for training is comfortable;

- **Style** – Pay attention to the learning styles of the different generations represented; and

- **Substance** – Be sure the training has real substance.

Karl Kapp, Professor of Instruction Design, adds that Baby Boomer knowledge is formal, structured, hierarchical, and based on a distinction between the interface and information whereas Millennial knowledge is informal, unstructured, non-hierarchical, and based on the assumption that the information is the interface.[77] With respect to the knowledge transfer that must occur as the Baby Boomers retire and the Millennials enter the workforce, Kapp recommends that organizations break out of the class mentality thinking in terms of specific training events. He quotes John Cone, former head of Dell Learning, as saying:

> The idea learning event at Dell has a class size of one, lasts 5 to 10 minutes, and takes place within 10 minutes of when someone recognizes that he or she needs to know something. Our challenge is to reduce learning to its smallest, most-useful increments and to put the learner in charge of the entire process.[78]

Cone indicates that the best way to support this type of incremental learning is to provide a combination of online (e.g., tutorials and frequently asked question forms) and phone support (e.g., Help Desk Hot-Line).

In Figure 9.3, Natalie Laderas-Kilkenny, an Instructional designer, reinforces this notion that generational cohorts have taken different approaches to constructing their own knowledge during their formative years.[79]

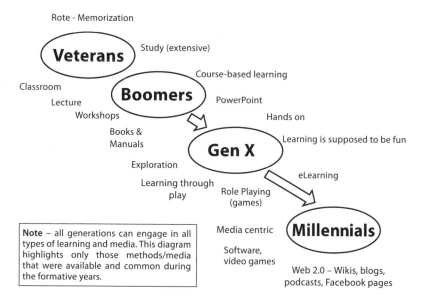

Figure 9.3. How Do (Did) They Learn?[80]

This diagram suggests that in adolescence the Mature (Veteran) and Boomer generations constructed their knowledge through the absorption and memorization of information (direct instruction) while the Gen X and Millennials constructed their knowledge by finding and manipulating information (constructivism). This constructivist or "learning by doing" approach suggests that people generate knowledge and meaning by reflecting on their everyday experiences.[81]

The goals and learning outcomes of workplace training have been traditionally defined in relationship to three primary domains: cognitive, affective, and psychomotor. The cognitive domain relates to the capacity to think or one's mental skills.[82] The affective domain is about emotions and feelings, especially in relationship to a set of values.[83] The psychomotor domain is concerned with the mastery of physical skills ranging from reflexive movements to exhibiting appropriate body language.[84]

A number of educational researchers have concerns that none of these domains are adequately addressed in most training contexts.[85] To begin, most training is focused on the cognitive domain rather than the affective or psychomotor domains.[86] And, even within the cognitive domain much more attention is paid to the lower half of the domain (remembering, understating, and applying) than is to arguably the more important upper half (analyzing, evaluating, and creating). This problem stems largely from the relative ease with which the skills encompassed in the lower half can be taught and tested within most fields or disciplines. Teaching and assessing the cognitive skills required for analysis, evaluation, and creation take more time and effort than many, if not most, instructors feel they have. In addition, Thomas Reeves, Professor Emeritus at the University of Georgia, suggests that an entire domain is being ignored with regards to a performance orientation for IT&E.[87] This is the *conative* domain, which is associated with action.[88] He states that "although someone may possess the cognitive capacity, affective values, and physical skills to perform a given task, whether the person possesses the will, desire, drive, level of effort, mental energy, intention, striving, and self-determination to actually perform at the highest standards possible remains an unanswered question."[89]

The conative domain focuses on conation or the act of striving to perform at the highest levels. With rare exceptions, the literature on IT&E is not informed by consideration of the conative domain. However, the roots of conation can be traced all the way back to Aristotle who used the Greek word "orexis" to signify striving, desire, or the conative state of mind. Kathy Kolbe,[90] Founder of the Center for Conative Abilities, contrasted the cognitive, affective, and conative domains as illustrated in Table 9.6.

Cognitive	Affective	Conative
To know	To feel	To act
Thinking	Feeling	Willing
Thought	Emotion	Volition
Epistemology	Esthetics	Ethics
Knowing	Caring	Doing

Table 9.6: Comparison of Cognitive, Affective, and Conative Domains[91]

In order to create effective IT&E environments, which address the conative do-main, focus on a performance orientation, and meaningfully engage Millennial learners, an international consortium of educational researchers have developed a list of ten principles for designing authentic IT&E tasks.[92] These principles are outlined in Table 9.7 below.

Principle	Description
Authentic tasks require real-world relevance	The learning tasks set for Millennial learners should match as nearly as possible the real-world tasks of professionals in practice rather than de-contextualized or academic tasks.[93] Authentic tasks should address the realistic economic, environmental, and social problems that Millennials must learn to solve if they are to thrive, not just survive, in the 21st century.
Authentic tasks are ill-defined, requiring students to define the tasks and sub-tasks needed to complete the activity	Problems inherent in the tasks set for Millennial learners should be ill-defined and open to multiple interpretations rather than easily solved by the application of existing algorithms. In the face of problems that approximate the complexity of the real world, learners must identify their own unique tasks and sub-tasks in order to complete the major task.[94]
Authentic tasks comprise complex tasks to be investigated by students over a sustained period of time	Tasks developed for Millennial learners should require work over days, weeks, and months rather than minutes or hours. These tasks should require significant investment of time and intellectual resources.[95] The design of authentic task based learning environments must break out of the rigid semester and course hour structures that limit contemporary innovations in higher education.
Authentic tasks provide opportunities for students to examine the task from different perspectives, using a variety of resources	Authentic tasks should be developed in ways that afford Millennial learners the opportunity to examine the problem from a variety of theoretical and practical perspectives, rather than encouraging a single perspective learners simply imitate to be successful. The use of a variety of resources rather than a limited number of preselected references requires students to distinguish relevant from irrelevant information and thus develop the high levels of information literacy as well as technological fluency they will need in the years to come.[96]
Authentic tasks provide the opportunity to collaborate	Collaboration should be integral to the tasks that Millennial learners must complete, both within the course and the real world, rather than achievable by an individual learner.[97] Developing the ability to lead and work in groups is essential for Millennial learners.
Authentic tasks provide the opportunity to reflect	Tasks should be designed to enable Millennial learners to make choices and reflect on their learning both individually and socially.[98] Self-reflection, meta-cognition, and self-regulated learning must be fostered.

Authentic tasks can be integrated and applied across different subject areas and lead beyond domain-specific outcomes	Tasks for Millennial learners should be designed to encourage interdisciplinary perspectives and enable students to play diverse roles thus building robust expertise rather than knowledge limited to a single well-defined field or domain.[99] Traditional course and discipline structures will need to be redefined for Millennial learners.
Authentic tasks are seamlessly integrated with assessment	Assessment of how Millennial learners perform in the face of an authentic task should be seamlessly integrated with that major task in a manner that reflects real world assessment, rather than separate artificial assessment removed from the nature of the task.[100] Grades that fail to represent the richness of achievements that Millennial learners must accomplish should be abolished and replaced with rich descriptions of the cognitive, affective, conative, and psychomotor progress made by these learners.
Authentic tasks create polished products valuable in their own right rather than as preparation for something else	The tasks set for Millennial learners should culminate in the creation of a whole product rather than an exercise or sub-step in preparation for something else.[101] Integrated with the principles of service learning,[102] these products should contribute to society at large whenever possible.
Authentic tasks allow competing solutions and diversity of outcome	Authentic tasks should allow a range and diversity of outcomes open to multiple solutions of an original nature, rather than a single correct response obtained by the application of rules and procedures.[103] Expert, peer, self, and public review of the solutions that Millennials create to the problems inherent in the authentic tasks set for them should be enabled and encouraged.

Table 9.7: Ten Principles for Designing Authentic IT&E Tasks[104]

Optimum Efficiency

The concept of optimal efficiency requires that performance objectives, delivery strategies, resource expenditures and the number of personnel requiring IT&E be controlled to ensure operational needs are achieved at minimum acceptable cost when IT&E is selected as a solution to a performance deficiency.

There are many creative ways to design high quality authentic IT&E tasks for Millennial learners. Technology Enabled Learning (TEL) and Distance Learning (DL) can potentially be used to facilitate this process in an effective and cost efficient manner. Kuhlmann, in a recent report entitled *Why E-Learning is So Effective* demonstrates how TEL and DL can support the goals of an organization and the development of individual learners with optimum efficiency. Table 9.8 summarizes Kuhlmann's findings.[105]

Supporting the Organization's Goals

Improved training costs.
Producing learning content is time consuming whether it's online or not. With e-learning, each time the course is accessed your return on investment improves because you are dividing the fixed production costs by number of uses. You also have savings through decreased travel, reduced material, and hopefully improved (and more efficient) performance.

Decreased material costs.
By creating the IT&E environment online and letting the learner practice, you never have to worry about the costs associated with physical set up, use, and clean up.

Increased productivity.
Because e-learning is not bound by geography or time, you can control IT&Es impact on production by training people during down times. In addition, with the current economy, you're asking people to do more with less. So e-learning is a great way to give them the tools and skills needed to enhance their performance.

Standardization.
You may have a great instructor, but that's no guarantee that the courses are presented the same across sessions. E-learning allows you to create a standardized process and consistency in the delivery of content. It also compresses delivery time. You can also combine e-learning courses with instructor-led sessions. E-learning can deliver consistent content and face-to-face sessions can be used for interactive case studies that apply the online content.

Supporting the Learner's Development

Real-time access.
Face-to-face IT&E events require that those who participate align their schedules to the training calendar. E-learning eliminates this because the course can be accessed anytime, anywhere. This can also happen without internet access. For example, learners can access CD-ROM and DVD content on a PC out in the field and then upload their completed task work when they are back online.

Freedom to fail.
All learning requires some failure before success is achieved (e.g., trial and error). But no one likes to fail in a classroom full of other people. E-learning lets you fail without fear. This encourages exploration and testing of ideas. With the right feedback you create a great learning environment. Worst case, you can always start over. Something you can't always do in class.

Improved retention.
The combination of multimedia and instructional design can produce a very rich learning experience that is repeatable. Throw in some good practice activities with feedback and you have a learning environment that's going to help your learners retain the course content which will produce results.

Personalized learning.
Learners want to be in the "drivers seat" for their IT&E experiences. E-learning allows you to offer control to the learners in a way that classroom learning doesn't (e.g., time, pace, and space).

Nurturing a Learning Organization & Community
Ongoing access to resources. If you take a class in the real world and need a refresher, you better hope that you took good notes. Otherwise, you're out of luck. That's not the case with e-learning. Ideally, you continue to have access to the online content and resources to brush up on what you learned.
Knowledge management. Many people see e-learning as only the authored courses. But e-learning includes all sort of online technologies. If you incorporate some of the tools that allow collaboration and conversation, you can capture organizational knowledge that is available for future learners.
Encourage sharing. The foundation of a learning community is built on sharing what you know with others. This is where incorporating a forum or wiki really adds value to your e-learning. Depending on how the course is structured, you can encourage sharing of resources and insight gained from the course.
Employer of choice. People want opportunities to grow. A cafeteria with high fat foods is one way. Another is a catalog with all sorts of e-learning courses. This allows them to explore other opportunities in the organization. During downtime, it would be great to spend fifteen minutes learning to better manage meetings or improve working with peers. Offering these opportunities to learn makes you a place people want to stay.

Table 9.8: Why E-Learning is Effective[106]

Technology Implementation

There has been an ongoing debate in the field of educational technology about the impact of various forms of media and technology on IT&E.[107] The debate began in 1983 when Richard Clark published a paper entitled, *Reconsidering Research on Learning From Media*, in which he stated that "studies clearly suggest that media do not influence learning under any conditions."[108] Seven years later, consultant Robert Kozma responded to Clark's assertion in a paper entitled *Learning with Media*, where he took the position that media do influence learning and, therefore, media selection is significant.[109]

Recent meta-analyses[110] indicate that no strong conclusions can be drawn about the impact of educational technologies on IT&E. This finding is supported by Russel who maintains a *No Significant Difference* website documenting a long history of media comparison studies in the field of educational technology.[111] A variety of digital technologies are being used to support training and the performance of workers belonging to Gen X and the Millennials but the bulk of the published research indicates that training delivery modalities such as TEL and DL versus classroom instruction yield similar results. What should make a difference is the instructional design (pedagogical methods) of a training event or environment. As argued by Clark, if the same instructional design is delivered via two different modalities, it makes no sense to expect different outcomes.[112] More recently, Clark and Estes have written about how to develop "authentic technologies" through the use of sound instructional design strategies.[113]

Thus, with regards to course development , instead of worrying about whether Gen Xers and Millennials will learn more from direct instruction or virtual reality games, training managers and instructional staff, working closely with practioners and subject matter experts (SMEs), should begin by identifying the specific training needs of Canadian Forces personnel, designing the best possible prototype training environments *in situ*, and then conducting iterative cycles of formative evaluation and refinement to optimize the training and reveal robust design principles.

To guide this process, Reeves' design-based research framework may be of use. This framework consists of the following nine stages:[114]

1. Identify critical training issues and problems;

2. Collaborate with practitioners to identify solutions;

3. Integrate theory and research on learning and teaching;

4. Conduct literature review and needs analysis to refine solutions;

5. Design the training intervention;

6. Develop, implement, and revise the training intervention;

7. Evaluate the impact of the training intervention;

8. Iterate the process; and

9. Report and disseminate the findings from the design-based research on the training intervention.

Reeves[115] adds that the success of any IT&E event is determined by the degree to which there is adequate alignment among eight critical factors:

1. Goals;

2. Content;

3. Instructional design;

4. Learner tasks;

5. Instructor roles;

6. Student roles;

7. Technological affordances; and

8. Assessment.

The alignment of these eight critical factors is portrayed in Figure 9.4:

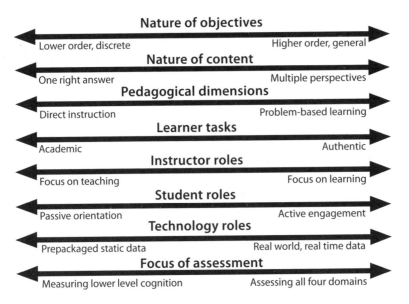

Figure 9.4: Critical Factors that must be Aligned in any Learning Environment[116]

Several authors have indicated that traditional training methods (e.g., drill and practice) are failing to engage all generational cohort learners and they advocate taking a systems approach to the instructional design of IT&E.[117]

Systems Approach

The Canadian Forces Individual Training & Education System (CFITES) is a "system" approach that ensures each part of IT&E is interconnected and affects the other.[118] The effectiveness of each part depends on how it fits into the whole system and effectiveness of the system depends on how each part functions. Figure 9.5 illustrates how quality control, quantity control and resource management are key components of CFITES and how they are impacted by the larger federal government and societal forces.

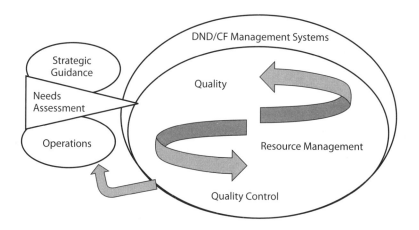

Figure 9.5: Systems Components[119]

Three factors that heavily influence a systems approach to IT&E are access, quality, and cost. These factors have been referred to as the "iron triangle" and indicate that IT&E goals of wide access, high quality, and low cost are not achievable with traditional models of training, which are based on classroom teaching in fixed locations.[120] They argue that in order to "break" the constraints of this iron triangle, organizations need to engage in TEL and DL that has been systematically designed, developed, implemented, and evaluated.

The systematic approach, as applied in CFITES, provides a proven methodology for analyzing the need for IT&E, determining the most appropriate instructional strategy, developing and implementing the IT&E, and evaluating and validating outcomes which provides feedback to initiate improvements.[121] Therefore, ongoing, continuous improvement is fundamental to CFITES. This focus on continuous improvement, by those who are entrusted to apply CFITES, is essential to its evolution as a management system that meets the requirements of the Canadian Forces.

Summary

Digital technologies can certainly be used as a catalyst to transform IT&E practices but they should always be considered as a "means to an end, rather than just an end". Interactive video games, simulations, virtual reality environments, and Web 2.0 applications such as podcasts, wikis, and social networking sites will surely have a role in future IT&E endeavors, but in order to harness the true potential of these technologies, they must be accompanied by appropriate instructional strategies, support for instructional staff, and sufficient resources to be truly effective.

1   Junguee Park, "A Profile of the Canadian Forces", *Perspectives*. Statistics Canada Catalogue, (2008, July), 75-001-X., 17-30.

2   Carolyn A. Martin and Bruce Tulgan, *Managing the Generational Mix – 2nd Edition* (Amherst: HRD Press, 2006).

3   Chuck Dziuban, Patsy Moskal and Linda Futch, "Reactive Behavior, Ambivalence, and the Generations: Emerging Patterns in Student Evaluation of Blended Learning" in Anthony G. Picciano and Charles D. Dziuban, eds., *Blended Learning: Research Perspectives* (Needham, MA: Sloan Center for Online Education, 2007), 179-202.

4   Thomas C. Reeves and Eunjung Oh, "Generation Differences and Educational Technology Research" in J. Michael Spector, M. David Merrill, Jeroen Van Merrienboer and Marcy P. Driscoll, eds, *Handbook of Research on Educational Communications and Technology*. (Mahwah: Lawrence Erlbaum Associates, 2007), 295-303.

5   Ibid.

6   Lynne Lancaster and David Stillman, *When Generations Collide. Who They Are. Why They Clash. How to Solve the Generational Puzzle at Work* (New York: Collins Business, 2002).

7   Neil Howe and William Strauss, *Millennials Rising: The Next Great Generation* (New York: Vintage Books, 2000).

8   Jean M. Twenge, *Generation Me: Why Today's Young Americans Are More Confident, Assertive, Entitled—and More Miserable Than Ever Before* (New York: Free Press, 2006), 2.

9   Ibid., 3.

10   Park, 18.

11   Regan Legassie, *Brief to IT&E Committee on CFSTG Training Modernization*, March 18, 2010, PowerPoint, slide 7.

12   Martin and Tulgan, 65.

13   Alice Springs School of the Air, retrieved on 12 Oct 2011 from <http://www.assoa.nt.edu.au/>.

14   Park, 18.

15   Robert W. Wendover, "From Ricky & Lucy to Beavis & Butthead: Managing the New Work-force", *Center for Generational Studies*, retrieved on 26 Jul 2011 from <http://www.generational-diversity.com/index.php?/free-articles.html>.

16   Dzuiban, Moskal and Futch, 183.

17   Douglas Coupland, *Generation X: Tales for an Accelerated Culture* (New York: St. Martin's Griffin, 1991).

18   Martin and Tulgan, 87.

19   Dzuiban, Moskal and Futch, 184.

20   Howe and Strauss, 42.

21   Lancaster and Stillman, 34.

22   Park, 18.

23   Neil Postman, *Amusing Ourselves to Death: Public Discourse in the Age of Show Business* (USA: Penguin, 1985).

24   Diana G. Oblinger and James L. Oblinger, *Educating the Net Gen* (Washington, D.C.: EDUCAUSE, 2005).

25   Dzuiban, Moskal and Futch, 187.

26   Marc Prensky, "Digital Natives, Digital Immigrants", *On the Horizon*, Vol. 9, No. 5, retrieved on 26 Jul 2011 from <http://www.marcprensky.com/writing/>.

27   Howe and Strauss.

28   Twenge.

29   Ibid., 2.

30   Park.

31   Susan Truscott, *Environmental Scan of CMP Strategic Planning Session*, 20 January 2010, PowerPoint, slide 18.

32   Don Tapscott, *Growing Up Digital: The Rise of the Net Generation* (New York: McGraw-Hill, 1998).

33   Dzuiban, Moskal and Futch.

34   Lancaster and Stillman.

35   Lancaster and Stillman.

36   Martin and Tulgan.

37   Robert Debard, "Millennials Coming to College" in Robert Debard and Michael D. Coomes, eds., *Serving the Millennial Generation: New Directions for Student Services* (San Francisco: Jossey-Bass, 2004), 33-45.

38   Debard.

39   Diane Billings and Karen Kowalski, "Teaching Learners from Varied Generations", *The Journal of Continuing Education in Nursing*, Vol. 35, No. 3 (2004), 104-105.

40   Susan Johnson and Mary L. Romanello, "Generational Diversity Teaching and Learning Approaches", *Nurse Educator*, Vol. 30, No. 5 (2005), 212-216.

41   Johnson and Romanello.

42   Amanda Lenhart, Kristen Purcell, Aaron Smith and Kathryn Zickuhr, *Social Media & Mobile Internet Use Among Teens and Young Adults* (Washington, D.C.: Pew Internet & American Life Project, 2010).

43   Prensky, 1.

44   Oblinger and Oblinger, 25.

45   Prensky, 1.

46   Mark Owen, *The Myth of the Digital Native*, retrieved on 12 Oct 2011 from <http://www2.futurelab.org.uk/resources/publications-reports-articles/web-articles/Web-Article561>.

47   Ibid., 1.

48   Marc Prensky, "Digital Natives, Digital Immigrants, Part II: Do They Really Think Differently", *On the Horizon*, Vol. 9, No. 6, retrieved on 26 Jul 2011 from <http://www.marcprensky.com/writing/>.

49   Jane M. Healy, *Failure to Connect: How Computers Affect Our Children's Minds - For Better and Worse* (New York: Simon & Schuster, 1998).

50   Sue Bennett, Karl Maton and Lisa Kervin, "The 'Digital Natives' Debate: A Critical Review of the Evidence", *British Journal of Educational Technology*, Vol. 39, No. 5 (2008), 775-786.

51   Aryn Karpinski and Adam Duberstein, "A Description of Facebook Use and Academic Performance among Undergraduate and Graduate Students" Paper presented at the *Annual Meeting of the American Educational Research Association* (San Diego, CA.), retrieved on 26 Jul 2011 from <http://www.aera.net/>.

52   Prensky, 2.

53   Marc Prensky, *Don't Bother Me, Mom – I'm Learning: How Computer and Video Games are Preparing your Kids for Twenty-first Century Success* (St. Paul: Paragon House, 2006).

54   Thomas C. Reeves, "Do Generational Differences Matter in Instructional Design?", *Instructional Technology Forum*. Discussion Paper No. 104, (January, 2008).

55   Craig A. Anderson and Brad Bushman, "Effects of Violent Video Games on Aggressive Behavior, Aggressive Cognition, Aggressive Affect, Physiological Arousal, and Pro-social Behavior: A Meta-analytic Review of the Scientific Literature", *Psychological Science*, Vol. 12 (2001), 353-359.

56   Healey, 56.

57   Simon Usborne, "Train Your Brain", *Third Age: Health and Wellness Newsletter* (April, 2008), retrieved on 12 Oct 2011 from <http://johnratey.typepad.com/blog/2008/04/third-age-healt.html>.

58   Mark S. Tremblay, Margot Shields, Manon Laviolette, Cora L. Craig, Ian Janssen and Sarah Connor Gorber, "Fitness of Canadian Children and Youth: Results from 2007-2009 Canadian Health Measures Survey", *Statistics Canada*, Catalogue no 82-003-X, (January, 2010).

59   John J. Ratey and Eric Hagerman, *Spark: The Revolutionary New Science of Exercise and the Brain* (NY: Little, Brown and Co, 2008).

60   James Paul Gee, *What Video Games Have to Teach us About Learning and Literacy* (New York: Palgrave Macmillan, 2003).

61   Ibid.

62   Douglas Rushkoff, *Playing the Future: What We Can Learn from Digital Kids* (New York: Riverhead Books, 1999).

63   Steven Johnson, *Everything Bad is Good for You: How Today's Popular Culture is Actually Making Us Smarter* (New York: Riverhead Books, 2005).

64   James Paul Gee, *Why Video Games are Good for your Soul: Pleasure and Learning* (Melbourne: The Learner Press, 2005).

65   Mark Prensky, *Don't Bother Me, Mom – I'm Learning: How Computer and Video Games are Preparing your Kids for Twenty-first Century Success* (St. Paul, MN: Paragon House, 2006).

66   Johnson, 41.

67   Stephanie S. VanDeventer and James A. White, "Expert Behavior in Children's Video Game Play", *Simulation & Gaming*, Vol. 33, No. 1 (2002), 46.

68   John C. Beck and Mitchell Wade, *Got Game: How the Gamer Generation is Reshaping Business Forever* (Boston: Harvard Business School Press, 2004).

69   Ibid.

70   Alice Mitchell and Carol Savill-Smith, *The Use of Computer and Video Games for Learning: A Review of the Literature* (London: Learning and Skills Development Agency, 2004).

71   John Eisenberg, "The Limits of Educational Research: Why All Research and Grand Plans in Education are Futile and Wasteful", *Curriculum Inquiry*, Vol. 25 (1995), 367-380.

72   James Belanich, Laura N. Mullin and J. Douglas Dressel, *Symposium on PC-based Simulations and Gaming for Military Training* (Arlington: U.S. Army Research Institute for the Behavioral and Social Sciences, 2004).

73   Victoria Rideout, Donald F. Roberts and Ulla G. Foehr, *Generation M: Media in the Lives of 8-18 Year-olds* (Kaiser Family Foundation, 2005), retrieved on 26 Jul 2011 from <http://www.kff.org/entmedia/upload/Generation-M-Media-in-the-Lives-of-8-18-Year-olds-Report.pdf>.

74   Clark Aldridge and Tom Parkinson, *Using Serious Games and Simulations: A Quick and Dirty Guide*, retrieved on 12 Oct 2011 from <http://clarkaldrich.blogspot.com/2009/12/using-serious-games-and-simulations.html>.

75   Eric Chester, *Getting Them to Give a Damn: How to Get your Front Line to Care about your Bottom Line* (Chicago: Dearborn Trade Publishing, 2005).

76   Lancaster and Stillman, 145.

77   Karl M. Kapp, *Bridging the Boomer/Gamer Knowledge Gap*, retrieved on 26 Jul 2011 from <http://www.karlkapp.com/materials/Lockheed_web.pdf>.

78   Ibid., slide 29.

79   Natalie Laderas-Kilkenny, *Generational Learning Styles and Methods*. retrieved on 26 Jul 2011 from <http://nkilkenny.wordpress.com/2006/08/30/generational-learning-styles-and-methods/>.

80   Laderas-Kilkenny.

81   Jean Piaget, *The Psychology of Intelligence* (New York: Routledge, 1950).

82   Lorin W. Anderson, David R. Krathwohl, Peter W. Airasian, Kathleen A. Cruikshank, Richard E. Mayer, Paul Pintrich, James Raths, Merlin Wittrock, *A Taxonomy for Learning, Teaching, and Assessing: A Revision of Bloom's Taxonomy of Educational Objectives* (New York: Longman, 2001).

83   David R. Krathwohl, Benjamin Samuel Bloom and Bertram B. Masia, *Taxonomy of Educational Objectives: The Classification of Educational Goals. Handbook II: The Affective Domain* (New York: David McKay, 1964).

84   Anita J. Harrow, *A Taxonomy of the Psychomotor Domain: A Guide for Developing Behavioral Objectives* (New York: David McKay, 1972).

85   Ken Bain, *What the Best College Teachers Do* (Cambridge, MA: Harvard University Press, 2004).

86   Murray Sperber, "How Undergraduate Education became College Lite – and a Personal Apology" in Richard H. Hersh and John Merrow, eds., *Declining by Degrees: Higher Education at Risk* (New York: Palgrave Macmillan, 2005), 131-143.

87   Thomas C. Reeves, "How Do You Know They are Learning? The Importance of Alignment in Higher Education", *International Journal of Learning Technology*, Vol. 2, No. 4 (2006), 294-309.

88   Richard E. Snow, Lyn Corno and Douglas Jackson, "Individual Differences in Affective and Cognitive Functions" in David C. Berliner and Robert C. Calfee, eds., *Handbook of Educational Psychology* (New York: Macmillan,1996), 243-310.

89   Reeves, 297.

90   Kathy Kolbe, *The Conative Connection: Acting on Instinct* (Reading: Addison-Wesley, 1990).

91   Kolbe.

92   Thomas C. Reeves and Jan Herrington, "Authentic Tasks: The Key to Harnessing the Drive to Learn in Members of "Generation Me" in Martin Ebner and Mandy Schiefner, eds., *Looking Toward the Future of Technology-Enhanced Education: Ubiquitous Learning and the Digital Native* (Hershey: Information Science Reference, 2009), 148-169.

93   John Seely Brown, Allan Collins and Paul Duguid, "Situated Cognition and the Culture of Learning", *Educational Researcher*, Vol. 18, No. 1 (1989), 32-42.

94   Cognition and Technology Group at Vanderbilt, "Anchored Instruction and its Relationship to Situated Cognition" *Educational Researcher*, Vol. 19, No. 6 (1990), 2-10.

95   John D. Bransford, Nacy Vye, Charles Kinzer and Victoria Risko, "Teaching Thinking and Content Knowledge: Toward an Integrated Approach," in Beau Fly Jones and Lorna Idol, eds., *Dimensions of Thinking and Cognitive Instruction* (Hillsdale, NJ: Lawrence Erlbaum Associates, 1990), 381-413.

96   Michael F. Young, "Instructional Design for Situated Learning", *Educational Technology Research and Development*, Vol. 41, No. 1 (1993), 43-58.

97   David Lebow and Walter W. Wager, "Authentic Activity as a Model for Appropriate Learning Activity: Implications for Emerging Instructional Technologies", *Canadian Journal of Educational Communication*, Vol. 23, No. 3 (1994), 231-144.

98   Rick Gordon, "Balancing Real-world Problems with Real-world Results", *Phi Delta Kappan*, Vol. 79 (1998), 390-393.

99   David Jonassen, "Toward a Design Theory of Problem Solving", *Educational Technology Research and Development*, Vol. 48, No. 4 (2000), 63-85.

100   Jan Herrington and Anthony Herrington, "Authentic Assessment and Multimedia: How University Students Respond to a Model of Authentic Assessment", *Higher Education Research and Development*, Vol. 17, No. 3 (1998), 305-322.

101   Sasha Barab, Kurt D. Squire and Anthony Dueber, "A co-evolutionary model for supporting the emergence of authenticity," *Educational Technology Research and Development*, Vol. 48, No. 2 (2000), 37-62.

102   Barbara Jacoby, *Service-learning in Higher Education: Concepts and Practices* (San Francisco: Jossey-Bass, 1996).

103   Philip Duchastel, "A Web-based Model for University Instruction", *Journal of Educational Technology Systems*, Vol. 25 (1997), 221-228.

104   Examples of learning environments that incorporate these authentic task design principles can be found on outlined above can be found at the Authentic Task Design web site (University of Wollongong, 2006 – retrieved on 26 Jul 2011 from <http://www.authentictasks.uow.edu.au/>).

105   Tom Kuhlmann, "Why E-Learning is So Effective", *The Rapid E-Learning Blog*, retrieved on 26 Jul 2011 from <http://www.articulate.com/rapid-elearning/why-e-learning-is-so-effective/>.

106   Kuhlmann.

107   Robert B. Kozma, "Learning with Media", *Review of Educational Research*, Vol. 61, No. 2 (1991), 179-211.

108   Richard E. Clark, "Reconsidering Research on Learning with Media", *Review of Educational Research*, Vol. 53, No. 4 (1983), 445.

109   Kozma, 183.

110   Robert M. Bernard, Philip C. Abrami, Yiping Lou, Evgueni Borokhovski, Anne Wade, Lori Wozney, Peter Andrew Wallet, Manon Fiset and Binru Huang, "How Does Distance Education Compare to Classroom Instruction? A Meta-analysis of the Empirical Literature", *Review of Educational Research*, Vol. 74, No. 3 (2004), 379-439; and May K. Tallent-Runnels, Julie A. Thomas, William Y. Lan, Sandi Cooper, Terence C. Ahern, Shana M. Shaw and Xiaoming Liu, "Teaching Courses Online: A Review of the Research", *Review of Educational Research*, Vol. 76, No. 1 (2006), 93-135.

111   Thomas L. Russell, *No Significant Difference Phenomenon* (NSDP) (Western Interstate Commission for Higher Education (WICHE), 2010), available online at <http://www.nosignificantdifference.org/>.

112   Clark, 445.

113   Richard E. Clark and Fred Estes, "How to Develop Authentic Technologies" in Richard E. Clark, ed., *Learning from Media: Arguments, Analysis and Evidence New Directions* (Greenwich, CT: Information Age Publishing, 2001), 241-262.

114   Thomas C. Reeves, "Design Research from the Technology Perspective" in Jan Van den Akker, Koeno Gravemeijer, Susan McKenney, Nienke Nieveen, eds., *Educational Design Research* (London: Routledge, 2006), 86-109.

115   Ibid.

116   Ibid.

117   Mike Bitten, *A History of Training Development in the Canadian Forces* (Canada: Canadian Forces Training and Development Branch Association, 2007).

118   Canadian Forces Individual Training & Education System, *Manual of Individual Training and Education: Volume 1: Interim Guidance – Introduction/Description* (Ottawa: Government of Canada, 1997).

119   Canadian Forces Individual Training & Education System.

120   John Daniel, Asha Kanwar and Stamenka Uvalic-Trumbic, "Breaking Higher Education's Iron Triangle: Access, Cost, and Quality", The entity from which ERIC acquires the content, including journal, organization, and conference names, or by means of online submission from the author. *Change: The Magazine of Higher Learning*, Vol. 41, No. 2 (2009), 30-35.

121   Canadian Forces Individual Training & Education System.

CHAPTER 10

CULTURE, IDENTITY AND CULTURAL INTELLIGENCE: LEADERSHIP AND LEARNING IN THE CANADIAN FORCES

Karen D. Davis

Cultural complexity is the operational context within which Canadian Forces leaders lead, whether that means conducting aid to civil power operations in Canada, developing whole of government strategies for international missions, motivating and influencing local civilians to cooperate with security efforts, or conducting combat operations within joint, inter-agency, multi-national, and public (JIMP) peace support contexts. Military leaders must be able to adapt to new cultural settings and to positively engage in a complexity of multi-cultural interactions within a dynamic landscape of potential belligerents and allies who represent the interests of military and civilian organizations, networks, and communities. Preparation to meet these challenges begins as soon as potential military recruits step inside the door of a recruiting centre. Enrolment in the military represents the formal beginning of an intense socialization process in which recruits are transformed into military members and develop a sense of belonging within the military family.

Cultural intelligence (CQ)[1] is a meta-competency which identifies the key competencies, attributes, and skills that contribute to the ability to effectively interact, adapt and make effective decisions within unfamiliar, and often complex, cultural environments. This chapter discusses the relationship between national culture, military culture and identity, cultural intelligence, and leadership development within the context of the CF, arguing that it is essential to ensure that CF leader development pay particular attention to the long term development of cultural intelligence, including its relationship to professional ideology and identity.

Canada, Culture and Military Identity

As Canadians and CF members, a particular range of values, beliefs, and experiences impact the ways in which individuals think about the self and their relationships to others in the CF, the community, the nation, and beyond. Military culture is a shared and relatively stable pattern of behaviours, values, and assumptions that military members learn over time as an effective means of defining membership, maintaining social stability and achieving military goals, and that are transmitted to new members, through professional development and military socialization, as the correct ways to perceive, think, and act.[2] The culture of the CF, which includes its learning, education and training systems, as well as employment and deployment environments, provides the cultural foundation and context within which individual members develop military occupational and leadership skills and expertise. Concurrently, they are testing and refining their worldview – the overarching belief system that gives coherence and uniqueness to the way that members of particular societies or cultures make sense of the world around them.[3] It is essential, therefore, to understand not only what comprises cultural intelligence, but also the relationship between CF culture, leader development and developing cultural intelligence.

Negotiating culture includes not only understanding those societies that are based upon shared ethnicity, religion or language, but also cultures that are rooted within domestic and international organizations such as non-government organizations, the media, other government departments and private industry. In understanding how military organizations work, it is important to recognize the ways in which it is both similar to and unique from other organizations in society. Virtually all organizations, including the military, are run as mainstream bureaucracies that can generally be described as large and formal complex organizations, which are organized through elaborate divisions of labour, under hierarchical structures of authority, and which operate according to explicit rules and procedures.[4] Joining, belonging, and becoming are key concepts related to the process of socialization[5] into and within an organization that are shaped by the relationship between individuals and the organizational environment.

The framework within which this relationship is shaped holds important keys to understanding how individuals learn in the organization. For example, from systems and ecological perspectives, individuals enter into an iterative relationship within which they negotiate meaning by learning and adapting to the rules of the organization. This iterative relationship allows space for individuals to use a toolbox of multiple sets of rules depending on the situation, thus assuming that there is no particular pressure on the individual to conform to the organizational environment;[6] in fact, deviance from norms is seen as a way of ensuring that the organization remains dynamic and responsive. In contrast, within a mechanistic model, individuals are encouraged to continuously respond to the rules and norms of the organization to the extent that their behaviour is almost completely shaped by the organizational environment.[7]

In recent decades, an increasing emphasis on transformational leadership in the CF has created opportunities for individuals to contribute to organizational discourse and decision-making as they learn, thus having an impact on the organizational environment. Learning and adaptation processes within the CF are shaped by the leadership and culture – both historic and contemporary. The CF is an institution, unique from generic organizations as a result of an enduring social structure with a distinctive set of norms and values which reflect and are reflected over time through professional attributes.[8]

CF leadership doctrine highlights the pervasiveness of leader influence on people as well as in shaping group and institutional characteristics. The development of professional ideology and the inculcation of military ethos is a primary responsibility of military leaders. This includes acting to align cultural values through a variety of mechanisms including institutional rites and rituals.[9] Given the potential cost of error in many military operations, organizational behaviour requires a sensitive synergy between control and innovation, and rules-based and values-based behaviour and learning. The CF Leader Development Framework (LDF),[10] with its emphasis on military expertise, cognitive, social, and change capacities, permeated at every level by professional ideology, was developed to address this very challenge.

As an institution, the CF has endured and evolved within the context of Canadian policy and strategic culture. The capacity of individuals to operate effectively within security environments, including as a member of the CF, is reliant upon a myriad of experiences, knowledge and identities that are formed within the Canadian cultural context. CF institutional culture, shaped within Canadian strategic culture, provides the context within which individuals gain knowledge and develop social identity as military members. Culture provides stability, a sense of belonging and identity, and creates commitment to something larger than self-interest.[11] Military organizations, including the CF, call it military ethos. Military ethos, as an expression of ideal cultural values, is essentially the social glue that holds the organization together by providing appropriate standards of behaviour, and guiding and shaping the attitudes and behaviours of members. In the case of the CF, this is presented as a doctrinal framework in *Duty With Honour: The Profession of Arms in Canad*a.[12] As a framework for understanding the significance of their role on behalf of Canada, military culture plays an important role in instilling a strong source of pride and identity for CF members that is strongly linked to who they are as Canadians and as members of the military. Canadian historical experience shapes national discourse on war and security, and has a long standing impact on the military traditions and heritage which continue to influence the character of CF culture today. National strategic culture is the product of a particular historical experience within a geographical context, which encompasses religion, ideology and culture, governance, the influence of different national cultures, and technology.[13]

In 1867, the *British North America Act* created a Canadian polity which recognized Québec and Ontario as equal and dominant partners[14] among the four founding provinces of Canada (New Brunswick, Nova Scotia, Ontario and Québec). The vision of Confederation formulated by Canada's first Prime Minister, Sir John A. MacDonald, and pursued by his successor, Sir Wilfred Laurier, was a predominantly British empire in terms of language and economic development.[15]

The roots of Canadian military identity were formed within this context, and through participation in military campaigns such as the Boer War, the First World War, the Second World War and the Korean conflict. As a result, Canadian military identity, including allegiance to the British crown, is largely based upon a predominantly British, Anglo and male foundation of traditions, structure, and governance.

Notwithstanding, Canadian philosopher John Ralston Saul suggests that George Étienne Cartier made a greater intellectual contribution to Confederation than MacDonald by explaining within parliamentary debates over Confederation that races should be brought together by ideas to form a political union independent of the national or religious origins of individuals.[16] Thus, according to Saul, persistent claims to Canada's predominantly Victorian roots, or to a Canada built upon two founding pillars – English and French – are misleading. He further asserts that the key tenets of Canadian civilization: egalitarianism, individual and group rights and obligations, balanced complexity, reconciliation, inclusion, continuing relationships, and minority rights are a reflection of the Aboriginal roots upon which the Canadian polity developed. By extension, Saul also links a uniquely Canadian attitude toward war, as well as Canadian military tactics and strategy to the historical underpinnings of Aboriginal philosophy.[17] Canadian military identity, although heavily influenced by a predominantly Anglo and male membership, has been shaped by a diverse and complex range of socio-historical actors and events including the historical participation of French Canadians, Aboriginal People, racial and ethnic minorities, and women in Canada's military efforts.[18]

The contemporary historical roots of today's CF can be found in the 1960s and the social transformation that followed the Second World War as a result of considerable economic expansion; the coming of age of the baby boom generation; an increase in state intervention in social, economic, and cultural affairs; the feminist movement; the emergence of political leadership and pressure for change from within Aboriginal communities in Canada; the Québec independence movement; and the arrival of over four million immigrants to Canada from 1945 to 1960.[19] Political response to demands for change resulted in several key political processes, including new legislation: the Royal Commission on Bilingualism and Biculturalism led to the *Official Languages Act* in 1969; in 1970, the Royal Commission on the Status of Women in Canada made 167 recommendations to Parliament to address inequalities between women and men; the government announced a federal Multiculturalism policy in 1971; the *Canadian Human Rights Act* was passed in Parliament in 1977; the *Canadian Constitution Act* came into effect in 1982; and in 1996 the CF became subject to the *Employment Equity Act*. As a result, individual and language rights are entrenched in law in Canada and must be recognized as such within the CF.

Historical identity reaching back to the 19th century and beyond, coupled with recent Canadian experience – significant social and demographic change, the Cold War, the end of the Cold War, and multiple peacekeeping, disaster relief and peace support operations have influenced the culture that is reflected in the military today. Within this strategic cultural context, Canadians bring a range of perspectives, experiences and identities to the military, and further develop their identity as Canadians and military members through military professional development and socialization.

From a post modern perspective, social identity is conceptualized as socially and historically constructed, complex, multifaceted, and subject to contradiction and change.[20] The relationship between individual identity and collective identity within organizations varies across context; however, the military invests extraordinary effort to create, maintain, and convey numerous traditions, symbols, policies and messages to encourage cohesion and commitment to the team, organization, and mission success. Similarities among individuals within groups are emphasized and individuals, motivated to belong, internalize the group norms.[21] The extent to which this does or does not take place has an impact on how individuals learn and develop within the organization.

Diversity, described by social identity theorists as a mixture of people with different group identities within the same social system,[22] has the potential to significantly enrich the learning environment in the CF. Research has found that diversity in and of itself enhances organizational inputs; however, the extent to which diverse members of an organization are comfortable with expressing unique opinions and perspectives is dependent upon sufficient communication, trust, and openness in the work environment.[23] Other research suggests that individuals with relatively high levels of ethnic identity are more likely to draw positive inferences of organizations,[24] suggesting a greater comfort level and increased likelihood of making unique contributions to organizational discourse and culture if diverse gender, ethnic, and cultural identities are valued, even fostered within organizations.

A diverse learning environment is of particular salience to the development of cultural intelligence; however, optimizing the benefits of diversity requires a reflective relationship between CF members and the institutional leadership and discourse that shapes understanding of internal and external cultural dynamics. CQ provides a framework for developing and enhancing that insight within the military.

Cultural Intelligence

CQ experts have invariably constructed CQ as a multi-dimensional model focusing on the relationship between numerous factors such as mental (cognitive and meta-cognitive), behavioural and motivational dimensions;[25] attitude, skills and knowledge;[26] and knowledge, mindfulness and skills.[27] Considering its various potential dimensions and contributors, CQ can be described as a meta-competency that integrates knowledge, cognition, motivation, behaviour, and mindfulness. The distinction between knowledge and cognition is similar to the distinction that CQ experts Christopher Earley and Soon Ang identified between the cognitive and meta-cognitive dimension; knowledge refers to what you know about a particular culture and cognition refers to how you think about thinking. It follows that CQ is unique from, but does encompass cultural awareness which reflects cultural knowledge. As a meta-competency, CQ provides a framework for developing the capacity to understand and act in complex cultural milieu beyond accessing factual knowledge and applying prescriptive behaviours.

Figure 10.1 provides an illustration of the predominant relationships and competencies, each discussed below, that contribute to CQ: motivation, cognition, knowledge, behaviour, and mindfulness. It is important to note that CQ results from the integrated power of this range of dimensions; that is, highly effective CQ cannot be achieved in the absence of any of these dimensions. Each dimension, as described below, is a unique contributor to CQ, but is not mutually exclusive from the others. Within each dimension, a plethora of knowledge, skills, and attributes (KSAs) can be brought to bear within complex cultural environments. The relative impact and weight that these more specific KSAs have on the contributing value of a particular dimension, and thus overall CQ, will vary by context. The quality and quantity of KSAs is important, but the overall capacity to adapt and act effectively within unfamiliar milieu is dependent upon the relationship between the five dimensions. Military culture is the experiential CF schoolhouse within which all formal and informal learning takes place, and, therefore, has a significant impact on how military members understand and adapt to cultural influences and challenges.

Figure 10.1: Cultural Intelligence, Concepts and Relationships[28]

Motivation

The motivational dimension represents concepts such as self-awareness, percep-
tual acuity, flexibility, openness, openness to learning, and goal setting, which
facilitate adaptable approaches in culturally unfamiliar or complex situations. A
motivated individual would be, for example, someone who strives toward self-
awareness and self-development in enhancing their effectiveness in different
cultural situations. According to CQ trainer, David Livermore, interest, drive and
energy have an important influence on how CQ is developed and the extent
to which it is developed; that is, if individuals are not interested in developing
the ability to adjust to cultural differences, it is not likely that they will increase
their effectiveness in unfamiliar cultural domain.[29] Similarly, the Canadian Foreign Service Institute, Centre for Intercultural Learning, identifies personal and
professional commitment, and knowledge of self as two of nine major competencies that describe an interculturally effective person.[30] Importantly, personal
and cultural values, including the emphasis and priority placed on developing
particular attributes and competencies within an organization such as the CF
will impact the motivational dimension.

Cognition

The cognitive dimension includes *how* you think about thinking and how you
gain new cultural knowledge, recognizing that different strategies might be required to learn about and adapt within different cultures. Ethnocentrism refers
to the tendency for individuals to assume that their own group or culture is
better or more natural than others.[31] Recognizing that ethnocentrism, whether
conscious or unconscious, has an immeasurable influence on how you think, is
critical. Cultural psychologist Harry Triandis notes, for example, that members
of different cultures will differ in the way that they sample, and give weight to,
information from different cultures.[32] The cognitive scripts that guide behaviour
are informed by cultural values which are stored in memory through gradual
internalization of prevailing cultural patterns. Social perception, within the cognitive sphere, includes, for example, perceptions of events and attributions of
their causes; that is, perceptions of what actually took place and why or what
led directly to a particular outcome. The relationship between identity development and cultural values systems informs the cognitive processes underlying
decision-making and moral reasoning. Military ethos and professional ideology
are important contributors to how CF members approach cultural learning and
perceive or make sense of cultural behaviours and patterns.[33]

Knowledge

The knowledge domain includes what you know about culture[34] including an understanding of the concept of culture and its pervasive influence on people and societies.[35] The cognitive dimension will have a significant impact on what knowledge is gained and how available information and knowledge are processed, prioritized and integrated. Cultural awareness or culture-specific knowledge, such as social and family structure, and notions of masculinity and femininity, falls within, but does not wholly comprise the knowledge dimension or fully constitute CQ. Strategic culture, also within the knowledge domain, includes much of what has been commonly understood as intelligence, and sometimes referred to as cultural intelligence in military communities – social, political, economic, religious, demographic, institutional and historical knowledge, as well as how such systems and their features and attributes interact and influence one another in a given society or security context.

Knowledge of language and how language is constructed and reflects cultural practices is also a component of the CQ knowledge domain. Language expresses not only what we think, but is also an expression of how we think. The extent to which an individual has mastered a language or become immersed in the culture that uses that language, will contribute to greater understanding of cultural practices that are expressed through nuances in language; that is, contribute to insight into the worldview of members of another culture. Also, CF members with different language and cultural foundations may approach cross-cultural learning and challenges with different questions and strategies. In numerous ways, language can be linked to the cognitive, knowledge, and behaviour dimensions of CQ.

Behaviour

The behaviour/skills dimension of CQ is the performance of integrated motivation, cognition, knowledge, and mindfulness; that is, the application of CQ reflecting capacity to appropriately adapt behaviour to respond to various and dynamic cultural contexts. Behaviour or self-presentation includes everything that is said or done in an unfamiliar cultural environment, including, for example, speaking another language, expressing interest in understanding another language by using a few key words, conveying respect for the concerns and perspectives of another organization, or adjusting body language to the context of the situation – specific examples of behaviours that are important aspects of inter-cultural communication skills, organizational skills, relationship-building skills[36], and decision-making skills in complex multicultural environments.

Mindfulness

Mindfulness, according to David Thomas, is a key component linking knowledge and behavioural capability.[37] When developed to a very high level, CQ relies upon the following cognitive activities comprising mindfulness:[38]

- being aware of our own assumptions, ideas and emotions;

- noticing what is apparent about the other person and tuning in on their assumptions;

- using all of the senses to perceive situations;

- viewing the situation from several perspectives, that is with an open mind;

- attending to the context to help understand what is happening;

- creating new mental maps of other peoples' personality and cultural background to assist us in responding to them;

- seeking out fresh information to confirm or negate the mental maps; and

- using empathy to understand the situation from another's cultural background.

Mindfulness highlights the inter-dependencies among the dimensions of CQ, as well as the importance of self and situational awareness. Importantly, mindfulness also places a particular focus on challenging assumptions, re-framing perspectives, and creating alternative constructions and analyses of cultural phenomena to re-interpret and discover the unfamiliar and the unknown.

There is conceptual overlap across the five dimensions of CQ discussed above. For example, the cognitive activities that Thomas describes as part of mindfulness are closely related to the cognitive dimension. Similarly, self-awareness contributes to motivation, but also has an impact on cognitive processes; decision-making influences cognitive processes, but is also a behaviour that is impacted by motivation, cognition and knowledge. While knowledge of a foreign language contributes to cultural knowledge, the ability to effectively apply language knowledge roles over into the behaviour dimension. The construction of distinctions across dimensions serves to highlight the key KSAs and processes that contribute to CQ; however, CQ is a meta-competency that derives its power from the integration of the five domains discussed above – the absence of one domain will considerably weaken the potential for the effective application of CQ to achieve mission success.

The competencies and attributes that contribute to CQ also overlap with the five capacities that comprise the CF LDF: expertise, cognitive capacities, social capacities, change capacities, and professional ideology.[39] Moreover, as presented in Table 10.1, many of the leader attributes identified within the LDF can be understood and articulated within the multi-dimensional model of CQ. For example, the cognitive capacities required to lead a group of people are much the same as those required for cultural adaptability and effective inter-cultural relations. One needs "left brain" – analytical – capabilities to prepare for intercultural encounters and one needs "right brain" – creative – capabilities to challenge conventional ways of thinking to create new mental maps of the culture and personalities of cultural outsiders. The social capacities needed for leadership, especially flexibility or open mindedness, communication skills and interpersonal proficiency, are also imperative to CQ, and relate to its cognitive and motivational elements.[40]

	CF LEADERSHIP	CQ
MOTIVATION	change capacities –self change capacities – group credibility & impact *learning organization*	*self-awareness* openness goal-setting open to learning commitment
COGNITION	moral reasoning strategic thinking analytic capacities creative capacities *internalized military ethos* systems thinking	*social identity* perceptual acuity flexibility empathy self-actualization sensory perception decision-making
KNOWLEDGE	military knowledge specialist knowledge *strategic culture*	*cultural complexity & influences* culture-specific knowledge language
BEHAVIOUR	team-building / collaboration communication skills partnering decision-making flexibility	communication skills culturally appropriate actions relationship-building
MINDFULNESS	paradigm shifting	*awareness of own assumptions, ideas, emotions* awareness of others using all senses to perceive open mind, viewing from all perspectives empathy create new mental maps; challenge own thinking attentive to context, activity and change within

Table 10.1: CF Leadership and CQ Attributes by Dimensions of CQ

Several attributes, identified in italics in Table 10.1, have a particular influence on the development of CQ: the CF schoolhouse and those characteristics which enhance it as a learning organization; the development of self-awareness through reflection, dialogue and feedback over a lifetime; awareness of the relationship between professional ideology/military ethos, social identity as a Canadian and

CF member, and the impact of Canadian strategic culture on Canadian military identity and military strategy; and knowledge and understanding of culture, including the ways in which it influences, and is influenced by, the behaviour of individuals and inter-related cultures and cultural systems. Finally, within the concept of mindfulness, developing self-awareness of the assumptions, emotions, and ideas that shape your worldview is essential to the development of CQ. This includes an understanding of how your worldview contributes to your perceptions of others, their motivations, and potential behaviours, as well as the way that others perceive you and your organization.

CF Identity, Culture and Developing CQ

Enhanced CQ among military leaders arises within the more general context of CF transformation and of a learning organization. The extent to which individuals will be motivated to develop cultural intelligence will be influenced by the value that the CF places on CQ, the support that is provided to assist members in developing CQ, and CF training and education that includes CQ. Given the relationship between CQ and leadership, the inclusion of CQ on leadership training would be particularly beneficial.

Within the five dimension CQ meta-competency model, there are numerous embedded connections and synergies among the attributes and characteristics within each dimension. Many of these attributes and characteristics are essential to leadership and well understood within the CF. This chapter suggests that there is a foundational relationship within the model; that is, those attributes and understandings that inform the worldviews that Canadians and CF members bring to bear in complex cultural encounters. Self-awareness, including an appreciation of the Canadian historical and military experience, and the processes and relationships within the CF that shape assumptions, values, beliefs and social identity, is the foundation upon which cultural intelligence develops.

---

1   Although CQ does not represent a mathematical relationship of capabilities in the same way as an intelligence quotient (IQ), it is a unique construct of intelligence that reflects adaptation to varying cultural contexts. Christopher Earley and Soon Ang, *Cultural Intelligence: Individual Interactions Across Cultures* (Stanford, California: Stanford University Press, 2003), 4.

2   Adapted from definition of culture in Canadian Forces leadership doctrine. See: Canada, *Leadership in the Canadian Forces: Conceptual Foundations* (Kingston, ON: Canadian Defence Academy, Canadian Forces Leadership Institute, 2005), 129.

3   Refers to what Max Weber referred to as Weltanshshauung. David Jary and Julia Jary, *Web-Linked Dictionary of Sociology*. 3rd Edition (New York: Harper Collins Publishers, 2000), 39 and 686.

4   Albert J. Mills and Tony Simmons, *Reading Organization Theory: A Critical Approach* (Toronto, ON: Garamond Press, 1995), 35.

5   Albert J. Mills and Stephen J. Murgatroyd, *Organizational Rules: A Framework for Understanding Organizational Action* (Milton Keynes and Philadelphia: Open University Press, 1991).

6   Ibid., 55-59.

7   Ibid., 55.

8   Canada, *Leadership in the Canadian Forces: Conceptual Foundations*, 3.

9   Canada, *Leadership in the Canadian Forces: Leading the Institution* (Kingston, ON: Canadian Defence Academy, Canadian Forces Leadership Institute, 2005), 5; 13-15.

10   Originally developed as the Professional Development Framework. See: Robert W. Walker, *The Professional Development Framework: Generating Effectiveness in Canadian Forces Leadership* (Kingston, ON: Canadian Forces Leadership Institute, Technical Report 2006-01, 2006).

11   Stephen P. Robbins and Nancy Langton, *Organizational Behaviour: Concepts, Controversies, Applications* (3rd Canadian Edition) (Toronto: Prentice Hall, 2003), 349.

12   Canada, *Duty With Honour: The Profession of Arms in Canada* (Kingston, ON: Canadian Defence Academy, Canadian Forces Leadership Institute, 2009).

13   See Bill Bentley, "Cultural Intelligence and Strategic Culture" in Karen D. Davis, ed., *Cultural Intelligence and Leadership: An Introduction for Canadian Forces Leaders* (Kingston, ON: Canadian Defence Academy Press), 28 for discussion of strategic culture which draws on the work of Colin S. Gray, *Another Bloody Century: Future Warfare in the 21st Century* (Oxford: Oxford University Press, 2005); Alistair Johnson, "Thinking about Strategic Culture" in *International Security* Vol. 19, No. 4 (1994-1995); and John A. Lynn, *Battle: A History of Combat and Culture* (Boulder: Westview Press, 2003).

14   Eric Waddell, "State, Language and Society: The Vicissitudes of French in Quebec and Canada" in Alan Cairns, *The Politics of Gender, Ethnicity and Language in Canada* (Toronto: University of Toronto Press, 1986), 74.

15   Ibid.

16   John Ralston Saul, *A Fair Country: Telling Truths About Canada* (Toronto: Viking Canada, 2008), 144.

17   Ibid., 64.

18   See, for example, Stéphane Roussel and Jean-Christophe Boucher, "The Myth of the Pacific Society: Quebec's Contemporary Strategic Culture", *American Review of Canadian Studies*, Vol. 38, No. 2 (2008), 165-187; James W. Walker, "Race and Recruitment in World War I: Enlistment of Visible Minorities in the Canadian Expeditionary Force", *Canadian Historical Review*, Vol. LXX, No. 1 (1989), 1-26; and Ruth Roach Pierson, *They're Still Women After All: The Second World War and Canadian Womanhood* (Toronto, ON: McClelland and Stewart, 1986).

19   Raymond Breton, "Multiculturalism and Canadian Nation-Building" in Alan Cairns, *The Politics of Gender, Ethnicity and Language in Canada* (Toronto: University of Toronto Press, 1986), 38-41.

20   Stuart Hall, "The question of cultural identity" in Stuart Hall, David Held and Tony McGrew, eds., *Modernity and its Futures* (Cambridge: Polity, 1992), cited in Stella M. Nkomo and Marcus M. Stewart, "Diverse Identities in Organizations" in Stewart R. Clegg, Cynthia Hardy, Thomas B. Lawrence, and Walter R. Nord, eds., *The Sage Handbook of Organization Studies, 2nd Edition* (London/Thousand Oaks/New Delhi: Sage Publications, 2006).

21   See M.A. Hogg and D.J. Terry, "Social Identity and Self-Categorisation Processes in Organizational Contexts", *Academy of Management Review*, Vol. 25, No. 1 (2000), 121-140, cited in Stella M. Nkomo and Marcus M. Stewart, "Diverse Identities in Organizations".

22   Stella M. Nkomo and Marcus M. Stewart, "Diverse Identities in Organizations", 522.

23   Ibid., 524.

24   Sandra Kim and Michelle Gelfand, "The Influence of Ethnic Identity on Perceptions of Organizational Commitment", *Journal of Vocational Behaviour*, Vol. 63 (2003), 396-416, cited in Stella M. Nkomo and Marcus M. Stewart, "Diverse Identities in Organizations", *The Sage Handbook of Organization Studies, 2nd Edition* (London/Thousand Oaks/New Delhi: Sage Publications, 2006).

25   Christopher Earley and Soon Ang, *Cultural Intelligence: Individual Interactions Across Cultures* (Stanford, California: Stanford University Press, 2003).

26   James P. Johnson, Tomasz Lenartowicz, and Salvador Apud, "Cross-Cultural Competence in International Business: Toward a Definition and a Model", *Journal of International Business Studies*, Vol. 37 (2006), 525.

27   David C. Thomas and Kerr Inkson, *Cultural Intelligence: People Skills for Global Business* (San Francisco: Berrett-Koehler Publishers, Inc., 2003).

28   Adapted from Karen D. Davis and Justin C. Wright, "Culture and Cultural Intelligence" in Karen D. Davis, ed., *Cultural Intelligence and Leadership: An Introduction for Canadian Forces Leaders* (Kingston, ON: Canadian Defence Academy Press, 2009).

29   David Livermore, *Leading With Cultural Intelligence* (New York: AMACOM, 2010).

30   Thomas Vulpe, Daniel Kealey, David Protheroe and Doug MacDonald, *A Profile of the Interculturally Effective Person* (Ottawa: Foreign Affairs Canada, Canadian Foreign Service Institute Centre for Intercultural Learning, 2000).

31   Peter G. Northouse, *Leadership Theory and Practice, Fifth Edition* (Thousand Oaks, California: Sage Publications, Inc., 2010), 337.

32   Harry Triandis, "Cultural Intelligence in Organizations", *Group & Organization Management*, Vol. 31, (2006), 23.

33   What is identified here as cognition is similar to what Earley and Ang (2003) describe as meta-cognition: strategic, high level thinking that may be unconscious or very subtle, and reflecting a sense or intuition about a situation. For discussions regarding cultural intelligence and identity development see Christopher P. Earley and Soon Ang, *Cultural Intelligence*, p.64; and Daniel Lagace-Roy and Justin C. Wright, "Cultural Intelligence and Identity Development" in Karen D. Davis, ed., *Cultural Intelligence and Leadership: An Introduction for Canadian Forces Leaders* (Kingston, ON: Canadian Defence Academy Press, 2009).

34   What is referred to here as the knowledge domain is similar to what Earley and Ang (2003) refer to as cognition.

35   Understanding the concept of culture and its impacts, and knowledge of host country and culture are two of nine core intercultural competencies identified by Thomas Vulpe *et al* (2000).

36   Organizational skills, intercultural communication skills, and relationship-building skills are three of nine core intercultural competencies identified by Thomas Vulpe *et al* (2000).

37   David C. Thomas, "Domain and Development of Cultural Intelligence: The Importance of Mindfulness", *Group and Organisation Management,* (2006), 78-99.

38   David C. Thomas, 85.

39   Robert W. Walker, *The Professional Development Framework.*

40   Kimberly-Anne Ford and Karen D. Davis, *Cultural Intelligence, Emotional Intelligence and Canadian Forces Leader Development: Concepts, Relationships, and Measures* (Kingston, ON: Canadian Forces Leadership Institute, Technical Memorandum 2007-01).

CHAPTER 11

CIVILIAN LEARNING AND PROFESSIONAL DEVELOPMENT SYSTEM

Natacha Saintonge and Danielle McMullen-Dubé

This chapter will closely examine the various attributes of the learning environment of civilian employees in the Department of National Defence. It will present an overview of the external and internal influences that provide strategic orientation for the conduct of civilian learning and professional development (LPD). It will then draw attention to important interdependencies within the civilian LPD system, describe its governance as a component of human resource (HR) management and outline the enabling infrastructure that is in place to support both individual employee LPD as well as the development of an organizational learning culture. In addition, this chapter will summarize the outcomes attributed to the system and illustrate the resulting benefits to the organization.

It is important to note, for clarity and standardization of terms, that the Treasury Board (TB) Policy on Learning, Training and Development defines professional development as "an activity that assists public service employees to further their careers and is aligned with departmental business priorities and management improvement objectives of the government. It includes courses, programs or learning events sponsored by a variety of service providers (e.g., in-house, the Canada School of Public Service (CSPS), academic institutions and the private sector)."[1] This definition also applies to civilian professional development in DND.

The Public Service Context

The changing nature of employees' roles as public servants, growing pressures in the labour market, technology, an increasingly diverse population mix and an aging population[2] are the key drivers of civilian LPD in the public service. These drivers influence how organizations, including DND, view LPD and its contribution to enhancing organizational performance and achieving their organizational missions.

In response to these pressures, the Clerk of the Privy Council identifies, through his/her action plan for public service renewal, employee development as one of the priority areas to be addressed by heads of departments. Emphasis is placed on leadership development with the aim of preparing public servants to work in new ways and be able to adapt to emerging challenges in order to maintain high organizational performance. In his Public Service Renewal Action Plan, the Clerk states, "it is critical for a high-performing organization to develop its talent through a systematic and integrated approach to managing performance and learning".[3]

In addition, the Clerk has stressed that "Employee development is the responsibility of both the individual and the institution, but it serves a single purpose: to improve effectiveness and productivity in current and future jobs. This requires going beyond coursework and classroom learning. The task is to consciously create learning environments where knowledge management is done well and where employees have ready access to the information they need to do their jobs".[4]

With regard to the modernization of the public service, organizations hold the responsibility to have "the people, work environment and focus on building capacity and leadership to assure its success and a confident future for the public service of Canada."[5] The TB Management Accountability Framework (MAF) provides Deputy Ministers (DM) with a vision of excellence in management and organizational performance. In terms of learning, innovation and change management, the MAF sets expectations for departments to manage "through continuous innovation and transformation, promote organizational learning, value corporate knowledge, and learn from their performance."[6]

The Departmental Context

DND civilian employees support the implementation of the *Canada First* Defence Strategy (CFDS) and share the Department's corporate responsibilities, with the CF, through their work at headquarters, bases, in the regions and overseas. They are committed to a variety of trades and occupations within the organization, for instance, plumbers, mechanics, policy analysts and specialists in information technology, finance, procurement, and communications, amongst others. "The knowledge and skills of this workforce ensure that, together with the Canadian Forces…valued defence services can be provided at home and abroad."[7]

Civilian employees are hired under the *Public Service Employment Act* and, as stated in the *Defence Administration Order and Directive (DAOD) 5005-1, Governance of Civilian Human Resource Management*, they are managed "in accordance with the relevant legislation, terms and conditions of employment, collective agreements, directions of central agencies and public service-wide values and principles of HR management."[8] When they are hired, DND civilian employees have already been found qualified for their specific position through a formal assessment. They typically progress to the next level by seeking promotion opportunities through competitive selection processes. Employees are therefore responsible for taking an active role in their own learning, professional development and career planning by discussing their career aspirations and co-developing a Personal Learning Plan (PLP) with their manager.

The DND/CF relies on the work and expertise of its personnel to ensure the CF's operational effectiveness. Accordingly, the CFDS, outlines *Personnel* as one of the four pillars responsible for building military capabilities. The Strategy, which is "based on an extensive and rigorous analysis of the risks and threats facing Canada in the years to come, as well as the government's vision for defence,"[9] stresses the importance of "encouraging the continued development of a knowledge-based workforce."[10]

Among the challenges facing its workforce, DND has identified two key corporate risks, within its Corporate Risk Profile, for which LPD becomes a mitigating and capacity building strategy. First, there is a risk that the Defence Program's effectiveness may be jeopardized by an inability to achieve the right balance and composition of the Defence team in terms of size, mix of skills and diversity of backgrounds. Second, there is a risk that the Defence Services Program's effectiveness may be compromised if the DND/CF does not have the capacity to respond to current and emerging challenges, capitalize on investments and innovations, and continually improve its management and support of the military and civilian workforce.[11] This highlights the importance of strategic investments in LPD.

In the same vein, the Defence Priorities (2011-2014) represent a focused number of areas where the department has decided to direct additional future efforts with the purpose of addressing corporate risks and gaps in capability or capacity. As part of the Strengthen the Defence Team priority, the Assistant Deputy Minister, Human Resources – Civilian [ADM (HR-Civ)], jointly with the Chief of Military

Personnel (CMP), have been identified as the Officer of Primary Interest (OPI) for three Defence Priority Elements: retain and strengthen capacity through succession planning; continue to build leadership through maximizing personnel potential to meet future challenges; and strengthen continuous LPD.[12]

Additionally, in order to help further alleviate identified risks associated with loss of knowledge and experience, the DND/CF Organizational Learning Strategy was developed. The strategy provides direction to ensure that senior military and civilian leaders are held accountable for shaping and nurturing the future organizational learning environment by establishing organizational learning processes with the purpose of enhancing the ability of DND/CF to improve its performance as an organization.[13] Moreover, the strategy describes an overarching intent to foster an enabling workplace and enhance learning infrastructures to ensure the continued development of employees.

Interdependencies in the Civilian Learning and Professional Development System

The DND civilian employee's LPD system derives from the more extensive public service HR system, which promotes values and ethics, integrates the public service's four Key Leadership Competencies (KLC) and links employee development to performance management and succession planning. These elements are the central foundation of the entire system in which employees hold primary responsibility for their careers and their professional development.[14]

A balanced framework of public service values guides professionalism and conduct for DND civilian employees. The following four clusters of values provide ethical standards that guide public servants in the performance of their professional duties and are therefore at the heart of civilian professional and leadership development:[15]

- Democratic Values: Helping Ministers, under law, to serve the public interest;

- Professional Values: Serving with competence, excellence, efficiency, objectivity and impartiality;

- Ethical Values: Acting at all times in such a way as to uphold the public trust; and

- People Values: Demonstrating respect, fairness and courtesy in dealings with both citizens and fellow public servants.

Civilian continuous learning and development activities are expected to support and be consistent with the integration of public service values to ensure Canadians are served by a professional workforce.

The cornerstone of professionalism in the public service lies with the KLC, which outline the leadership skills, abilities, characteristics and behaviours that are required by managers and employees at all levels to meet standards of professional conduct. "From a foundation of values and ethics, public service leaders and employees deliver results through strategic thinking, engagement, and management excellence."[16] Managers and employees may use the profiles as a part of the performance review process, to identify professional development needs and to create PLPs based upon the KLC.[17]

In DND, the *DAOD 5006-0, Civilian Performance Planning and Review* (CPPR) provides direction toward an integrated and employee-oriented approach to civilian performance management and employee development. A key element of the CPPR process is to provide appropriate learning activities that will assist DND employees in attaining their work objectives. Managers and supervisors are expected to provide guidance to their civilian employees concerning their LPD and career interests, while DND employees are expected to engage in discussions with their managers and participate in the development of a PLP, which must be aligned with work objectives.[18] As the Clerk of the Privy Council acknowledged in his *Fifteenth Annual Report*, "The development of public servants as leaders, managers, professionals and empowered employees is central to a high performance institution [...] Our performance in coming years will depend hugely on the skills, knowledge, seasoning and judgment of our employees, and on how well they grow as leaders and knowledge workers."[19] This highlights the importance of succession planning.

Succession planning is defined as "an integrated, systematic approach to identify, recruit, develop and retain talent for key positions and is done in line with current and projected business objectives."[20] It is a process designed for various levels across the organization and is not exclusive to the executive level or leadership positions. Succession planning is critical to ensuring that high-quality candidate pools exist in order to effectively fill the organization's vacancies.[21] The principal objective of succession planning in DND is to increase organizational capacity, which includes developing the knowledge and leadership competencies required to make certain that the DND/CF has the capabilities needed to meet its essential commitments related to defence and security.

The basis of the DND Succession Planning Framework is Competency-Based Management (CBM), which provides a starting point to map out employee development needs as part of a succession plan. It derives from the TB KLC and "is a system or process for gathering, documenting and analyzing data about the knowledge, skills and abilities required for a position".[22]

Additional considerations linked to succession planning relate to the TB-specific requirements for second language training (SLT) as per the Policy on Official Languages for Human Resources Management.

Governance of Civilian HR Management

As per *DAOD 5005-1, Governance of Civilian Human Resources Management,* the governance structure for civilian HR management, including LPD, consists of accountabilities, authorities, supporting committee structure, functional direction and guidance, as well as performance measurement.[23]

Accountabilities

The *Financial Administration Act* (FAA), within the framework of the *Public Service Modernization Act*, places direct responsibility for people management in the hands of deputy heads. By virtue of the FAA, the DM has direct legislated authority to "determine the learning, training and development requirements of persons employed in the public service and fix the terms on which the learning, training and development may be carried out".[24]

The Privy Council Office provides further clarification to DMs on exercising their role through the publication *Guidance for Deputy Ministers*. This document indicates that effective departmental management requires that employees be properly trained to carry out the duties of their position and that DMs must promote responsibility and accountability for good HR management in the departments so that the necessary staff with an appropriate balance of skills is maintained. It is also stated in the *Guidance for Deputy Ministers* that the DM has the

responsibility to "improve the management practices within his or her department by creating the conditions which will foster an environment of continuous
learning in which public servants strive for excellence in management."[25]

The TB Policy on Learning, Training and Development supports deputy heads in
upholding their accountability. With regard to Professional Development, "deputy heads are responsible for ensuring that: their organizations have a learning
policy to align departmental business priorities with the management improvement objectives of government; their learning policy supports their mission and
mandate, including requirements for job-related training and learning plans that
align individual learning with departmental business priorities; and employees
at all levels have learning plans to acquire and maintain the knowledge, skills
and competencies related to their level and functions."[26]

The TB also sets specific requirements for SLT through the Policy on Official
Languages for Human Resources Management and the Directive on the Staffing
of Bilingual Positions. The organization must provide access to SLT for incum-
bents of bilingual positions who need to acquire the skills in order to meet the
language requirements of their positions to effectively communicate in both
official languages and provide bilingual services to the public as well as meet
language of work requirements, when appropriate. It further requires that the
organization provide access to SLT for employees who wish to develop their
second-language skills in order to advance their careers and possibly fill bilingual positions in the future. In support of this TB Policy, DND has issued the ADM
(HR-Civ) Directive on Access to Second Language Training, which states roles
and responsibilities for managers.

Authorities

As per *DAOD 1000-0, Corporate Administrative Direction*, the DM delegates
authority for civilian LPD to the ADM (HR-Civ). The ADM (HR-Civ) exercises functional authority by setting standards; communicating clear expectations and is-
suing functional direction in Defence Administrative Orders and Directives; providing advice and functional guidance; consulting and obtaining feedback; as
well as monitoring compliance with functional direction. As a result, managers
at all levels follow this functional direction, conducting their activities in support
of the DM's authority within the realm of their management responsibilities as
well as their financial and HR accountabilities. They have responsibilities towards

sound stewardship of resources, including people, which take into account the development of their employees. Managers play a key role in orchestrating the needs of the organization and those of their employees through their facilitation of an alignment process.

Committee Structure

The DM and ADM(HR-Civ) provide direction through a committee structure that is in place to support policy and decision-making on HR management processes, including civilian LPD. Some of the main committees with specific mandates to address LPD issues as part of their outlook on civilian HR management include the Defence Management Committee, the Civilian Human Resources Committee, the Union Management Consultative Committee's HR-Sub Committee, and the Regional Civilian Human Resources Planning and Coordination Committees.

Functional Direction and Guidance

DAOD 5031-0, Learning and Professional Development,[27] is issued under the authority of the ADM (HR-Civ) and the CMP. It reinforces the DND/CF commitment to provide DND employees and CF members with the LPD necessary to support the mission to defend Canada and Canadian interests.

In line with the requirements for the effective management of learning within the public service, *DAOD 5031-50, Civilian Continuous Learning and Professional Development*[28] provides senior management, managers, supervisors, training providers and DND employees with clear direction and guidance in relation to their responsibilities pertaining to LPD issues.

Management Principles of LPD in DND

The ADM (HR-Civ) has defined the terms on which civilian LPD is to be carried out within the department through the Civilian Learning and Professional Development Management Framework. The LPD Management Framework introduces a principle-based approach and provides indicators of successful practice that help Level 1 organizations and Operational Commands as well as DND/CF managers plan, manage, and leverage civilian learning effectively in their organizations. The principles guiding civilian LPD are: aligning learning with corporate and business plans and priorities; integrating learning with business and HR processes; fostering a learning culture; providing appropriate learning options; managing learning effectively; supporting the application of skills in the workplace; and evaluating learning systematically.

The last LPD management principle outlines how evaluation supports the DM's sound stewardship of investments in civilian LPD. For this reason, the Civilian Learning and Professional Development Evaluation Framework and accompanying Toolkit have been implemented to guide the development of LPD evaluation strategies.[29] Both documents promote the following six levels of evaluation: relevance, appropriateness, reaction, learning, performance, and outcomes. They also support training providers in the development and implementation of evaluations for their civilian training activities.

Performance Measurement

The Treasury Board policy on *Management, Resources and Results Structures* (MRRS) "supports the development of a common government-wide approach to the identification of programs and to the collection, management, and reporting of financial and non-financial information relative to those programs".[30] According to the policy, departments are expected to manage their programs for results, define measurable strategic outcomes, establish a program activity architecture (PAA) and demonstrate accountability by reporting on their performance to Parliament.

In DND, the Civilian Learning and Professional Development Management Framework supports two PAA strategic outcomes: Internal Services as well as Care and Support to the CF and Contribution to Canadian Society. Under Internal Services, the sub-sub activity entitled HR Management Services encompasses activities undertaken to determine LPD strategic direction, define processes, conduct risk analysis and ensure that programs and services comply with applicable Acts, policies and governmental plans. The second strategic outcome, Care and Support to the CF and Contribution to Canadian Society, includes the sub-activity Learning and Career Centre and entails granting employee access to LPD from anywhere at any time, in order to build their knowledge, skills and competencies. PAA strategic outcomes are supported by performance indicators and managed through a comprehensive departmental Performance Management Framework (PMF).

The PMF enables DND to monitor the achievement of the expected results of the PAA. This includes reporting on civilian LPD within the annual Departmental Performance Report (DPR), which is linked to the Defence Priorities identified in the Report on Plans and Priorities (RPP). DND reports specifically on its programs and initiatives in support of employee learning, civilian PLP completion rate as well as the percentage of the Salary Wage Envelope (SWE) spent on LPD.

In addition, the Treasury Board requires DND to submit annual MAF assessments which detail the Department's management strengths and weaknesses.[31] The People Management element of the MAF includes an employee learning component and a particular focus on building leadership capacity. Sources of evidence for this area of assessment include data collected through the Public Service Employee Survey and from departmental administrative data systems.

Enabling Infrastructure

Within DND, "learning is a shared responsibility; employees are to take charge of their learning and professional development and managers/supervisors are to provide resources and an environment conducive to such learning and professional development."[32] All indeterminate employees are required to develop PLPs; complete required courses as per the Treasury Board policy on Learning, Training and Development and the Defence Leadership Curriculum; address their second language training needs; as well as participate in learning activities that allow them to develop their knowledge, skills and competencies and prepare them for their future positions.

The PLP is the planning tool used to assess and identify immediate and future employee learning needs that are linked to organizational learning needs and priorities; work commitments; competency and knowledge gaps; and individual learning objectives. In DND, the PLP is used to open a communication channel through which supervisors/managers and employees agree on the learning, training and development required to fulfill the DND mission and meet the personal LPD needs of employees.[33]

The TB Policy on Learning, Training and Development "reflects the government's commitment to ensure a skilled, well-trained and competent public service workforce".[34] The Policy and the Directive on the Administration of Required Training (RT) outline the requirements related to RT for employees new to the public service, first time supervisors, managers and executives as well as functional specialists in the fields of procurement, material management, real property and finance.

The Defence Leadership Curriculum (DLC) was designed to outline departmentally focused required and suggested learning activities for DND's civilian executives, managers and employees. The DLC is aligned with the Treasury Board's four KLC. It provides leadership development opportunities to employees at all levels and empowers them in playing an active role in their own professional development.

The SLT program is an important component of the LPD system in the context of succession planning and employee career development. The DND provides opportunities, through its corporate program, for civilian employees to participate in full-time or part-time training to develop their second language competencies. The SLT program aims to build the department's capacity for filling bilingual positions while supporting the advancement of its employees.[35]

Within DND, the Learning and Career Centre Network (LCCN) provides courses across Canada, thereby facilitating access to learning opportunities. The LCCN was established to provide a departmental infrastructure that would contribute necessary resources in support of a continuous learning culture for Defence team members. The LCCN focuses on providing learning and career advisory services, resource libraries and computer labs as well as the delivery of courses, lunch-and-learn sessions and seminars to assist individuals with their professional development.[36]

Civilian employees may also access classroom courses through the CSPS. The CSPS is mandated by the *Canada School of Public Service Act* to assist deputy heads in addressing the learning needs of their organizations and to provide development programs for public servants.[37] The School is also the sole provider of required training as per the TB Policy on Learning, Training and Development.[38]

A variety of self-paced online professional development courses is available to civilian employees through DNDLearn; a departmental learning management platform that is co-managed by the CMP and ADM (HR-Civ). DNDLearn responds to the need "to train faster and in less time, to provide the right training at the right time, to integrate training with workplace activities, to reduce the amount of time spent away from home on training, to harmonize the military and civilian training and education policies and services".[39] The CSPS e-learning portal, currently entitled My Account, also provides a platform for access to a variety of online professional development products.

DND encourages employee development in the workplace through informal learning options such as ad hoc problem solving, job shadowing, assignments, peer learning and mentoring. Informal learning is defined as "the unstructured transfer of work-related skills, knowledge and information, usually during work".[40]

To further facilitate workplace learning, the DND Mentoring Program was established to provide civilian employees throughout the department with the means to build mentoring relationships. The objective of the program is to "create a mutually beneficial relationship, where both the mentor and the mentee can use each other's insights to achieve their own learning goals for their professional development."[41]

In terms of leadership development, the TB published a new Leadership Development Framework for the Public Service in 2010. The objectives of the framework are to define the general approach to leadership development throughout the Public Service, define the responsibilities of deputies and central agencies, as well as outline specific goals, expected results and accompanying performance measures for assessing those results.[42] DND's corporate leadership development programs are currently being reviewed to align DND with the new Leadership Development Framework in order to ensure they better meet the need of the department and its managers.[43]

The funding for DND's civilian LPD is determined through the integrated business and HR planning process which grants managers at all levels the opportunity to identify and assess critical workforce issues affecting their ability to meet strategic objectives and operational goals. The *Instrument of Delegation of Labour Relations, Compensation and Benefits Authorities for Civilian Public Service Employees of National Defence* outlines which positions within the organization have authority over the approval of LPD related requests.

Resulting Benefits of the Civilian LPD System

The LPD system relies on a framework of cohesive and coherent policy instruments, strategies, guides, tools and advisory services that support managers and facilitate access to LPD activities for civilian employees. A key effect of the system is that employees have access to LPD activities, enabling them to be effective in the exercise of their current functions and preparing them for future organizational challenges. Managers have access to directives, advice and support, enabling a competent staff working in a supporting organization capable of adapting to a changing organizational context. The civilian LPD system promotes opportunities for employees to develop their individual careers. The system is also in place to ensure that the department is compliant with its legislative obligations linked to LPD, and that the funds invested in learning respond to organizational requirements and corporate priorities.

The overall outcome is that LPD in DND contributes to developing people and their potential to effectively support the implementation of the CFDS.

Conclusion

The focus of this chapter has been on how both the public service and departmental contexts provide effective strategic direction for the management of the civilian LPD function. The LPD system is the result of external and internal requirements, outlined in Acts and policies, which provide a unifying framework and guide the implementation of the governance structure, learning options and enabling infrastructure required to support employee development. The four KLC, rooted in distinctive public service values and ethics, are central to the civilian LPD system. The KLC are pivotal in the integrated processes of employee performance management and development as well as in the context of succession planning as they provide direction for the development of LPD roadmaps that are reflective of individual and organizational capability requirements. This chapter reflected on how, within the civilian HR structure, employees are empowered to take the lead in the development of their own career and professional development. Given that civilian employees are a part of the greater pool of federal public service employees, their learning and career development may span across different departments and agencies. All organizations, as part of the broader public service, retain the responsibility for creating an environment that is conducive to the enhancement of competencies that are aligned with identified priorities. The primary benefit to the system as a whole will be a productive, versatile and innovative civilian workforce capable of responding to the current and future needs of not only DND, but also the public service.

1   Government of Canada, Treasury Board of Canada Secretariat, *Policy on Learning, Training, and Development*, 1 Jan 2006, retrieved on 21 Nov 2011 from <http://www.tbs-sct.gc.ca/pol/doc-eng.aspx?id=12405&section=text#cha4>.

2   Nicole Jauvin, *Demographic Challenges Facing the Federal Public Sector*, 17 Apr 2007 <http://www.tbs-sct.gc.ca/nou/n20070417-eng.asp>.

3   Governement of Canada Clerk of the Privy Council, *2010-11 Public Service Renewal Action Plan*, retrieved on 17 Nov 2010 from <http://clerk.gc.ca/local_grfx/docs/2010-11_PS_Renewal_Action_Plan.pdf>.

4   Wayne G. Wouters, *Seventeenth Annual Report to the Prime Minister on the Public Service of Canada* (Canada: Clerk of the Privy Council and Secretary to the Cabinet, 2010) retrieved on 17 Nov 2010 from <http://clerk.gc.ca/local_grfx/docs/reports/17rpt-eng.pdf>.

5   Treasury Board of Canada Secretariat, *Integrated Planning Handbook for Deputy Ministers and Senior Managers*, retrieved on 13 Dec 2010 from <http://www.tbs-sct.gc.ca/gui/iph01-eng.asp>.

6   Treasury Board of Canada Secretariat, *TBS management Accountability Framework*, retrieved on 16 Nov 2011 from <http://www.tbs-sct.gc.ca/maf-crg/overview-apercu/overview-apercu-txt-eng.asp>.

7   Department of National Defence, *Managing Civilian Human Resources* (Ottawa, ON: Department of National Defence On-Line Course).

8   Department of National Defence, *DAOD 5005-1, Governance of Civilian Human Resources Management*, 28 Feb 2003, retrieved on 21 Nov 2011 from <http://admfincs.mil.ca/admfincs/subjects/daod/5005/1_e.asp>.

9   Department of National Defence, *Canada First Defence Strategy*, 3, retrieved on 15 Nov 2011 from <http://www.forces.gc.ca/site/pri/first-premier/June18_0910_CFDS_english_low-res.pdf>.

10   Ibid., 16

11   Department of National Defence and Canadian Forces, *Defence Corporate Risk Profile*, November 2010, retrieved on 11 Nov 2011 from <http://vcds.mil.ca/sites/CProg/Resources/DDFP%20files/Corporate%20Risk%20Profile%20(EN).pdf>.

12   Department of National Defence, *Defence Priorities (2011-2014)*, retrieved on 26 Nov 2010 from <http://vcds.mil.ca/sites/CProg/Resources/DDFP%20files/Defence%20Priorities%202011_2014.pdf>.

13   Department of National Defence, Knowledge Management (DDSM), *Organizational Learning Strategy*, retrieved on 18 Jan 2011 from <http://vcds.mil.ca/sites/page-eng.asp?page=4771>.

14   Treasury Board of Canada Secretariat, *Learning and Leadership Development*, retrieved on 9 Nov 2010 from <http://www.tbs-sct.gc.ca/chro-dprh/dev-eng.asp>.

15   Treasury Board of Canada Secretariat, *Values and Ethics Code for the Public Service*, retrieved on 9 Nov 2010 from <http://www.tbs-sct.gc.ca/pubs_pol/hrpubs/TB_851/vec-cve1-eng.asp#_Toc46202802>.

16   Treasury Board of Canada Secretariat, *Key Leadership Competencies*, retrieved on 9 Nov 2010 from <http://www.tbs-sct.gc.ca/tal/kcl/intro-eng.asp>.

17   Ibid.

18   Department of National Defence, *DAOD 5006-1, Civilian Performance Planning and Review Instructions*, retrieved on 29 Apr 2005 from <http://admfincs.mil.ca/admfincs/subjects/daod/5006/1_e.asp>.

19   Governement of Canada Clerk of the Privy Council, *Fifteenth Annual Report to the Prime Minister on the Public Service of Canada*, retrieved on 17 Nov 2010 from <http://www.clerk.gc.ca/eng/feature.asp?featureId=19&pageId=216#3.3>.

20   Department of National Defence, *DND Succession Planning Guide for Managers: Organizational Capacity Building - May 2010*, retrieved on 9 Nov 2010 from <http://hr.ottawa-hull.mil.ca/hrciv/documents/pdf/EX_SP_guide_e.pdf>.

21   Ibid.

22   Ibid.

23   Department of National Defence, *DAOD 5005-1, Governance of Civilian Human Resources Management*, retrieved on 28 Feb 2003 from <http://admfincs.mil.ca/admfincs/subjects/daod/5005/1_e.asp>.

24   Canada, Minister of Justice, *Financial Administration Act*, 12.(1)(a), retrieved on 14 Dec 2010 from <http://laws.justice.gc.ca/PDF/Statute/F/F-11.pdf>.

25   Governement of Canada Privy Council Office, *Guidance for Deputy Ministers*, retrieved on 20 Jan 2011 from <http://www.pco-bcp.gc.ca/index.asp?lang=eng&page=information&sub=publications&doc=gdm-gsm/doc-eng.htm>.

26   Government of Canada Treasury Board of Canada Secretariat, *Policy on Learning, Training and Development*, retrieved on 1 Jan 2006, retrieved on 11 Nov 2011 from <http://www.tbs-sct.gc.ca/pol/doc-eng.aspx?id=12405&section=text#cha1>.

27   Department of National Defence, *DAOD 5031-0, Learning and Professional Development*, 31 Jan 2003, retrieved on 11 Nov 2011 from <http://admfincs.mil.ca/admfincs/subjects/daod/5031/0_e.asp>.

28   Department of National Defence, *DAOD 5031-50, Civilian Continuous Learning and Professional Development*, 30 Jan 2004 <http://admfincs.mil.ca/admfincs/subjects/daod/5031/50_e.asp>.

29   Department of National Defence, *Civilian Learning and Professional Development Evaluation Framework*, retrieved on 20 Jan 2011 on <http://hr.ottawa-hull.mil.ca/hrciv/documents/pdf/Civ_LPD_Evaluation_Framework_e.pdf>.

30   Government of Canada, Treasury Board of Canada Secretariat, *Policy on Management, Resources and Results Structures*, retrieved on 23 Feb 2010 from <http://www.tbs-sct.gc.ca/pol/doc-eng.aspx?id=18218&section=text#cha1>.

31   Treasury Board of Canada Secretariat, *TB Management Accountability Framework*, retrieved on 31 Dec 2010 from <http://www.tbs-sct.gc.ca/maf-crg/index-eng.asp>.

32   Department of National Defence, *Director General Learning and Professional Development - Welcome*, retrieved on 5 Jan 2011 from <http://hr.ottawa-hull.mil.ca/hrciv/dglpd/dlpdsp/plp/en/home_e.asp?reference=110970001>.

33   Department of National Defence, *Guide to Civilian Personal Learning Plans (PLPs)- April 2011*, retrieved on 16 Nov 2011 from <http://hr.ottawa-hull.mil.ca/hrciv/documents/pdf/plp_guide_e.pdf>.

34   Government of Canada, Treasury Board of Canada Secretariat, *Policy on Learning, Training, and Development*, retrieved on 1 Jan 2006 from <http://www.tbs-sct.gc.ca/pol/doc-eng.aspx?id =12405&section=text#cha4>.

35   Department of National Defence, *ADM(HR-Civ) Directive on Access to Second Language Training*, retrieved on 15 Nov 2011 from <http://hr.ottawa-hull.mil.ca/hrciv/documents/word/ SLT_directive_e.doc>.

36   Department of National Defence, *Director General Civilian Human Resources Management Operations – Welcome*, retrieved on 20 Dec 2010 from <http://hr.ottawa-hull.mil.ca/hrciv/ dgchrmo/lcc/en/home_e.asp?reference=110850001>.

37   Canada, Department of Justice, *Canada School of Public Service Act* (1991, c.16), 4.(f), retrieved on 16 Nov 2011 from <http://laws.justice.gc.ca/eng/acts/C-10.13/page-2.html#h-4>.

38   Government of Canada, Treasury Board of Canada Secretariat, *Policy on Learning, Training, and Development*, 1 Jan 1 2006, retrieved on 21 November 2011, from <http://www.tbs-sct. gc.ca/pol/doc-eng.aspx?id=12405&section=text#cha4>.

39   Department of National Defence, *Defence Learning network project*, retrieved on 4 Feb 2011 from <http://cmp-cpm.forces.mil.ca/dln-rad/index-eng.asp>.

40   P. Derek Hughes and Alison Campbell, *Learning and Development Outlook 2009: Learning in Tough Times* (Canada: The Conference Board of Canada, 2009), 6. See also: <http://www.ntab. on.ca/wp-content/uploads/downloads/2010/02/LearningDevelopment2009v1.pdf>.

41   Department of National Defence, *DND Mentoring Program - Mentoring at DND*, retrieved on 4 Jan 2011 from <http://hr.ottawa-hull.mil.ca/hrciv/dglpd/dlpdps/mentoring/en/home_e. asp?reference=111020011>.

42   Treasury Board of Canada Secretariat, *A Leadership Development Framework for the Public Service of Canada*, retrieved on 21 Jan 2011 from <http://www.tbs-sct.gc.ca/chro-dprh/ldf-cpl-eng.asp#Toc234979998>.

43   Department of National Defence, *Leadership Development - Director Civilian Executive Services*, retrieved on 5 Jan 2011 from <http://hr.ottawa-hull.mil.ca/hrciv/dgcesp/dces/en/ home_e.asp?reference=110480169>.

CHAPTER 12

LEARNING ABOUT ORGANIZATIONAL LEARNING IN DEFENCE

Dr. Grazia Scoppio

Organizations learn only through individuals who learn.
Individual learning does not guarantee organizational learning.
But without it no organizational learning occurs.[1]

Organizations, just like individuals, should never stop learning. As individuals, we commit to lifelong learning in order to progress in our careers, become better people and avoid repeating mistakes. This learning can occur consciously, unconsciously, formally, informally, through education, training, self-study or experience. If we stop learning, we fail to improve in our jobs and in life. The same is true for organizations. Given that organizations are made up of people, they need to draw on individuals' learning in order to continuously improve and evolve as institutions, remain relevant, and avoid becoming obsolete. Translating individual learning into organizational learning, however, is a challenge that many organizations face and struggle with. Organizational learning is difficult to achieve due to several factors that can include: insufficient understanding of these concepts; unclear leadership guidance; not enough support; lack of buy-in; scarce human and financial resources; time limitations; and inadequate enabling processes (i.e., lessons learned and knowledge management processes).

The Department of National Defence and the Canadian Forces have put in place strategic guidance, lessons learned directives and processes, and a knowledge management system to support organizational learning. However, there are still some challenges and gaps that need to be addressed (i.e., limited resources, inadequate knowledge management tools, and lack of buy-in from the Defence community).[2] Ultimately, it is critical for the DND/CF to further and fully embrace a culture that fosters individual and collective learning, knowledge sharing, and learning from experience, in order to become a true learning organization.

Although there are separate bodies of literature unique to organizational learning, lessons learned and knowledge management, these concepts and related practices are interlinked and overlap each other; that is to say, lessons learned and knowledge management are key processes to enable successful organizational learning.

Organizational Learning

Organizational learning is not a new idea and numerous definitions are found in the literature. Two American scholars, Donald Schon, a professional learning theorist, and Chris Argyris, an organizational behaviour expert, were among the first to write about organizational learning and defined it as "the detection and correction of error".[3]

Notwithstanding this important contribution, it was Peter Senge, an American engineer and world expert in organizational development, who made the concept of organizational learning vastly popular. In his seminal book *The Fifth Discipline: The Art and Practice of the Learning Organization*, he defined a learning organization as one:

> …where people continually expand their capacity to create the results they truly desire, where new and expansive patterns of thinking are nurtured, where collective aspiration is set free, and where people are continually learning to see the whole together.[4]

Senge developed a model that can be applied to any organization, including DND/CF, to help it transform into a true learning organization. His model includes five "disciplines", that is to say, principles and practices that we study, master and can integrate into our lives:

- Personal mastery, which involves clarifying and deepening our vision, focusing energies, developing patience, and seeing reality objectively;

- Mental models, which are assumptions and generalizations that influence how we see and understand the world and how we act;

- Building a shared vision, that is to say, having commitment and engagement rather than compliance;

- Team learning, which means establishing a dialogue and truly thinking together without making assumptions; and

- Systems thinking, the fifth discipline that integrates the other four: in other words, the ability to think in a holistic way about complex systems and the interrelationships within systems.[5]

Simply put, organizational learning is about people learning and sharing their knowledge and experience. In the context of the DND/CF, personal mastery applies to the competence of its members, developed through career-long training, education, self-development and experiential learning. To do so requires that DND/CF members develop the ability to question deeply ingrained mental models or assumptions that could hinder positive change in the organization. They also must be open to innovation and new ideas, put aside old ways of thinking, develop shared goals, and work together as a team to achieve that goal. Finally, organizations are complex systems; therefore, DND/CF personnel members need to develop the ability to think holistically, to comprehend and address the whole, and to examine the interrelationship between the parts.

There is a wide range of activities and initiatives related to organizational learning, lessons learned and knowledge management occurring within the DND/CF. As a result, a certain level of success has been achieved in these areas to include the promulgation of an organizational learning strategy; the development of a knowledge management system; and, the on-going use of after action reviews and lessons learned reports in operations and exercises.

Despite the progress made, there remain some deficiencies in these areas, as revealed by two studies conducted by the Canadian Defence Academy.[6] These deficiencies include: lack of budgetary authority; insufficient human resources; deficient software management tools; and unclear future direction. In addition, organizational learning concepts are not always well understood, nor are the linkages between organizational learning, lessons learned and knowledge management. Further, lessons learned processes are rarely used outside of operations. The new DND/CF Organizational Learning Strategy states:

> Although many organizational learning initiatives and programs are in place, many leaders are not aware of the opportunities that are offered. As a result, many of the programs are not being used to the extent that

they could be. Overall, organizational learning remains a poorly under-stood concept throughout much of DND/CF.[7]

As such, there is acknowledgement within Defence leadership that organiza-tional learning was initially seen only as a conceptual framework at the strategic level, and was not clearly understood nor linked to processes at the operational and tactical level (i.e., such as lessons learned and knowledge management).

More recently, efforts have been made to establish firm linkages between these concepts and related processes. These connections are well illustrated in an arti-cle by Lieutenant-Colonel Christina Evans and Michel Lavallée of the Directorate of Defence Strategic Management (DDSM), Chief of Programme, responsible for leading and coordinating the DND/CF Organizational Learning Working Group and other related activities:

> Organizational learning is about learning from experience and learning from others in order to do things better. Within Defence, the lessons learned process and after-action reviews allow units to learn from expe-rience (their own and others'), to avoid repeating errors and to build on successes, and can be used to enhance organizational learning. We all know that these tools have proven their value in operations—lives have been saved—but they can be applied in other settings as well.[8]

Evans and Lavallée also provide practical examples of successful information sharing and knowledge management within Defence. For example, the new *Counter Improvised Explosive Device Task Force Web Site* allows personnel to share and access the latest information about IEDs, request specific information, and provide feedback to the task force. As a second example, the Defence de-partment remains concerned with the future loss of knowledge that may occur as the Baby Boomers retire. To prevent this, various organizations within Defence are using knowledge transfer tools to identify critical at-risk knowledge, as one element of succession planning.

The DND/CF Organizational Learning Working Group in itself represents an ex-cellent example of information sharing. As mentioned, it is headed by DDSM on behalf of the Vice Chief of the Defence Staff (VCDS) who is the Defence Team's Champion for organizational learning. The working group meets on a regu-lar basis throughout the year and is attended by representatives of Level One organizations, and a few Level Two, across the DND/CF.[9] Recently, the working group revised the 2008 DND/CF Organizational Learning Strategy and Guidelines; in 2010 the new strategy and guidelines were approved and disseminated.[10] In the new strategy documents, organizational learning is defined as:

> The capability or processes within an organization to create, acquire, capture and share knowledge, skills or attitude. It involves the intentional use of learning processes at the individual, group and system level to find new and better ways of achieving the organizational mission.[11]

The Organizational Learning Strategy aims to achieve the following six goals:

a. **Enhance Collaboration** – through the interactions of people actively sharing data, information, knowledge, and concepts when working together toward a common purpose;

b. **Manage Content Effectively** – using document and record management to allow users to easily find content previously created in order to leverage it;

c. **Learn from Our Own Experience** – reviewing and assessing successes and failures to increase efficiency and prevent failure;

d. **Learn from Other Organizations** – looking outside our environment and studying the experience of similar organizations to gain insights and new perspectives;

e. **Leverage Our Knowledge** – ensuring critical knowledge is not lost through retirements, employee relocation, job changes and recruitment by other organizations; and

f. **Foster a Culture of Continuous Learning and Innovation** – empowering employees to think, ask questions, and participate actively.[12]

The strategy also includes clear outcomes and practical illustrations of how to achieve these outcomes. For example, the expected outcome of the first goal is to use collaboration as a "knowledge-multiplier" in order to improve efficiency, innovation and decision-making. This outcome can be achieved by promoting and rewarding participation in internal and external networks, communities of practice and other collaborative organizations to facilitate the exchange of knowledge. As well, the DND/CF should exploit the use of online tools to facilitate collaboration and the exchange of knowledge (e.g., DNDLearn – the DND/CF learning platform, SharePoint, the Knowledge Management System, wikis, blogs, and expertise locator systems).[13] Finally, the strategy includes a section on evaluation to provide direction on how to assess progress through performance management mechanisms.

Lessons Learned

As mentioned, lessons learned processes and related tools are enablers to organizational learning and many organizations involved in operational missions have lessons learned systems in place. In military organizations, lessons learned systems are critical to operations: lessons learned in theatre, if addressed in training, can help to better prepare troops, and ultimately save lives. There are also lessons learned systems in various military organizations, at the national and intra-national level, such as: the United States Center for Army Lessons Learned; the French Army Research and Lessons Learned Division; and the North American Treaty Organization Joint Analysis and Lessons Learned Centre.[14]

The National Aeronautics and Space Administration (NASA) was among the first organizations to recognize the importance of learning from the past to ensure future mission success (through the use of various mechanisms to capture and disseminate lessons learned).[15] However, a few mission failures have occurred and NASA has recognized that some past lessons were not always being applied to current programs and projects. Consequently, the General Accounting Office was asked to assess the effectiveness of lessons learned policies, procedures and systems, and make recommendations for improvement.[16] It was hoped that these efforts will diminish if not eliminate future mission failures.

In the DND/CF, formal lessons learned policies and joint doctrine are in place to define the context, requirements, authorities and process for lessons learned in Defence.[17] Lessons learned have been widely adopted in current operations and exercises, such as the recent mission to Afghanistan and the 2010 Vancouver Winter Olympics (e.g., using after action reviews). According to the DND/CF policy a lessons learned is defined as:

> ...the adding of value to an existing body of knowledge, or seeking to correct deficiencies in areas of concepts, policy, doctrine, training, equipment or organizations, by providing feedback and follow-on action.[18]

The lessons learned process involves five main steps: observe; collect; analyze; direct and recommend; and change.[19] Therefore, a lesson is not considered learned, until a change has been directed, and implemented.

There are well established lessons learned organizations in the various CF Environmental Commands and Joint Commands including the Army, Royal Canadian Navy and Royal Canadian Air Force, Canada Command, Canada Expeditionary Force Command and the Strategic Joint Staff. The CF Joint Warfare Center Lessons Learned Branch, on behalf of the Chief of Force Development, provides governance and coordination of the DND/CF lessons learned community, including heading the DND/CF Lessons Learned Working Group, in support of the Department's goals as a learning organization.[20] The DND/CF Lessons Learned Working Group, similar to the Organizational Learning Working Group, includes representatives from various organizations who usually meet bi-annually.

At the tactical level, the DND/CF has become very effective at learning lessons from operations, such as Afghanistan, in order to identify deficiencies in procedures or equipment in theatre, look for root causes, recommend solutions, and implement changes. Addressing strategic level lessons has proven to be significantly more difficult, as stated in a document of the Strategic Joint Staff:

> At "higher" levels, learning lessons often involves addressing issues that span multiple Commands/Departments or implementing either long-term or large-scale solutions. Further, validating that changes have had the desired impact can be elusive. Nonetheless, a great many strategic-level lessons are being learned from CF Operations, and the trend is improving.[21]

Not surprisingly, some examples of identified, but unresolved, strategic-level lessons fall in the area of Whole-of-Government operations, such as inter-departmental information sharing, planning and cooperation. The fact that not all civilian government departments have well established lessons learned organizations and processes likely compounds the problem of inter-agency lessons learned implementation. In addition, even when lessons learned processes are in place in Other Government Departments (OGDs), the lessons are not always shared as various departments have different knowledge management tools.

Knowledge Management

Also related to organizational learning and lessons learned, is the concept of knowledge management. This term appears to have been first used by Karl Wiig, an American management consultant who has wrote extensively on the discipline of knowledge management.[22] Based on his theory, knowledge is the foundation of the whole enterprise; people in organizations create, represent and use knowledge; and organizations must manage this knowledge through specific methods and practical approaches.

Knowledge management includes three phases: the construction, representation, and transfer of knowledge. Knowledge construction refers to the creation of knowledge within an organization and includes both social and scientific inputs. This knowledge is then represented through various means, both formally (e.g. programs, documents, databases, etc.) and informally (e.g. people's interactions, social networks, etc.). The last and most difficult phase is knowledge transfer; that is the communication of knowledge from one individual or group to another. What makes this difficult is that while some knowledge can be explicit and easily taught tacit knowledge is less teachable and generally more complex. According to Michael Polanyi, a Hungarian-British scientist who coined the term tacit knowledge, people "can know more than they can tell".[23] Polanyi believes that most of the knowledge people possess cannot be put into words, such as sensory information about what see around us; for example, attempting to describe the face of someone we know. In the context of organizations, transferring tacit knowledge is challenging due to the fact that it is often informal knowledge, its difficult to codify, it includes employees' experiences, thoughts and corporate memory. On the other hand, explicit knowledge is formal, can be categorized, easily communicated and shared; it can include books, documents, databases, and policies. In other words, the tacit knowledge of an organization such as the DND/CF is arguably the richest and most valuable body of knowledge. Unfortunately, it is also the most difficult to capture and share.

The DND/CF Knowledge Management System (KMS) is the "official" lessons learned tool for the Defence Department. The goal of the DND/CF KMS is to:

…track the staffing of observations and LL [Lessons Learned] derived from CF operations, training, exercises and experiments. It is a tool used to monitor the progress of the action plan from the identification of an issue to a Lesson Identified and finally a Lesson Learned as endorsed by the appropriate Commander.[24]

However, not all lessons learned organizations within Defence utilize it. For example, the Canadian Army uses the Army Lessons Tracker as the repository of potential lessons and best practices identified in operations. It should also be noted that the KMS is mainly used by organizations responsible for lessons learned, such as the CF Joint Warfare Center Lessons Learned Branch; the broader Defence community employs other tools to work collaboratively and share information, such as Microsoft SharePoint,

Discussion

There is considerable activity in DND/CF in the areas of organizational learning, lessons learned and knowledge management that includes the development of policies, doctrine and tools. Notwithstanding these positive developments, there are several issues that require attention as highlighted in the two aforementioned research studies conducted on behalf of the Canadian Defence Academy.[25] Some of the challenges include:

- Limited resources, both human and financial, allocated to organizational learning and lessons learned;

- People's inability or unwillingness to share knowledge with others because they believe "knowledge is power";[26]

- Lack of time to dedicate to organizational learning and lessons learned due to the priority of operations;

- Loss of corporate memory caused by high turnover, people changing jobs or retiring, and/or not being able to transfer their knowledge;

- Lack of buy-in from the wider DND/CF community, rooted in the belief that organizational learning and lessons learned are the sole responsibility of specific organizations;

- Limited understanding of the benefits of organizational learning and lessons learned, since "people don't know what they don't know";

- The DND/CF KMS being used primarily by lessons learned personnel instead of the whole Defence community;

- The KMS is not self-intuitive or user-friendly, and consequently, not exploited enough; and

- Knowledge is often not shared across OGDs due to the inability or unwillingness to do so: this results in knowledge stove-pipes and it is in contrast with the current Whole-of-Government approach to operations.

In addition to these challenges, there are social trends that will further impact the ability of the DND/CF to retain corporate knowledge, transfer knowledge, and remember the lessons learned. A large segment of the DND/CF personnel are of the Baby Boomer generation (born between 1946 and 1964); thus, they are considering or are close to retirement. Consequently, many employees who have been educated/trained, acquired considerable experience and corporate knowledge, are leaving the organization and, in many cases, it is difficult to manage this loss of knowledge efficiently. As this cohort retires, there is great potential for a significant loss of knowledge and as a result, the increased probability of repeating mistakes. The problem is compounded when personnel are not replaced, or are replaced without a proper handover to transfer their corporate knowledge. This is especially true in Defence organizations where military members rotate every two or three years with little or no time to conduct a proper handover. Often the civilian and reserve personnel are the keepers of the corporate "tacit" knowledge.

It is particularly difficult to capture tacit knowledge; it is simpler to manage and transfer explicit knowledge, although even explicit knowledge is at times not easily retrievable, unless it is efficiently managed. There are various systems or "tools" to capture, store, and share explicit knowledge. These systems have had varying degrees of effectiveness (e.g. KMS, shared drives, Microsoft SharePoint, databases, etc); however, there also needs to be a systematic way to capture and transfer tacit knowledge.

Finally, it is essential to foster an organizational culture that encourages and facilitates individual and collective learning. The assumption that an automatic improvement in performance will occur by institutionalizing organizational learning through formal policies, processes and tools, is flawed. While it is important to have the right policies, programs and tools in place, developing the right organizational culture is essential for success. If there are cultural barriers, such as resistance to knowledge sharing and intolerance for mistakes, organizational learning will not occur. This is true for any organization, even those with mature lessons learned and organizational learning systems, such as NASA. For example, a NASA survey identified that cultural barriers exist to the sharing of lessons learned and there is a need to "adopt a culture that admits frankly to what really worked and didn't work".[27]

Summary

While much progress has been made in the areas of organizational learning, lessons learned and knowledge management within Defence, much remains to be done. This reality is amplified when considering the impending loss of the Baby Boomers tacit knowledge as they retire. A clear vision, strong leadership support and appropriate resources are needed to successfully institutionalize these processes and develop the right enabling tools. In doing so, the organization will have created the necessary conditions to continuously learn and evolve.

These processes, however, should not be limited to select groups. Rather, they should be integrated into all areas of Defence at every level: tactical, operational and strategic. In the context of Whole-of-Government operations, more sharing of knowledge and lessons among various government departments is required. By sharing information, all organizations can better detect problems, determine the causes, and find solutions to address and avoid future mistakes in the future. Best practices adopted by others should also be shared and, where appropriate, implemented within one's own organization.

In addition, personnel must be informed and educated on these concepts and processes, and have a clear understanding of their importance to improve current and future operations as well as non-operational activities and programs. All personnel, regardless of rank or position, need to be engaged so that each person can see: "how can my knowledge and experience contribute to the success of the organization?'"

To become a true learning organization, the DND/CF must foster a culture that values and supports: individual and collective learning; the creation, capturing, and transferring of knowledge; learning from experience; and leveraging best practices. If we agree that "knowledge is power", then sharing knowledge is even more empowering, as it ensures that lessons learned are not forgotten.

---

1   Peter Senge, *The Fifth Discipline: The Art and Practice of the Learning Organization* (New York, NY: Currency Doubleday, 1990), 139.

2   The Defence community, also referred to as the Defence Team, includes military and civilian members of DND/CF organizations.

3   Chris Argyris and Donald Schön, *Organizational Learning: A Theory of Action perspective* (Reading, MA: Addison-Wesley, 1978), 2.

4   Senge, 3.

5   Ibid.

6   Andrew B. Godefroy, *Lessons Learned About Lessons Learned, an Analysis of Policies, Organizations, and Processes in the Department of National Defence and the Canadian Forces* (Kingston, ON: National Defence, Canadian Defence Academy, Directorate of Learning and Innovation, 2009), retrieved on 15 Nov 2011 from <http://www.cda-acd.forces.gc.ca/LITER/doc/Reports%20-%20LL%20Research/LL%20About%20LL/LL%20About%20LL%20report.pdf>.; Roger Vandomme, *From Lessons Identified to Lessons Learned, A Proposition for Integration of Lessons Learned into Canadian Forces Professional Development* (Kingston, ON: National Defence, Canadian Defence Academy, Directorate of Learning and Innovation, 2010), retrieved on 15 Nov 2011 from <http://www.cda-acd.forces.gc.ca/LITER/doc/LL_Integration_into_PD_FINAL.pdf>.

7   Department of National Defence, "Department of National Defence & Canadian Forces Organizational Learning Strategy", *Knowledge Management (DDSM) - Organizational Learning*, retrieved on 15 Nov 2011 from <http://vcds.mil.ca/sites/CProg/Resources/DDSM/KM/Revised%20Strategy%20and%20Guidelines/Revised%20Org%20Lrg%20Strategy%20version%201.7_%204%20Oct%202010.pdf>.

8   Lieutenant Colonel Christina Evans and Michel Lavallée, "Organizational Learning and Gold Medals", *The Maple Leaf*, Vol. 13, No. 6, (Feb. 2010), retrieved on 15 Nov 2011 from <http://www.forces.gc.ca/site/commun/ml-fe/article-eng.asp?id=5947>.

9   Level One organizations are responsible directly to the Chief of the Defence Staff and/or the Deputy Minister of Defence and include: Chief of the Maritime Staff, Chief of the Land Staff, Chief of the Air Staff, Vice Chief of the Defence Staff, Chief of Military Personnel, and various Assistant Deputy Ministers. Level Two organizations are those reporting to their corresponding Level One. For example, the Canadian Defence Academy is a Level Two organization reporting to Chief of Military Personnel.

10   Department of National Defence, "Department of National Defence & Canadian Forces Organizational Learning Strategy"; National Defence, "Department of National Defence & Canadian

Forces Organizational Learning Guidelines", *Knowledge Management (DDSM) - Organizational Learning*, retrieved on 15 Nov 2011 from <http://vcds.mil.ca/sites/CProg/Resources/DDSM/KM/Revised%20Strategy%20and%20Guidelines/Org%20Lrg%20Guidelines%20Rev%20v5.5_4%20Oct%202010%20with%20new%20definitions.pdf>.

11   Department of National Defence, "Department of National Defence & Canadian Forces Organizational Learning Guidelines", A-3.

12   Ibid., 6.

13   Ibid., 7.

14   United States Army Combined Arms Center, *Center for Army Lessons Learned*, retrieved on 15 Nov 2011 from <http://usacac.army.mil/cac2/call/index.asp>.; Ministère de la Défense et des anciens combattants, Centre de doctrine d'emploi des forces, "The Research and Lessons Learned Division", retrieved on 15 Nov 2011 from <http://www.cdef.terre.defense.gouv.fr/organismes/drex/drex_english.htm>; NATO Joint Analysis and Lessons Learned Center, *Welcome to NATO's Joint Analysis & Lessons Learned Centre (JALLC)*, retrieved on 15 Nov 2011 from <http://www.jallc.nato.int/>.

15   NASA Engineering Network, *Overview*, retrieved on 15 Nov 2011 from <http://llis.nasa.gov/llis/search/home.jsp>.

16   United States Government, General Accounting Office, *NASA: Better Mechanisms Needed for Sharing Lessons Learned*, GAO-02-195 (Washington, D.C.: United States Government, 30 January 2002), retrieved on 15 Nov 2011 from <http://www.makingstories.net/NASA_case_study_knowledge_management_stories.pdf>.

17   Department of National Defence, "DAOD 8010-0, Lessons Learned", *National Defence and the Canadian Forces*, retrieved on 15 Nov 2011 from <http://www.admfincs-smafinsm.forces.gc.ca/dao-doa/8000/8010-0-eng.asp>; Department of National Defence, "DAOD 8010-1, Operational Lessons Learned Process", *National Defence and the Canadian Forces*, retrieved on 15 Nov 2011 from <http://www.admfincs.forces.gc.ca/dao-doa/8000/8010-1-eng.asp>; Government of Canada, Chief of the Defence Staff, *Canadian Forces Joint Doctrine Note JDN 04/08: The Lessons Learned (LL) Process*, retrieved on 15 Nov 2011 from <http://cfd.mil.ca/websites/Resources/dgfda/Pubs/CF%20Joint%20Doctrine%20Notes/JDN_04_08_%20Lessons_Learned_Process_En.pdf>.

18   Department of National Defence, "DAOD 8010-0, Lessons Learned", 1.

19   Department of National Defence, "DAOD 8010-1, Operational Lessons Learned Process".

20   Department of National Defence, "Lessons Learned - CFWC Lessons Learned Mission", National Defence and the Canadian Forces, retrieved on 15 Nov 2011 from <http://www.cfd-cdf.forces.gc.ca/sites/page-eng.asp?page=1688>.

21   Department of National Defence, *Strategic Lessons Learned from CF Operations*, Discussion Primer, Strategic Joint Staff – Internal document (Ottawa, ON: Government of Canada, February 2009), 1.

22   Karl Wiig, *Knowledge Management Methods: Practical Approaches to Managing Knowledge* (Arlington, TX: Schema Press, 1995); Karl Wiig, *Knowledge Management: The Central Management Focus for Intelligent-Acting Organizations* (Arlington, TX: Schema Press, 1994); Karl Wiig, *Knowledge Management Foundations: Thinking about Thinking – How Organizations Create, Represent and Use Knowledge* (Arlington, TX: Schema Press, 1993).

23   Michael Polanyi, *The Tacit Dimension* (London, UK: Routledge & Kegan Paul), 4.

24   Department of National Defence, "KMS - Knowledge Management System", JOALL, retrieved on 15 Nov 2011 from <http://cfd.mil.ca/sites/page-eng.asp?page=1744>.

25   Godefroy, *Lessons Learned About Lessons Learned, An Analysis of Policies, Organizations, and Processes in the Department of National Defence and the Canadian Forces*; Vandomme, *From Lessons Identified to Lessons Learned, A Proposition for Integration of Lessons Learned into Canadian Forces Professional Development.*

26   "Knowledge is power" means that new knowledge, inventions and discoveries are the forces that drive history; this idea was developed by Sir Francis Bacon an English lawyer, historian and philosopher who wrote on the advancements of learning and technological progress. See: David Simpson, *Francis Bacon (1561-1626)*, Internet Encyclopedia of Philosophy – A Peer-reviewed Academic Resource, retrieved on 15 Nov 2011 from < http://www.iep.utm.edu/bacon/>.

27   United States Government, General Accounting Office, 3.

PART III

EDUCATION

CHAPTER 13

PERSPECTIVES AND THEORIES ON TEACHING AND LEARNING

Dr. Beverlie Dietze

When educators and learners are asked to describe teaching and learning, it becomes clear that there is not a consistent response among them. Some suggest that effective teaching is being able to plan and deliver a lecture that will provide students with key information needed to advance their knowledge on a particular subject. Others suggest that teaching and learning is about guiding students in the examination of theory to application. And others view teaching and learning as building a learning community that supports individuals and groups in acquiring new knowledge, abilities, and skills needed to perform particular roles. The myriad of perspectives underlines the reality that teaching and learning is an evolving process. It changes as society changes.

The blueprint for higher education was originally developed to meet the needs of an egalitarian and industrial economy.[1] Individuals learned what they required for adulthood during their early years through formal schooling or with adult role models. Academic programs were the "delivery systems" whereby "experts" transmitted the knowledge on the subject matter to the student. As society evolved and the level of change accelerated, the learning acquired during youth was insufficient to meet the diversified knowledge demands necessary to function in the new world. The industrial-based economy was replaced by an informational-based economy, which in turn was replaced by our present knowledge-based society. In this new age, there are calls for educators to incorporate technology into learning environments and to be familiar with the up-to-date research on how learning occurs. Educational institutions require accountability processes, and teaching and learning techniques that address community and individual diversity that put global learning into practice. Employers and consumers expect learning environments to be "relevant, competitive, accessible, and accountable" as lifelong learning becomes the reality for all adults whether you are an educator, auto mechanic, a soldier, or a volunteer in the community.[2]

The paradigm shift in adult education is not only being influenced by the information and knowledge-based society, it is being ignited by the revolutionary field of cognitive science. New research on how learning occurs and how learning options can be best designed and facilitated to meet individual and group needs is changing the face of institutional education and workplace learning. The design and delivery of curricula, as well as the role of the learner, is having a direct impact on the theoretical framework for teaching and learning experiences. For example, adults now enter learning venues expressing their expectations, identifying what their needs are, and knowing what type of learning environment will best support their learning style. Learners bring a range of knowledge and technical skills to the environment. They expect facilitators to challenge them with new knowledge and skills that they may effectively transfer to their workplace.

One of the key attributes of the Canadian Forces is their commitment to continuous learning for their members. For both internal and external educators, the learning audience is a diverse group. The diversity may include a multigenerational audience that presents differences in life and work experience, learning styles, culture, phase of career and rank achieved. As a result, educators require a variety of teaching and learning strategies that will address the needs of each member of the learning environment. For example, younger learners who have grown up with technology learn differently from older adults who are known as the technology immigrants. Younger learners come with specific expectations for their learning environment. As a result, the younger computer and TV student generation is influencing the new realities of teaching and learning in both the institutional setting and workplace environment. This student group does not tolerate learning environments that are lecture based. They require fast-paced interaction and entertainment. Mid-twenty and early thirty year-old students expect the learning experience to be relevant and consist of more than "theory dumping". They see education as a collaborative process rather than a "top down" teacher experience. And, older students require opportunities to share their knowledge and experience. They expect the details to be presented in a logical format from a subject expert and in a timely manner. Educators who develop skills in observations, assessment, teaching and learning methods, and flexibility in delivery strategies have the best success in meeting learner needs and the goals of the curriculum.

Educators and learners must also be cognizant of employer needs and expectation. Employers internal or external to the CF expect employees to join the workplace with critical thinking skills, problem solving skills, effective human interaction skills, and the ability to apply theory to application in a variety of situations. Research suggests that these skills are developed through interactive education rather than from a "top down, expert based" model for learning. Learning environments are no longer homogeneous, which makes the learning environment more complex. This chapter provides an introduction to a variety of teaching and learning theories and perspectives. This information forms the foundation for the developmental of one's philosophical orientation and teaching and learning practice.

In response to the changing educational tides, institutions and workplaces are in the midst of transforming their learning cultures. Many strategies are being utilized to respond to the needs of learners, including: applying new technology to teaching and learning; investing in curriculum that has defined learning outcomes, content, and assessment measures; building community and industry partnerships; and, adopting frameworks that support educational and human resource development objectives and processes. These changes require educators to continuously work with their learners to ensure that the learning environment will advance the level of learning that is conducive to the needs of the membership, the area of study, and the overall organizational goals and objectives.

A Framework for Teaching and Learning – Andragogy, Pedagogy, and Learning-Centred

There are many aspects in the literature on adult teaching and learning methodologies among educators about the most appropriate ways to implement teaching and learning.[3] At the same time, there is a body of literature that outlines the ongoing debate on whether adults, pre-adults and children learn in similar ways or if learning principles for each age group are distinctly different. As some educators grapple with the meaning of characteristics and needs of learners, there are other adult educators who suggest there are defined differences and approaches between teaching adults and children, resulting in them adopting an andragogical approach to teaching adults. They assume that this is the only model that should be used for executing learning. Other adult educators suggest that some subjects require the learners to receive information, (such as specialized skills and processes) in a more traditional, pedagogical model. More recently, there has been a surge in the literature suggesting the need for adult educators to return to a cognitive, constructivist educational approach that was initially favoured by philosophers including John Dewey, Leo Vygotsky and Jean Piaget. As one reviews the literature, it becomes clear that educational theory, beliefs, and practice are not uniform among researchers, theorists, practitioners, or institutions. Rather, there are many factors and facets that influence one's framework for teaching and learning.

Most adult educators are influenced by one's past experience, culture, learning style, beliefs, and subject matter expertise. Adult educators benefit from examining a variety of perspectives on teaching and learning as it contributes to them determining their philosophical foundation. Being able to articulate one's philosophical beliefs is essential as one's philosophy guides practice – it establishes a foundation from which all actions and experiences emanate. A personal philosophy informs practice. The concepts of andragogy, pedagogy, and learning-centred are presented. Think about how each of these concepts and orientations influence your values and beliefs about teaching and learning.

The Concept of Andragogy

The term "andragogy", originally used by the German educator Alexander Kapp[4] in 1833, is defined as the process of engaging adult learners in learning experiences. The eminent adult educator, Malcolm Knowles rejuvenated the term in the late 1970s and defined it as "the art and science of helping adults learn." He contrasted andragogy with pedagogy known as "the art and science of helping children learn."[5] He distinguished adult learning from pre-adult schooling and children's learning because he believed the more life experience one has, the more knowledge and skills that individual has to bring to the learning environment.

Over the past twenty years andragogy has become an alternative approach to a teacher-directed education known as pedagogy. Andragogy now refers to a learner-focused education for people of all ages. In this context, learner-centred refers to educators recognizing that each learner comes to the environment with internal needs and a unique learning style. Educators practicing an andragogical approach design learning experiences that build confidence, support diverse learning styles, take away fears of the unknown, and support learners in acquiring answers to their questions regarding the content and the process of implementation.

Knowles outlined six assumptions that are foundational concepts to be considered when planning programs or learning experiences with adults.[6] They are:

1. Self-concept: As adults mature their self-concept moves from being dependent toward one of being a self-directed human being.

2. Experience: As adults mature they accumulate experiences that become an increasing resource for learning.

3. Readiness to learn: As adults mature their readiness to learn becomes oriented to their developmental tasks associated with their social roles.

4. Orientation to learning: As adults mature their time perspective changes from one of postponed application of knowledge to immediacy of application. Accordingly their orientation toward learning shifts from one of subject-centredness to one of problem centredness.

5. Motivation to learn: As adults mature their motivation to learn becomes more internal than external.[7]

6. The need to know about learning: As adults engage in learning, they need to know why they are learning it and how it will help them.

Knowles suggested that each of these assumptions requires examination when designing, implementing, and assessing learning experiences with adults.[8] For example, in order to support the adult learner in exhibiting independence and self-directedness toward their learning, the learning environment should cause "adults to feel accepted, respected, and supported"; further, there should exist "a spirit of mutuality between teachers and students as joint inquirers."[9] Knowles identified that four of the five key assumptions are relevant to adults and children. One of the primary differences between working with children and with adults is that children have fewer life experiences, beliefs, and perspectives to draw upon and therefore require some structure and curricula that will provide foundational information from which they build upon. Adults generally have more life experiences, knowledge and perspectives to use in connecting new information to their knowledge base.

Educators clearly recognize that there are definite teaching and learning differences used when facilitating and leading children's learning experiences and adult learning. Children require foundational information and skills before they can grasp more complex skills. Educators lead the child in gaining concrete foundational information through skill development techniques such as guided exploration experiences, memorization and practice and drill exercises. For example, children are required to learn social communication skills including listening, taking turns, and being respectful in their dialogue with others. In order to support children in developing these skills, using pedagogical approaches, educators ensure that the children perform to a specified standard. This may require the adult to lead them toward establishing predetermined life skills by correcting them and redirecting them until the children have internalized the concepts of what is right and what is wrong in social communication.

Educators lead adults in different ways from children. Adults require educators that lead them by coaching, supporting, and offering them a respectful environment that will allow them to practice, make mistakes, evaluate, gain new information, and synthesize the information and new learning with previous learning. Adults achieve more learning when they are led by leaders who allow and encourage them to discover new information and knowledge through experiential opportunities. Educators tap into adult learners' internal and external motivators in a formal learning situation.

As noted earlier, Knowles initially identified andragogy as helping adults learn and pedagogy as helping children learn. By 1984, Knowles altered his descriptors of andragogy and pedagogy. He identified pedagogy as a content model and andragogy as a process model. For example, adults are more motivated by and interested in specific projects and problems relevant to their work and career goals than discipline-oriented knowledge. A process model can become a motivator for adults through the authentic projects that connect new knowledge with previous knowledge and skills.

The distinction between content and process has merit among many educators and trainers; although not total congruence. Educators are increasingly interested in the relationship of learning and learning results that are achieved through both individual and group learning options that are prevalent in process learning models. For example, there are benefits in integrating knowledge areas such as economics and learning theory with culture, policy, group processes, and social cohesion. This approach mirrors the tenets of the social capital theory. Some studies on the social capital theory reveal that when groups learn collectively, they build a sense of trust, norms and networks which facilitate collective action. The group norm becomes reciprocity, which encourages bargaining, sharing of knowledge, and compromise; all skills necessary to prepare individuals for the workplace. Adults continuously gain and refine these skills with their life experience. Such skills are less likely to be exhibited in young children.

The content versus process models and debate stretches across the educational and organizational development and training domains. For example, human resource educational professors Joseph Kessels & Rob Poell suggest that andragogy, in conjunction with social capital theory transforms the workplace into a community of learning workplace.[10] The social capital theory based on "social networks, mutual trust, communities of practice, and relational forms of capital" combined with the principles of andragogy increase the quality in the facilitation of learning in the workplace. The quality increases because of the strong motivational aspects of self-directedness and the network of meaningful relationships. These combined components support the concept for learning to be integrated into the social contexts of the day-to-day work environment and with a group of learners.

Ralf St. Clair indicates that as "adult education programs have become more instrumental and employment focused, training and development in the business world have increasingly emphasized the holistic development of workers."[11] Consistent with the modern approach to the andragogy model, learners benefit from:

- Knowing why it is important for particular information to be learned;

- Connecting the topic to the learners' experiences;

- Having experience and support in transferring new learning to the workplace;

- Gaining skills in being able to find information and to work through what the information means; and

- Having facilitators who assist learners in overcoming inhibitions and behaviours that may be interfering with learning.

Many educators, including St. Clair, consider Knowles's six assumptions as good instructional practice for all ages, especially adults.[12] St. Clair indicates "It does not give us the total picture, nor is it a panacea for fixing adult learning practices. Rather, it constitutes one piece of the rich mosaic of adult learning."[13] Another piece of mosaic is ensuring that there is framework for teaching and learning, opportunities for problem-solving skills and critical thinking skills to be practiced and applied, and that the learning is just-in-time learning.[14]

It is important to make a distinction between just-in-case learning and just-in-time learning. Just-in-case learning describes learning that will be done in case a learner requires it in the future. This is consistent with the knowledge and skills in child related curricula, such as history courses. Just-in-time learning occurs as required to advance knowledge or skills needed to augment current practices or processes and to be able to conduct business in new ways. This just-in-time methodology is particularly important to areas that change or evolve at a rapid pace such as being able to integrate new technological processes as they become available. Finally, it has also been suggested that most adults are highly motivated when engaged in just-in-time learning that is needs based and facilitated by knowledgeable professionals.[15]

Much of the debate surrounding andragogy is whether to classify it as a theory of learning, principles of learning, or assumptions about how adults learn. There is no definitive answer to this question. In searching for meaning, however, individuals bring forth perspectives, ideologies, and assumptions; each of which strengthens individual and group discussions and beliefs about teaching and learning with adults.

The Concept of Pedagogy

Throughout history there have been varying views on what pedagogy is, what it means, and who it includes; that is, does it focus on children, adults or both? Despite the research conducted and literature available, pedagogy means different things to different educators. Giving meaning to the term is often influenced by one's experience, knowledge, and perspective about teaching and learning. For example, as identified earlier in this chapter, Knowles described pedagogy as the art or science of being a teacher and of educating children.[16] It has also been suggested that the educational literature in the United States, Canada, and the United Kingdom identifies the term "pedagogy" as being synonymous to "teaching". Pedagogy is described as a "catch-all term for such things as teaching procedures, teaching practice, instruction and so on."[17] Max Van Manen describes the concept of pedagogy encompassing more than teaching.[18] He sees it as the art and science of educating children, "focusing on the relationship between learning and teaching such that one does not exist as separate and distinct from the other."[19] In essence, the term pedagogy is influenced by a number of factors including educational background, experience in the educational domain, and philosophy about learning.

The adult education literature generally aligns the term pedagogy with the education of children not adults; although there are many educators working with adults who use the term pedagogy to describe teaching and learning rather than andragogy. This may be due in part to the educational backgrounds and experiences that educators have been exposed to.

The execution of a pedagogical philosophy is embedded in the adult's self-understanding about teaching and learning and how they view roles that educators and students in the learning environment. A large body of literature on pedagogy suggests students come to the learning environment ready to learn what their society believes they ought to learn. Students are generally dependent on the teacher, while teachers assume the responsibility for making decisions about what will be learned based on standardized, subject-centredness curricula. Teachers determine the content, the timing of content delivery and how the information will be delivered to the learners. The teacher is viewed as an authoritarian leader, directing the learning and evaluation based more on the experience of the teacher than on the knowledge and experience that learners bring to the learning environment.

Since the turn of the 21st century, various levels of governments and educational institutions both in Canada and the United States have rekindled their focus on examining how children learn and how institutions support children in acquiring the skills and knowledge deemed necessary for today's society. There is a movement for the more traditional teacher-directed learning strategies to be reconfigured so that children have access to a variety of learning strategies that support diverse learning styles and curricula outcomes. For example, professor Fred Korthagen indicates that many teachers are framing learning experiences based on a combination of factors including curricula and the teacher and student relationships and interests.[20] This personal approach between teachers and students "is crucial as identity formation and personal growth combine to shape the nature of pedagogy itself."[21] Many educators are advocating for this approach to be adopted across educational systems as this connectedness is aligned with student engagement and success. From an adult education perspective, if learners become accustomed to this type of learning strategy during their elementary and secondary school experiences, they will come to expect this as a normative process in their lifelong learning endeavours.

Finally, similar to the discussions on andragogy, there is evidence to suggest that the debate will continue among educators on the breadth and depth of what the pedagogical framework should look like in order to effectively meet the needs of learners and educators today.

The Concept of Learning-centred

Research on teaching and learning continuously brings forth new ideas, perspectives, and teaching and learning methodologies. Over the past fifteen years, one of the most prominent theoretical constructs being discussed in higher education is the concept of learning-centred education. Many writings suggest that learning-centred education has the potential to meet the diverse needs of learners and educators. Similar to the androgogical perspective, learning-centred teaching draws upon a variety of teaching and learning strategies that complement the learning outcomes to be met, the diverse learners within the learning community, and most importantly, offering learners ways to develop their knowledge, skills, and abilities, while being active participants in their developmental learning path. In essence, this discussion focuses on the principles of learning rather than teaching processes.

The learning-centred concept, with its roots in constructivism, experiential learning theories, and the progressive education movement of the 1900s is not entirely a new concept.[22] It is a resurgence of examining how individual people and groups of people learn. For example, Educator Howard Gardner identifies that "human minds do not all work in the same way, and human beings do not have the same cognitive strengths and weaknesses."[23] As educators examine the learning-centred perspective, the debate encompasses how to shift from a well engrained instructional model that focuses on teaching to one that emphasizes learning.[24] The learning-centred perspective places the student at the centre of the educational experience. It focuses on what students are expected to know and be able to do in the context of the field of study. The challenge for educators and institutions is to "not simply...offer instruction but instead to produce learning as an outcome."[25] This requires educators and learners to think about learning from an outcome based perspective – what is it at the end of a learning session that learners should know and be able to apply.

Learning-centred education differs from the learner-centred concept. Learner-centred implies that the learner has control over the content coverage, learning strategies, and assessment methodologies. Learning-centred education is built on the premise that a community of learners is established and that the learners and their facilitator explore topical issues within a carefully designed, scaffolded curricula with defined learning outcomes. Throughout the process, learning occurs on both an individual and collaborative process, with a major emphasis of theory and application being integrated. Learners acquire learning through the investigation of problem-based processes using general skills of inquiry, high levels of critical thinking, analysis, synthesis and evaluation of information and experimentation.

Although many researchers and educators view learning-centred as an innovative teaching and learning strategy, this social learning model is not new. John Dewey identified the importance of individuals having learning options in both a social setting and individually in the early 20th century.[26] He advocates that that social learning provides learners with more in-depth knowledge and experience because of the breadth of knowledge gained from others. Building on Dewey's perspective, contemporary learning-centred principles outlines the roles of teachers as guides and partners in learning. More specifically, the learning-centred framework identifies the following:

- Adults learn from a variety of teaching and learning strategies and by being active participants in the learning process.

- Adults learn at different rates and in different ways.[27]

- Adults benefit from a flexible, multi-faceted approach to learning which allows them to gain meaning and content knowledge through individual and interpersonal exploration, reflective of their learning style. Learners become co-producers of learning as they progressively take responsibility for their learning direction.

The term "the learning college" has also been used as a generic reference to all educational institutions and workplace learning venues, indicates that learning institutions must place "learning first and provides educational experiences for learners anyway, anyplace, anytime."[28] The learning college is structured on the following six key principles:

- The learning college creates substantive change in individual learners;

- The learning college engages learners as full partners in the learning process, with learners assuming primary responsibility for their own choices;

- The learning college creates and offers as many options for learning as possible;

- The learning college assists learners to form and participate in collaborative learning activities;

- The learning college defines the roles of learning facilitators by the needs of the learners; and

- The learning college and its learning facilitators succeed only when improved and expanded learning can be documented for its learners.

Learning-centred shifts the power from a practice of teacher-centredness to one that places the learner at the centre of the paradigm, with shared power between the learner and the educator. This architectural framework creates a learning environment that reflects established functions, structures, and activities that are active, creative, concrete, challenging, rigourous, and responsive to the various learner styles, needs, and rhythms of the learners. The educator becomes a partner in learning, guiding learners to discover the new learning needed to meet established learning outcomes.

Learning-centred experts indicate that no singular curriculum model or teaching approach supports all learners or academic settings.[29] The emphasis is on learners and educators formulating learning communities, curricula being integrated across disciplines, topics, and workplaces, and that a variety of teaching and learning strategies be used that support clearly defined learning outcomes. The learning outcomes are clearly defined and structured to communicate what the learner is expected to know or be able to do in the context of the area of exploration.

According to educators Patricia Lawler and Kathleen King, the role of the facilitator is significant in the implementation of learning-centred education.[30] Facilitators require skills in creating a positive environment and a broad repertoire of teaching and learning strategies in order to address the needs of individual learners and groups of learners, while maintaining the integrity of the required learning outcomes. Being able to scaffold learning, present probing questions, and assess skills and knowledge accurately are key attributes for facilitators in learning-centered environments.

Table 13.1 provides an overview of some of the distinct differences between a learning-centred and instructor-centred model of teaching and learning.

Learning-centred	Instructor-centred
Learners are called participants or learners.	Learners are labeled students.
Facilitators support learners – "they are guides on the side".	Teachers are the "sage on the stage" or expert in the field.
Independent learning style encouraged.	Dependent learning style encouraged.
Goals and learning outcomes evolve and are flexible based on the needs , interests and life application of the learners.	Goals and objectives are predetermined by the teacher. Curricula organized by subjects.
Learners are encouraged to share their knowledge and experiences with the learning community.	Teachers share their knowledge and experiences relative to the curricula. Students provide limited input.
Experiential learning methods used with a variety of problem-centred strategies evident.	Traditional, didactic teaching methods used.
Learners and facilitators collectively guide pace of learning.	Teacher controls pace of learning.
Learners bring ideas, resources and examples to the learning environment.	Teacher is the primary resource for ideas and examples.

Table 13.1: Models of Teaching and Learning

Shifting the paradigm to a learning-centred environment is not an easy process for institutions, educators, or learners. To be successful, educators must be willing to give some level of control to the learners. It requires a shift in thinking about the roles and responsibilities of learners and educators. And it requires educators and learners to be familiar with a variety of interactive learning experiences that will support learners in achieving defined learning outcomes.

Comparing Pedagogy, Andragogy and
Learning-centred Environments

Adult educators generally agree that they wish to be student-centred; that is to help students learn and develop new knowledge and skills. How we create learning environments is dependent on a number of variables, including teaching and learning experiences, role models, and philosophy. Adult educators benefit from having a thorough understanding of pedagogy, androgogy and learning-centred. In this next section, we summarize the core principles of each of the orientations.

Pedagogy

Generally pedagogy is teacher-centred and known as a traditional model of delivery. The course information is designed and delivered to the students by the teacher. The teacher makes the judgments about the teaching method, the depth of inquiry, what the right information is, and how students will be assessed, regardless of previous knowledge, skills or abilities of students. Students are able to predict the learning environment.

This traditional teaching model is efficient for disseminating content to large audiences but often compromises supporting students in developing hypothesis-based inquiry, which is an essential skill in military operations. Pedagogy is generally viewed as a one-way delivery model, leading to surface or superficial learning rather than deep learning. Students tend to become passive and disengaged. It often reduces the development of internal motivation that is needed for transferring learning concepts to various scenarios. Some learning outcomes may not be achieved which may contribute to some learners being unsuccessful or exiting the learning environment, including withdrawing from the military.

Andragogy

The roles and responsibilities of the learner and the facilitator in an andragogical model can be less clear than those using a pedagogical model. Students are leaders in this process and take on more responsibility for their learning successes and failures based on their needs and interests. This model may cause disequilibrium for learners because of the lack of structure or the change in the power structure. It may be either very successful or chaotic for learners. This is a particularly challenging model for learners who have come from a pedagogi-cal learning environment because of the shift in power from the educator to the student. Some experts including Robert Barr and John Tagg[31] suggest that that the optimal approach involves having facilitators shift the power from the teacher to the learner on a gradual basis rather than all at once.

Learning-centred

The learning-centred approach focuses on the construction of knowledge that supports clearly defined goals and learning outcomes. Building knowledge is a multi-faceted process. It is a shared process among students and educators whereby the students become engaged with theoretical explorations and ac-tivities that connect theory to practice. Students become motivated to want to learn through their input into the learning options and meeting the unique needs and learning-styles that they bring to the environment.

Learning-centred education requires facilitators to develop effective skills in de-signing learning that is active and inquiry-based. This learning process empha-sizes interactions with peers, the facilitator, and at times community experts. In-dividual students, peers, and the facilitator are consistently engaged in exploring concepts, seeking feedback, and applying new knowledge in real or simulated environments. As identified earlier in the chapter, a learning-centred environ-ment shifts the focus from teaching to learning. Educators Knight and Wood suggest that this model can lead to improved student attitudes while achieving increased learning outcomes relative to a learning that occurs in either a peda-gogical or andragogial environment.[32]

Table 13.2 further illustrates differences between pedagogy, androgogy and learning-centred perspectives.

Pedagogy	Andragogy	Learning-Centred
Building Knowledge: Knowledge comes from the teacher to the students, using a lecture format. The focus is on content delivery. The students are passive recipients of information.	Building Knowledge: Knowledge building is lead by the student, with guidance from the facilitator. The student explores areas that will lead to acquiring knowledge, skills, and application of theory in area of interest. The students are actively involved in seeking out knowledge and determining how the knowledge applies to their learning interest.	Building Knowledge: The student and the facilitator combine efforts to build knowledge needed to support learning outcomes using problem solving, critical thinking, and inquiry options. The focus is on using the content to inform application or practice. The students and the facilitator are actively involved in seeking new knowledge and determining through active inquiry how to transfer knowledge to real life situations.
Assessing Knowledge: The assessment strategies are usually summative in nature, are administered after specific units have been delivered. Students are required to be able to clearly delineate the right answer from the wrong answer. Testing is used to acquire the level of knowledge that the student has attained. The assessment is used to monitor academic performance.	Assessing Knowledge: A formative assessment process is used. Project based and self-reflective assessments are prevalent, such as journal writing and portfolio development. Students engage in a reflective process that gives focus to the intended learning outcomes, the methods and processes of meeting the learning outcomes, and an analysis of the learning that has occurred. The facilitator examines the project as it evolves, offering probing questions that are intended to support the learner in examining interrelated issues, or topics, in more depth.	Assessing Knowledge: A formative assessment process is generally used that involves students in engaging in a self-reflective and group process with peers and facilitator for the purpose of examining learning and enhancing areas requiring further knowledge or practice. This is an ongoing process, intertwined with new knowledge and practices. A variety of assessment strategies are used including tests, portfolios, performance experiences, student observation, and presentations. The assessment is used to determine areas of strength and areas requiring further development.

cont...

Teachers make choices about what students need to learn.	Learners make many choices about their learning options.	Learners and facilitators make choices based on learning outcomes.
Students are passive receivers of teacher information.	Learners determine level of activity and ways of learning.	Learners and facilitators collectivly make decisions about learning content and methods relative to the learning outcomes.
Teachers have the power for determining learning.	Learners have the power over their learning options, depth of learning and assessment methods.	Learners and facilitators share power – they find an effective balance to meet learning outcomes and needs of the learners.

Table 13.2: Differences Between Pedogogy, Androgogy, and Learning-Centred

The purpose of this section has been to introduce you to the conceptual frameworks that influence how and why different learning options are utilized in learning environments. The teaching and learning research literature provides useful descriptions of ideals, theories, principles, and assumptions. These perspectives impact educators and learners in a variety of ways; from the structure of the learning environment to the teaching and learning strategies implemented, to the roles and responsibilities of the members of the learning community.

It should be duly noted that there is some overlap and some distinct differences among the three orientations presented. At times, educators may use different aspects from each of the perspectives with learners or they may clearly focus on one perspective. Teaching and learning decisions are often influenced by the learners, the context or learning outcomes, or conscious decisions that educators make when they shift their teaching and learning orientation.

It is clear that the use and interpretation of these frameworks are influenced by one's philosophical orientation. That is, what one believes is important in a teaching and learning environment. In essence, philosophy guides practice.

Teaching and Learning Perspectives

Understanding the dynamics of programming and teaching and learning is a complicated process. Each teaching and learning perspective is influenced by life experiences, personality traits, preferred learning style, attitudes toward learning, and environmental conditions. The experience that a person has with both formal and informal learning, combined with other life experiences, influences their values and beliefs about learning and what they personally bring to the learning environment. How a person learns is unique to each individual. Merlin Wittrock, indicates that learning is a process of acquiring new information that contributes to making "relatively permanent changes in understanding, attitude, knowledge, information, ability and skill through experience."[33] Learning requires individuals to embrace new information and adjust to or eliminate previous beliefs, behaviours or ways of knowing. This is a complex process, influenced by educators, co-learners, and the learning environment.

There are a number of philosophies, perspectives, and disciplines that exist about programming and in teaching and learning in both institutional and workplace learning environments. Every facilitator and learner comes to a learning environment with different views and perspectives about both a subject matter and about how learning should occur. Becoming familiar with one's educational philosophical orientation has a direct impact on how teaching and learning occurs. This section examines adult program disciplines, followed by Pratt's five perspectives on teaching and learning.

Adult Program Disciplines

There are five major philosophies that influence adult program disciplines. Most educators have a clear leaning toward one philosophy, while utilizing aspects of the other philosophies. As you review each orientation, it is helpful for you to explore answers to the following questions:

- What is the purpose of education, training, and learning?

- What do you envision the role of the learner to be?

- What is the most effective role for the facilitator to exhibit?

- Is the role of the facilitator always the same? Why or why not?

- Is the role of the learner always the same? Why or why not?

Liberal Education

This philosophy emphasizes the arts, learning for the sake of learning, and developing intellectual breadth. This perspective, popular among adult educators in institutional settings, view liberal education as a process whereby learners with basic information about local, national and world events are challenged to acquire analytical skills and abilities to synthesize a situation in order to make informed decisions. Liberal education is more focused on broadening perspectives than on teaching specific skills of a discipline or skills needed to meet objectives of a workplace. E-learning displays many of the characteristics of liberal education.

Progressive Education

Progressive adult education emphasizes training that focuses both on skill development and utilitarian training that advances the knowledge and skills of individuals, society, and the workplace or community of practice. The training programs are learner-centric, emphasizing strategies and processes that support the learner achieving the goal through a problem-based process, advancing from simple to more complex concepts in design. Learners exhibit self-directed characteristics, while the adult educator plans an environment that is supportive of exploring learning from a variety of perspectives and is a partner in learning.

Behaviourist Education

The Behaviourist adult education model is prevalent in corporate training because of the clearly defined behavioural goals and objectives content generated from a gap analysis. The competency-based model utilizes observable and measurable outcomes. It incorporates drill and practice learning and is often linked to specified skill training needed in a workplace setting. It offers less emphasis on critical thinking and problem solving than other models and more on being able to produce particular actions or skills.

Humanistic Education

This philosophical orientation examines the development of the whole person, with an emphasis on the affective domain. The focus is on the learner taking responsibility for their learning. Facilitators act as guides using a probing process in both theoretical and application exploration. Individual and group learning experiences are emphasized. Each learner may have a unique learning path with specialized areas of exploration and learning outcomes. Collaborative exploration and communication discoveries are inherent in this humanistic perspective.

Radical Adult Education

Radical adult education focuses on advancing social, political, and economic changes through education. This orientation views education as a means for consciousness-raising, critical thinking, and social change. Curriculum evolves from the consciousness of the oppressed and the disadvantaged. The facilitator is a partner in learning and "the methodology is a dialogical encounter that leads to praxis – that is, reflective thought and action."[34]

Table 13.3 provides an overview of each perspective including their roots from theorists who have influenced educational perspectives from as early as the 1900s.

	Liberal	Progressive	Behaviourist	Humanistic	Radical
Theorist	Socrates, Plato, Aristotle	Pestalozzi, Dewey, Bergevin, Lindeman	Skinner, Watson, Thorndike	Rousseau, Tough, Maslow, Knowles	Holt, Kozol, Reich, Freire, Illich
Purpose	To develop intellectual breadth, moral and spiritual development	To transmit culture & promote social change through advanced knowledge, critical thinking and problem solving skills	To change behaviour to reflect societal & individual needs	To enhance personal growth & development & self-esteem	To advance social, political, & economic changes in society through education.
Learner	A lifelong learner seeking knowledge that will provide theoretical understanding of concepts and perspectives	Learner needs, interests, & experiences are built upon through a variety of educational experiences	Learner is an active participant in practicing new behaviours. Feedback from expert is used to improve skill acquisition	Learner is self-directed, motivated & assumes responsibility for learning	Learner and teacher share power in learning process; reflection on knowledge about people, history, & culture occurs.
The Role of the Educator or Facilitator	Is the "expert" in the field of study and transmits knowledge to learners.	Is the organizer & guide in the learning process through experiential learning. Probes & stimulates learning options that lead to new knowledge development.	Is the controller of learning & designer of the learning outcomes that reflect desired skills and behaviours.	Is a facilitator, promoter, guide, and partner in learning. Creates a rich, flexible learning environment.	Is a partner in learning. Supports learners in determining their desired direction for learning. Stimulates discussion.
Teaching & Learning Methods	Lecture, critical reading, study groups, dialectic	Problem-based, experimental, experiential	Specified task completion, assisted or programmed instruction	Team tasks & teaching, experiential, group processes, discovery, & self-directed	Group exploration, discussion groups, debates, problem posing & discovery

Table 13.3: Educational Perspectives

The adult program disciplines are interconnected to how adults view teaching and learning. Adults benefit from exploring each discipline to determine where their values and beliefs fit within each of the perspectives outlined. Adult educators who engage in determining their beliefs and values on teaching and learning are better able to effectively plan and deliver learning opportunities that are reflective of their style. This act of knowing becomes a segment of the anchor for curricula delivery and learner success.

Five Perspectives on Teaching

Pratt identifies that "our perspectives on teaching are cultural views of teaching, powerful but largely invisible frames of reference through which all of us make meaning of our worlds" and suggests that our perceptions and assumptions remain constant and invisible until we encounter a basis for comparison.[35] He outlines five perspectives on teaching and learning and suggests that educators generally have one dominant perspective that guides their practice. Each perspective is outlined below. Theses include:

    a. The Transmission Perspective;

    b. The Apprenticeship Perspective;

    c. The Development Perspective;

    d. The Nurturing Perspective; and

    e. The Social Reform Perspective.

The Transmission Perspective

This traditional teacher-centred model is used by educators with experience in a specified field. The educator is focused on students acquiring content mastery, through a lecture format. The educator, using clear objectives, is expected to know the content well enough to deliver it with confidence, answer questions, provide clear explanations and examples, exhibit a level of authority in the content presentation, and develop objective strategies for assessing learning.

Educators with this perspective focus on:

- Adequately covering the content within a specified time frame, regardless of the learners' ability to grasp the concepts in the time allotted;

- Assuming that their material is integrated with other parts of a course or program. The content is taught based on the curriculum taught previous or forms the foundation for future courses and content;

- Teaching information in a step-by-step process in a structured format; and

- Having limited interaction about the content among learners or educators and learners.

Pratt suggests that teachers who favour this method view learning as a process that occurs as a result of gathering a body of information followed by reproducing that information on tests and assignments. Effective teaching is based on the content expertise of the educator.

The Apprenticeship Perspective

The apprenticeship model has long been associated with learning skills and knowledge in workplace settings under the guidance of an expert in the field such as those with a trade, a vocation, a profession or a cultural group. Pratt identifies this as a process of enculturating learners into a specific workplace or community and its success is based on "intensive, diversified and prolonged participation in the work and social relations of the community."[36]

Educators with this perspective focus on:

- Coaching learners to build skills and acculturate them into the profession;

- Supporting learners in acquiring discipline competence and social relations in the community of practice;

- Scaffolding learning from simple to complex by breaking tasks into small steps or processes;

- Engaging learners' within their "zone of development";

- Preparing learners to combine their learning with self-directed responsibilities and coaching; and

- Supporting and encouraging learners to progress from dependent learners to self-directed learners and independent workers.

This perspective is based on the teacher sharing and transferring the knowledge and values of the workplace or community to others. The learning is focused on the context and situation within which it is learned. Apprentices, through guided practice and success on identified tasks acquire skills and abilities within the context and application learned. Authentic forms of representing the content is often implemented by using case studies and project oriented assignments that simulate the workplace or community of learning.

The Developmental Perspective

The developmental perspective is consistent with the tenets of a learning-centred environment. It is derived from cognitive psychology and based on each learner having a cognitive map that is used to guide his/her perspective on the world. The learner uses prior knowledge and ways of thinking and learning to examine new information and knowledge. For example, when a learner acquires new information or situations, he/she attempts to align it with their current knowledge or skills. If learners are unable to assimilate the information with their current knowledge, they are put into a state of disequilibrium. This leads the learner to revise their cognitive map, reconstruct a new cognitive map, or dismiss the new information.

Educators with this perspective focus on:

- Challenging learners with new information and perspectives as a trigger to cause the learner to reconsider perspectives and adjust their cognitive map;

- Examining the learners' current level of knowledge and content to guide a probing process that will provide new knowledge and advance new thinking.

- Creating stimulation and growth opportunities through critical thinking and problem solving skills, while using the content as the background for discussions and in the development of new ways of thinking;

- Moving the learner to think like experts in the field of study by using probing questions and effective examples as they evolve from mastering simple tasks to complex structures.

- Supporting learners in acquiring a qualitative change in both understanding and in the thinking process relative to the theory and application;

- Exhibiting respect to the learner for the knowledge and thinking processes they bring to the learning environment;

- Assessing the learners' knowledge, skills, and abilities relative to the proposed learning outcomes and building upon areas requiring further development; and

- Taking direction from the learners as a starting point in the process of expanding each learner's ways of thinking.

Pratt identifies that learning based on this perspective is "a change in the quality of one's thinking rather than a change in the quantity of one's knowledge."[37] It requires educators to clearly articulate to learners that the learning process is based on probing questions, thoughts and perspectives in a collaborative environment, rather than the educator giving the learner the required information or template for the expected knowledge. Prior knowledge and ways of thinking are foundational to determining what individuals will learn next.

The Nurturing Perspective

This perspective, aligned with the work of Malcolm Knowles, has its roots in adult teaching and learning. This perspective is built on learner motivation, knowing what influences learning, how learning occurs for individuals and groups, and when there is a fear of failure. Learning is strongly influenced and affected by the learner's self-concept and level of self-efficacy. Learners need to be able to understand why new knowledge is useful. They require a level of confidence that they can learn the content and transfer content to application.

Educators with this perspective build a balance of professional and caring relationships with learners. Pratt describes caring as "empathizing with learners while providing support and encouragement as they attempt to learn; challenging means holding to expectations that are both achievable and meaningful for learners."[38] There is a high degree of trust and respect among the educator and the learner. Educators with this perspective focus on:

- Supporting learners in gaining confidence and becoming self-sufficient in their learning;

- Encouraging learners to take responsibility for their learning successes based on their efforts and abilities;

- Listening to and responding to the emotional and cognitive needs of the learners;

- Providing for and supporting learners in establishing clear expectations and goals;

- Building the self-esteem and self-concept of each learner; and

- Assessing learners needs on individual growth and absolute achievement.

The content supports learners in meeting certain goals and in acquiring first-hand knowledge of their capabilities to learn and to become self-reliant in learning new information.

The Social Reform Perspective

The Social Reform perspective is gaining popularity among educators and employers who have a focus on trying to create a better society. Each principle evolves from a core or central system of beliefs, usually based on an ethical code, a religious doctrine, or a political or social ideal. The learner and the content are less important than the broader agenda and the teaching and learning process focuses on the collective group rather than the needs of individual learners. Educators with this perspective focus on:

- Seeking to change society by challenging current beliefs and status quo activity;

- Highlighting macro concerns rather than micro issues;

- Addressing or changing underlying value systems of learners to reflect those of the educator;

- Devising discussion based on who has created knowledge and for what purposes, rather than the specific knowledge created;

- Moving from an individual perspective to a collective focus;

- Facilitating cognitive and personal development in issues of moral or political topics; and

- Using probing questions to bring learners from diverse communities of practice to examine topical issues from a variety of perspectives.

The content provides learners with the freedom to exhibit a critical perspective and power so that they are empowered to take social action. Educators support and encourage learners in exploring topics from a broad perspective and in using non-conventional strategies to examine the subject.

As you will note throughout this chapter, there is no one theory that represents adult learning; rather there are a number of frameworks that guide practice. These perspectives are intended to provide educators with a framework from which to think about teaching and learning and the various roles that educators and learners exhibit. As you will explore in the next section of this chapter, one's philosophical orientation influences the approach taken in teaching and learning. By engaging in a reflective process, whereby educators think about what they believe, what they do, and why they engage in particular strategies, the process facilitates discoveries about the potential of good or poor teaching strategies that they bring to the learning environment. Being aware of one's skills, strengths, and opportunities for expanding teaching and learning expertise will enhance the learning environment, which ultimately contributes to learner success.

Teaching and learning is a complex process with a wide range of individual needs and talents. As a result, there is no one theory or process that will encompass quality learning experiences. The planning and implementation of learning experiences should take into consideration the learners' learning styles, the curricula, the transference of knowledge and skills to a variety of workplace settings, and ways of supporting learners in being successful. To be effective, educators require knowledge about teaching and learning in general and a variety of specific teaching and learning strategies that support diverse learning needs and styles.

Examining Your Teaching and Learning Philosophy

The meaning of the phrase "to teach" differs among educators and students. Some might argue that it means "to impart knowledge" while others might suggest it is a "process of supporting learners [to] discover new knowledge, skills and abilities". Some suggest that you can learn to teach, while others suggest you are born with those innate skills. Generally, it is our philosophy that guides our perspective and informs practice.[39]

A facilitator's philosophy about teaching and learning impacts both the quality and the depth of the learning experience of individuals and groups. How a facilitator thinks about learners has a significant impact on the teaching methods used, the connectedness to learners, how the program is designed, delivered, and evaluated and the overall success of learners. Facilitators are more likely to align their teaching practices to reflect adult learning principles when they have invested time to examine and reflect upon their philosophy and beliefs about teaching and learning.[40] Conversely, when facilitators are not clear on their philosophy, their ability to align the content, learning outcomes and evaluation is less likely to occur in practice.

Facilitators benefit from having a personal philosophy statement about teaching and learning because a philosophy statement presents the ideal that an individual strives to reach. For example, "it establishes a basic premise from which all actions and experiences emanate. It is a returning point, a centering, in a time of crisis."[41] A teaching and learning philosophy is based on core values related to what the individual believes about teaching, learning, their role in their position and in the lives of others, and their responsibility as members of a community and society. Examples of core values include:

- Each individual in a learning environment is unique and is respected for what they bring to the learning environment;

- Each member of the military has foundational information upon which to build;

- Learning occurs in environments that support and respect learners and colleagues;

- Collaborative and individual learning opportunities are important; and

- Learning is complex and differs for each person.

Adult educators who are able to articulate their perspective on how individuals learn appear to be able to correlate their philosophy about teaching and learning with their practice. Facilitators use their philosophy to:

- Guide their practice while becoming aware of beliefs, biases, and future goals;

- Support their decision-making on approaches to curriculum design and delivery, assessment, and student success;

- Contribute to their personal authenticity, professional practice, and commitment to teaching and learning; and

- Support learners in meeting their goals and objectives.

When facilitators utilize teaching and learning methods that are incongruent with the principles of adult education or one's philosophical orientation, valuable learning opportunities are jeopardized. When facilitators do not have an established philosophical orientation, their teaching and learning strategies will either be inconsistent or rigid, resulting in disequilibrium for the learners.

Developing a personal philosophy requires individuals to engage in a self-reflective process. There are many ways to engage in self-reflective practice. For example, responding to clearly defined questions helps educators begin to engage in a self-reflective process. There are many questions that can be explored that bring clarity to your philosophy. The questions and answers will evolve and change as you engage in teaching and learning. Experience and continuous learning will affect and should influence a philosophy, thus making one's philosophy fluid in nature.

Examples of questions that help bring clarity to one's beliefs and philosophy include:

- What are best practices and quality indicators that are essential for learning?

- What do you want learners to say about your learning environment?

- How do your ideas and values influence what you do with learners?

- How do you implement your philosophy?

- How do your experiences in learning situations reflect your philosophy?

When one's philosophy is clear, educators are able to articulate and execute their beliefs in teaching and learning experiences. Philosophy statement considerations might include:

- I believe the purpose of teaching and learning is to…

- I believe that individuals learn best in environments that…

- I believe facilitators should offer…

- I believe that the learning environment should…

- I believe I bring qualities such as…

In summary, each person's philosophy and perspective on teaching and learning illustrates their personal beliefs and values. A philosophy guides how a facilitator establishes curricula, how curricula are delivered and how learners are assessed.

Developing an Effective Learning Environment

There are many aspects of the learning environment that impact learning. For example, when adult learners feel that they are being respected by the facilitator, the learning process will be more effective. The strategies that facilitators use to approach learners, how learners are guided throughout the learning process, the method, depth, and timing of feedback given to learners all contribute to learner success or failure.

The facilitator of learning establishes the constructs of the learning environment – from the level of rapport with learners to the complexity of the theoretical concepts delivered. The constructs of the learning environment contributes to learner motivation and learner success. More specifically, facilitators and learners benefit from physical environments that:

- Ensures the learning space is comfortable from the perspective of room temperature, lighting, and work space. Materials are conducive to the types of learning options extended to learners.

- Exhibits a positive, open flowing feeling tone among facilitators and learners. Furniture and accessories are arranged to encourage effective communication among the learners. The room arrangement reflects equality and inclusion of the community of learners.

- Is clean, uncluttered, and inviting to the participants.

In addition to the physical environment, the goal of teaching and learning among facilitators and learners is to build effective learning environments within which learners engage in building knowledge and skills through inquiry. Inquiry advances their learning from a surface level to one of demonstrating deeper forms of learning. There are a number of strategies that are evident in effective learning environments. They include:

- Facilitators that recognize learners are not "receptacles" of knowledge. Learners each have a unique way of creating meaning from their learning. Learners focus on assimilating new information with existing knowledge. When the learning environment is correct, this transforming process contributes to learners developing flexible thinking skills and problem solving processes, while using a variety of creative thinking and learning processes. Incorporates a learner's goals, needs and previous learning into the planning and implementation of the learning experience.

- Supporting learners in devising learning strategies for given situations that will allow them to engage in constructing ways of knowing that are reflective of their needs and congruent with defined learning outcomes. Learning occurs at different times and with varying levels of understanding among each learner. Too much stimulation or insufficient stimulation reduces learning opportunities.

- Providing opportunities for learners to acquire a thorough understanding of their strengths and areas requiring further development. This requires individuals to be constantly assessed with tools that are reflective of the established learning outcomes and for learners to have opportunities to re-work ideas, processes, as well as knowledge base and learning structures.

- Offering the correct levels of problem-based learning options that combine varying levels of challenge and advanced learning for participants. This process requires the theoretical concepts to be aligned with its application to real life situations. Forging new connections increases critical thinking and new knowledge development.

- Advocating for learners to embrace cultural and human diversity in their learning circles broadens thinking and learning options. Facilitators and learners create a social milieu environment that embraces respect, risk-taking, debate, and new insights among a community of learners.

- Creating a collaborative learning space. Facilitators and learners have equal power in carving out learning options, strategies, teaching and learning methodologies and assessments. Responsibilities for discussions and explorations are shared among the learning community membership.

- Using self-reflective practice to support learners in acquiring an understanding of their beliefs, values, opportunities, and ideologies.

- Using a variety of teaching and learning strategies to support learners in retaining information, developing an understanding of its usage, and being able to apply and transfer the information correctly to different settings or situations.

It is important to acknowledge that teaching and learning is a challenging process. Although a number of ideas and perspectives have been outlined, no one facilitator or learner will be successful in creating an effective learning environment at all times. What is important for learners and facilitators is to examine those times when the learning environment has not met the needs of the learners or the facilitator and to analyze some of the environmental, human characteristics and teaching and learning strategies that may have contributed to the situation. When this reflective process occurs, new growth opportunities about teaching and learning, and beliefs and values evolve.

Summary

This chapter has outlined some key concepts and frameworks that formulate the foundation for the teaching and learning process when working with adults. It highlights the collective importance of educators and learners in establishing environments that meet the needs of the learners, that exhibits respect for the learners, and that challenges learners to expand their current knowledge by assimilating and incorporating new knowledge and ideals into their framework of ways of knowing.

The chapter outlines the importance of adult educators gaining insight into how knowing about adult education perspectives, disciplines, and frameworks become guiding elements toward gaining an understanding of what we know about how complex and multi-faceted teaching and learning is. There is no one method of practice that is correct or guarantees learners will be successful in attaining the intended learning outcomes or skills. It is clear from the information presented that the field of adult education is vast and varied. It continues to evolve, which requires adult educators to establish a philosophical orientation that is fluid in nature.

There are a number of key competencies that facilitators exhibit. They include: creating and exhibiting a caring, respectful environment, expertise in designing and implementing curricula that is conducive to the needs of individual learners and groups of learners, and teaching and learning methods that support learners in engaging in deep learning through critical thinking, problem solving and creative thinking.

Effective facilitators examine their beliefs and values about teaching and learning and they take their responsibility for advancing learning very seriously. They challenge learners, they engage in becoming partners of learning and they promote reflective practice both personally and among learners. In essence, they set the framework for learners engaging in new learning options.

1   Terry O'Banion, *A Learning College for the 21ˢᵗ Century* (Westport, CT: American Associa-tion of Community Colleges. Oryz Press, 1997).

2   Sharon Merriam, Rosemary Caffarella and Lisa Baumgartner, *Learning in Adulthood: A Comprehensive Guide* (San Francisco, CA: Jossey-Bass, 2007).

3   Daniel D. Pratt, *Five Perspectives in Teaching Adult and Higher Education* (Malabar, FL: Krieger Pub Co, 1997).

4   Alexander Kapp, *Platon's Erziehungslehre, als Paedagogik für die Einzelnen und als Sta-atspaedagogik* (Minden und Leipzig: Ferdinand Essmann, 1833).

5   Malcolm Shepherd Knowles, *The Modern Practice of Adult Education: from Pedagogy to Andragogy* (New York: Cambridge Book Co, 1980), 43.

6   Malcolm Knowles, *The Adult Learner: A Neglected Species* (Largo, FL: Gulf Publishing, 1984), 12.

7   Ibid., 12.

8   Malcolm Knowles, *The Modern Practice of Adult Education: from Pedagogy to Andragogy* (New York: Cambridge Books, 1980), 47.

9   Ibid., 47.

10   Joseph Kessels and Rob Poell, *Andragogy and Social Capital Theory: The Implications for Human Resource Development*, retrieved on 15 Jan 2012 from <http://www.kessels-smit.com/files/Artikel_2004_kessels__poell_-_andragogy_and_social_capital_theory.pdf>, 6.

11   Ralf St. Clair, in Sharon Merriam, Rosemary Caffarella and Lisa Baumgartner, *Learning in Adulthood: A Comprehensive Guide* (San Francisco, CA: Jossey-Bass, 2007), 92.

12   Ibid., 93.

13   Sharon Merriam, Rosemary Caffarella and Lisa Baumgartner, *Learning in Adulthood: A Comprehensive Guide* (San Francisco, CA: Jossey-Bass, 2007), 92.

14   Kevin Jarrett, *Just-in-time versus Just-in-case Learning*, NCS-Tech Blog. Retrieved on 15 Jan 2012 from <http://www.ncs-tech.org/?p=2229>, 1.

15   Ibid., 1.

16   Malcolm Knowles, *The Modern Practice of Adult Education: From Pedagogy to Andragogy* (Cambridge Books, 1980).

17   John Loughran, *Developing a Pedagogy of Teacher Education: Understanding Teaching and Learning about Teaching* (Abingdon: Routledge, 2006), 2.

18   Max van Manen, *The Tact of Teaching. The Meaning of Pedagogical Thoughtfulness.* (Albany, NY: State University of New York Press, 1991), 2.

19   Ibid., 2.

20   Fred Korthagen, *Linking Practice and Theory: The Pedagogy of Realistic Teacher Education* (Mahwah, NJ: Lawrence Erlbaum Associates, 2001), 2.

21   Ibid., 2.

22   David A. Kolb, *Experiential Learning: Experience as the Source of Learning and Develop-ment*, (Upper Saddle River, NJ: Prentice-Hall, 1984).

23   Howard Gardner, *The Disciplined Mind: Beyond Facts and Standardized Tests*, the K-12 Education that Every Child Deserves, (New York, NY: Simon and Schuster, 1999), 166.

24   Robert Barr and John Tagg, "A New Paradigm for Undergraduate Education" *Change* (November/December 1995), 12-25.

25   Jim Reynolds, "Learning-Centered Theory: Theory into Practice", *Inquiry*, Vol. 5, No. 2 (2000), 2.

26   John Dewey, *Democracy and Education: An Introduction to the Philosophy of Education* (New York, NY: Macmillan, 1963).

27   Paul Ramsden, *Learning to Teach in Higher Education* (New York, NY: Routledge, 1994).; and Judith Grunert, *The Course Syllabus: A Learning-Centered Approach* (San Francisco, CA: Jossey-Bass, 1997).

28   Terry O'Banion, *A Learning College for the 21ˢᵗ Century* (Westport, CT: American Association of Community Colleges. Oryz Press, 1997), 22.

29   Harry Hubball and Helen Burt, "An Integrated Approach to Developing and Implement-ing Learning-Centred Curriculum", *International Journal for Academic Development*, Vol. 9, No. 1 (2004), 51-65.

30   Patricia Lawler and Kathleen King, *Planning Effectively for Faculty Development: An Adult Learning Perspective* (Malabar: Florida: Kreiger Publishing, 2000).

31   Barr and Tagg, 16.

32   Jennifer K. Knight and William B. Wood, "Teaching More by Lecturing Less", *Cell Biology Education*, Vol. 4, No. 4 (2005), 298-310.

33   Merlin Wittrock, in Deo H. Poonwassie and Anne Poonwassie, eds., *Fundamentals of Adult Education: Issues and Practices for Lifelong Learning*, (Toronto, ON: Thompson Educational Pub-lishing, 2001), 76.

34   Bruce Spencer, *The Purpose of Adult Education: A Short Introduction* (Toronto, ON: Thompson Educational Publishing, 2006), 12.

35   Daniel D. Pratt, 37.

36   Ibid., 43.

37   Ibid., 47.

38   Ibid., 49

39   Beverlie Dietze, *Foundations of Early Childhood Education: Learning Environments and Childcare in Canada* (Don Mills, ON: Pearson Education Canada, 2006).

40   Tara Fenwick and Jim Parsons, *The Art of Evaluating Adult Learners: A Handbook for Educa-tors and Trainers* (Toronto, ON: Thompson Educational Publishing, 2000).

41   Barbara Crossley, Beverlie Dietze and Joyce Hume, *Staff Development Options in Early Childhood Education* (Bellevillle, ON: Loyalist College, 2001), 1.

CHAPTER 14

HIGHER EDUCATION AND THE PROFESSION OF ARMS: EXPLAINING THE LOGIC

Dr. Bill Bentley and Colonel Bernd Horn

The question often arises amongst senior officers as to what is the requirement for higher, or more accurately, graduate education. Although few, if any, would deny the value of such an investment, the barrier is always time. For individuals who are exceptionally busy, the issue continues to be the trade off between time spent on studies and time available to clear the ever present day-to-day workload. Many default to a position that time spent in an appointment or rank adequately prepares the individual for the challenges they encounter or will face in the future. So what exactly is the requirement for graduate education for senior officers?

There is no "silver bullet" answer to the question; no quantifiable data that can categorically provide comprehensive proof. Rather, the response to the question lies in the logic – the argument for the critical importance of education for senior officers in the profession of arms. The starting point stems from the great Prussian theorist Carl von Clausewitz. He clearly identified that "If we pursue the demands that war makes on those who practice it we come to the realm of intellect."[1]

Simply stated, all members of the profession of arms in Canada must possess a deep and comprehensive understanding of the necessity, if we profess to truly consider ourselves a profession in Western society, to possess a deep understanding and comprehension of a relevant body of knowledge. More exactly, as Eliot Freidson, a leading scholar on the subject of professionalism, identifies, "A profession has a formal program that produces the qualifying credentials, which is controlled by the profession and associated with higher education."[2]

And, there is good reason. The failure to abide by this tenet could have serious repercussions as the institution discovered in the 1990s. By 1997, Doug

Young, the Minister of National Defence, General Maurice Baril, the Chief of the Defence Staff, and the Louise Frechette, the Deputy Minister, were all seriously concerned that the balance among the four pillars of professional development – training, education, experience and self-development – had become distorted and very problematic. Missing was an emphasis on education, particularly higher learning.[3] The MND confirmed, "Without higher education you're not tuned into what's happening in the larger society." He concluded, "That's where we lost the ball."[4]

As a result, Young, supported by monographs written by four eminent Canadian scholars – Jack Granatstein, Desmond Morton, Albert Legault and David Bercuson – oversaw the production of *The Defence Minister's Report to the Prime Minister on Leadership and Management in the Canadian Forces.*[5] The centre of gravity of this Report was the importance of higher education. Among the most important results were the stand-up of the Canadian Defence Academy, *Officership 2020*, *NCM Corps 2020* and the creation of the Applied Military Science Course and the National Security Studies Course at the Canadian Forces College. However, that was over a decade ago and predates the Canadian Forces' involvement in Afghanistan, the Indian Ocean and Libya. If anything, today's security environment is much more challenging, complex and unpredictable than at the close of the 20th century. Arguably, the need for higher education is even greater today.

But the logic, or requirement for graduate education for senior officers goes beyond the failing of the past due to a lack of higher education or the more complex security environment. A second critical characteristic of any true profession is captured by scholar Andrew Abbott, another expert on the subject of professions. He observes that "In any profession practical skill grows out of an abstract system of knowledge, and control of the profession lies in control of the abstractions." Abbott asserts, "This characteristic of abstraction is the one that best identifies the professions." He explains, "Only a knowledge system governed by abstractions can redefine its problems and tasks, defend them against interlopers, and seize new problems."[6] For the Canadian Profession of Arms, this abstract system of theory-based knowledge at the core of the profession is the General System of War and Conflict illustrated in Figure 14.1.

FORMAL EDUCATION

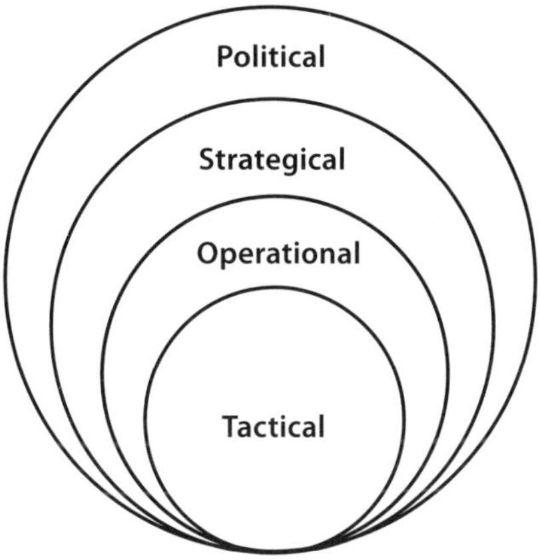

Figure 14.1: The General System of War and Conflict

This system must be understood as a complex adaptive system as described in complexity science. The system becomes less linear and more complex as one ascends from the tactical to the politico-strategic level. Formal education becomes the mechanism that allows and individual to better comprehend and understand the integrated, multifaceted, intricate and complex context of the military profession within the larger world it exists in. It is critical to mastering the necessary body of knowledge.

This requirement has long been understood by those studying the profession. Renowned strategist Colin S. Gray identifies a key abstraction within the realm senior officers exist. He states, that "Strategy is virtual behaviour, it has no material existence." Gray explains, "Strategy is an abstraction, though it is vastly more difficult to illustrate visually than are other vital abstractions like love and fear."[7] Israeli strategist Shimon Naveh makes a similar, if more abstruse, point. He insists, "Military strategy evolves in a dynamic learning environment of praxis, which is a spatial reflection of the tensions between the ontological analysis of reality and the epistemological understanding of institutional knowledge, between conceptualization and application, theorizing and performance, institutionalization and change."[8]

Importantly, operational art, the playground of senior officers, is only slightly less abstract than strategy. Naveh asserts, "We can legitimately argue that the conceptualization of operational art transformed military science in a pattern resembling relativity and quantum mechanic."[9] He notes, "The development of operational art as a neoteric field of knowledge provided for the first time in the history of modern military thought an intermediate environment for discourse, which bridges harmoniously over the traditional cognitive gap between the conventional fields of military knowledge."[10]

The central point is that officers, particularly general officers, require knowledge and understanding at a higher level once they leave the tactical level of operations and staff appointments. They need a wider and deeper understanding of human behaviour, politics and the world around them, to mention just a few areas, in order to be able to operate effectively. Given this increasing complexity as one ascends the hierarchy in the General System of War and Conflict, higher education becomes a necessity. Military strategist Barry Watts underscores the requirement. He affirmed, "The cognitive skills exercised by combatants with tactical expertise differ fundamentally from those required of operational artists and competent strategists."[11] In fact, Watts identified a cognitive boundary as illustrated in Figure 14.2.

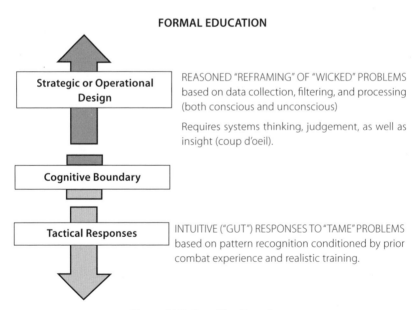

FORMAL EDUCATION

Strategic or Operational Design

REASONED "REFRAMING" OF "WICKED" PROBLEMS based on data collection, filtering, and processing (both conscious and unconscious)

Requires systems thinking, judgement, as well as insight (coup d'oeil).

Cognitive Boundary

Tactical Responses

INTUITIVE ("GUT") RESPONSES TO "TAME" PROBLEMS based on pattern recognition conditioned by prior combat experience and realistic training.

Figure 14.2: Cognitive Boundary

In essence, the boundary is between the tactical level and the operational level. Therefore, crossing this boundary and operating as operational artists and military strategists requires advanced education, specifically graduate level education. Gray drives this point home persuasively. He argues, "Because strategy is uniquely difficult among the levels of war and conflict, few, indeed, are the people able to shine in the role of strategist." He insists, "Their number can be increased by education though not by training, and not at all reliably by the experience of command and planning at warfare's operational and tactical levels."[12] Henry Yarger, yet another expert in the field, supports Gray's thesis. He points out that "strategy remains the domain of the strong intellect, the lifelong student and the dedicated professional."[13]

In short, senior officers of all ranks can never stop studying and learning if they are to lead and act as stewards of the profession into the future. Moreover, the General System of War and Conflict discussed above always takes place in a real world, within a contemporary context that is ever changing and evolving. Importantly, this context is accessed, created and understood through the study of conventional academic disciplines such as geo-politics, international relations, history, sociology, anthropology, economics and science and technology. Given the nature of the abstract theory-based body of knowledge at the core of the profession of arms, the old paradigm that is based on the concept that successful tactical command equals promotion must be rejected. The new paradigm for the 21st century quite simply is – successful tactical command, plus higher education, equals promotion.

Respected American commander and warfighter, and current Director of the US Central Intelligence Agency, General David Petraeus, confirmed the need of graduate level education for senior commanders. He believes "Such experiences are critical to the development of the flexible, adaptable, creative thinkers who are so important to operations in places like Iraq and Afghanistan." Moreover, he concluded that graduate studies "provide a fair amount of general intellectual capital and often provides specific skills and knowledge on which an officer may draw during his or her career." Importantly, Petraeus insisted, "graduate school inevitably helps U.S. military officers improve their critical thinking skills."[14] It is no different for Canadian officers.

And so, a summary of the logic for higher education for CF officers is as follows:

- All officers need an undergraduate degree.[15]

- All lieutenant-colonels and colonels employed at the operational or strategic levels need a graduate degree(s) from as wide a selection of universities as possible.

- All general officers/flag officers (GO/FO) require a graduate degree.

- A PhD is desirable (but not mandatory) for a GO/FO but it should be acquired prior to promotion to Flag rank.

- All GO/FOs should be involved in a comprehensive program of secondments, seminars, two week courses, three, six and twelve month programs, fellowships, etc. This program could be administered by the Canadian Defence Academy but must be directed by the CDS as the Head of the Profession of Arms in Canada.

The investment in graduate and post-graduate education in both time and resources is undisputedly high. However, the responsibility of senior officers to navigate the institution through an often ambiguous, perpetually changing, and always complex and dangerous world, imposes the obligation on its stewards. After all, those who claim the title of professional, and who society has entrusted with the safety of the nation and the lives of its sons and daughters, are obliged to ensure they are as prepared as possible to provide advice to the government and lead the nation in harm's way.

---

1   Carl von Clausewitz, *On War,* ed. by Michael Howard and Peter Paret (Princeton, NJ: Princeton University Press, 1976) 135.

2   Eliot Freidson, *Professionalism* (Chicago: Chicago University Press, 2001) 127.

3   Only 53.3 percent of officers had a Bachelor's degree and only 6.8 percent had graduate level education at the time.

4   Vice-Admiral Larry Murray, interview with Dr. Bill Bentley and Colonel Bernd Horn, PhD, 6 October 2010.

5   Doug Young, MND, *Report to the Prime Minister on the Leadership and Management of the Canadian Armed Forces* (Ottawa: DND, 1997).

6   Andrew Abbott, *The System of Professions* (Chicago: Chicago University Press, 1988) 9.

7   Colin S. Gray, *The Strategy Bridge: Theory for Practice* (Oxford: Oxford University Press, 2011), 61.

8   Shimon Naveh, "Discursive Command- Operators – Systemic Operational Design: A New Framework for Strategic Epistemology," 1. <http://home.no.net/tacops/taktikk/kadettarbeld/hovan.htm.2005>, accessed 10 October 2011.

9   Ibid., 2.

10   Ibid.

11   Barry Watts, "US Combat Training, Operational Art and Strategic Competence," Center for Strategic and Budgetary Assessments, Washington, D.C., 2008, 52.

12   Gray, 61.

13   Henry Yarger, *Strategic Theory for the 21st Century* (Carlisle, PA: Strategic Studies Institute, US Army War College, 2006), 8.

14   Ibid., 18.

15   This was mandated by the MND in 1997. However, see Bernd Horn, "A Rejection of the Need for Warrior Scholars?" *Canadian Military Journal*, Vol. 11, No. 2 (Spring 2011), 48-53, for an explanation of why education is essential for officers.

CHAPTER 15

THE VALUE AND PURPOSE OF EDUCATION IN THE CANADIAN FORCES

Dr. Molly McCarthy-Senebald

The Purpose of Education

What is the value and purpose of education? When questioned, most people will acknowledge that education has value in and of itself. Within the CF, we educate not just because of ministerial direction that all officers will have degrees (i.e., be educated), but rather, because we value education as a significant component of the CF professional development system (CFPDS)[1] that together with the other components, facilitates the development of intellectual ability in both officers and non-commissioned members. The CFPDS is in effect the key enabler of the profession of arms through continuous career-long intellectual development provided via specific training, education, experience and self-development. Education provides a base of knowledge and intellectual skills upon which information can be correctly interpreted and sound judgement exercised. Training provides technical and procedural knowledge and skills required in the performance of assigned duties; it is often described as the development of a predictable response to a predictable situation; it is a continuous, career-long process. Experience reinforces education and training and extends personal and professional capabilities. Self-development seeks to develop the individual professionally, above and beyond that which is provided for them by the organization. Self-directed education, training, or experience is supported by the organization because it enhances both personal and professional capabilities.

Foundational documents including the *Report to the Prime Minister on Leadership and Management in the Canadian Forces; Military HR Strategy 2020: Facing the People Challenges of the Future; Officership 2020 and NCM 2020*[2] recognized the gap created by an almost singular focus on skills training and highlighted considerable deficiencies in the organization's leadership, military ethos, and training. The CFPDS was envisioned to address that gap and as one of the means to develop and promote a defence culture of continuous learning within a learning organization.

The CFPDS identifies the core elements which define what we must know, what we must be able to do and what it means to be a member of the Profession of Arms. These core elements include: leadership, warfighting and a professional body of knowledge based on our doctrinal literature: the *Duty with Honour: The Profession of Arms in Canada* manual, *Leadership in the Canadian Forces: Conceptual Foundation*s, and the Strategic Operation Concept and Joint Doctrine manuals.[3] The CFPDS was intended to address the demands of a progressive career in a professional military force and meet the requirements of a dynamic and evolving military profession using processes that were more responsive to anticipate asymmetrical and other non-traditional threats. In addition, as a result of comprehensive reviews, the Officer Professional Development System (OPDS) and the Non-Commissioned Member Professional Development System (NCMPDS) frameworks were modified to include the same duty areas:

a. Leadership in peace and war;

b. Operations and warfighting;

c. Communications;

d. Defence management; and

e. General service requirements.

The new specifications and the CFPDS emphasized developing and integrating at all levels, a defence culture of professionalism focused on developing critical thinking, responsibility and accountability balanced with intelligent risk-taking, innovation and an appropriate repertoire of leadership tools and styles … as well as the capacity to motivate people and generate trust and confidence.[4] It also abandoned the traditional distinction between junior officers and NCMs in favour of a common approach recognizing the convergence of the responsibilities at the leading people level but recognizing continued differences at the executive – leading the institution level.

The renewed focus on education was intended to develop CF members capable of transcending the deeply embedded cognitive orientation towards linear, analytical and reductionist thinking and to produce people with the capacity to deal with chaotic, non-linear problems also known as "wicked problems" in a holistic manner.[5] A variety of new methods and tools were suggested to bridge this gap, including cognitive tools such as Soft Systems Methodology (SSM), Recognition Primed Decision-Making Theory and Systemic Approaches to Operational

Design. It was suggested that these types of alternate methodologies should be introduced at an early stage in one's career and refined as members progress through career development programs. In addition, the emphasis on the Operational Planning Process (OPP) in the CF training and education system should be examined due to a reported inadequacy in dealing with the types of complex problems faced by deployed forces in the contemporary security environment. It was also suggested that a new competencies-based framework was required to identify the full range of competencies necessary and to describe how these should be addressed progressively at the tactical, operational, military strategic and politico-strategic levels. The Professional Development Framework (PDF)[6] was developed to address this need. The PDF addresses five meta-competencies spanning four levels – junior, intermediate, advanced and senior, and these correspond generally to the tactical, operational, military strategic and politico-strategic levels of war and conflict. The five meta-competencies are: expertise, cognitive capacities, social capacities, change capacities and professional ideology. The PDF does not dispense with the general specification (GS) system. Rather, the GS requirements are fully integrated into the PDF.[7]

To ensure maximum effectiveness, education systems need to continuously improve to meet changing requirements. Our contemporary operating environment has changed significantly since the CFPD was initially established and there are questions as to whether the education system is keeping pace. As Ronald Barnett, a professor of higher education, observed, we live in an age of supercomplexity in which the demand for change is ever present.[8] Nowhere is this more true than in the educational sphere; for example, there is vigorous pressure from learning theorists and learners to incorporate multiple learning options and alternate pathways in post-secondary education including more online learning. These pressures are often driven by leading edge research, advances in technology, globalization including threats without borders such as global warming, narco-terrorists, oil spills, and epidemics such as SARS and AIDS. The challenge for educational institutions and educators is to develop and implement new strategies. In effect we must evolve to meet these challenges or risk losing our credibility as a cutting edge, forward leaning, learning organization.

Measure What We Value – Value What We Measure

As stated above, the CFPDS has been in place for a number of years and there have been some attempts at its assessment.[9] Any attempt to assess the effectiveness of education in meeting our desired outcomes involves a values-based judgement related to the aims and purposes of education. To make judgement calls about the effectiveness of education, for instance, we must first ask: effective for what and effective for whom?[10] To respond to those questions we must examine the functions of education. Gert Biesta suggests a framework of three functions that overlap in the form of a Venn diagram:

a. qualification – the provision of knowledge, skills and understanding for example to support life roles and specific jobs or professions as is the case in the CF;

b. socialization – the process of enculturation into a specific social network or organization; the means by which we acquire our cultural norms, values and traditions within a particular organization such as the CF or how we learn the ways of being and doing in a particular group; and

c. subjectification – or individuation, the opposite of socialization whereby the individual learns to become more independent in thinking and acting, (i.e., separate from yet accepting of the group norms).[11]

In the CF we tend to focus on measuring qualifications – how many; how often and over what period of time? While we are concerned with socialization and individuation, we are constrained in our ability to measure these qualities except through indicators which rarely results in the precise kinds of measures required for full financial or program accountability. Nevertheless, considerable research is available that reports on the value of post-secondary education. For instance, researchers have performed a comprehensive review of over 2600 studies covering the period 1991 to 2005; this research compendium reports in detail on the impact that attending college has on student development and academic abilities. Factors assessed include:

a. degree of change, how much and in what direction;

b. net effects, what effects are attributable to attending college;

c. between college, any institutional differences;

d. within colleges, effects at any specific type of college;

e.   conditional; effects, based on individual characteristics; and

f.   long term effects, durability.[12]

These researchers concluded, as in an earlier review, that in the areas of learning and cognitive changes, students' competencies in the areas of critical and abstract thinking improved as a result of attending college; in addition, students were able to think in more complex and reflective ways. For instance, studies showed a shift from making judgements based simply on beliefs to relying on evidence which is a prerequisite to dealing effectively with ill-structured problems, as well as a shift from conventional to principled reasoning which results in qualitative advances in moral development; hence, they concluded that there was holistic change within college students' growth from year one to year four.[13] Furthermore, they concluded that:

> On nearly all dimensions …a statistically significant part of that change was attributable to attending college. Exposure to post-secondary education not only appeared to significantly enhance students' general verbal and quantitative skills as well as oral and written communication skills, but also had a statistically significant and positive net effect on their general intellectual and analytical skills, critical thinking, their use of reason and evidence in addressing ill-structured problems (reflective judgement-thinking), and their intellectual flexibility. Further, these effects could not be explained by maturation or differences between those who attended and those who did not attend college in tested intelligence, academic ability, or other precollege characteristics.[14]

The researchers also reported an impressive number of net effects attributable to the post-secondary experience and not to other factors such as maturation; for instance, multiple studies demonstrated improvements in academic and cognitive factors such as:

a.   verbal and quantitative skills – content knowledge, critical thinking, reflective judgement and principled moral reasoning;

b.   psychosocial skills – academic and social self-concept, self-esteem, independence, sense of control, interpersonal skills and leadership skills;

c.   attitudes and values – increase in engagement in civic and community; diversity and racial understanding, support to gender equality; and

d.   career/economic advantages – improvements in employment, earnings and job satisfaction, along with overall quality of life improvements.[15]

Regardless of factors such as college type, size, ranking, or selectivity, the net effect on students is equal or improved cognitive growth and development. In sum, those who attend college learn better, know and earn more, which led the authors to conclude that post-secondary education acquired through college and/or university studies adds value.

In terms of specific competency development in the area of critical thinking, related research offers positive findings as well. For instance, research has found three factors relevant in the development of critical thinking: faculty encouragement of student ideas, the amount and cognitive level of student participation in class, and the amount of interaction among students in a course.[16] Lisa Tsui,[17] an expert on higher education, found that critical thinking is linked to an emphasis on cooperative exploration of knowledge and that it encourages divergent thinking. It has also been noted that growth in critical thinking was positively related to having papers critiqued by instructors, conducting independent research as well as working on a group projects, giving class presentations and completing essay exams; however, critical thinking was negatively related to multiple-choice exams.[18] Tsui focused on instructional techniques used in developing critical thinking and noted that the ability to think critically is a higher order cognitive skill that is required to prepare individuals to tackle a multitude of challenges and it fosters lifelong learning.[19] This research reported that although gains in critical thinking from college experience may be overestimated in terms of perception versus actual test results, college experiences were particularly helpful where courses used strategies such as analyzing articles with essays to identify logic flaws, ambiguity and the misuse of data and to identify assumptions, and uncritical and unsound thinking. In this instance, critical thinking was defined as the students' ability to identify issues and assumptions, recognize important relationships, make correct inferences, evaluate evidence or authority and deduce conclusions.[20]

Extending from this earlier research, Tsui noted that exercises emphasizing writing and rewriting, with critiques from faculty and peers, promote development of critical thinking.[21] Rewriting is used to encourage synthesis, analysis and refinement of ideas. In addition class discussions were reported as a critical factor linked to the exchange among students and with faculty. Discussions and debates were identified as important because they require attention, focus and the active processing of a multitude of ideas, opinions and materials, and all of these strategies are viewed as much better than lecture based methods. On the other hand, it was noted that these types of studies do not conclude causality due to methodological limitations in the use of observation and self-reports rather than specific measures of critical thinking; however, the results still support the higher value of active learning methods.

Implications for Teaching and Learning

These findings suggest important implications for the CF training and education system. For example, Ernest Pascarella and Patrick Terenzine emphasize enhancing the tried and true rather than replacing everything old with something new.[22] Specifically, this research compendium supports the evolution of teaching and learning approaches away from teacher-dominated delivery of instruction to more student-centred learning models. The traditional teacher-directed model has driven curriculum design, course scheduling, teacher selection and the nature of student-teacher/faculty interaction. The research suggests that the teacher-centred model has controlled what goes on and what does not in the classroom. In this model, the teacher decides what will be learned, how, when and where; teachers do the teaching and learning is considered an essentially passive activity that requires students only to acquire knowledge, not necessarily to actively participate in its discovery or construction. As Marcia Baxter-Magolda reported, this approach results in a separation of teacher from student, knowledge from experience and curricular from cocurricular life.[23]

Others, also cited in this research, advocate a learning-centred model wherein learning is the central focus.[24] Tsui further suggests that if we want to achieve and promote teaching and development of critical thinking at the institutional level, we must invest in faculty development and teaching reform efforts via workshops, seminars and training sessions that must be held on a regular re-occurring basis, not a one time shot only. Reform efforts must be an ongoing part of professional development for faculty to promote, encourage and support development and use of active learning strategies to replace more passive methods such as lectures.[25]

Findings such as these are driving a revised view of the role of colleges and that of teachers and students. It is now recognized that students teach and learn from one another as well as from faculty and that instruction involves learning guides and facilitators rather than knowledge dispensers. In addition, the research strongly supports the value and power of cooperative and collaborative learning models in promoting higher-order learning, including critical thinking and moral reasoning.[26] Studies emphasize the importance of and need for strong teacher skills, particularly with respect to organization and preparation for the learning experience. In addition, the level of academic effort and engagement of students was found to be a key factor in benefits gained. In terms of overall achievement, persistence and educational attainment proved to be a key predictor, (i.e., past behaviour predicts future success and engagement).

Finally, student learning style, in particular cooperative learning, produced more pronounced positive effects on higher or more complex levels of cognitive functioning over approaches such as lecture-discussions.[27] This type of evolution in higher education is supported in empirical studies because it challenges students to learn and to engage actively in learning and this type of learning experience results in change. Research also demonstrates that learning is not bound by time and space; that it occurs continuously in a variety of locations and often unpredictably, and that it is maximized when both the activities and outcomes have meaning for the learner.[28]

In addition, growing evidence indicates that learning is not a solitary activity; it thrives on social relationships and takes place when students engage in tasks with each other and through informal interaction with peers and family. It is informal as well as formal. Learning is holistic rather than segmented; students develop academically and cognitively outside classroom as well as within it.[29] Most effective teaching and learning requires opportunities for active student involvement and participation. It involves encountering people and ideas that challenge beliefs which trigger learning, especially where the learner is actively engaged.

Furthermore, knowledge acquisition, skill development and psychosocial change are most likely to occur when learners find meaning in both the activities and the outcomes of the college experience. That is not to say we should totally discard the lecture; it is an efficient means of transmitting information and it is effective in promoting knowledge acquisition and cognitive skill development among college students. However, effectiveness in using the lecture method is linked prominently to teacher skills such as clarity, expressiveness, organization and preparation. That said, new approaches may be even more effective, if not as efficient, because innovative, active collaboration, as employed in cooperative and constructivist instructional approaches shape learning more powerfully in some instances by substantial margins, than do conventional lecture-discussion and text-based approaches.[30]

Organizational structures also affect outcomes, for example, interdisciplinary experiences have been shown to be more powerful than separate and distinct departments and faculty,[31] as is often the case with CF schools that are based on single or small groupings of occupations. The aim for learning experiences that cut across disciplines is especially important if we expect to promote joint and integrated perspectives in complex environment such as those involving whole of government players and international allies and agencies.

From an institutional perspective, it may be necessary to rethink course design, teaching methods and teacher selection at the institutional level. In addition, more emphasis should be placed on the ability to facilitate learning versus dispensing knowledge to pass tests and acquire qualifications. The overall aim of training and educational experiences should be focused on promoting better teaching and greater learning.

Conclusion

It is evident from this limited review of related literature that the value of education depends primarily on the purpose for which one promotes and undertakes education. Considerable research indicates that undertaking post-secondary education adds value in terms of improved intellectual capability, professional opportunities and overall quality of life. Furthermore higher education contributes to a wide variety of graduate attributes and capabilities such as the ability to:

    a. acquire work-related knowledge and skills and general industry awareness;

    b. speak and write clearly and effectively;

c. think critically and analytically;

d. analyze and solve complex problems;

e. use computing and information technology;

f. work effectively with others;

g. learn effectively on their own;

h. understand people of diverse ethnic backgrounds;

i. understand different social contexts;

j. develop a personal code of values and ethics; and

k. contribute to the welfare of the community.

In terms of CF aims for education, it is safe to assume that by focusing specifically on promoting educational achievement and lifelong learning, we are achieving the benefits originally established for the CFPDS. Nevertheless, we must also recognize the need for continuous improvement in our academic approach. Evidence supports the need to shift from the industrial school model we have relied on to establish our skills training foundation to a comprehensive student-centred tutorial approach which blends learning activities with experiential opportunities, offered through a variety of pathways, coached and monitored by subject matter experts, and tracked via learning management systems (LMS) including e-portfolios for accreditation and qualification management.

It is suggested that the CF must become more proficient at leveraging the training and educational systems, processes and programs for the individual student and organization benefit. Concerns related to the time, cost and lack of responsiveness in training and education in terms of meeting the demands of the contemporary operating environment provide the impetus for transformation and modernization, that is to say, most involved in training and education agree that almost all aspects of the design and delivery of training and education including teaching and learning models and activities must evolve from passive to active approaches.

Further, new approaches must promote innovations available through alternate approaches and technological advances such as the use of e-portfolios for qualification and experience management in an effort to maximize accreditation and transfer credits. The CF accrues significant benefits and value from education, but all social systems require continuous improvement and evolution. Current efforts to transform training and education would be wise to focus on improving the quality of student learning while reducing and optimizing the overall cost of training and education including time, numbers of people dedicated to teaching and learning efforts and administrative processes.

1   Robert W. Walker, *The Professional Development Framework: Generating Effectiveness in Canadian Forces Leadership* (Kingston, ON: Canadian Defence Academy Press, Canadian Forces Leadership Institute, Technical Report 2006-01, 2006).

2   Department of National Defence, *Report to the Prime Minister on Leadership and Management in the Canadian Forces* (Ottawa, ON, 1997).

3   Department of National Defence, *Duty With Honour: The Profession of Arms in Canada* (Kingston, ON: Canadian Defence Academy, Canadian Forces Leadership Institute, 2009); and Department of National Defence, *Leadership in the Canadian Forces: Conceptual Foundations* (Kingston, ON: Canadian Defence Academy, Canadian Forces Leadership Institute, 2005).

4   Kathleen Currie, *HR2020 Internal Assessment* (Ottawa, ON: ADM HR, Directorate of Strategic Human Resources, 2003).

5   CFLI Project Team. *Broadsword or Rapier? The Canadian Forces Involvement in the 21st Century Coalition Operations* (Kingston, ON: Canadian Defence Academy Press, Canadian Forces Leadership Institute, Technical Report 2008-01, 2008).

6   Walker, 17.

7   Department of National Defence, *Leadership in the Canadian Forces: Conceptual Foundations*, (Kingston, ON: Canadian Forces Leadership Institute, 2005).

8   Ronald Barnett, "University Knowledge in an Age of Supercomplexity", *Higher Education*, Vol. 40 (2000), 409-422.

9   Kathleen Currie, *HR2020 Internal Assessment* (Ottawa, ON: ADM HR, Directorate of Strategic Human Resources, 2003); and Wendy Darr, *Content Validation of the Leadership Development Framework* (Ottawa, ON: Director General Military Personnel Research & Analysis, DGMPRA TN 2009-025, 2009).

10   Gert Biesta, "Good Education in an Age of Measurement: On the Need to Reconnect with the Question of Purpose in Education", *Education Evaluation Association Springer Science*, Vol. 21 (2009), 33-46; and Ira Bogtoch, Luis Miron and Gert Biesta, "Effective for What; Effective for Whom? Two Questions SESI Should Not Ignore" in Tony Townsend, ed., *International Handbook of School Effectiveness and School Improvement* (Dordrecht/Boston: Springer, 2007), 93-110.

11   Ibid., 40-41.

12   Ernest Pascarella and Patrick Terenzine, *How College Affects Students: A Third Decade of Research* (San Francisco: Jossey-Bass, 2005), 577.

13   Ibid., 577.

14   Ibid., 579.

15   Ibid., 578-626.

16   Daryl G. Smith "College Classroom Interactions and Critical Thinking", *Journal of Educational Psychology*, Vol. 69 (1977), 180-190.

17   Lisa Tsui, "Effects of Campus Culture on Students' Critical Thinking", *Review of Higher Education*, Vol. 23 (2000), 421-441.

18   Lisa Tsui, "Courses and Instruction Affecting Critical Thinking", *Research in Higher Education*, Vol. 40 (1999), 185-200.

19   Lisa Tsui, "Fostering Critical Thinking Through Effective Pedagogy: Evidence from Four Institutional Case Studies", *The Journal of Higher Education*, Vol. 73, No. 6 (2002), 740-763.

20   Ibid., 747-748.

21   Ibid., 747-748.

22   Ernest Pascarella and Patrick Terenzine, *How College Affects Students: A Third Decade of Research* (San Francisco: Jossey-Bass, 2005), 608-610.

23   Marcia B. Baxter-Magolda, *Knowing and Reasoning in College: Gender-Related Patterns in Students' Intellectual Development* (San Francisco: Jossey-Bass, 1992).

24   Robert Barr and John Tagg, "From Teaching to Learning: A New Paradigm for Undergraduate Education", *Change*, Vol. 27 (1995), 13-25; and John Tagg, *The Learning Paradigm College* (Bolton: Anker, 2003).

25   Tsui, "Fostering Critical Thinking," 759.

26   Pascarella and Terenzine, 608-610.

27   Ibid., 622.

28   Ibid., 645-646.

29   Ibid., 645-646.

30   Ibid., 646.

31   Ibid., 647-649.

CHAPTER 16

THE POWER OF DIVERSITY IN DEFENCE: THE LEARNING AND EDUCATION PERSPECTIVE

Dr. Grazia Scoppio

Globalization, migration, improved travel, and technological advancements, have brought people of different nations closer together than ever before. As such, populations within nations have become increasingly diverse. Consequently, organizations need to reflect the diversity of the society in which they exist and serve. Moreover, they must draw on the diverse skills of their personnel in order to remain competitive and effective. This is true for any organization, private, public, not-for-profit, civilian, or military.

Although not yet fully representative of the Canadian population, the Canadian Forces and the Department of National Defence have a very diverse membership (i.e., in terms of gender, ethnicity, language, religion, ability, etc.). This greater organizational diversity has been achieved over the course of many years, dictated at times by legal action or social change (e.g., such as the inclusion of women in all CF occupations). Importantly, currently, there are many policies and programs in place to support and enhance organizational diversity in the DND/CF.

This chapter is intended to be an overview of the foundational concepts and issues related to diversity in the global, Canadian and DND/CF environments – a resource for learners, instructors, and leaders in Defence. As well, the chapter will highlight the impact of diversity on organizations and the importance of diversity education and other learning opportunities to develop leaders and members who are "diversity smart," that is to say, having the appropriate competencies and skills to work effectively in a diverse environment.

Definitions and Concepts

In order to fully understand diversity, it is vital to first define and understand several related concepts that include *culture* and *organizational culture*. Scholars and practitioners have suggested different definitions of culture. The

Dutch social psychologist Geert Hofstede, considered an expert in the study of cultures in organizations and across nations, defines culture as:

> the collective programming of the mind which distinguishes the members of one group or category of people from another... it is learned, not inherited.[1]

Hofstede's definition is consistent with CF doctrine as outlined in the manual *Leadership in the Canadian Forces: Conceptual Foundations* where culture is described as:

> a shared and relatively stable pattern of behaviours, values, and assumptions that a group has learned over time as an effective means of maintaining internal social stability and adapting to its environment, and that are transmitted to new members as the correct ways to perceive, think, and act in relation to these issues.[2]

To put it simply, we can define culture as a shared system of meaning, ideas and thoughts transmitted from generation to generation through socialization, and which gives people a sense of belonging and identity. Culture influences the way we do things, view life, and behave in our private sphere or at work.

Organizational culture has also been defined in various ways. Edgar Schein of the MIT Sloan School of Management, one of the founders of organizational psychology, defines organizational culture as:

> a pattern of shared basic assumptions that the group learned as it solved its problems of external adaptation and internal integration, that has worked well enough to be considered valid and, therefore, to be taught to new members as the correct way to perceive, think, and feel in relation to those problems.[3]

Organizational culture can be visible, in terms of observable attributes, behaviours and physical infrastructures, as well as invisible, that is, the espoused values promoted by the leadership, and people's underlying assumptions that guide their actions. In other words, organizational culture refers to those things that one is expected to do and value in order to fit in an organization. The CF, as other military and para-military organizations, has a strong organizational culture, with distinct officer and non-commissioned member cultures, Regular and Reserve Force cultures, environmental cultures (i.e., the navy, army and air force), as well as numerous occupational sub-cultures. Civilian personnel add yet another "layer" of culture to the overall Defence Team.

The term *diversity* has a broader meaning than culture, and can refer to all the differences that make people unique including culture, gender, ethnicity, language, religion, ability and disability, education, socio-economic background, and sexual orientation. Diversity is not just about cultural diversity or specific groups, it is about everyone.[4]

Diversity can refer to individuals as well as groups, organizations, or entire societies. *Organizational diversity* refers to both the internal diversity of the members within an organization, as well as the external diversity of the workforce, stakeholders, partners and clients external to the organization.[5]

Having provided some definitions to clarify the meaning of diversity and related concepts, it is important to explain the Canadian legislative framework for diversity.

Canadian Legislative Framework for Diversity

In the Canadian context, there is a legislative requirement to ensure that the workplace reflects Canadian diversity. To this end, the Canadian *Employment Equity Act* (EEA) has the purpose to:

> achieve equality in the workplace so that no person shall be denied employment opportunities or benefits for reasons unrelated to ability and, in the fulfillment of that goal, to correct the conditions of disadvantage in employment experienced by women, aboriginal peoples persons with disabilities and members of visible minorities by giving effect to the principle that employment equity means more than treating persons in the same way but also requires special measures and the accommodation of differences.[6]

The EEA defines Aboriginal People as persons who are Indian, Inuit or Métis, while visible minorities are defined as ethnic minorities, other than Aboriginal People, who are non-Caucasian in race, or non-white in colour.[7]

Prior to the EEA, Canada was the first country to adopt an official *Multicultural-ism Policy* in 1971 which was later made into an act of Parliament. The *Multicul-turalism Act* recognizes the diversity of Canadians and is meant to preserve and enhance our multicultural heritage while working to achieve the equality of all Canadians in the economic, social, cultural and political life of Canada.[8]

The equity and multiculturalism policies are at times perceived negatively. They are often the result of special measures being used to increase representation of specific groups. For example, if the CF used special measures to recruit quali-fied Aboriginal People, women or visible minorities, these measures could be viewed by some as "reverse discrimination" against members of majority groups. These principles and policies, however, should be viewed as being more inclu-sive, rather than exclusive. In the past, "equity" was a term linked to the notion of treating everyone the same; for example, recognizing "equal pay for equal work". The current approach, however, recognizes that by ignoring differences we also ignore individuals' legitimate needs (i.e., spiritual accommodation, dietary needs, dress accommodation, or needs related to ability). Equity and equality are about fairness, not about equal treatment of people.[9] It is also critical to recognize that racisim, sexism, discrimination and harrasment exist in Canadian society includ-ing Defence, despite its zero tolerance policy, as they are microcosms of the larger society.

The principles of diversity, multiculturalism and equity, along with related con-structs, should inform Defence values, doctrine, practices, and professional de-velopment. This holistic approach will allow for the development of personnel able to successfully perform in the context of internal organizational diversity, as well as external global diversity. It is also important for the DND/CF, and other organizations, to respond to the challenges of diversity in a way that is proactive, rather than reactive.

Organizational Responses to Diversity

Organizations currently face three main types of diversity:

1. Workforce diversity;

2. Structural diversity; and

3. Business diversity.

Workforce diversity refers to the differences among individuals and groups to include gender, language, ethnicity, religion, sexual orientation, physical ability, age, family status, socio-economic status, education, and geographic background. It also includes differences in behaviours, including communication styles, work styles, career aspirations and learning styles.

Structural diversity refers to differences among divisions, levels, and functions. It is important to look at this aspect of diversity when organizations examine ways to become more flexible, less layered, and more team-based.

Business diversity refers to the diversity in the environment within which the organization is operating, the diversity of customers that the organization is serving, and the way the organization is responding to clients' diverse needs.

In the case of the CF and other military organizations whose purpose is non-profit, but the application of force on behalf of the government, the need for embracing diversity still applies. Military organizations must reflect the diversity of the nation and population they serve (i.e., societal values, demographics changes, and legislation – external diversity), and at the same time, they need to adapt to and draw from the internal diversity of their personnel (i.e., the composition and values of members and new recruits – internal diversity).

Organizations adopt various approaches to address diversity issues. According to organizational behaviour research conducted by David Thomas and Robin Ely,[10] two internationally recognized professors of organizational behaviour at the Harvard Business School, the three main approaches or paradigms adopted are:

1. Discrimination-fairness;

2. Access-legitimacy; and

3. Learning-effectiveness.

Organizations that fall under the first paradigm (i.e. Discrimination-fairness), focus on compliance with legislation, to meet recruitment and retention goals. This approach focuses on increasing the representation of certain groups without giving value to or taking into consideration the different needs and perspectives that diverse members bring to the organization. This colour-blind, gender-blind, and culture-blind approach, which is based upon the assumption that all people must be treated the same way regardless of circumstances is unlikely to succeed in the context of today's diverse workforce.[11] This can be considered a *compliance* and *reactive* approach.

The second paradigm (i.e. Access-legitimacy), is focused on the requirement to match the internal diversity of the workforce to the external diversity of its customers. For example, if a company wants to attract customers among the American-Mexican community, it is important for them to recruit Spanish-speaking employees. This can be considered an approach based on *business requirements* (i.e., financial and marketing). However, while this approach is founded on the principle of acceptance of cultural differences, these differences are not clearly analyzed or understood.

Organizations that adopt the third paradigm (i.e., Learning-effectiveness) value pluralism by incorporating diversity into their mission, work, and culture. This is a more *proactive* approach which encourages the development of new ideas, strategies, missions, and practices, which reflect the diverse cultures of its members.

The challenge for the CF and other military organizations is that they have strong organizational cultures that are based on historic military traditions, hierarchical structures, a defined chain of command, and linear planning and rigid operating procedures; consequently, these organizations have a more "closed" organizational culture. As such, they are more likely to resist culture change and diverse perspectives. For instance, a DND doctrinal publication acknowledges:

> In a mature organization like the CF, which possesses a deeply ingrained culture or family of cultures, achieving significant cultural change is a difficult undertaking at any time.[12]

Shifting a paradigm requires a cultural change in the organization. Change, however, can be challenging for the CF and other military organizations. In organizations with closed cultures, the approach towards newcomers is usually one of "assimilation" whereby new recruits are expected to conform to the organization. This approach may work for new members who are similar to the majority, but does not necessarily work well for "minority" groups that are significantly different from the mainstream. Thus, the assimilation approach needs to be re-visited due to the increasing diversity of the workforce, greater immigration and human capital mobility. Conversely, newer organizations with horizontal struc-tures, less-linear planning, and more flexible operating processes, have a more "open" organizational culture and are more likely to embrace change and diverse ways of thinking.[13]

Globalization and Diversity

Having provided a series of definitions and a framework for understanding di-versity, culture, equity and organizational responses to diversity, attention now shifts to the wider context of globalization and how it affects diversity.

The term "globalization" is not new. It gained prominence in the early 1980s in response to business and economic trends, such as the phenomenon whereby multinational corporations operate in and sell their products worldwide. In ac-tual fact, economic trends represent but one factor of globalization. There are several inter-related aspects to globalization; greater movements of people and goods, the free flow of information facilitated by the internet and modern tech-nology, and faster world-wide communications. Thus, we can broadly define glo-balization as the "widening, deepening and speeding up of connections across national borders".[14]

Globalization affects diversity in that it creates an increasing flow of human capital across borders, including the migration of people from developing to industrialized countries; many migrants move due to economic, political, social, and environmental reasons, others are refugees. While experiencing increasing immigration, industrialized countries such as Canada, are at the same time un-dergoing a decrease in growth due to low birth rates and aging populations. These factors contribute to the growing diversity of the global workforce and as a result, organizations must face the reality of competing to attract quality hu-man capital. The DND/CF, one of the largest departments in the Canadian federal government, also faces the challenge of attracting competent recruits from an increasingly diverse labour force.

The Canadian Workforce

The Canadian population is extremely diverse and multicultural, made up of Anglophones, Francophones, Aboriginal People, and immigrants. Based on the

2006 Census, Canada's population reached 31.6 million and has the fastest growing population among G8 countries, with a 5.4 per cent growth rate.[15] However,
this growth is not due to natural increase, rather, it mostly derives from immigration. Canada has an active immigration program with an annual intake of about
230,000. Almost 20 percent of our population is foreign-born; the second highest foreign-born rate in the world after Australia. Approximately 58 percent of
new immigrants come from Asia and the Middle East; 16 percent from Europe;
10 percent from the Caribbean, Central and South America; and 8 percent from
Africa. As a result, the visible minority population in Canada has increased to
over 5 million. The Aboriginal population is also increasing due to high birth
rates and is now over 1.2 million.[16]

Not surprisingly, over 20 percent of the labour force is foreign-born and about 50
percent are women. Aboriginal participation in the workforce is also increasing
as this is one of the fastest growing groups in Canada. This increasing diversity of
the Canadian workforce poses a particular challenge for the CF, as the traditional
pool of recruits of white, young males is shrinking while more women, visible
minorities and Aboriginal People join the Canadian work force. The CF in the
past responded reactively to challenges posed by internal and external diversity;
however, it has recently been more proactive in its approach as demonstrated by
the wide range of diversity programs recently implemented, for example the CF
Aboriginal programs such as the Aboriginal Opportunity Year (ALOY) delivered
at the Royal Military College of Canada.

Diversity and Employment Equity in Defence

As of 2002, the Canadian Forces falls under the EEA, although there are specific
regulations to account for the operational effectiveness of the Forces. There are
two separate directorates in Defence dealing with diversity and Employment
Equity (EE). The Directorate of Human Rights and Diversity (DHRD) is responsible
for military personnel, while the responsibility for Defence civilian personnel falls
under the Director of Diversity and Well-Being (DDWB).

These two organizations operate independently in matters concerning EE; however, they come together on matters concerning broad diversity issues. Strategic
level responsibilities include providing inputs for the annual EE and Multiculturalism reports and the coordination of the Defence Diversity Council (DDC). The
DDC provides a unified forum on matters related to diversity for the DND/CF

informed by the Defence Advisory Groups, to help identify issues, challenges and systemic diversity barriers.

While the Defence civilian population is fairly representative of the labour force, similar to other civilian departments in the federal government, the composition of the CF does not yet reflect the gender and ethnic diversity of the Canadian labour force. The majority of CF membership is still predominantly male, white Anglo-Saxon and French-Canadian. Representation rates of women, visible minorities and Aboriginal People in the CF are lower than federal government rates and significantly below labour force representation rates. The Reserve Force has higher representation of women and visible minorities than the Regular Force. According to Statistics Canada:

> Overall, the Canadian military is predominantly male. However, women's representation has risen in recent decades. In 2002, 15 percent of all personnel were women… A very small proportion of CF personnel were members of visible minorities—only 6 percent of all CF members (5 percent of regular forces and 11 percent of reservists) were visible minorities compared with 17 percent of the civilian working population. This is much lower than the U.S. military's rate of 33 percent. Only 3 percent of officers in the regular forces were members of visible minorities.[17]

The issue of low representation of women and minority groups is not unique to the CF; it is a challenge faced by other military organizations in allied nations.[18] Having said that, the study also showed that the CF has implemented several initiatives to remove enrolment barriers and facilitate access for various groups. For example:

- opening combat occupations to women;

- creating policies for dress and dietary accommodation;

- allowing homosexual members to be open about their sexual orientation;

- creating Aboriginal recruiting and training programs; and

- establishing Advisory Groups.

Some of these initiatives are based on the *compliance* approach. For example, opening combat occupations to women and accommodation policies were legislative requirements. On the other hand, Aboriginal programs and Advisory Groups are more in line with the *business* approach; these initiatives are influenced by demographic trends and aim to reach out to certain communities that are not well represented in the CF. The CF needs to become more proactive and shift its diversity paradigm to "learning – effectiveness" (a values-based model) by valuing the diversity of each team member, and tapping into their unique skills to make the CF more effective and better capable of accomplishing its mission.[19]

The business case for diversity in the CF can therefore be linked to an operational imperative. Given the greater diversity of the Canadian workforce and the competition to recruit qualified candidates, the CF has no choice but to attract, recruit and retain appropriate numbers of skilled candidates that represent Canada's multicultural mosaic. These candidates must have the ability to develop the skills necessary to operate successfully in different functions within the context of diversity and globalization. A wide range of learning opportunities, in particular formal education, are key factors in preparing newly recruited members to respond to a wide range of unpredictable situations and meet the challenges of a diverse and constantly changing global environment.

The Role of Diversity Education and Training

A globalized world calls for people who are adaptable to change, dynamic, analytical, flexible, technologically literate, creative, able to speak foreign languages, and "diversity smart". These skills and competencies must be acquired through a combination of experience, education, training and self-development, using a lifelong approach to learning.

Due to the requirement to develop these new skills, the CF has developed various learning events to increase diversity and EE awareness among its members. The initial program developed to provide common training to all CF members was the Standard for Harassment and Racism Prevention (SHARP). This program, however, was looked upon as a "tick in the box" and it was often considered reactive and uncoordinated. Since then, no single program has been developed to replace the mandatory SHARP training. However, select learning initiatives are provided as needed to include:

- cross-cultural workshops for select CF members deployed to certain foreign countries;

- briefings for deploying units on the cultural, geo-political, and social characteristics of the country where the unit is to be deployed;

- diversity lessons/presentations included in the common portion of the National Recruiters Course;

- a cross-cultural awareness training seminar developed by the Canadian Forces Northern Area (CFNA) to familiarize personnel deployed to the Northern communities with the cultural differences in the lifestyles and attitudes of Aboriginal People;

- a course focusing on Aboriginal Awareness;

- a course on diversity and EE for practitioners;

- the graduate course "Leading and Working in a Diverse Environment" delivered on-line through the Royal Military College of Canada; and

- several Defence publications in the field of diversity, including on culture, religions, and gender.[20]

As of 2006, the CF has started to integrate diversity and EE topics into some common professional development programs. In 2009 and 2010, the CF Officer and NCM General Specifications were reviewed; this review included updating the tasks, skills, knowledge and attitudes related to EE, human rights, diversity and ethics. In response to changes in the CF officer and NCM specifications, it is expected that more diversity and EE development topics will be included across all CF common professional development programs.

It is necessary for the CF to continue to place effort and assign resources to diversity education to ensure that all CF personnel develop an increased aware-ness and understanding of culture and diversity; first, through awareness of their own culture; second, through appreciation of cultural differences among indi-viduals, organizations, and societies. It is crucial for CF leaders to be aware of and be sensitive to the cultural differences of its members, allied nations and host countries, including differences in communication styles, ways of thinking, or leadership styles.

While it is important to acknowledge cultural differences, we need to avoid stereotypes, prejudice and discrimination. Stereotypes are based on what we know and have experienced; they are the "lenses" through which we see the world and process information. When we meet people we see them through these lenses or "templates"; we need to realize, however, that these are assumptions based on generalizations. As such, we must revisit these perceptions and change the way we think and behave.

However, change is difficult to implement, both at the individual and organizational level. It is easier to maintain the *status quo* than to undergo change. Nonetheless, it is essential to go through the process of change and break down any existing barriers in order to build a more inclusive workplace in the organization. To do so, organizations such as the DND/CF must ensure that all personnel are afforded the relevant learning and experiential opportunities to develop the required skill set, which includes "hard" and "soft" skills, as illustrated in the following section.

Diversity Competencies and Soft Skills

Traditionally, military training is focused on the development of hard skills, that is to say, technical and military skills. More recently, attention has also been afforded to developing soft skills, namely an individual's career attributes, personal qualities, skills and abilities that set him/her apart from others with similar technical or hard skills.[21] Other terms used to refer to these skills are: non-academic skills; transferable skills; employability skills; or emotional intelligence. While some soft skills are considered innate, such as empathy, most soft skills can be learned. In the military context, soft skills are defined as those abilities that fall in the range of human dynamics, interpersonal communications and personal relations, rather than combat skills associated with engaging the adversary by fire and manoeuvre or other kinetic means.[22] Soft skills include: building trust, communication, cultural awareness, conflict resolution, and interpersonal skills. Many soft skills are similar to "diversity competencies" which are required by leaders in the DND/CF in order to be "diversity smart", that is to say, to be able to successfully work in a diverse organization and a global environment.[23]

Diversity competencies and soft skills can be acquired progressively through a combination of formal, informal and experiential learning, over the course of a member's career. The CF Professional Development System (PDS) provides a well-balanced framework for the development of soft skills as it is based on the four pillars of education, training, experience and self-development. The PDS is now more focused on competencies, in line with the Leadership Development Framework, previously referred to as the Professional Development Framework. The LDF includes five leader elements: expertise, cognitive capacities, social capacities, change capacities and professional ideology.[24] If we "map" diversity and soft skills competencies within the LDF, they fall mostly under cognitive capacities, social capacities, and professional ideology. Having said that, it is equally important for leaders to build a foundation of knowledge on diversity, therefore the element of "expertise" is also involved.

Summary

As populations and organizations are becoming increasingly diverse, it is critical for the DND/CF to harness and capitalize on the diversity of the workforce. To do so, it is necessary for the organization to continue to shift from a reactive to a proactive approach towards diversity.

While legislative requirements exist and must be taken into consideration, diversity should not be viewed as an obligation or a constraint. Instead, it should be considered as an opportunity to do the right thing and an operational necessity. The spectrum of initiatives in the diversity domain should not be limited to increasing representation through recruiting of certain groups, retention strategies, or accommodation policies. Although these are steps in the right direction, it is equally important to create a more open organizational culture that values the perspective of members from different backgrounds, encourages new ideas, and supports career-long learning. Organizations that welcome and promote diversity are ultimately more successful and competitive in our diverse and rapidly changing "global village".

Through appropriate learning events, leaders and followers can develop the necessary diversity competencies and soft skills to operate successfully in diverse environments, both within and outside the organization; as a result, they can become "diversity smart".

The way ahead is not "one-shot", "one-size fits all" diversity training, which has proven to be inadequate and ineffective in the past. Rather, there is a need for a career-long learning approach that includes a combination of diversity education and training, as well as relevant experience and self-development.

Ultimately, it is through a lifelong learning process that minds can be influenced and behaviours can change.

---

1   Geert Hofstede, "Culture and organizations", *International Studies of Management and Organizations*, Vol. 10, No. 4 (1981), 15- 41.

2   Department of National Defence, *Leadership in the Canadian Forces: Conceptual Foundations* (Kingston, ON: Canadian Forces Leadership Institute, 2005), 129 retrieved on 15 Nov 2011 from <http://www.cda.forces.gc.ca/cfli-ilfc/doc/DND_Conceptual-eng.pdf>.

3   Edgar H. Schein, *Organizational Culture and Leadership* (San Francisco, CA: Jossey-Bass, 1992), 12.

4   Grazia Scoppio, *Leadership in a Diverse Environment: Diversity Strategies in Military and Police Forces in Canada, Australia, the United Kingdom, and the United States,* Final Report (Kingston, ON: Canadian Defence Academy, 2007). Retrieved on 15 Nov 2011 from <http://www.deomi.org/EOEEOResources/documents/Research_Report_Leadership_Diversity.pdf>.

5   Ibid.

6   Department of Justice Canada, *Department of Justice - Employment Equity Act* (S.C. 1995, c. 44) Part 2, retrieved on 15 Nov 2011 from <http://lois-laws.justice.gc.ca/eng/acts/E-5.401/index.html>.

7   Ibid.

8   Department of Justice Canada, *Department of Justice - Canadian Multiculturalism Act* (R.S.C., 1985, c. 24 (4th Supp.)), retrieved on 15 Nov 2011 from <http://laws-lois.justice.gc.ca/eng/acts/C-18.7/>.

9   Judge Rosalie Abella, *Royal Commission Report – Equality in Employment* (Ottawa, ON: Canadian Government Publishing Centre, 1984).

10   David A. Thomas and Robin J. Ely, "Making Differences Matter: A New Paradigm for Managing Diversity", in R. Rosevelt Thomas, David A. Thomas, Robin J. Ely & Debra E. Meyerson, *Harvard Business Review on Managing Diversity* (Boston, MA,: Harvard Business School Press, 2002).

11   In the past, the approach towards a diverse workforce was limited to treating everyone the same way (e.g., giving equal pay for equal work regardless of gender or ethnicity). It is now widely recognized that this approach is no longer enough and that if we ignore people's differences, we ultimately ignore their individual needs.

12   Department of National Defence, *Leadership in the Canadian Forces: Conceptual Foundations.*

13   Grazia Scoppio, Ray Idzenga, and Sharon Miklas, *Learning together: Lessons on Canadian Forces Skill Sets for Multinational, Inter-agency Operations.* (Kingston, ON: Canadian Defence Academy, Department of National Defence, 2009).

14   Organization for Economic Co-operation and Development (OECD), *Trends Shaping Education 2010*, retrieved on 15 Nov 2011 from <http://www.oecd.org/dataoecd/40/13/46447355.pdf>, 10.

15   At the time of writing this chapter the data from the 2011 Census by Statistics Canada was not yet available to the public.

16   Statistics Canada, *Statistic Canada - Census 2006*, retrieved on 15 Nov 2011 from <http://www12.statcan.gc.ca/census-recensement/2006/rt-td/index-eng.cfm>.

17   Jungwee Park, "A profile of the Canadian Forces", *Perspectives- Statistics Canada Catalogue no. 75-001-XIE,* Vol. 9, No. 7 (July 2008), retrieved on 15 Nov 2011 from <http://www.statcan.gc.ca/pub/75-001-x/2008107/pdf/10657-eng.pdf>.

18   Scoppio, *Leadership in a Diverse Environment*, 2007.

19   Grazia Scoppio, "Diversity Best Practices in Military Organizations in Canada, Australia, the U.K., and the U.S.", *Canadian Military Journal*, Vol. 9, No. 3 (2009), 17-30, retrieved on 15 Nov 2011 from <http://www.journal.forces.gc.ca/vo9/no3/doc/05-scoppio-eng.pdf>.

20   See for example: *Challenge and Change in the Military: Gender and Diversity Issues*, F. Pinch, A. MacIntyre, P. Browne, and Alan Okros (Eds.) (Kingston, On: Canadian Forces Leadership Institute, National Defence, 2004); *Women and Leadership in the Canadian Forces*, K. Davis (Ed.) (Kingston, On: Canadian Defence Academy Press, National Defence, 2007); *Religions in Canada* (Ottawa, ON.: Directorate of Military Gender Integration and Employment Equity (DMGIEE), National Defence, 2003).

21   Grazia Scoppio, *The Importance of Culture: Soft Skills for Interagency, Complex Operations.* Research report (Kingston, ON: Canadian Forces Leadership Institute, National Defence, 2011), retrieved on 15 Nov 2011 from <http://www.cda.forces.gc.ca/cfli-ilfc/Reports-eng.asp>.

22   Victor M. Rosello, "Soft Skills for 21st Century Land Dominance", Landpower Essay No. 09-1, AUSA Institute of Land Warfare (January 2009), retrieved on 15 Nov 2011 from <www3.ausa.org/marketing/SoftSkillswebsite0209.pdf>.

23   Scoppio, "Diversity best practices in military organizations in Canada, Australia, the U.K., and the U.S.".

24   Robert Walker, *The Professional Development Framework: Generating Effectiveness in the Canadian Forces Leadership* (Kingston, ON: Canadian Forces Leadership Institute, National Defence, Technical Report 2006-01, 2006), retrieved 15 Nov 2011 from < http://www.cda.forces.gc.ca/cfli-ilfc/Reports-eng.asp >.

CHAPTER 17

THE CANADIAN FORCES
PROFESSIONAL DEVELOPMENT SYSTEM

Major Frédéric A.C. Brulier and
Lieutenant-Colonel Dennis G. Hartnett

The success of any organization, particularly a military one, rests on the capability of its members. For the Canadian Forces its success had been dependent on highly trained well-educated personnel that have been able to respond correctly to a myriad of complex, dangerous and ever-changing circumstances in diverse environments. However, the success has not been by chance. It has been a direct result of the CFPDS, which is the product of an evolutionary process extending over many years. This system is responsible for the professional development of CF members. PD is sequenced throughout an individual's CF career to impart skills, knowledge and attitudes necessary to rank and responsibilities and to allow each member to exercise sound judgement. The CFPDS is a career-long, comprehensive, integrated and sequential development process of education, training, self-development, and experience. In essence, the CFPDS provides a continuous learning environment to develop and enhance the capabilities and leadership of CF members.

The CFPDS is a critical component of CF effectiveness. Its purpose is the ethical, social and intellectual development of CF personnel and the accumulation of a sufficient Professional Body of Knowledge (PBK) to deal with the broad range of leadership and staff responsibilities throughout the full spectrum of military activities that can be anticipated during an individual's career.

The CFPDS is rooted in a doctrinal foundation and is guided by a number of strategic directions. The documents below provide the strategic level guidance for PD and the theoretical foundation for leadership in the CF. The CFPDS provides the education and training detailed in these documents to the CF:

  a. *Defence Strategy 2020*[1] (also called *Strategy 2020*), a keystone document, was a major milestone in developing a strategic plan to shape future PD in the CF. The CFPDS was developed in support of *Strategy 2020* to position Defence as an employer of choice for Canadians by expanding the knowledge and skills base of our personnel and by providing them with progressive opportunities for development, career mobility and recognition for service;

b. *Officership 2020*[2] is the strategic guidance for reshaping the Officer Corps to meet the anticipated challenges of the future. It is the next step in achieving the PD objectives outlined in *Strategy 2020* for the Officer Corps. The CFPDS was designed to develop an ethical, highly intelligent and proactive Officer Corps;

c. *NCM Corps 2020*[3] provides the strategic guidance for the professional development of the NCMs for the next 20 years and is the companion document to *Officership 2020*. The PD objectives described in *Strategy 2020* and *Officership 2020*, are incorporated in *NCM Corps 2020*. The CFPDS was developed to support a distinctive NCM PD while reinforcing the common elements of the officer/NCM team;

d. *Canadian Military Doctrine (CFJP-01)*[4] is the Canadian Forces capstone doctrine publication and is published under the authority of the Chief of the Defence Staff. This manual specifies the roles and missions assigned to the CF; provides the fundamentals of warfare and guidance for command, control and organization of the CF; describes authorized command relationships and the authorities that military commanders can use; and formulates guidelines for operational activities embodied in CF strategic policy. Also provided is the doctrinal basis for interdepartmental and interagency coordination. The guidance contained in *Canadian Military Doctrine* serves as the foundation upon which the CFPDS is designed;

e. *Duty with Honour: The Profession of Arms in Canada*[5] is a cornerstone document within the CFPDS. It provides an understanding and vision of the Canadian military profession and establishes the intellectual and doctrinal basis for all personnel and PD policies in the CF;

f. *Leadership in the Canadian Forces: Conceptual Foundations*[6] provides a broad conceptual understanding of military leadership and a systems overview of the requirements of leadership in the CF. It also represents

the primary source for the development of leader training and education programs in all CF Centres of Excellence for PD;

g. *Leadership in the Canadian Forces: Doctrine*[7] is a companion document
   of *Duty with Honour: The Profession of Arms in Canada*. It is the authoritative guide to leadership training, education, and practice throughout
   the CF. It provides a unified doctrinal basis for all officer-NCM leadership training and education in the CF. The CFPDS serves as a roadmap
   to leadership development at all levels as defined in *Leadership in the
   Canadian Forces: Doctrine*;

h. *Leadership in the Canadian Forces: Leading People*[8], which has drawn
   from *Leadership in the Canadian Forces: Doctrine* and *Leadership in
   the Canadian Forces: Conceptual Foundations*, is a doctrinal and theoretical foundation to provide CF military professionals with the practical
   guidance to effectively lead people. This manual is used extensively in
   all PD centres across the CF. The CFPDS provides officers/NCMs with a
   graduated leadership development within the first four developmental
   periods (DPs); and

i. *Leadership in the Canadian Forces: Leading the Institution*[9] provides
   guidance to those senior officers and NCMs who serve in key/senior
   appointments, their staffs, and others with the abilities and commitment to contribute to CF strategy. It offers direction for one to attain
   the knowledge, leader capacities, skills and professionalism required for
   becoming an effective institutional leader. The CFPDS provides the leadership development necessary for those institutional leaders in DP5.

Undisputedly, the CF is committed to providing CF members with PD throughout their military careers and promoting a continuous learning environment
with a view to imparting new knowledge and developing skills and attitudes as
the basis for enhanced mental agility, innovation and judgement. PD is a shared
responsibility between commanders and commanding officers on one hand,
and individual CF members on the other hand. As bilingualism is intrinsic to CF
leadership, ability in both official languages becomes increasingly important for
progression through the DPs.

The CFPDS is designed to ensure that CF members meet the applicable
work and job requirements identified in the appropriate Military Employment

Structure (MES)[10] specifications: to ensure that CF members are capable of critical thinking, managing change, effective leadership and resource management, across the full spectrum of military service; to strengthen understanding of the military profession; to enhance general, environmental and occupational expertise; to enable CF members to develop professional competencies and attitudes required to successfully perform their duties and tasks; to prepare CF members for the demands of a progressive career; and, to prepare retiring CF members for transition to civilian life.

CF Doctrine provides the fundamental principles upon which the CFPDS is based, including: the *Professional Body of Knowledge* comprising core knowledge, supporting knowledge and specialized knowledge; the *war fighting skills* required to conduct the full spectrum of military operations from the tactical to the strategic level; and, the required *leadership competencies* that span from leading people to leading the institution. They are contained in the Leader Development Framework.

The basis upon which PD is achieved during a career in the CF are the four pillars of the CFPDS:

    a. Education allows for a reasoned response to an unpredictable situation through the provision of a base of knowledge and intellectual skills upon which information can be correctly interpreted and sound judgement exercised. The cognitive ability to reason, acquired through academic education and practice, enables individuals to think through a problem and formulate a reasoned solution;

    b. Training is a learned response to a predictable situation, that is the skills and knowledge to perform specific duties and tasks;

    c. Employment Experience. Training and education must be reinforced by the practical application of acquired skill and knowledge through job experience; and

    d. Self-development, which may take the form of education, training or experience; however, it differs from conventional learning in that it is based on the self-motivation of each officer/NCM. Self-development is taking personal responsibility for one's own learning and development through a process of assessment, reflection, and taking action.

Figure 17.1: Canadian Forces Professional Development System

Professional development incorporates two distinct components: formal education and training directed, conducted, or sponsored by the CF; and self-motivated or self-directed improvement. For professional development to be effective, the officer must first accept responsibility for career-long involvement in all aspects of his/her professional development, whether it is in activities related to either training, or education, or experiential learning, or self-development. Subject to service requirements, the CF will encourage and support the seeking by individual officers of training and education opportunities over and above those offered by the CF. While the employment/experiential learning component of development is ultimately dependent on service requirements, individuals will be given and are expected to take an active role in the planning of their employment. This individual responsibility for career-long self-improvement also applies to the Reserve Force to an extent proportional to their service employment.

The orders, policies and instructions that govern the CFPDS are contained within CF Defence Administrative Orders and Directives, CDA Policies with respect to PD and CF Military Personnel Instructions (CF Mil Pers Instr). They were developed in consultation with the Designated Training Authority (DTA), Training Authorities (TAs)[11] and other major stakeholders and approved by AFC. They constitute the CFPDS policy framework which is applicable to all officers and non-commissioned members.

The CFPDS delivers PD across five DPs for officers and NCMs. A DP is a timeframe in a career during which an individual is trained, employed and given the opportunity to develop specific occupational or professional skills and knowledge. DPs are distinguished by progressive increase in the levels of accountability, responsibility, authority, competency, military leadership ability and the knowledge of operations and war.

The CFPDS is also comprised of several elements; one of these elements is the Canadian military professional ideology consisting of two components: the theory-based body of knowledge defining the profession's specialized expertise; and the profession's value system. The former is referred to as the General System of War and Conflict (GSoWC), and the latter is the Canadian Military Ethos.

In any profession, practical skill grows out of an abstract system of knowledge and control of the profession lies in control of the abstractions that generate the practical techniques. In the profession of arms the abstract system of knowledge is represented by the GSoWC, which is divided into four levels: tactical, operational, strategic and political. The CFPDS is designed to provide CF members with the right PD at the appropriate DP to ensure understanding of the GSoWC at the tactical, operational, strategic and political level(s).[12]

The military ethos, the second component of professional ideology, comprises values, beliefs and expectations that reflect core Canadian values, the imperatives of military professionalism and the requirements of operations. It acts as the centre of gravity for the military profession and establishes an ethical framework for the professional conduct of military operations. In establishing desired norms of behaviour, the military ethos acts as an active and unifying spirit that brings all members of the Canadian Forces together from their different Environments and branches. The uniquely Canadian military ethos is made up of three fundamental components: beliefs and expectations about military service, Canadian values and Canadian military values. The CFPDS was designed to ensure that the PD of CF members throughout their careers takes into account these components, establishing the desired institutional culture of the CF in which CF members perform their mission and tasks to the highest professional standards, meeting the expectations of Canadians at large.

Key to the development of the CFPDS is the fact that all members of the CF must be capable of performing the common tasks contained in the Officer and NCM General Specifications (OGS & NCMGS). These common tasks are universal in nature and pertain to fundamental expertise, cognitive, social, change and professional ideology competencies, which when combined deliver the appropriate leadership and management capacities. To perform these duties/tasks effectively, which involve activities outside their occupation and environment, members of the CF must attain levels of competencies commensurate with their rank. These common competencies complement and reinforce the environmental and occupational skills and knowledge acquired through occupational training and enable members of the CF to perform effectively at all levels in the CF. It is these specifications that call up the type, timing, and quality of PD required by each officer/NCM at each stage of their development and consequently form the foundation of PD in the CF as reflected by the design of the DPs within the CFPDS.[13]

The CFPDS provides the knowledge and skills unique to the leadership and management of armed forces in war and peace, commonly referred to as military arts and science. This PD, integrated and shaped by employment experience in the military environment, is recognized as the CF Professional Body of Knowledge.

The CF PBK is unique to the Profession of Arms in Canada. It is comprised of Core, Supporting and Specialized bodies of knowledge. The CF's Core and Supporting bodies of knowledge are those items that are required to operate within the GSoWC model and are what make a member of the CF a "professional" within the "Profession of Arms". The Core and Supporting bodies of knowledge are described as follows:

    a. Core Knowledge – is the unique, theory-based body of knowledge at the core of the profession of arms as it is related to the GSoWC. This knowledge includes tactics and tactical doctrine, the broad and deep discipline of operational art, the operational, technological, logistical and social dimensions of strategy, civil-military relations, command and leadership theory and practice, and the theory and practice of military professionalism. Imparting this core body of knowledge begins in the early socialization process and becomes increasingly more substantive as the member's career progresses. At the individual tactical level, the content of the core body of knowledge may be as different as the fighting skills of an infantry section commander compared to those of a navy destroyer captain or a CF-18 pilot. Orchestrating the battle at higher tactical levels and leading these forces at the operational level, however, requires different skills that have a great deal in common. At the strategic and politico-strategic levels, a sophisticated understanding of the two types of strategy described in *Leadership in the Canadian Forces: Leading the Institution*, the strategy of annihilation and the bipolar strategy, is essential;

b. Supporting Knowledge – includes everything necessary to support a large organization whose primary function is to operate effectively across the spectrum of conflict, up to and including combat. This expertise is normally organized through highly differentiated systems of support, such as the communications, logistics, human resources, legal, and professional development systems. Also in this category is a very wide range of expertise encompassed in such disciplines as Canadian history, military history, political science, psychology, sociology, anthropology, and management theory, among others. The division of expertise between the core and supporting fields of knowledge characterizes the collective nature of the profession of arms. Only through the collective, professional application of all of the expertise at the organization's disposal can operational effectiveness and mission success be achieved. Regardless of rank, role or technical speciality, each member makes an indispensable contribution to the collective whole. Each is a member of the profession of arms first and foremost. These two distinct bodies of knowledge rely heavily on each other as without the sum of the two, the CF cannot truly be considered "professional"; and

c. Specialized Knowledge – the profession of arms in Canada is also characterized by the presence of groups whose expertise is not specific to the military, but organized in its own right by civilian professions. Doctors, lawyers, clergy, engineers and psychologists, to name a few, belong to external professional associations and hold themselves responsible to a second professional ethic as well as the military ethos. In effect, groups external to the military profession can legally discipline these professionals under certain circumstances. As dual professionals, such people provide specialized advice and services to the chain of command on issues that relate to the well-being of individuals and on collective matters in support of the organization. Furthermore, leaders in turn require specialized assistance to deal effectively with the unique demands and burdens that military service imposes. Medical, legal, spiritual and a wide range of other personnel services are essential to the well-being of the individuals who collectively make up the organization and hence to the health of the organization itself. Dual professionals are bound by the military ethos and their responsibility to the Canadian Forces to resolve circumstances where there is a conflict between operational imperatives and other professional considerations. They must understand and accept the commander's overriding responsibility for mission accomplishment. Operating within the limits of their civilian professional expertise, they have an ethical duty to balance the needs of the individual against the needs of the group. They must, however, understand and conform to operational objectives and direction unless these are clearly unlawful. In turn, leaders throughout the chain of command must understand the importance of the services provided by dual professionals and carefully weigh the consequences to the individual and the organization when defining the operational imperative and seeking to accomplish the mission.

Important to note is that the CFPDS does not operate in isolation. A governance structure provides direction and guidance to the CFPDS as follows:

a. <u>Professional Development Council (PDC)</u>. The PDC is a senior-level council established to provide strategic guidance and oversight of the CF Officer and NCM PD Framework, including IT&E. The PDC is chaired by the Commander (Comd) CDA; members of the PDC include Director General Military Personnel Requirements (DGMPR), Comd Land Forces Doctrine and Training System (LFDTS), Comd 2 Canadian Air Division, Director General Military Personnel (DGMP), Director General Integrated Force Development (DGIFD) and the CDA CWO. The PDC serves as a forum for the provision of strategic direction and integration of pan-CF PD/IT&E issues. A major area of focus is improvement of the DP framework and content for officers and NCMs. The Council assists the CMP in providing functional direction concerning CF PD, including IT&E.

b. <u>Individual Education and Training (IT&E) Committee</u>. The IT&E Committee is established to coordinate pan-CF PD. It is chaired by CDA Chief of

Staff (COS) Strategic Training and Education Programs (STEP) with membership from the CF TAs and DTAs. The IT&E Committee advises CMP and other senior staff on CF PD issues and manages the implementation, coordination and verification of the IT&E activities. The guiding principle of the IT&E Committee is to promote cohesion, collaboration and efficiency in the identification of PD needs and in guiding the lessons observed to lessons learned process.

c. <u>CDA/CFC Curriculum Review Board (CRB)</u>. The CRB is an oversight mechanism to monitor the delivery of CF common senior officer professional development programs conducted by CFC and the Non-Commissioned Member PD Centre (NCMPDC). The Board is established to ensure that the specified CFC and NCMPDC programs provide valid, consistent and reliable training and education that is responsive and relevant to current officer and senior NCM professional development needs.

In addition, CF Institutions/Training Establishments (TEs) are responsible for the development and delivery of Common Professional Development. The CDA TEs are as follows: CFC, RMCC, Collège militaire royal de St-Jean (CMR St-Jean), CFC NCMPDC, and Canadian Forces Leadership and Recruit School (CFLRS). In addition, the Canadian Forces Naval Operations School (CFNOS) Seamanship Division, the Canadian Forces Fleet School Esquimalt (CFFS (E)) Seamanship Division and the Air Command Academy (ACA) Borden deliver a single program, the Primary Leadership Qualification, on behalf of CDA.

Key to the CFPDS, as already briefly mentioned, is the concept of developmental periods. A DP is a timeframe in a career during which an individual is trained, educated, employed and given the opportunity to develop specific occupational or professional skills and knowledge. DPs are distinguished by a progressive increase in the levels of accountability, responsibility, authority, competency, military leadership ability and the knowledge of operations and war. The nature of the military profession is such that officers'/NCMs' capabilities must be developed to meet the demands and broader responsibilities of the employment associated with increased rank. The relatively narrow focus of skills and perspective associated with the limited responsibilities of the early employment must, with time, be expanded to include a greater breadth of perspective, increased cognitive skills and professional military knowledge for in-depth problem assessment and the broader professional judgement needed to deal with increasingly complex issues. Accordingly, the CFPDS is designed to meet the unique developmental needs of the officer/NCM. It is defined by five DPs, each of which encompasses one or more ranks. Training, education and experience within a DP prepare the Officer/NCM not only for effective employment in that DP but also for progression to subsequent DPs.

For officers, the purpose of the DP1 is to develop the required skills and knowledge for CF entry level employment and further training. The formal developmental requirements include achievement of the Basic Military Officer Qualification (BMOQ), environmental and occupational qualifications. Second official language education training (SOLET) may also occur but, with the exception of military college cadets, this is normally limited to DP1 training and employment with specific linguistic requirements. After achieving the developmental requirements of DP1, officers are deemed to be occupationally employable at the introductory level.

Progression into DP2 takes place when the member joins a unit and leaves the Basic Training List (BTL). PD during DP2 is very demanding with the emphasis on training and job experience oriented to occupation and environmental requirements. The CF common requirements for this DP are met, in part, through the Officer Professional Military Education (OPME) Program. The OPME Program is intended to orient the junior officer to selected topics within a professional body of knowledge related to the military profession. From this body of knowledge, officers will begin to enhance their critical thinking skills and develop innovative responses to a myriad of issues. In addition, environmentally conducted residency and self-study programs are conducted to meet the specific needs of the environments. Development within each occupation and environment continues with On the Job Training (OJT). Mentoring and coaching by directing supervisors encourages development. In addition, learning from experience plays a large part. Finally, selected officers may also participate in other formal developmental courses such as SOLET, management training and postgraduate education.[14]

The PD program for DP3 is the Joint Command and Staff Program Residential (JCSP RESID) and Joint Command and Staff Program Distance Learning (JCSP DL) conducted at CFC Toronto. The aim of the Joint Command and Staff Program (JCSP) is to prepare selected senior officers of the Defence Team for command and/or staff appointments in a contemporary operating environment across the continuum of operations in national and international settings. Through a range of professional educational activities, both the residential and distance learning (DL) versions of the program develop officers to a level of knowledge and competence appropriate to the aim.

Next, is DP4, which takes the form of the National Security Program (NSP), which is conducted at CFC Toronto. The NSP is designed to prepare participants for employment as strategic-level leaders and managers and to prepare military officers as operational-level joint task force commanders and senior staff. This 10-month residential program is intended for the following participants: CF colonels and naval captains, officers of similar rank from allied nations, civilian executives from within the Department of National Defence and other government departments, public security agencies, non-governmental organizations and academic institutions. DP4 is characterized by its focus on the national and international environment, decision-making within states and their civil-military interface. The NSP includes the study of strategic leadership and the management of resources at the national level. It examines issues regarding the design, direction and conduct of security operations, ranging from domestic security response to military operations in a war zone.

The aim of the Officer DP5, the Executive Leaders' Program (ELP), conducted at CFC Toronto, is to provide newly-promoted generals and flag officers, as well as key appointment senior Chief Petty Officers First Class and Chief Warrant Officers, and invited senior executives from DND civilian and other government departments with an understanding of what it means to be an Executive Leader. The educational framework of the ELP is based on an andragogical, active learner-centred approach to education with the emphasis on shared learning through participation. Participants are challenged to think critically and analytically about issues facing the Canadian Forces in general and the Canadian government in particular. A significant part of the learning experience comes from interaction with subject matter experts, fellow participants and mentors within a privileged platform environment.

ELP Program Goals set the framework for the session. These entail two major areas of study:

   a. <u>Senior and Executive Leadership</u>. The objective of this program goal is to further develop the executive leaders' ability to evaluate and apply the principles of institutional leadership, in shaping the profession of arms and in sustaining the military ethos. Engaging executive leaders at the early stages of their new role as institutional leaders allows them to address the demands placed on the CF and DND, in the context of competing outcomes and the challenges of the future security environment.

b. <u>Canadian Government and Society</u>. The second ELP program goal is intended to further develop the executive leader's ability to understand the framework of government organization, how the CF operates within that framework and where possible, influence the government's policies and priorities through direct advice. Additionally, this goal seeks to broaden the senior/executive leader's knowledge of how the impact of domestic and international trends create the conditions for operational and professional success.

It is worth noting that a new Officer DP5 program, called the Executive Development Program (EDP), is under development. The intent is to prepare GO/FOs for the highest levels of operation and institutional command and management responsibilities. The EDP is envisioned to consist of four modules, as follows:

a. <u>Introductory Session</u>. An Introductory Session, based on the current GO/FO Executive Leader Program at CFC is designed to prepare newly selected GO/FO for their responsibilities with a view to maximizing their effectiveness;

b. <u>Continuing Development Program</u>. This module consists of an individually focused, centrally managed program of continuing development designed to broaden the perspectives of GO/FOs, and to prepare them for employment in specific competency streams and positions;

c. <u>Mentoring/Executive Coaching</u>. The intent of this module is to develop a structured but informal program of mentorship designed to enhance the effectiveness of the GO/FO by providing support for individual growth and peer consultation; and

d. <u>Team Building for Institutional Effectiveness</u>. This module consists of a variety of group activities that provide the opportunity for GO/FOs (and civilian partners) to work together to solve problems in a focused group setting.

The figure below captures the holistic nature of the Officer DP program.

DP1	DP2	DP3	DP4	DP5
				Flag/ General Officers
			Capt(N)/Col	
		Cdr/LCol		
	Lt(N)/Capt LCdr/Maj			
NCdt/OCdt A/Slt/2Lt	SLt/Lt			
• Basic Military Officer Qualification (BMOQ) • Environmental Training • Basic Occupational Training	• Intermediate Occupational & Environmental Quals • Officer Professional Military Education (OPME) • Joint Staff Operations Program (JSOP)	• Advanced Occupational Quals (as required) • Joint Command and Staff Program (JCSP) • Post Grad • Canadian Security Studies Program (CSSP)	• Develop Advanced Management & Institutional Leadership Ability • National Security Program (NSP) • Post Grad • Second Language Training (as required)	• Develop Executive Level Management & Institutional Leadership Ability • Executive Leader Program • Executive Development Program (EDP) (4 modules – under development) • Second Language Training (as required)

Figure 17.2: Canadian Forces Development Periods, (Officers)

A similar construct exists for the NCM. For NCMs the purpose of DP1 is to focus development towards achieving the required skills and knowledge for CF entry level employment and further training. The formal developmental requirements include achievement of the Basic Military Qualification (BMQ), environmental and occupational qualifications. Development of second language ability may also be indicated but only to the extent necessary to fill position-related linguistic requirements. After achieving the developmental requirements of DP1, NCMs are deemed to be occupationally employable at the introductory level. Progression into DP2 takes place when the member joins a unit and leaves the BTL.

The purpose of DP2 is to prepare NCMs for supervisory employment related to the member's environmental affiliation and occupation. The focus of development in DP2 is twofold: to consolidate and reinforce previous training and employment experience leading to enhanced individual occupational capabilities and to develop leadership potential. The formal development requirements for DP2 are the Primary Leadership Qualification (PLQ) and environmental and occupational qualifications. Training strategies to achieve these qualifications may include both distributed learning and residential components.

Subsequently, DP3 is designed to prepare NCMs for employment as supervisors in an occupationally related employment, matching the members' environmental affiliation. While building on further occupational training and experience, the focus of DP3 is to further develop leadership and management skills through experience and increased responsibilities. Formal development requirements for DP3 are the Intermediate Leadership Program (ILP) and the environmental and occupational qualifications. Education/training strategies to achieve these qualifications may include both DL and residential components. During DP3, NCMs gain leadership experience and proficiency through employment in jobs with increased span of control and responsibilities. NCMs who exhibit high leadership skills and potential are selected for promotion to Petty Officer Second Class/Sergeant (PO2/Sgt).

Next, DP4 prepares NCMs for employment as supervisors and managers, with an increasing probability of employment outside the member's occupation or environment. As well, the level of operations associated with employment changes from the tactical level encountered in the previous DP to the operational level. The focus of development in DP4 is leadership, management and staff skills for employment as a member of a command team and for staff level duties within headquarters. The formal development requirement for DP4 is the Advanced Leadership Program (ALP) while the Senior Leadership Program (SLP), delivered in DP4, develops prospective NCMs for leadership, staff and advisory positions in DP5.

Finally, DP5, the Senior Appointments Program (SAP), prepares NCMs for varied employment assignments to include unit, joint or combined operational employment, employment within a command team at a base, wing or staff positions within higher HQs. The CPO1/CWO occupies a unique position within the framework of the CF. The traditional role of the CPO1/CWO has been to act as the custodian of the NCM corps, and as a co-steward of the CF Profession of Arms. The CPO1/CWO is instrumental in the formulation of a strong officer/NCM team, and fosters an atmosphere of partnership. The focus of development in DP5 is the ability to provide advice on the human factors uniquely associated with military organizations and operations as well as providing input to plans, programs and policies at the senior staff level. The level of operations associated with employment in DP5 can range from tactical to strategic, but is predominantly at the operational level progressing to the strategic level for selected individuals. The CPO1s/CWOs appointed to senior appointments and key positions, through succession planning, will receive education specifically tailored to prepare them for these appointments. During DP5, NCMs gain experience in positions which are often outside their occupation and/or environment.

The figure below captures the holistic nature of the NCM DP system.

DP1	DP2	DP3	DP4	DP5
				CPO1/CWO
			CPO2/MWO	
		PO2/Sgt	PO1/WO	
	LS/Cpl	MS/MCpl		
OS/Pte (B)	AB/Pte (T)			
• Basic Military Qualification (BMQ)	• Environmental & Occupational Quals	• Environmental & Occupational Quals	• Second Language Training (as required)	• Develop Advanced Management & Leadership Ability
• Environmental & Occupational Quals	• Develop Leadership Potential	• Develop Management & Leadership Ability	• Develop Advanced Management & Leadership Ability	• Second Language Training (as required)
	• Primary Leadership Qualification (PLQ)	• Intermediate Leadership Program (ILP)	• Advenced Leadership Program (ALP)	• Selection for Key/ Senior Appointment
			• Environmental & Occupational Quals	• Senior Appointment Program (SAP)
			• Senior Leadership Program (SLP)	• Executive Leader Program (ELP)

Figure 17.3: Canadian Forces Development Periods (Non-Commissioned Members)

Summary

In summary, the CFPDS fully supports the mission of both the officer and NCM corps. In the case of the officer corps, the development of the abilities of all officers to exercise command and staff functions effectively and efficiently in war or other operational settings is the pre-eminent precept guiding the conduct of OPD. For NCMs, the CFPDS delivers tactical, technical and operational skills exemplifying the Canadian military ethos with its bonds of tradition, comradeship and mutual respect. The CFPDS plays an essential role in creating and maintaining the concept of a strong officer/NCM team dedicated to supporting the CF mission and selflessly serving Canada with pride and distinction.

---

1   *Shaping the Future of Canadian Defence: A Strategy for 2020* (Ottawa: DND, 2006), 12.

2   *Canadian Officership in the 21ˢᵗ Century: Strategic Guidance for the Canadian Forces Officer Corps and the Officer Professional Development System* (Ottawa: DND, 2001), 16.

3   *Strategic Guidance for the Professional Development of the Canadian Forces Non-Commissioned Members* (Ottawa: DND, 2003), 18.

4   *CFJP- 001 Canadian Military Doctrine* (Ottawa: DND, 2009), 86.

5   *Duty with Honour: The Profession of Arms in Canada* (Ottawa: DND, 2009), 87.

6   *Leadership in the Canadian Forces: Conceptual Foundations* (Ottawa: DND, 2005), 165.

7   *Leadership in the Canadian Forces: Doctrine* (Ottawa: DND, 2005), 50.

8   *Leadership in the Canadian Forces: Leading People* (Ottawa: DND, 2007), 98.

9   *Leadership in the Canadian Forces: Leading the Institution* (Ottawa: DND, 2007), 174.

10   The MES is the arrangement of CF Jobs into structural elements consisting of Career Fields, Occupations and sub-occupations that collectively provide the necessary management framework for the Personnel Cycle of Activities across all components of the CF, and throughout the spectrum of conflict. A Career Field is defined as a single occupation or a group of occupations that is organized to provide for career progression.

11   The TA performs the qualification management of assigned CF common, environmental, occupation/sub-occupation and/or specialty qualifications. DTA is an authority other than a TA that due to functional, environmental and/or special accountabilities has been designated responsibility for qualification management of Individual Training and Education for specific Career Field occupation/sub-occupation and/or specialty qualifications. DTAs perform the same qualification management responsibilities as TAs.

12   The GSoWC is a distinctly human activity system and a social activity. It is a complex system rather than a complicated one and like all complex systems it is interactive and non-linear. In this system policy is defined as a set of actions and objectives prescribed by or on behalf of the Prime Minister and Cabinet that governs decisions and activities of Ministers and other officials in implementing the government's agenda or in providing public administration.

13   The OGS and NCMGS are integrated policy and quality control documents that describe the common and environmental requirements, including professional development requirements, that apply to all CF officers and NCMs. They are the foundation documents of the OPD and NCMPD system.

14   The PME Program is a combined DP1/DP2 program. The completion timeline depends on the entry plan. For example, during DP1 RMCC Cadets complete the OPMEs prior to graduation. However, most junior officers, such Direct Entry Officers, Regular Officer Training Plan Civilian University and Continuing Education Officer Training Plan will do their OPME during DP2.

CHAPTER 18

THE LEADERSHIP DEVELOPMENT FRAMEWORK, COMPETENCY DEVELOPMENT & CFITES: LEVERAGING THE CFITES FOR COMPETENCY DEVELOPMENT

Lieutenant-Commander (Ret) Randy Purse

Introduction

Arguably, the Canadian Forces is under a state of transition. Individual Training and Education modernization, learning architectures, learning-centred approaches, technology-enhanced learning environments, recruiting and attrition challenges, and a plethora of other influences are pressures for change to existing personnel development systems such as the Canadian Forces Individual Training and Education System. As the Chief of Military Personnel has stated, the CF must have a learning and development system that will "ensure a competent, committed and professional work force is available to accomplish the operational mission."[1] To be sure, there have been a number of criticisms levelled against the CFITES.[2] To delve into each of the various criticisms in this chapter would be well off the point. Suffice to say that many of the initiatives within the training and education community, including IT&E modernization, are intended to evolve existing policies, processes and practices so that the system can be responsive to, and keep pace with, personnel development requirements. That said, perhaps the single most influential concept introduced in the past decade that affects personnel development and, consequently, the CFITES, is the Leadership Development Framework.

Endorsed at the highest levels of the CF, the LDF is the basis for leader development in the CF and has been adopted as the framework for the CFPDS. The LDF's utility goes beyond PD.[3] It has been applied to ongoing Military Personnel Systems review and revision projects[4] and is the foundational concept upon which the trinity of performance assessment, succession planning, and professional development can be accomplished in a coherent, progressive manner throughout all CF members' careers. In time, the LDF and its competency-based approach will help to unify the currently disparate personel systems.

For PD and specifically for T&E, the LDF and its competency-based approach provides a more holistic perspective on, and deeper understanding of, human performance requirements, thereby facilitating better learning and development. The larger cohesive effect of integrating the LDF and the competency-based approach cannot be understated. Despite the evident benefits, recent efforts to integrate the LDF into the Officer and Non-Commissioned Member PD programs have identified a key challenge in determining how the CFITES can support competency development. Accordingly, this chapter will provide an overview of the LDF, introduce key supporting concepts that are core to understanding competency development and then show how CFITES can be leveraged to better support competency development.

The Leadership Development Framework

The changing nature of society, the global security environment, and technological innovation necessitate an aggressive approach to the continuous PD of our CF leaders. These leaders must see the world in terms of its paradoxes and contradictions in order to balance the competing institutional demands and to generate CF effectiveness. Seeing institutional dynamics in this manner requires a systemic perspective and flexibility in outlook. Current and ongoing CF initiatives magnify the demand for tenacity, decisiveness and versatility in CF leaders, reflect the increasing challenges for professionalism in leadership, and underscores the pronounced need to enhance leader capacities through effective learning and development.

The CF is a hierarchic and bureaucratic organization with an embedded profession of arms. The integration of these two components, the organization and the profession, is necessary to achieve institutional effectiveness. From the leader's perspective, this is accomplished through leading people, mainly at the tactical level, and leading the institution at the operational and strategic levels. Accordingly, leaders collectively require strong cognitive capacities, social capacities, the capacities to respond to and shape change in a transformational organizational setting, with technical expertise and institutional knowledge. This is infused with a professional ideology that supports mastery within profession of arms. These comprise the five leader meta-competencies within the LDF.

The LDF, originally named the Professional Development Framework, was created as an early consequence of almost a decade of Canadian Forces Leadership Institute leadership research.[5] The resulting CFLI Technical Report (2006) identified the five LDF meta-competencies intended to support the PD of CF members at all ranks and levels. The origins of the LDF are rooted in the work completed to produce *Officership 2020: Strategic Guidance for the CF Officer Corps*.[6] Two other CF products also contributed important dimensions to the LDF, those being *Duty with Honour: The Profession of Arms in Canada* (2003) and the suite of four *Leadership in the Canadian Forces* manuals – *Conceptual Foundations* (2005), *Doctrine* (2005), *Leading the Institution* (2007) and *Leading People* (2007).[7]

Extensive consultation throughout the CF confirmed that the extant occupational and task-based approach was inadequate as it did not capture many of the underlying requirements that characterize effective CF leadership and performance. The complex, dynamic, non-linear and hazardous security environment demanded a metacompetency-based PD system that allowed for progressive, clearly specified, development throughout an individual's career. The Strategic Objectives and Strategic Initiatives identified in *Officership 2020* were highly suggestive with regard to how these competencies should be grouped into meta-competencies. Importantly, sound leadership was identified not as a discrete competency within the LDF, but rather, as a cumulative endstate resulting from the development and application of all five meta-competencies:

- The ordered application of military force called for the highest levels of *Expertise* in the prosecution of the full range of operational roles;

- Critical thinking and ongoing intellectual development spoke directly to the development of *Cognitive Capacities*;

- Cultivating linkages across service boundaries, throughout the Whole-of-Government, and to Canadians at large, indicated the need for more advanced and sophisticated *Social Capacities*;

- Embracing and managing change and institutional transformation called for *Change Capacities*; and

- The highest standards of professionalism and military ethos meant that *Professional Ideology* was the key concept to link all of the required meta-competencies into a complete whole: a dedicated member of the Profession of Arms in Canada.

As shown in Figure 18.1, Professional Ideology occupies a privileged position in the LDF. The other four meta-competencies across the top of the Framework are present in most effective organizations. Only when these meta-competencies are shaped by a professional ideology do all five coalesce into a collective, interdependent perspective of effective leader meta-competencies needed for achieving complete institutional effectiveness within the CF.

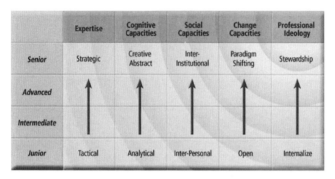

	Expertise	Cognitive Capacities	Social Capacities	Change Capacities	Professional Ideology
Senior	Strategic	Creative Abstract	Inter-Institutional	Paradigm Shifting	Stewardship
Advanced					
Intermediate					
Junior	Tactical	Analytical	Inter-Personal	Open	Internalize

Figure 18.1: The LDF – Five Leader Meta-competencies & Four Leader Levels

So, with these five LDF meta-competencies identified – Expertise, Cognitive Capacities, Social Capacities, Change Capacities, Professional Ideology – the issues of levels of development were addressed. Here the General System of War and Conflict was a determining factor, for it consisted of four sub-systems – tactical, operational, strategic and politico-strategic in ascending order. CF members rising in rank and/or appointment needed to be developed to excel at each level, culminating at the politico-strategic level at the interface between policy and strategy, the realm of national security formulation. These levels generally mapped onto the existing PD developmental periods: DP1 and DP2 at the tactical level, DP3 at the operational, DP4 at the strategic and DP5 at the politico-strategic level. The final stage in the development of the LDF was the "populating" of each of the five meta-competencies with the specific competencies. As the LDF is further integrated into PD, it is important to rationalize how each competency is best developed, whether through education, training, experience and/or self-development (or by combinations of these four pathways to learning).

In summary, an understanding of the implications of the LDF show that it provides a broad view of leader meta-competencies that enable deeper exploration of the requisite competencies and the various enablers for effective leadership. Most importantly, for this volume, the LDF serves as a "comprehensive model for expanding the depth and breadth of leadership and leader learning."[8] It further introduces the concept of competency development to the T&E community and initiates the dialogue on the implications to learning and the CFITES. However, prior to delving into this discussion, it is beneficial to define competency development and identify two key supporting concepts that provide important context.

Defining Competency Development

The CF/DND has two definitions of a competency with the common elements being demonstrable knowledge, skills, and abilities that enable successful performance on the job:

- the set of knowledge, skills, abilities or other characteristics which may vary among individuals that contributes to effective performance (CFITES);[9] or

- knowledge, skills, abilities and other personal qualities that:
  - underlie effective or successful job performance;
  - are observable and measurable; and
  - are distinguishable between CF members who perform at superior versus average levels (DAOD 5031-8).[10]

Competencies are represented collectively in a profile that is based on a position, function or role which defines Proficiency Levels (PL) in terms of mastered performance at each level.

Development is the process of growing or developing, a stage of growth or advancement.[11] The competency profiles and PLs provide the structure to assess individual capabilities against mastered performance and determine individual development requirements to meet that desired level of performance. So, competency development is simply determining what competencies an individual needs development in and how this should best occur. The process of competency development typically includes the following:

- Identifying the required competencies for successful performance in a given position, function or role (these are normally defined in a competency profile);

- Assessing an individual's current proficiency level in required competencies;

- Determining the gap between an individual's current and required proficiency; and

- Identifying and deploying the means to develop an individual's competencies to the required level.

Critical Supporting Concepts

There are a myriad of theories, concepts and assumptions that can be extended to the competency development discussion, thus confusing even some of the most experienced learning and development professionals. Competency development discussions can be significantly streamlined through a common understanding of learning and development. There are two interrelated concepts that are key to establishing the CF T&E context for competency development: learning as process; and development as a continuum.

Learning as Process

Learning is often seen to be synonymous to training and/or education. It is not. There are many definitions of learning used, but the Treasury Board Secretariat definition serves best: learning is "the acquisition of new knowledge and ideas that change the way an individual perceives, understands or acts."[12] As the definition suggests, learning is largely a voluntary endeavour that is ongoing (i.e., continuous) that involves sensing, acquiring, perceiving, understanding, and, as one inclines, accepting and acting upon information received.

As shown in Figure 18.2, the learning process is a critical component of competency development. Each individual arrives in the organization with his/her own traits and characteristics. They also bring with them prior skill and knowledge from life, work and educational experiences. This forms the baseline for learning. Individuals then acquire additional knowledge, skills and abilities through the learning process that contributes to their competency which, in turn, enables performance. This process continues until the desired competency level is achieved. Note that the learning is a necessary component of development that precedes competent performance and mastery.

Figure 18.2: A conceptual learning and development model[13]

From this, an important distinction is drawn – learning is essential for competency development whereas T&E (a.k.a. formal learning) are not. T&E are activities that support learning, but do not constitute learning. How and where the learning occurs is not specified because it can occur in a wide range of formal and/or informal settings. Competency development often occurs in absence of any formal T&E through workplace activities and other experiential settings. The hope is that T&E supports effective learning and, by consequence, competency development.

Development as a Continuum

Within organizational settings, learning and development are inextricably intertwined. Individuals learn as they develop; if they are not learning, they are not truly developing. So, learning is a core component of competency development.

Within the CF and other organizations, development (or PD) is often seen as a series of courses or training programs. This is reinforced within the CF through diverse approaches to managing PD and T&E. These dynamics create an artificially segmented view of development. Just as learning is considered to be an ongoing activity, development should viewed as a continuum where individuals are seen to be continuously learning, improving and developing whether or not they are in a formal learning setting. As alluded to above, formal learning is only one component that supports competency development. The majority of the learning occurs beyond formal T&E where individuals are exposed to authentic work situations.[14] To engender the most effective approach and assure alignment of objectives within formal, informal and workplace learning settings, the workplace should be recognized as part of the *extended learning environment* where formal learning is reinforced through workplace activities that enhance competency development (Figure 18.3).

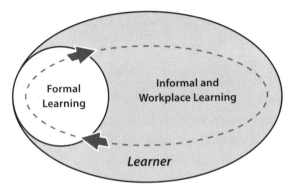

Figure 18.3: The Extended Learning Environment

Summary

The two key concepts discussed above, learning as a process and development as a continuum, are fundamental to competency development discussions as they reflect qualities of the "continuous learning environment" reflected in CF policies. These provide important context for discussions on how CFITES can better support competency development.

The CFITES Support to Competency Development

If there is anything to be echoed from the now numerous articles, summaries and references to the LDF, it is that CF members need to be developed in professional and leader capacities for an evolving and complex world of conflict.[15] The operating environment is becoming so complex and evolving so quickly that the current "task-based" model of learning and development, upon which the PD system is largely based, cannot reliably deliver the required level of human capability needed. The analysis within the task-based model is based on minimal acceptable performance (a.k.a. the "first day on the job" or "job ready" standard) where only those tasks to be trained are introduced into formal learning environments; important tacit functions, relationships, and context is often missing.

Alternatively, the LDF provides the context in which to better identify required competencies needed to meet CF requirements. The CF competency analysis is based on what an individual needs to "excel" on the job. It reveals important information regarding psychological, social, cultural and environmental aspects of work across a spectrum of activities or situations that are not normally captured in task-based descriptions.[16] So, in addition to the knowledge and skills needed for concrete tasks, a competency-based approach includes the range of cognitive, social, change and professional capabilities that provide a more holistic and a more comprehensive picture of the requirements for successful human performance.

Conceptual work on integrating the LDF and competency-based approach into CF personnel management systems is ongoing. The current practice is that competencies are identified for positions, functions or roles which are, in turn, rolled up into competency dictionaries based on occupation/job families.[17] As these competency profiles and dictionaries become available, those working within the sub-disciplines within personnel management need to determine the impacts on their current systems and how they will support a competency-based approach.

Over the past few years, CDA has been conferring with T&E stakeholders across the CF to assess the impact of adopting the LDF and its in-built competency-based approach on the CFPDS and the CFITES. The primary consideration is how the CF T&E community will support competency development. In fact, a key challenge discovered during preliminary work on the officer and NCM PD programs was identifying how the CFITES could evolve to better support competency development. While there has been some discussion of replacing the CFITES, there have been no valid arguments presented that outweigh the costs and effort in doing so. In fact, the CFITES is considerably more agile than most in the T&E community believe. As will be shown in the overview below, the CF has a significant investment in the CFITES and it provides reliable training and education that generally meets operational requirements. Instead of abandoning a proven, effective system, the following is presented in the spirit of continuous improvement and introduces some ideas on how core CFITES processes can be adapted to better support competency development.

Overview of CFITES

The CFITES is a CF/DND management system that is intended "...to optimize the quality and quantity of individual training and education (IT&E) while minimizing the resources dedicated to IT&E programmes."[18] The five fundamental principles of CFITES are: performance orientation; a systems approach; systematic process; optimum efficiency; and continuous improvement.[19]

The CFITES is comprised of a quantity control process and a quality control, each with integrated resource management functions. In simple terms, the quantity control cycle identifies who receives the T&E and when they will receive it (a.k.a. production). The quality control cycle identifies what T&E is required and how it will be provided. The adoption of a competency-based approach development has the greatest impact on the quality control cycle. Accordingly, the following explores how the CFITES can support competency development through the Needs Assessment process and the remaining quality control cycle (Figure 18.4).

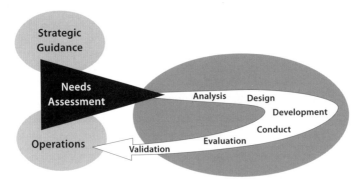

Figure 18.4: The CFITES Quality Control Cycle and Inputs

Needs Assessment and Competency Development

> Regardless of how much we want a solution or resource, they are not needs. They are potential ways to meet needs. Leaping to select solutions or resources before identifying the needs (gaps in results) is to choose "quasi-needs" which are frequently solutions in search of problems.[20]

External to the CFITES, needs assessment is the systematic study of a problem or innovation incorporating data and opinions from varied sources in order to make effective recommendations or to propose valid solutions.[21] During the needs assessment, the key question is what is the need and how can it best be addressed. Done correctly and objectively, the needs assessment defines the human performance gap based upon the "desired state" which readily equates to "mastered" performance discussed within the competency framework. The gap analysis should survey the breadth of solutions, including T&E, that will contribute to the desired performance. For example, in determining the desired end state for a pilot, one will find that there are certain abilities or characteristics that a pilot must bring to the job which cannot be trained such as visual acuity, hand/eye coordination and spatial appreciation. Consequently, the "solution" is to have a rigourous selection process to ensure that all candidates have these abilities and characteristics before T&E begins. Of course, to generate an effective military pilot, some T&E will be required as there will be a remaining competency gap. But, the example highlights the benefits of looking holistically at problems and developing solutions that will efficiently meet the full organizational need. In the context of competency development, the needs assessment process will define those developmental activities that will support individual learning and development to achieve "mastered" level of performance (i.e. desired state). Formal learning may not be required. Only once it has been decided that formal learning is required is the CFITES implemented.

Analysis

> The purpose of the analysis phase is to specify the required training and education outcomes in terms of essential on-job performance.[22]

The analysis phase identifies the required level of performance and translates it into performance (or educational) objectives. As a part of the more holistic picture of the required performance, information in competency profiles on a role, position or function can be included in the analysis of the performance requirements and better inform what should be trained or educated and to what degree. This more comprehensive picture of desired performance will inherently result in some degree of competency development being embedded within formal T&E. Should competencies not be specifically defined, then a competency analysis can be conducted.[23]

One caution for the analysis phase is that every effort should be made to define the breadth of the learning requirements that may support development of identified competencies. Referring back to the LDF and the meta-competencies, it is evident that not all competencies will result in explicit behaviour upon which the current task-based approach relies. True attention to competency development requires greater insight and analysis of learning requirement for tacit performance and the reinforcing concepts, beliefs, values and expectations. As a result, tacit performance can consume more analytical energy than explicit performance which is readily observable (Figure 18.5). There are many tools that can help ferret out tacit performance such as cognitive task analysis to help define expert level processes and practices thereby creating a richer picture of the true performance requirements.

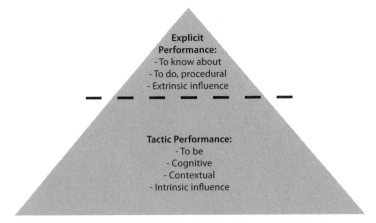

Figure 18.5: Learning and Level of Effort in Determining Explicit and Tacit Performance

Design and Development

The purpose of the Design phase is to select or describe a learning program/activity and an environment which will enable the learner to achieve, at optimum cost, the performance objectives defined in the analysis…[24]

and the intent of the Development phase is to

…provide effective instructional materials that will preserve the design intent and prepare for the delivery of the instructional program.[25]

It follows that with a more comprehensive picture of the performance requirement, instructional designers and developers will be able to provide T&E more consistent with the on-job requirement. T&E can be constructed that recognizes relationships, influences, activities and abilities that would typically go unexplored in the traditional task-based approach and therefore attend to the breadth of capacities/competencies needed to support mastered performance. As design and development are focused on creating learning environments, the emphasis should be on balancing traditional organizational objectives (successful performance in assigned tasks) and the learners' learning and developmental needs (appropriate and active engagement in learning opportunities). This is otherwise known as a *learning-centric approach*. More specifically, two design intentions consistent with competency development are:

- Contextual learning. Similar to *anchored instruction* or *situated learning*, contextual learning requires learners to apply their skills and knowledge in an authentic work context. This type of learning environment significantly aids learning transfer to the workplace. It supports competency development in that learners are required to *think* and *respond* with an appreciation of the given context. Clearly supportive of traditional performance objectives, this type of learning environment also ensures that tacit capacities are engaged that are not typically elicited in the more traditional learning settings; and

- Active learning methods. As discussed by Jennifer Bennett, a new professional development model using more active methods of delivery is based on precepts that mirror other competencies of CF leaders.[26] Instructional design that supports competency development relies heavily on adult learning methods such as problem-based learning, simulations, gaming or cooperative learning that ensure learners actively engage in the learning process. These methods provide greater potential for learning transfer to the workplace.

In short, a small shift in design and development practices that require use of more context-driven and active learning methods will improve learning transfer and inherently support competency development.

Conduct

The purpose of the Conduct phase is to enable personnel to successfully achieve the performance or education objectives associated with a specific job and/or training and education requirement.[27]

Conduct is where the "rubber hits the road" as analysis, design and development culminate in the provision of a learning activity aimed at producing learners who have achieved the desired outcomes. A well thought-out design is only as good as its delivery. Therefore, the greatest support that can be offered to competency development during the conduct phase is to ensure that all instructional professionals support the intended design.[28] In many cases, this requires them to move beyond their traditional views of learning and instruction which are largely based on a "transmission perspective" of learning.[29] Some principles of instruction related to competency development are:

- Learning is understood to be continuous and that T&E is only one part of the overall developmental requirement that contributes to individual mastery;

- Learners' existing competencies are known, appreciated and leveraged;

- Learning is based on the premise that all *properly screened* participants can master the required competencies given sufficient time, constructive feedback and guidance (even though the organization may not wish to invest that time);

- Learning events that exercise skills or tasks reinforce related competencies;

- Learning methods are active, engaging and contextual thereby eliciting competencies within the learning environment (learn by doing);

- Multiple means and methods are used to address learner diversity and exercise learner perspective and insight into what is being learned; and

- Assessment includes feedback to better guide development.

Evaluation and Validation

The purpose of the Evaluation phase is to ensure the optimal effectiveness and efficiency of an instructional programme.[30]

This is supported by the Validation phase which seeks,

...to determine whether the objectives themselves satisfy the performance requirement for which the program was initially produced.[31]

Evaluation, including validation, within the quality control cycle generally mirrors Kirkpatrick's four levels of evaluation: learner reaction, learner achievement, learning transfer to the job, and any organizational impact (e.g. return on investment/expectations).[32] The latter three are of particular importance in terms of both performance and competency development.

- Learner Achievement – This asks *did the requisite learning occur?* This is perhaps one of the most complex aspects of T&E and, done poorly, can have significant impact on both the individual and the organization. Fundamentally, the CF needs to ensure that the learner has met the required standard for performance on the job and that the T&E has achieved the desired results. While traditional assessment instruments can be applied to the task-based requirements, assessment of proficiency in a particular competency is more difficult. It requires more effort to identify the required proficiency level, the indicators of successful performance, and the consequences or actions taken when an individual does not meeting the desired level. This is made more complex since not all competencies (or components thereof) are observable/measureable. Assessment of competencies needs to consider the learner entry point, the time and opportunity for development within T&E and the CF's expectations upon completion of T&E. For example, assessed proficiency in a competency may not contribute to pass or fail, but will more likely be used to provide constructive feedback that can guide further development. Suffice to say that given the potential impact of "unsuccessful" T&E in the eyes of the organization, this particular aspect of evaluation needs a well thought-out approach to assessing learner achievement to ensure all stakeholders are properly addressed. Again, there are a myriad of tools available to aid designers in developing assessment tools;[33]

- Learning Transfer to the Job – This asks *did the learning result in the required change of behaviour needed on the job?* Without doubt, this is the most valid indicator of learning and competency development. Mechanisms for measuring and recording this aspect of learning include personnel evaluations, monitoring and observation, peer reviews, etc. However, those working within T&E rarely get the feedback needed to adjust to meet the needs of dynamic work environments. A competency-based approach provides another layer of complexity that will need some additional thought, discussion and collaboration within the personnel management disciplines to determine what evaluation strategies would be most effective and efficient; and

- Organizational Impact – This asks *what value has the T&E had on organizational performance?* Also viewed as return on investment (ROI) or return on expectations (ROE), the results of concrete skills or knowledge development within T&E are often immediately apparent in the workplace. On the other hand, because competencies develop over time and are primarily developed within the workplace, it may be difficult to get tangible measures that can be directly tied back to T&E. Existing validation methods may support measures for competency development, but further exploration of this issue should occur in conjunction with discussion of how other personnel management functions support competency development.

In summary, within the CFITES and, more specifically, throughout all phases of the quality control cycle there exists potential to support competency development without significant changes to current processes or procedures. The key challenge will be to have the T&E community shift from traditional perspectives on learning and development to a more agile and responsive approach using the concepts and practices discussed within the CFITES context.

Conclusion

The LDF introduced an integrated view of leader development through meta-competencies and attending capacities and competencies. The efforts to integrate a competency-based approach across the spectrum of personnel management processes, including T&E are ongoing. The critical concepts that relate to competency development are learning should be understood as a process and that development should be recognized not as an event but as a continuum. They provide a foundational baseline for understanding both the CF's approach to competency development and the implications on T&E and, by extension, the CFITES.

As shown though the examination of the quality control cycle, the CFITES can effectively contribute to competency development through all phases with very few changes to existing processes or practices. Certainly, there are challenges beyond minor changes to CFITES. The most significant of these challenges is likely to be the reticence to change the existing approach to T&E towards something that is seemingly less tangible. Perhaps the most influential activity that can help prepare the T&E community is to generate more dialogue on the emerging concepts and find the means for all to better understand the benefits of a competency-based approach for both the organization and the learners.

1   Department of National Defence. National Defence and the Canadian Forces. *About Chief Military Personnel*, retrieved on 15 Nov 2011 from <http://www.cmp-cpm.forces.gc.ca/acm-scp/index-eng.asp>.

2   Numerous criticisms of the CFITES from a variety of sources within the CF challenge both the relevance and responsiveness of the system. This chapter does not intend on addressing the various challenges but instead looks forward toward improvement of the system. It is important to note, however, that the CFITES is based on traditional Instructional Systems Design (ISD) models. Many of the criticisms of the CFITES echo similar challenges, see also: Ron Zemke and Jack Gordon, "Attack on ISD", *Training Magazine*, Vol. 37, No. 4 (April 2000), 42. The main conclusion is that many of the criticisms leveled against ISD are unfounded and symptomatic of the craftsman blaming their tool, as Donald Clark so succinctly put it in his response published in 2004 at <http://www.nwlink.com/~donclark/history_isd/attack.html>.

3   Departmant of National Defence. *DAOD 5031-2, Individual Training and Education Strategic Framework,* retrieved on 15 Nov 2011 from <http://www.admfincs.forces.gc.ca/dao-doa/5000/5031-2-eng.asp>, describes Professional Development as a composite of training, education, self-development and experience.

4   Such projects include regeneration of the Officer and Non-Commissioned Member General Specifications, revision of the CF Personnel Appraisal System, development of a CF-wide succession planning methodology, and utilization of the LDF for creating and structuring, competencies dictionaries.

5   Robert W. Walker, *The Professional Development Framework: Generating Effectiveness in Canadian Forces Leadership, CFLI Technical Report 2006-01* (Kingston, ON: DND, 2006).

6   Canada. *Canadian Officership in the 21st Century: Strategic Guidance for the Canadian Forces Officer Corps and the Officer Professional Development System* (Officership 2020) (Ottawa, ON: DND, 2001). Background, perspectives and applications related to the LDF were provided by Dr. L. W. (Bill) Bentley, Director CFLI. *Officership 2020* identified eight Strategic Objectives to achieve an agreed vision of the officer corps of 2020, with five relating to the individual officer and *three* relating to the PD system itself. The five individual officer Strategic Objectives were the ordered application of military force, sound leadership, the highest standards of professionalism, critical thinking, and the embracing and managing of change. The three Strategic Initiatives most related to the LDF for achieving these five Strategic Objectives were to ensure intellectual development, strengthen military ethos, and cultivate external linkages.

7   The suite of Leadership in the Canadian Forces manuals can be found on the Canadian Defence Academy website at <http://www.cda-acd.forces.gc.ca/pub/index-eng.asp>.

8   Walker, 49.

9   Department of National Defence. *A-P9-050-000/PT001 Canadian Forces Individual Training and Education System Manual of Individual Training and Education*, Vol. 1, No. 1 (2007), Glossary.

10   Department of National Defence. *DAOD 5031-8, Canadian Forces Professional Development*, retrieved on 15 Nov 2011 from < http://www.admfincs.forces.gc.ca/dao-doa/5000/5031-8-eng.asp>.

11   Catherine Soanes and Angus Stevenson, eds, *Concise Oxford Dictionary 11th Edition (Revised)* (Don Mills, Ontario: Oxford: University Press, 2008), 392.

12   Government of Canada Treasury Board of Canada Secretariat, *Policy on Learning, Training, and Development*, retrieved on 2 Nov 2010 from <http://www.tbs-sct.gc.ca/pol/doc-eng.aspx?id=12405&section=text#cha4>.

13   Adapted from U.S. Department of Education 2000, "A Conceptual Learning Model" in Elizabeth Jones, Richard. A. Voorhees, and Karen Paulson, *Defining and Assessing Learning: Exploring Competency-Based Initiatives. Report of the National Postsecondary Education Cooperative Working Group on Competency-Based Initiatives in Postsecondary Education* (Washington, D.C: National Center for Education Statistics, U.S. Department of Education, 2001), 8.

14   Throughout the Learning and Development discipline it is common to see phrases that indicate that only 20% of formal learning is actually transferred to the workplace. In truth, such a generalization cannot be applied across the board. In the CF's case, the training development processes and performance orientation would most assuredly reflect a higher percentage of transfer. However, the point is that formal learning only partially prepares an individual for effective performance on the job. See Jay Cross, *Informal Learning: Rediscovering the Natural Pathways That Inspire Innovation and Performance* (San Francisco: John Wiley & Sons, Inc., 2007); Don Clark, *Knowledge Jump - The Cost of Informal Learning*, retrieved on 19 Oct 2010 from <http://www.knowledgejump.com/learning/cost.html>; Sally-Ann Moore, *Time-to-Learning, Digital Equipment Corporation*, retrieved from <http://en.wikipedia.org/wiki/File:Ttp_samoore.gif>.

15   Walker, 11.

16   Michael F. Burnett and David J. McCracken, "Characteristics, Procedures, and Results of Two Job Analysis Techniques", *Journal of Vocational Education Research*, Vol. 7, No. 3 (Summer 1982), 1-10; as cited in Robert Bacal, *Task Analysis Strategies and Practices, Practice Application Brief*, retrieved on 1 Nov 2010 from <http://www.thetrainingworld.com/wp/training-wisdom-or-training-foolishness/learning-theory-to-practice/task-analysis-strategies-and-practices-practice-application-brief/>.

17   This was the process being explored at the time of writing this chapter. There are numerous ways to capture the competency requirements. Regardless of approach used, the critical output should be a coherent description of competencies common to key roles/functions as well as the proficiency levels that can be used to guide development to successive levels within each role/function.

18   Department of National Defence, *Canadian Forces Individual Training and Education System Manual of Individual Training and Education* (A-P9-050-000/PT001) (Ottawa, 2009), 1, 8.

19   Ibid., 9.

20   Roger Kaufman and Jerry Herman, *Strategic Planning in Education: Rethinking, Restructuring, Revitalizing* (Lancaster, PA: Technomic Publishing Co., Inc, 1991), 28.

21   Department of National Defence, *Canadian Forces Individual Training and Education System Manual of Individual Training and Education* (A-P9-050-000/PT001) (Ottawa, 1997), 2 – Needs Assessment.

22   Department of National Defence, *Canadian Forces Individual Training and Education System Manual of Individual Training and Education* (A-P9-050-000/PT003), (Ottawa, 2003), Vol. 3 – Analysis of Instructional Requirements, 2.

23   Tools and templates are widely available for competency analysis that will provide an appreciation of what competencies may be engaged in task performance.

24   Department of National Defence, *Canadian Forces Individual Training and Education System Manual of Individual Training and Education* (A-P9-050-000/PT004) (Ottawa, 1999), Vol. 4 – Design of Instructional Programmes, 2.

25   Department of National Defence, *Canadian Forces Individual Training and Education System Manual of Individual Training and Education* (A-P9-050-000/PT005) (Ottawa, 2001) Vol. 5 – Development of Instructional Programmes, 2.

26   Jennifer J. Bennett, "Effective Professional Development Strategies for Institutional Leaders" in Robert W. Walker, ed., *Institutional Leadership in the Canadian Forces: Contemporary Issues* (Kingston, ON: Canadian Defence Academy Press, 2007).

27   Department of National Defence, *Canadian Forces Individual Training and Education System Manual of Individual Training and Education* (A-P9-050-000/PT006) (Ottawa, 2002), Vol. 6 – Conduct of Instructional Programmes, 2.

28   Instructional professionals are those specifically employed in learning delivery include instructors, teachers, professors, instructional facilitators and standards staff.

29   The transmission perspective in adult learning is the most common perspective held within secondary and adult learning settings and is reflected in traditional teacher-student dynamics that involve delivery of official content from an expert teacher to the student who is primarily seen to be in "receive" mode. See Daniel D. Pratt. *Good teaching: one size fits all?*, retrieved on 11 Oct 2010 from <www.teachingperspectives.com/PDF/goodteaching.pdf>.

30   Department of National Defence, *Canadian Forces Individual Training and Education System Manual of Individual Training and Education* (A-P9-050-000/PT011) (Ottawa, 2003), Vol. 11 – Evaluation of Instructional Programmes, 2.

31   Department of National Defence, *Canadian Forces Individual Training and Education System Manual of Individual Training and Education* (A-P9-050-000/PT008) (Ottawa, 1998) Vol. 8 – Validation of Instructional Programmes, 2.

32   For further information see Kirkpatrick's Philosophy and Model retrieved on 9 Jan 2011 from <http://www.kirkpatrickpartners.com/OurPhilosophy/tabid/66/Default.aspx>.

33   There are many online and text based tools for "competency assessment" that can guide tool development. Within the CF, perhaps the most efficient means would be to first determine if the Personnel Selection community have already developed an assessment tool for recruiting and selection that might be adapted to the T&E environment. This would ensure reliability of assessment throughout the developmental process.

PART IV

TRAINING

CHAPTER 19

FROM SECOND LANGUAGE TRAINING (SLT) TO SECOND OFFICIAL LANGUAGE EDUCATION AND TRAINING (SOLET): NEW APPROACHES TO MEET NEW DEMANDS

Dr. Richard D. Monaghan

Introduction

There are few issues that generate a more passionate response in the Canadian Forces than second language training (SLT). Some see the ability to work in both languages as an enormous advantage, while others see it as a huge burden. Everyone who expects to advance in a career understands, if required, that they will be subjected to regular doses of SLT, but few want to "lose the time" to learn the language well. Lack of SLT is routinely blamed for stalled careers, others' otherwise inexplicable advancement, and reduced prospects of personal advancement. Of the many myths and misapprehensions about learning another language, the most prevalent is the notion that a few weeks of training will make one bilingual. We think of acquiring languages by "putting in the hours," no matter that the hours are months or years apart. The fact is that one can no more *acquire* language proficiency passively than one can *acquire* fitness passively. It's a hard road to get there, but once you are there, it's fairly easy, with discipline, to maintain.

Language *training* works for short-term memorized responses. Language learning, on the other hand, involves the active development of listening and speaking skills, of memory, of associations, and of modified behaviour. Over the past three decades, language professionals have learned a lot about how language is developed, how it is maintained, and how it is lost. And while training worked well enough to help individuals develop minimal competence in the 1980s and 1990s, new and more complex linguistic demands are being made on leadership at all levels today. Some language demands are operational, while others are occupational, while still others speak to the responsibilities of leadership. Add to that the pressing demands of operational tempo and continuous transformation as it affects the entire organization, and it is easy to see that the old "bums-in-seats" model is less effective today and that SLT just does not work any more. This is true of Individual Training and Education in general.

By virtue of the fact that we can speak a language, we all assume we are experts in language. Those lucky enough to have a facility in learning languages cannot imagine what all the fuss is about. And as in most contexts that are complex, the less we know, the more we think we do. Second, Official Language (OL) proficiency is hard to come by, often relying on a set of unlikely conditions (availability, access, and motivation, as a start), falling into place at the right time. In the CF, for those who enter monolingual, proficiency in a second OL is expensive in terms of time, effort, and commitment. Getting on course is hard enough, and then there is the challenge of learning itself. Learning another language involves rewiring one's brain[1] – it is time-consuming, frustrating, and leads to extraordinary revelations about oneself and one's perceptions and limitations. It expands ones capacity to interact with others and broadens cultural horizons. Ultimately, it is rewarding on a very personal level. It is, in a word, complex.[2]

Current Situation

The politics of language learning in the CF has generated a fair amount of ink,[3] but there is very little published within the CF about language learning itself. The current Military Second Language Training Program (MSLTP), officially implemented in 1988 but developed over the previous decade, has deep roots in the tradition of training. The key distinction between officers' language learning and other ranks' is clearly enunciated in the *Instruction*: "For Non-Commissioned Members (NCMs) bilingualism will be treated strictly as a skill. The new aim of language training for NCMs is to produce sufficient bilingual personnel to man each NCM bilingual position (MSLTP)."[4] The distinction between NCMs and officers' learning has shifted since then, but the perception of language education as language training persists. While the initial stages of learning another language can be efficiently managed by the institution relying on traditional training, a student's development of anything beyond survival skills requires a much more sophisticated approach than a training model provides. This simple truth is well recognized by language teachers everywhere. The goal of the MSLTP was to fill a specified number of positions with linguistically qualified personnel (qualified at that time meant a proficiency level of, roughly speaking, either

AAA or BBB).[5] While the goal of SLT was to provide all officers and some selected NCMs with basic instruction to acquire certification, the MSLTP served us well. A study conducted by the Office of the Commissioner of Official Languages in March 2004 makes the astute comment, "Meeting a linguistic profile does not necessarily mean that the second language will be used."[6]

The goal, however, has changed. Language proficiency rather than certification is the current focus. It has changed through policy and the commitment of leaders. Aside from the goals themselves, our awareness of the complexity of language learning and the management of that learning has grown enormously in the past two decades. Linear concepts of learning that characterize a training model have been supplanted by complexity theory which stresses the interaction of systems. Research on the arts and sciences of learning has flourished. Since the mid-eighties, developments in instructional technology, in teaching techniques, in assessment of linguistic competency and proficiency, in several fields of linguistics (including psycholinguistics, sociolinguistics, neurolinguistics and linguistic policy), and in program management theory and practice have grown exponentially.[7]

Other chapters of this *Handbook* explore these dimensions of learning in other contexts. And while there is a common though mistaken perception that the requirement for Second Official Language learning is driven solely by legislation, the operational requirements for the use of second languages sits right at the core of CF readiness and interoperability, as it always has. In this chapter, the term "operational" is used to encompass operations, deployment, occupation, and work-related language use.[8] Rapid deployment in concert with other NATO and UN troop contributing nations in the Balkans and Afghanistan, and now in North Africa, have underlined our reliance on shared communication protocols. At the same time the development of standardized instruments to certify levels of language proficiency in international HQs and in theatre have become more important than ever.[9]

More sophisticated operational capacity, demanding high levels of skills and knowledge today put a much higher premium on the mobility of CF members, and the linguistic demography of the CF has adapted to meet this challenge internally as well as internationally. To meet national and international demands on Canada's Forces, language is a key enabler and a core competency.[10] As an enabler, language learning is an integral part of the Professional Development

System of the CF;[11] competency in other languages is a distinct operational advantage as well as a leadership qualification. By dispelling some of the myths about learning and using a second language, and showing why select members of the CF are expected to work in their second language, this section of the *Handbook* intends to clarify the roles of IT&E as it relates to Official Languages, Foreign Languages, and Aboriginal Languages in the CF.

Like the rest of IT&E, CF Language Programs are in the throes of Modernization. A quick overview of strengths and weaknesses is in order. Sweeping changes to CF policies to enhance compliance with the Official Languages Act, as promulgated by the Official Languages Program Transformation Model (OLPTM) and recent DAODs and CANFORGENs,[12] are difficult to effect because of policy gaps between CF Policy (based on functions) regarding Language IT&E and the Military Employment System (based on positions). Working groups have been established in the past year to identify those policy gaps and to address them.[13] Governance remains unsettled but stakeholders are working together to resolve conflicts and gaps. Management of programs has been centralized, but course design is still largely training-based while new curricula are being designed for English courses and refined for French courses. Maintenance packages are under development but poorly funded, and the pressing need for online computer adaptive testing has no support.[14] The current training delivery model is inadequate to meet language education and training demands, but is slowly adapting itself to the demands of the CF and the demands of learners.

Teachers, on the other hand, are professional, dedicated, and innovative, and make up for lapses in outdated or incomplete curricula. Foreign Language programs, essential for operations, make do by relying on NATO partners for testing and learning materials, but have restricted capacity to conduct independent internal research and development.

The languages of Canada's First Nations are not recognized as Official Languages, and are not recognized as Foreign Languages. They lie somewhere in limbo. The advantages of having CF members familiar with proficiency in these languages and the cultures they represent are clear strategically, yet we have no mechanisms to recognize them.[15] In the end, all IT&E faces the same sorts of pressures emanating from policy, governance, management, and delivery; language simply lines up with the others in competition for diminishing resources.

The current situation in the three sets of language programs managed by CDA follows.

Policy

Government policy on access to services and support in both Official Languages is identified in the *Official Languages Act* (OLA). The application of that act in government departments and agencies is further refined in Treasury Board guidelines. Within Defence, the CF Official Languages Program Transformation Model (2007-2012), promulgated in 2006, outlines the OLA responsibilities as they apply to Defence team.[16] As 2012 approaches, a new model is in the works. Foreign Language policy is dictated by the CF mission and changes according to government priorities and interests. The International Program policy resides with ADM (Pol) and the Director of the Military Training Cooperation Program (DMTCP).[17]

Governance

The Governance Framework for Second Official Language Education and Training (SOLET), as a sub-set of IT&E, is set out in DAOD 5031/2 *Individual Training and Education Strategic Framework*.[18] The role of the Director Official Languages (DOL) is defined separately (see below). The following is a very brief summary of roles and responsibilities as they apply to CF SOLET.

Chief Military Personnel

Chief of Military Personnel is the Functional Authority for SOLET and defines the requirements for the CF. CMP delegates the DOL to develop and maintain the OL policy framework, and to establish and provide departmental direction and guidance on SOLET for CF members. CMP has delegated functional authority for all IT&E in the CF, including SOLET, to the Canadian Defence Academy.

Director of Official Languages

The DOL carries out the day-to-day functions of the CMP with regard to: developing SOLET policy, specifications and related instruction/documents; establishing and publishing annual guidance and direction on CF SOLET consistent with the departmental strategic planning process; formulating the annual CF SOLET requirements; verifying that delivery of SOLET achieves identified goals; and providing advice where needed.[19]

Canadian Defence Academy

CMP delegates CDA to act as the Training Authority for all common IT&E, including Language Education and Training. CDA is the technical authority for all language learning in the CF and as such defines the training standard and monitors and reports on all language learning activities in the CF, whereas the implementation (training delivery) is decentralized between the Training Establishments, which are the three Environmental Commands (ECs), the Canadian Forces Language School (CFLS), and the Royal Military College of Canada and the Collège militaire royal de Saint-Jean.

The TA is responsible for:

- managing, overseeing and coordinating CF-wide language training delivery;

- providing second official language education and training and certification testing services to members;

- managing the administration and delivery of testing by the Public Service Commission (PSC);

- developing and maintaining SOLET standards for Program delivery;

- ensuring the effectiveness and efficiency of the different training programs and services and their delivery options used in the CF;

- developing, validating and establishing second language retention and maintenance tools and strategies, and ensuring that the provision of relevant refresher training is available;

- conducting research in language learning, teaching and testing, and program management; and

- ensuring that SOLET is provided in accordance with the priorities established by the Functional Authority (FA).

Schools

Each Training Establishment is responsible for:

- delivering SOLET in an effective and efficient manner in accordance with the standards established by the TA;

- inputting and maintaining accurate data;

- reporting on SOLET through the chain of command;

- arranging PSC Second Language Education (SLE) testing; and

- responding to additional tasks.

Environmental Commands

ECs are responsible for:

- managing, overseeing and coordinating SOLET assigned to their Command;

- providing SOLET and certification testing services to members;

- coordinating the administration and delivery of testing by the PSC;

- participating in research activities in language learning, teaching and program management;

- reporting on SOLET to TA;

- in consultation with the FA and Director General Military Careers (DGMC), providing SOLET requirements;

- ensuring that SOLET is provided in accordance with established priorities;

- establishing second language learning strategies in collaboration with the TA and DGMC; and

- collecting and maintaining data on SOLET.

Management

CDA HQ houses two Language Program units: Language Planning and Policy (LPP), which addresses strategic planning and policy issues in collaboration with stakeholders, and Language Program Delivery (LPD), which conducts the day-to-day management of CF language training and education programs.

LPP is responsible for horizon 2-3 planning for language programs, which includes liaison with the IT&E Modernization Initiative, for recommending resolution of policy gaps to integrate language into the Professional Development System, and for commitments within NATO for language coordination.

LPD manages CDA Standards Company in Kingston, St-Jean and Asticou Centre to design, develop, and monitor curriculum and testing. LPD also manages contracted services for language delivery resources across Canada and selected OUTCAN locations, and the Memorandum of Understanding with the Public Service Commission and other agencies for language assessment and certification. It also manages distributed language learning for the CF, Foreign Languages, and the International Program.

Delivery: A Bird's-eye View of CF Language Programs

The CF has three distinct language learning programs, all managed centrally by CDA. Opportunities to learn English and French are provided at bases by Environmental Commands, and centrally through CFLS and both RMCC and CMR St-Jean. Foreign Languages are managed by CDA and delivered by CFLS. The International Program (English and French as foreign languages for foreign nationals) is managed for DMTCP by CDA and delivered by CFLS.

OL

There are only two Official Languages, English and French. English is the Declared First Official Language (FOL) of 73 percent of the CF, while French is the Declared FOL of 27 percent.[20] Some trades, but not all, require members to work in English, some require members to work in both languages. French-speaking units (FU) require members to work in French while English-speaking units (EU) require members to work in English. Bilingual units (BU) expect members to function in both languages. The linguistic designation of units is established by

DOL. The language of work, language of instruction, and language of service are all defined and protected by the OLA and applied in DND by the OLPTM. While there is a defined requirement for functions, positions, and jobs to be performed in one or the other, or both Official Languages, there is officially sanctioned requirement for any member to be taught either English or French. The CF simply develops the capability internally to meet need. Medical staff, psychological services, legal staff, and providers of central services, for instance, all deal with members of both linguistic communities on a regular basis.[21] Pilots or ship drivers are expected by international law and convention to function in English. Outside of Canada, the OLA does not apply to other nationals, so the language of operations is the language of the lead nation or body. In NATO, the language of operations is English, while the language of staffing is officially both English and French, but predominantly English. On deployment, in nations where French is a shared or dominant *lingua franca*, the language of operations is French.

The CF offers both language courses and language services. Courses of study in English and French have been developed and continually refined over decades to encourage efficient and effective language learning for CF members. Courses are conducted in classrooms by qualified language teachers who are either civilian Defence employees or contracted. Courses lead to qualifications, as well as to a language proficiency certification measured by the Public Service Evaluation (PSE). The results of a PSE assessment are recorded in every Member's Personnel Record Resume (MPRR) and account for points on merit boards.[22]

Language services, on the other hand, are learning activities which do not lead directly to qualifications or to certification – they are essential to either establishing a pool of students ready to advance to courses leading to qualifications, or to maintain their acquired proficiency. Services include modules in single skills (Writing or Oral Interaction, for instance) as well as maintenance activities (one-on-one, classroom, or on-line modules) to help members maintain acquired proficiency in B or C levels. Services also include refresher courses designed to prepare individuals to sit exams for recertification. A range of services is being rolled out on-line during 2011, including tutor-assisted distributed-learning and self-directed learning (through the ALLIES program developed in St-Jean), and licensed commercial packages, the purpose of which is to provide universal access to language learning opportunities for CF members. An updated list of courses and services is available on the CDA Official Language Delivery website.[23]

Advanced courses leading to C-level certification in French are offered by CFLS and RMC, and on specific bases by Chief of the Land Staff (CLS) and Chief of the Maritime Staff (CMS). C-level English courses are not yet available. Intermediate courses leading to B-level certification are offered at many bases in both languages as well as at St-Jean-sur-Richelieu. Basic courses in both languages are offered where and when numbers warrant, but most bases have the capacity to offer them.

There is not yet an integrated central registry of language courses and services that would allow members to quickly and easily determine what courses and services are available to meet their PD needs. Base and wing coordinators of Official Languages do have immediate access to environmental course listings. Members are normally selected for courses by Director Military Careers (DMilC) to meet CF priorities established annually by DOL. Members are selected for services by their Chain of Command for scheduled events, or self-selected for on-line self-directed learning.

Assessment of language proficiency in the CF has been conducted since 1995 by the Public Service Commission. Although successful completion of a course results in gaining a qualification in a member's MPRR, only PSC certification is taken into account for decisions concerning employment and advancement. Certification guarantees that a member has demonstrated a level of proficiency at the time of testing and is recognized throughout Canada.[24] The evaluation process conducted by the PSC is referred to as the Public Service Evaluation.

Foreign Languages (FL)

Foreign Languages are taught at CFLS at the Asticou Centre in Gatineau. Selected CF members are assigned to international postings, education abroad, intelligence, or operations and they are often required to have different levels of proficiency in Foreign Languages. Defence Attachés and their staff, arms control verification officers, and members working closely with in-country staff abroad account for the majority. Members are selected by DMilC or commands for these courses. CDA coordinates the delivery of the programs. The CF can provide courses in up to thirty foreign languages to meet CF Mission needs. Testing for these languages is also provided to verify levels of proficiency against international standards. A bi-annual call for members to identify proficiency in foreign languages is issued by the VCDS.

Specialized services (i.e., such as a course for Interpreters, or Somali phrasebooks) are designed, developed and delivered for Commands at their request.

International Program

The International Program is currently offered at St-Jean and Borden for defence staff of foreign governments. The program is fully supported by the DMTCP[25] and averages four hundred students or so per year in English as a Foreign Language, French as a Foreign Language, and Language Teacher Training. The program cements established relationships between Canada and other governments and builds strategic alliances by enhancing interoperability. The Language Teacher Training program prepares defence teachers from other countries to deliver English language courses.

History

How did we get here?

Until the 1940s, the dominant language was English at both the strategic and operational levels, while French dominated the tactical militias from Quebec. Long before the *Official Languages Act*, the use of both languages in Canadian military units was a recognized operational requirement. A simple example suffices. During the War of 1812, a few companies of French-Canadian fencibles, Voltigeurs, and Amerindians under the command of a retired British officer, Lieutenant-Colonel Charles-Michel d'Irumberry de Salaberry, repulsed the advance of General Wade Hampton 26 Oct 1813 just south of Valleyfield in Lower Canada and prevented the American forces from cutting the supply lines to Upper Canada. Salaberry's force was comprised of French and English speakers, as well as First Nations.[26]

Back then, the reality of command required leaders to communicate in both languages. In 1899, a militia order was issued to encourage all those who were in command, or aspired to be in command, to learn and use French.[27] But until the 1940s, senior leadership was almost exclusively English-speaking; with some exceptions, leaders communicated in English to their subordinates. It took several generations of political intervention by both French and English senior officers, deputy ministers and ministers, against the same resistance and intransigence witnessed in Canada as a whole, to establish the expectation of bilingualism in the CF.[28]

It was operational requirements that fostered the first language programs in the CF. The first Foreign Language courses were in Japanese during the Second World War:

> From January 1944 to July 1946, the first Canadian military language school operated in Vancouver, British Columbia; it was called the Canadian Army S-20 Japanese Language School. In December 1950, a small Russian language-training program operated with selected personnel, under the sponsorship of the Directorate of Air Intelligence. Known as the 'Royal Canadian Air Force (RCAF) Russian Language School'... located on Victoria Island in Ottawa, Ontario. The school trained 25 officers and non-commissioned members from the RCAF while the Army trained personnel in the USA and the Navy in Great Britain.[29]

The first courses in what came to be called Official Languages were offered by the youngest branch, the Air Force, to train French speaking technicians in Quebec to service aircraft during the Second World War and immediately afterwards:

- second language training in the Canadian Forces began in the 1940s with English courses organized in Montreal and Quebec to make French speaking recruits fluent enough to receive their military training as well as work in English since it was the only language of operations in the CF at that time. The first second language school was called the Royal Canadian Air Force School of English. It opened in 1949 at Trenton and moved to St-Jean-sur-Richelieu two years later. In 1964, it began to teach French to officers.

- Before the unification of the three forces the Army, Air Force and Navy were offering their own language courses at different military locations through Canada. In 1967, it was decided to gather all language courses at St-Jean and, one year later, the RCAF School of English was abolished and replaced by L'École des langues des Forces canadiennes (LFC St-Jean). The establishment of the *Official Languages Act* in 1968 prompted DND to give more impetus to language training.

- The teaching of second language official languages thrived and a testing section was created in 1968 whose mandate was to develop and administer tests in both languages in order to determine students' level of bilingualism. During the following years, always with the intention of improving the quality of instruction, a curriculum section was formed.

The profound contribution of Quebec units to the war efforts in Europe and Asia convinced the Land Forces to follow suit, primarily to ensure interoperability. The thrust of language training until 1967 was to offer English courses to French-speaking members. The Laurendeau Dunton Commission (The Royal Commission on Bilingualism and Biculturalism) stood up in 1963 and got the ball rolling; the impact of that report still resonates.[30] The insistence of the Pearson government on the right of French and English Canadians to grow professionally and culturally in their own language added a legislated dimension to the operational requirement for bilingualism in the CF. The legislation has been assiduously applied by all subsequent governments.

The institutional vision of bilingualism within the CF paralleled the recognition of the bilingual nature of Canada that was growing within the larger community, and reflected the regionalism that characterized the country. Once the *Official Languages Act* was passed in September 1969, the response of the CF was to establish a fifteen-year plan to meet the requirements of the Act. The Wenz Report of 1973 identified the state of CF compliance with the Act and recommended measures to meet the requirement as it was then defined.[31] A submission was presented to Treasury Board; it was rejected. A second submission was submitted for one third the resources required to meet the requirement: it was approved by Treasury Board in 1980. In 1981, Treasury Board suggested that DND redefine its operational targets in order to meet the OL objectives. A study was commissioned 1 Feb 1982 by ADM(Per) on *Official Languages Command and Control, Training and Infrastructure (Military)* – commonly known as the *McLaws Report* after its chair, Brigadier-General D.J. McLaws, Director General Recruiting, Education and Training (DGRET).[32] At a meeting of the NATO advisory body on language matters (the Bureau for International Language Co-ordination – BILC) at St-Jean in 1985, the CF plan to completely revitalize language training in the CF was unveiled.[33] It was implemented over the following years.

The older program, instituted in the 1970s, was based on formal grammar and vocabulary taught by the Public Service Commission and loosely joined with the military programs; it had a separate evaluation protocol. At that time, language education and training was conducted in two phases (I and II) and competence was measured by a four-component standard (listening, speaking, reading, and writing) to four levels: no competence, contact, functional, and integral. The establishment of the Language Standards Control Detachment at St-Jean in 1968-1969, which eventually became Standards Company, was followed by the introduction of both part-time and intensive courses at St-Jean in French and Borden in English. PSC teachers came under the control of the CF in 1977. Military vocabulary exercises were integrated into the civilian curriculum and intensive courses were decentralized and provided initially at bases for six months, followed by six months at St-Jean.

The *McLaws Report* acknowledged "a lack of overall coordination of effort," and, consequently, "dismal" results – no increase in the number of bilingual Anglophones in a decade. The report recommended sweeping changes to policy concerning selection and posting of members, the identification of bilingual positions, as well as to the design and delivery of language education and training.

There were forty-four recommendations in the *McLaws Report*. Those which were implemented resulted in, among other things:

- the approval of SLT for all regular force members;

- the development of a military curriculum (MSLTP) in both French and English;

- the identification of training specifications based on communicative competence (completed in 1985; signed in 1989);

- the development of tests;

- the General Officer/Executive program and immersion; and

- the identification of the linguistic requirement of all military positions.

The *McLaws Report* and the subsequent *McLaws II* (twenty-nine recommendations),[34] were the foundation the Military Second Language Training Plan which is currently at the core of CF Language Programs. In addition to the results listed above, the report also established the application of rigorous standards, as well as the notion of a bilingual officers corps to support leadership. The General Officer/Colonel (GO/Col) program (language maintenance services for senior officers) paralleled the Executive (EX) programs being offered in the National Capital Region (NCR) to civilians with a recognized need to become bilingual. The design to generate a bilingual officer corps relied on the provision of an initial six-month introduction to the second language; this was intended to provide officers with a solid foundation in their second language at the onset of their careers. This program was eliminated in 2008 to accelerate officer training for deployment to International Security Assistance Force (ISAF) and has not been reinstigated. The initial six-month course was to be complemented in following years by block courses to achieve the target functional level. For NCMs, the approach was rather different. The approach was to define language use by NCMs as a "skill" and apply a training regimen to program delivery. Four sets of priorities were identified: 1) trades with little requirement for bilingualism; 2) trades with a "normal" need, 3) trades with a "high need," and 4) bilingual trades. The quota for "high need" trades was 40% of the recruits to become bilingual, while designated bilingual trades would require 100% bilingual members. It did not work.[35] The delta between allocation and requirement, as well as an overly complex method of integrating language education and training in trades, was too much to sustain. The institutional vision, which dreamed of 1400 Anglophones enrolled in year-long courses for a stretch of fifteen years, at a cost of $42.5 million and 1300 Person Years, was unattainable. The operational vision, which dreamed of a seamless training system enthusiastically endorsed by highly motivated leaders at all levels and a system that prioritized language education and training, was unrealistic. Neither the institutional nor operational vision had been very successfully implemented.

By 1986, decentralized courses to Phase I were offered outside of St-Jean by the CMS in Halifax and Esquimalt, by the Chief of the Air Staff (CAS) in Comox, and by the CLS at Gagetown, Petawawa, and Borden. In 1990, the two phase program was replaced by a three phase program which recognized beginner, intermediate and advanced levels but restricted the delivery of decentralized programs to the beginner level (this practice persisted until 2009). Decentralized intermediate level programs were managed centrally but delivered by contractors on bases, needlessly duplicating resources.

In April 1993, a decade beyond the *McLaws Report*, another CF "Service Paper on Second Language Training" (generated by the Director of Professional Development: Language Training), identified the following deficiencies in Learning Programs (LP): annual goals were not determined, accountability for achieving goals was not defined, a low level of training was provided to many rather than having fewer members educated to an acceptable level of proficiency, those closest to becoming bilingual were not prioritized, inadequate performance data were available, and success rates were unacceptably low. Many of the same concerns expressed by McLaws were still prevalent. In 1996, the transfer of testing and certification from the CF, with its four-component standard and numeric scale, to the Public Service Commission, with its three-component standard (Reading Comprehension, Writing, and Oral Interaction) and an alphabetic scale, put an end to the need for a CF testing cell devoted to OL certification.

The CF lost the hard-won expertise to develop and maintain independent military certification tests for second language at that point. Simultaneously, force reduction gutted the centralized authority that managed SLT and left the programs delivered by the three environments and the components of the CFLS to fend for themselves. A new working model for Language Program delivery evolved to meet demands for recognition of Quality of Life issues, a reordering of priorities for second-language billets, and falling enrolments.

Restructuring CFLS provided an acting Managing Authority for LP in 2000, and a new attempt to identify requirements and rationalize programs was introduced by the Directorate of Official Languages in the DND OL Strategic Plan for 2001-2006. The Strategic Plan attempted to reconcile operational and institutional CF OL requirements through a broad and ambitious program that had the immediate effect of re-emphasizing the rights and responsibilities of the CF with regard to official languages. Ultimately, however, this Plan was overtaken by a more focused compliance-based Transformation Model proposed to and accepted by AFC and the Deputy Minister in 2006.

The Department of National Defence Official Languages Program Transformation Model[36] defines the responsibilities of DND in meeting the spirit and the letter of the OLA. Previous attempts to do so have conflated operational and institutional goals and have succeeded in meeting neither. The OLPTM identifies three target areas: communication, consultation, and redefinition.

The linguistic rights and responsibilities of all members of the CF are ill understood and applied, even after forty years of the OLA. A strategy to communicate the legal obligations and rights of the CF and its members has been identified as essential to complying with the OLA and is being implemented. The role of Co-ordinators of Official Languages as consultants to base commanders and higher commands has not been adequately defined or implemented; a strategy to raise the profiles and responsibilities of coordinators has been identified as essential to ensuring DND compliance with the OLA. The CF had been using civilian standards based on static positions to identify compliance with the OLA: a strategy to implement a functional rather than positional approach to complying with the spirit and letter of the OLA has been initiated. Intentions to develop these strategies are proposed in the OLPTM. The implications for the delivery of SOLET within the CF are broadly identified by the OLPTM in a statement of priority of access to SOLET programs and services for CF members. A greater emphasis on language retention (to capitalize on the investment in learning) through distance learning and continuing education is clearly identified. The OLPTM also sets five key areas of priority for access to SOLET:

- leadership and supervision;

- providers of services to the public;

- providers of central services;

- the instructional cadre; and

- Professional Development.

The OLPTM is the first attempt to quantify OL institutional requirements in two decades. Nevertheless, loading of courses continues to occur without any direct reference to the stated priorities.

DOL has recognized that the institutional requirement needs to be complemented by an operational model in order to fully meet the needs of the CF. In other words, language tied to the work people do is as important as language tied to managing people. CF members move vertically through ranks and horizontally through postings with, from the point of view of the Public Service, astonishing rapidity. For instance, a technician working in Bagotville today may be posted to Italy next week and then to Ottawa or Comox in December. The language requirement for that person to perform meaningful work changes quickly. Operationally, the language of international operations and the staffing of international HQs is predominantly English, and institutionally the language requirement of increasing rank and responsibility becomes proficiency in both OLs. The Audit of IT&E conducted by the Office of the Commissioner of Official Languages at the request of the CF concurs.[37] This is where the new model comes in.

SOLET

After decades of an institutional focus on Official Languages, the challenge to re-focus on operational requirements is welcomed. The next five years will present significant challenges to all language programs within the CF. Transformation of Language Programs will result in a new model of program design, delivery, and follow-up. The new SOLET model will be provided by a network of agencies delivering programs and services to meet requirements identified by the Departmental Authorities. The transformation that has occurred in civilian institutions since the early 1990s provides guidelines for the CF.

New Model

Second Language Education and Training requires an androgogy designed to provide opportunities for learning language and retention through communicative strategies grounded in but not hobbled by the Canadian Forces Individual Training and Education System. Adult learners are clients whose motivation and need for concrete results demands a teaching and learning style that is engaging and driven by concrete goals: learning activities must be relevant. Educational research over the past two decades has identified approaches and processes for adult learners that will be integrated into current curricula as well as into the professional development of language teachers. SOLET must become more client-driven than teacher-driven.

Learning a language for everyday use is not a training activity that relies on rote and repetition, it is an educational activity that engages intellect and involves, physically, rewiring of the human brain. Learning a language to actually use it in human interaction requires a continual and incremental commitment. Language training involves learning set responses to predictable situations, such as demanding passports or asking whether someone is armed, giving orders or asking for specific information. These are rote activities that involve minimal interaction, minimal cultural awareness, and minimal effort. Language education provides a learner with the tools and processes to generate new meaning or to process complex spoken or written spontaneous communication. Labelling language learning as "training" results in inaccurate and inappropriate expectations. It assumes that training effected is training maintained, that information delivered once has been communicated for always, and that a rote response is always correct. When using language to interact, nothing could be further from the truth. Although there is always an element of training in the early stages of language learning, it is an element that diminishes as the learner masters new skills, new information, and new attitudes about what works and what does not. For these reasons, Language Education and Training is the new focus of CF Language Programs. SOLET is not SLT. And what applies to OL applies equally to foreign languages.

Network of Agencies

The management of learning is – here is that word again – *complex* and consequently demands a systems approach. The management of learning language for large numbers of individuals over a geography and demography as vast and varied as ours is challenging in many ways. A centralized managing authority or Education and Training Provider supplies standards of achievement and program delivery, but courses of study and services need to be delivered across time zones and for differing requirements. The CF network comprises RMCC and CMR St-Jean, CFLS and its campuses, Language Training Centres under the control of the ECs, contracted suppliers, virtual classrooms (coming soon), collaborative professional development for teachers and managers, self-directed and tutor-supported learning, collaborative learning among learners, and a well regulated testing administration system. Selection of learners and recording of qualifications and certification are part of the puzzle as well.

The network is connected through:

- clear and consistent policy statements and foundation documentation;

- well articulated governance structures with requirement defined by the Department Authority, program and service management conducted by the Training Authority, and delivery conducted by Training Establishments;

- mission command management structures sharing common goals, responsibilities, and integrated performance measurement procedures;

- shared learning materials, shared best-teaching practice encouraged through a communication strategy involving conferences, seminars, and newsletters, and a shared pool of electronic, print, and multimedia resources; and

- central support through iterative curriculum development, test development and delivery, teacher and management training and recognition, performance measurement tools, and assistance visits conducted by the TA in close collaboration with the ECs.

Programs and Services

A new client base (Gen X), new learning environments (online, mobile, and social networking), and new demands call for renewed programs of study and services to members. In general, recruits are much better educated than in the past and have higher expectations of the Training Authority. They expect directly relevant learning activities, immediate feedback on progress, access from anywhere at any time, and individual support as it is needed. CF language programs are about a decade behind post-secondary programs in the provinces and are only beginning to catch up. Language maintenance activities need not be designed using the same mould as training curricula, and can therefore afford the luxury of being topical and authentic. Recommended strategies will be more than sufficient for most motivated members, but teachers, as facilitators of learning, will need to be provided with recommended resources from branches. The loss of the DP1 SOLET needs to be addressed as well, with a shorter course more focused on strategies to develop language skills and the use of resources to do so. The responsibility of members themselves to develop and maintain skills requires a greater emphasis on facilitating learning rather than directing learning for course designers, students, and teachers alike. Although commercial off-the-shelf software is now being used as a stop-gap measure to compensate for an incomplete English curriculum, the eventual migration of the English curriculum to ALLIES will fill a costly and embarrassing void in the CF military language curriculum, and will open more opportunities for strategic partnerships. Motivation to learn can be enhanced by establishing links between general linguistic proficiency and the vocabulary and procedures of specific trades can be established through on-the-job training either physically through special arrangements between TEs and branches or bases, or virtually through DNDLearn. Teaching and management staff in language programs need to be kept abreast of the changing landscape – communication among players can be enhanced through newsletters, communities of practice, and a journal devoted to best practice (the journal *Contact* published by CDA has served this purpose in the past).

Program development and maintenance is already being addressed through restructuring, more aggressive business planning, and new standing offers. The use of developing learning technologies has begun but resources and infrastructure are lagging. Programs that do not produce results are being reviewed. New courses and new services and new partnerships are being explored. The advent of Distributed Learning (DL rather than Alternative Training Delivery) in the CF opens opportunities for program development in both OL as well as in Foreign Languages, not only with the CF but within DND, in the Public Service, and perhaps beyond our borders.

And finally, access to programs, which has been rigidly constrained by classroom learning, has begun to expand through DL initiatives, education reimbursement (ER) for some language maintenance activities in approved programs of study, and pilot projects exploring blended learning activities. The Tutorat-à-distance (TAD) project at CFLS matches tutors with broad language experience and students following the web-base ALLIES on-line course. The results to date are very encouraging. Joining ALLIES with employment-specific on-line learning in both OL through DNDLearn will open new doors for CF students around the globe, and new opportunities for teachers and developers as well.

Requirement

From the 1970s, there has been a disconnect between what the OLA requires and what the CF needs in order to function. The OLPTM has addressed some of the more egregious gaps, but there still remains a significant disconnect between OL IT&E functional approach and the MES positional approach.

Although general expectations have been expressed clearly and at times eloquently by successive commands, the CF has been singularly unsuccessful in defining the bare bones requirement for education in one's second official language. The Wems and McLaws reports, the DOL Strategic Plan, and Instructional DAODs have struggled with defining the who, where, when, and to what level. The current OLPTM is not yet any more successful than previous attempts, but it provides some direction that will allow the different components of the CF to join the practical considerations necessary for sound business planning and practice to the implications for the CF and DND of the OLA.

When we need to know (as we do) that twelve Lieutenant-Colonels/ Commanders (the **who**) need to reach a CBC profile to command bilingual units (the **to what level**) between January 2012 and December 2012 (the **when**), that four are in Esquimalt and Shearwater, two are in Kingston, and six are in the NCR (the **where**); when we know the profiles of each and have verified them, then we know the requirement and we know how to coordinate resources to meet that requirement. The Annual Military Occupation Review (AMORs) process has been recommended[38] as a means of defining what the annual (and year-out) requirement will be; procedures to use that process are now being developed.

On the other hand, without a defined requirement, we can still ask if the program is internally sound. Judging from the results of some courses, notably those for the Senior Officer Second Language Selection Planning Committee (SSPC) candidates, most certainly – the program is internally sound. For the C-level course, the Qualification Standard (QS), Training Plan (TP), lesson plans and assessment instruments all lead to a satisfactory result – senior officers with the ability to work effectively in their second language.[39] Judging from other activities, such as the ill-defined GO/Col, the foundation documents and learning events do not coincide. Some learning events have no baseline, no expected target, and the curriculum itself shifts from definition to definition with an astounding rapidity. Are internal checks being applied? Again, in some cases they are; in others, they are not. The most common cause of failure in courses and in entire programs, even today, as it was when McLaws made his report and the Service Paper was published in 1993, is inappropriate selection; students who are ineligible or have no discernable requirement are routinely loaded into courses. This lapse is indicative of the complexity of the language education and training system overall and the lack of coordinated effort to make best use of scarce resources. The current process of loading of students on courses is only beginning to take into account the DOL annual targets and OLPTM recommendations.

The OLPTM goes a long way to set the stage for a quantifiable annual requirement. But at this time there is no language specification for the CF, which makes developing a training specification, qualification standard, and training plan virtually impossible. As the functional requirement is defined and refined, the development of a CF Language Specification becomes feasible. Processes to establish a quantifiable requirement are being developed and tested by branches through the AMORs process and will be recommended as Standing Operating Procedures (SOPs) to the IT&E Committee, which DOL attends[40]. At this time, senior leadership has specific linguistic requirements, commandants of national schools have specific requirements, some employment requires facility in English (in particular maritime or aviation trades), certain occupations (such as legal, medical, security and public affairs) have defined linguistic requirements, and some members with responsibility for providing central services or services to the public have defined requirements. Defining the broader requirement for all functions, for operations, for employment, and for succession planning is the next challenge. The CF has not been able to do that successfully in the past fifty years. The selection process for foreign languages is guided by strategic need and the relatively low numbers involved allow for tighter control of resources, curricula, and assessment. There are few opportunities for members to acquire proficiency in foreign languages and no incentives to do so.

No aboriginal languages, neither First Nations nor Inuit, are officially recognized, and there is neither incentive nor motivation for members to self-identify.

Conclusion

The modernization of Language Programs in the CF relies on the same processes as does IT&E modernization. Policy gaps and disconnects need to be identified and corrected, governance streamlined by better defining roles and responsibilities, management improved through better communication and an aggressive elimination of redundancy, and delivery improved by recognizing the strengths that exist and developing learning materials and processes that recognize the needs of the CF and its members. Formalizing performance measurement, providing professional development of teaching and management staff to meet a greater demand, building and maintaining partnerships within the language learning theory and practice community at home and abroad will keep the CF language programs current.

The strengths of the current system are numerous. A dedicated and professional teaching staff sits at the very core of our programs. Our French curriculum is sound. A Performance Measurement System has been developed internally and reporting is timely. We have built the foundations of online learning and language maintenance through the ALLIES Learning Management System developed at St-Jean, and CFLS has developed the capacity to provide tutor support, an expertise that can be extended to the ECs. But more importantly, the SOLET delivery community shares a common understanding of the operational focus of SOLET, and its foundation in history.

In 2011, there is still no defined CF language requirement, and no annual goals are set. The consequence of not achieving goals has become a major factor in promotion to higher ranks, both for officers and NCMs. More than half of the SOLET delivered is aimed at low levels of achievement. There is no correspondence between access to SOLET and OL targets. In contrast with the reported shortfalls identified in the 1993 Service Paper cited above, processes are now under way to define the requirement and set annual goals, and SOLET is becoming much more closely aligned to Professional Development, to succession planning, and to posting than it has ever been. A side effect, curiously enough, is closer compliance with legislated requirements.

---

1   For an overview of language development, see Harvard psychologist: Steven Pinker, *The Language Instinct* (NY: Harper Collins, 1994); *How the Mind Works* (NY: Norton, 1999); and The Stuff of Thought, (NY: Viking, 2007).

2   Diane Larsen-Freeman and Lynne Cameron, *Complex Systems and Applied Linguistics* (Oxford Allied Linguistics, Oxford University Press, 2008). For a compressed version of her argument, see: Larsen-Freeman, "Chaos/Complexity Science and Second Language Acquisition", *Applied Linguistic,* Vol. 18, No. 2, (1997). See also: Paul van Geert, "The Dynamic Systems Approach in Study of L1 and L2 Acquisition: An Introduction", *The Modern Language Journal,* Vol. 92 (2008), ii.

3   Three volumes from the CMP History section cover the history of French Canadians in the CF: Jean Pariseau and Serge Bernier, *French Canadians and Bilingualism in the Canadian Armed Forces: Vol 1 1763-1969: The Fear of a Parallel Army* (DND, 1988); and Serge Bernier and Jean Pariseau, *French Canadians and Bilingualism in the Canadian Armed Forces: Vol II 1969-1987 Official Languages: National Defence's Response to the Federal Policy.* Minister of Supply and Services, (Ottawa: 1988), and Armand Letellier *Reforme linguistique a la Defense nationale: la mise en marche des programmes de bilinguisme,* 1967-1977. (1987) are a start.

4   *Military Second Language Training Plan (MSLTP) – Implementation*, CF Military Personnel Instructions 06/85, issued December 31, 1985, retrieved on 12 Jul 2011 from <http://hr.ottawa-hull.mil.ca/mpi-ipm/06-85-eng.asp>.

5   The standard was 2122 or 3233 at the time, based on a four scale standard. That numeric PSC standard was based on the International Language Roundtable (ILR) scale, since adopted and refined for NATO use as STANAG 6001 (ed 4).

6   Office of the Commissioner of Official Languages, "Walking the Walk: Language of Work in the Federal Public Service", March 2004, retrieved on 1 Sept 2011 from <http://www.ocol-clo.gc.ca/docs/e/work_travail_2004_e.pdf>.

7   Many of these trends are covered in *The Handbook of Educational Linguistics*, edited by Bernard Spolsky and Francis M. Hult in the *Blackwell Handbooks of Linguistics* series, Wiley-Blackwell, 2010. There are chapters on neurobiology, psycholinguistics, sociolinguistics, and language assessment, among many other topics. Spolsky has also published *Language Management*, Cambridge, 2009. There is no need for me to cite the many sources available for current developments in management theory and practice, but two key conceptual frameworks used widely within DND are Peter Senge's *The Fifth Discipline* (new edition 2006) and Kaplan and Norton's *The Balanced Scorecard* 1996.

8   NATO distinguishes between Allied Command Transformation (ACT) and Allied Command Operations (ACO), and CDA HQ distinguished similarly between Strategic Training and Education Programs and Formation Operations Support and Management (FOSM). In this chapter, I use the terms "operational requirement" and "operational language" to refer to the day-to-day use of either or both official languages.

9   The standard employed by NATO is STANAG 6001 ed. 4.

10   CDS direction concerning "Regular Force general/Flag officer and Colonel/Captain(Navy) Succession Planning" 5 January 2009. "In fact … linguistic requirements are effectively part of core competencies…."

11   The IT&E Modernization Initiative recognizes this, as does the OGS (2-12) and NCM GS (2-17).

12   CANFORGENs 117-10, 151-10, and 115-10, instruct Merit Boards on the allocation of points for language certification of members; DAOD 5039-1 and 5039-7 address access to testing and to SOLET. An audit of OL compliance within the IT&E System was conducted at the request of the CF by the Office of the Commissioner of Official Languages and published in June 2010. It identified several areas where immediate action is required to comply with the provisions of the Official Languages Act.

13   An IT&E SOLET Working Group was stood up in September 2010 to advise the IT&E Committee on SOLET issues. At the same time, a SOLET Priorities Committee chaired by COS FOSM was established to keep lines of communication between CDA and DOL open.

14   A full range of learning maintenance activities has been developed by CDA to support English-speaking members who have been certified at the CBC or above level. The package cannot be used because policy dictates that a parallel package must be developed and made available for French-speaking members with the same certification, even though it is extremely unlikely that the package would be used by French-speaking members who are inundated daily with communications in English. Nevertheless, there are similar English-language learning materials developed and delivered by the Canada School of Public Service for the EX-level public service which could be adapted for use by the CF. Computer-adaptive testing, which would assess candidates over a range of levels with a single test, can be used as an assessment tool across the CF for diagnostic, formative and summative testing. Currently, tests are single-level and used for either formative or summative assessments. They are conducted face-to-face and using paper tests requiring the physical presence of assessors. Like so many other initiatives in modernizing IT&E, the development of computer-adaptive tests demand resources that are in very short supply, but would streamline and standardize reliable language assessment from recruiting to pre-course diagnostics to summative assessment for access to the PSE.

15   Karen Davis and Denise Kerr call particular attention to the importance of domestic cultural awareness in the context of the Oka situation. They also call attention to the increased

awareness in the CF of First Nations and the introduction of new programs to encourage recruiting and retention (Karen Davis, ed., *Cultural Intelligence and Leadership: An Introduction for Canadian Forces Leaders* (CDA Press, 2009), 123-125). Meanwhile, aboriginal languages are virtually ignored because they do not fit in either the Official or Foreign Language boxes.

16   Department of National Defence. *The Official Language Transformation Program*, retrieved on 1 Sep 2011 from <http://www.ocol-clo.gc.ca/docs/e/work_travail_2004_e.pdf>.

17   Department of National Defence. *The Directorate – Military Training & Cooperation*, retrieved on 1 Sep 2011 from <http://www.forces.gc.ca/admpol/mtcp-eng.html>.

18   Department of National Defence. *DAOD 5031-2, Individual Training and Education Strategic Framework*, retrieved on 1 Sep 2011 from <http://www.admfincs.forces.gc.ca/dao-doa/5000/5031-2-eng.asp>. The directive outlines the roles and responsibilities of stakeholders in CF education and training. COMD CDA, for example, is identified as the delegated Functional Authority for all IT&E as well as the Training Authority for common (i.e., pan-CF) IT&E, while the other three Training Authorities (RCN, CA and RCAF) are responsible for environmental IT&E.

19   The role of DOL is elaborated in Department of National Defence. *DAOD 5039-7 Second Official Language Education and Training for CF Members*, retrieved on 1 Sep 2011 from <http://www.admfincs.forces.gc.ca/dao-doa/5000/5039-7-eng.asp>.

20   Members are required to identify either English or French as their Official Language. The other language, by default, becomes their Second Official Language.

21   The OLA specifies that Canadians can expect to be provided with government services in the language of their choice.

22   Points are awarded according to direction provided in Department of National Defence. *CANFORGEN 115/11*, retrieved on 1 Sep 2011 from <http://vcds.mil.ca/vcds-exec/pubs/canforgen/2011/115-11_e.asp>.

23   Department of National Defence. CDA, *COS FOSM Language Program Delivery*, retrieved on 1 Sep 2011 from <http://cda-acd.mil.ca/lang/index-eng.asp>.

24   Public Service Commission of Canada. *Second Language Evaluation*, retrieved on 1 Sep 2011 from <http://www.psc-cfp.gc.ca/ppc-cpp/sle-els/index-eng.htm> DAOD 5039 "SOL Assessment" (in draft at this stage) defines access to testing and describes the levels of proficiency. Meanwhile, CANFORGEN 104/04 has not yet been superseded. Retrieved on 1 Sep 2011 from <http://vcds.mil.ca/vcds-exec/pubs/canforgen/2004/104-04_e.asp>.

25   The language programs are described at Canadian Forces Language School, *Military Training & Cooperation Program (MTCP)*, retrieved on 1 Sep 2011 from <http://cfls.mil.ca/mta-pai/index-eng.asp>, while the DMTCP programs are described at National Defence, *Directorate – Military Training & Cooperation*, retrieved on 1 Sep 2011 from <http://www.forces.gc.ca/admpol/mtcp-eng.html>.

26   Wikipedia, *Charles-Michel d'Irumberry de Salaberry*, retrieved on 29 May 2011 from <http://fr.wikipedia.org/wiki/Charles-Michel_d%27Irumberry_de_Salaberry>. See also: John Grodzinski, "Charles-Michel d'Irumberry de Salaberry", *The Canadian Encylopedia*, retrieved on 29 May 2011 from <http://www.thecanadianencyclopedia.com/index.cfm?PgNm=tce&Params=A1ARTA0007123>. A portrait of de Salaberry hangs in the Senior Staff Mess at RMC.

27   Pariseau, 62. Details of the CF response to the OLA in the section below are drawn from Bernier pp 551-619, who relied heavily on research conducted by Liliane Grantham.

28   Pariseau, Chapters 6 to 8, 143-238 traces the growing awareness of the value of French in the CF. Bernier, 425. Recounts one example concerning translation, and another 548-549 gives a snapshot of a single incident of friction (many more appear in the study) that centres around schooling of French-speaking members' children.

29   Department of National Defence. *History. Foreign Languages*, retrieved on 1 Sep 2011 from <http://www.cfls-elfc.forces.gc.ca/au-ns/history-histoire-eng.asp>.

30   Graham Fraser, *Sorry, I Don't Speak French* (Toronto: McClelland and Stewart, 2006). Fraser provides an intimate narrative of the genesis and impact of the Commission on Canadian culture.

31   Bernier, 369 ff.

32   The report was issued in December 1985. See note 4 above.

33   The annual report of Canada for 1985 to the BILC is available on the BILC website under archived conference proceedings retrieved on 1 Sep 2011 from <www.bilc.forces.gc.ca>.

34   The Senior Review Board established to implement the recommendations of the McLaws study grouped the recommendations ito eight "activities" which were subsequently expanded to thirteen Military Language Training Improvement Program (MLTIP) activities, each encompassing several recommendations. McLaws II consisted of a set of administrative reform recommendations that would "some fundamental policy and other issues to be resolved, such as: the voluntary aspect of SLT the balance between the individual's responsibility and that of the CF, SLT program priorities, and continued research on selection and motivation of candidates. These issues were addressed in a subsequent study, dubbed McLaws II . . . completed in July 1984 and gave rise to new recommendations primary among which was recognition of the requirement for different approaches towards language training for Officers [and] Non Commissioned Members" – from the preamble to the MSLTP. The source for this information is a copy of a mimeographed set of presentation notes on the implementation of the activities formerly in the possession of Mme Irene Copping of the Standards Coy in St-Jean and now in my possession.

35   Bernier, Chapter 15, 309-414.

36   Director Official Languages, *National Defence Program Transformation Model*, retrieved on 1 Sep 2011 from <http://hr.ottawa-hull.mil.ca/dgmp-dgpm/dol-dlo/kd-dc/ndolptm-dnmtplo-eng.asp>.

37   See the discussion leading to Recommendations 8 and 9.

38   The Office of the Commissioner of Official Languages (OCOL) *Audit* Recommendations 1 and 2.

39   Informal discussions with graduates of the course indicate that more work-related tasks (composing briefing notes, delivering presentations, and financial analysis) would enhance what is otherwise excellent delivery.

40   The CF Action Plan related to Recommendation 5 of the Audit states that DOL is a full member of the IT&E Committee (*Audit*, 37).

CHAPTER 20

ALTERNATIVE TRAINING DELIVERY: THE OPTIONS, OBSTACLES AND OPPORTUNITIES

Major Mark Russell

Alternative approaches to CF training and education have been considered and pursued for many years... and as a responsible department, we are expanding this type of activity. These initiatives have been driven in part to control training costs – a desirable objective given our current economic environment.[1]

General John de Chastelain

Transforming how Canadian Forces personnel train and determining what to train has been a subject of much strategic examination and review through the years. The words of General John de Chastelain, at the time the Chief of the Defence Staff, provided at the outset of this chapter, are part of the background for a study exploring alternative approaches for Canadian Forces Individual Training and Education. The study was centred on the IT&E requirements for individual occupations and it focused largely on initial occupation related IT&E, given this is where the largest expenditures are typically made. The directive was released in 1989 and over the next twenty years there would be several more pan-CF strategic reviews investigating the application of alternative approaches to satisfying IT&E requirements.[2]

The more recent focus on alternative approaches for CF IT&E delivery evolved from the pressures to find innovative solutions to increase CF personnel production and the overall capacity of the CF IT&E system. The rapid expansion of the CF force structure as well as the need for additional personnel to sustain the campaign in Afghanistan, and other operations, created the imperative for change in how CF IT&E is delivered.[3] Following a decade of reductions and cutbacks through the 1990s incremental personnel became the instructor cadre lifeblood in support of the CF IT&E system. As the operational tempo increased this source of expertise to support IT&E delivery was no longer an option. Concurrently, CF recruiting efforts were stepped up and the challenges being faced by the CF IT&E system became more apparent. In 2002, the Office of the Auditor (OAG) observed that, "bottlenecks in the system are beginning to show… the waiting time is increasing between the end of basic training and the start of instruction to become a skilled technician."[4] The OAG revisited this issue in 2006 and noted that little had changed: "…we found that limitations in the capacity of the training system remain an issue…instructors are often in short supply because they are needed to fill operational demands in the Forces."[5]

The implementation of alternative IT&E approaches allowed the CF personnel production system to respond to the increased intake of recruits and force expansion targets were ultimately achieved.[6] As recruiting intake normalizes, the CF IT&E system is poised to examine the lessons learned and begin to face new challenges. Over this past decade the CF context has evolved considerably and it is very likely that the need for alternative IT&E approaches will accelerate as new capabilities are introduced through the *Canada First Defence Strategy* and additional personnel, from within the CF's current personnel structure, are required to support them.

The examination of training alternatives that took place in 1989 was mainly a cost saving exercise and it became part of the eventual downsizing of the CF. The conditions have evolved considerably since it was completed. Perhaps the most significant change is that uniformed personnel have become a much more valued, and in demand, resource. Operations are such that it is no longer a question of "if" there is mission which will require CF support to that of prioritizing which mission Canada will support. The increasing demand for CF personnel to support operations internationally, and also at home, has resulted in a renewed focus towards the core mission of Canada's military. Going forward the scrutiny of in-service delivered IT&E is likely to continue as efforts are made to determine how best to employ uniformed personnel within the CF's IT&E system.

This chapter will examine alternative IT&E strategies and it will do so by providing a synopsis of the options applicable to the CF. This will be followed by an examination of the imperatives driving the need for change and a review of the forces that can present a barrier. Finally, this chapter concludes with an exploration of the potential for leveraging external service providers and especially the opportunities available through the post-secondary institutions that form Canada's network of community colleges. The college system is often identified as a potential course of action for CF personnel generation. While some CF IT&E requirements are now being satisfied through this approach there remains scepticism and questions as to the fit with CF needs.

The Options - Sorting Through the Alternatives

The majority of what has become the CF's modern occupation training capability began to emerge in the 1950s and 1960s. Significant investment created a contemporary self-sustaining training capability complete with dedicated personnel, infrastructure and equipment. The system constructed was intended to provide the environment that would meet the evolving needs of Canada's different armed services and it had to be scalable in order to support rapid force mobilization, which was a concern heightened by the Cold War.

Whereas at one time there appeared to be few alternatives to the in-service model, the broader training and education landscape has evolved considerably and as a result, there are now several viable options. A scan of the alternative IT&E activity ongoing within the CF was completed in 2009 as part of a report intended to provide recommendations to Armed Forces Council concerning the future of Alternate Training Delivery (ATD) within the CF.[7]

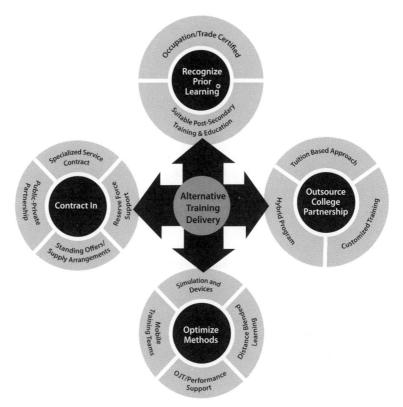

Figure 20.1: Alternative Training Delivery Strategies

An attempt to provide order to the various forms of ATD is outlined in Figure 20.1, and this is an updated version that was published previously in the 2009 report.[8] Regardless of the approach selected the effects to be achieved through CF IT&E remain the same. That is, to produce the right number of professional military personnel who are employable and deployable, at the right time and cost for the CF. The alternative strategies are summarized as follows:

- **Recognize Prior Learning:** This is a more learner-centred approach, the aim being to tap into an already skilled and suitably trained workforce. The intent is to avoid the unnecessary duplication with in-service IT&E delivery. By assessing a learner's profile of already acquired competencies and adjusting IT&E delivery accordingly there is a considerable opportunity to avoid delivery costs and this also leads to the production of operationally ready CF personnel in a significantly shorter period of time. CF IT&E may not be completely avoided; however, it can be reduced considerably and as a result, there are tangible benefits for the CF.

- **Contract In:** This approach involves augmenting the existing in-service IT&E cadre with instructors or other forms of support. This approach can be used to reduce the reliance on uniformed personnel and, through longer term contracted arrangements, may even incorporate an investment in new infrastructure and equipment as well as other support services which are combined with the delivery of training. Contracting-in usually takes the following forms:

  - **Specialized Services Contracts**. This involves contracting expertise to deliver specific courses, portions of courses and/or provide unique support which isn't typically resident within the CF IT&E environment.

  - **Standing Offers and Supply Arrangements**. Standing Offers and Supply Arrangements are used to augment resident training capability through a pool of incremental contractors available on an as required, call-up, basis. A Standing Offer is a proposal from a qualified supplier to provide services at pre-arranged prices, under previously set terms and conditions, when and if required. No contract exists until a request order, or call-up, is made against the Standing Offer. This approach provides flexibility to expand and reduce the IT&E cadre as required. Supply Arrangements are often less specific in terms of deliverables than Standing Offers. Supply Arrangements may include many potential providers and tend to result in greater contract administration when it comes to finalizing terms, conditions and other details. Standing Offers have emerged as preferred instruments for contracting-in the services of qualified civilians to augment in-service IT&E delivery.

- **Reserve Force Support**. This approach involves augmenting the IT&E environment with qualified Reserve Force personnel often filling vacant Regular Force positions. The process is completed on an individual hire basis and the duration of the contracts vary. In some cases Reserve Force personnel are used on a part-time basis. Reserve Force support proved essential during force expansion.

- **Public-Private Partnerships**. This represents a cooperative venture built on the expertise of each partner in order to best meet clearly defined needs. The belief is that the capacity of government to meet current and future infrastructure and major equipment needs as well as service obligations can be enhanced through public-private partnership. Public-private partnerships evolve into complex contracting arrangements with terms that typically extend over many years and include the appropriate allocation of resources, risks and rewards. The initial investment can be considerable hence it is amortized over time in order to make the venture affordable. The Royal Canadian Air Force has made significant use of this strategy in support of the production of trained pilots.

- **Outsource and College Partnership**: Through this approach the day-to-day execution of IT&E delivery is transferred, either as a whole or in part, to a post-secondary institute or other vocational training provider. This can also extend to tapping into foreign military IT&E opportunities. The CF generally retains management and oversight functions which vary based on the approach selected. This approach often, but not always, requires a contractual relationship to be established. The outsourced partnership may be used to augment current CF training capacity or replace it entirely. This approach can also position the CF to reduce longer term physical infrastructure needs and other support costs. Outsourced delivery generally takes the following forms:

- **Tuition Based Approach**. These models are commonly used in conjunction with post-secondary institutions in which CF members self-enrol and self-administer. This includes college programs as well as courses offered to the general public through private training providers. Under this approach there is no contract involving the Crown. The contract exists between the institution and the individual CF member. The individual member is later reimbursed for expenses. A waiver allowing for the disclosure of academic information, which is common practice in post-secondary institutions, becomes essential in order for the CF to monitor student progress. In some situations a Memorandum of Understanding is used in order to ensure current CF members have access to high demand and highly competitive programs within a post-secondary institution.

- **Customized Training Contracts**. This involves contracting external agencies to deliver training in accordance with CF requirements. There may also be guidelines regarding specific CF practices which are to be adhered to. This form of outsourced partnership can take many forms and varies in length of contract, training service specifics and other elements based on CF requirements.

- **Hybrid Programs**. This consists of contracting external agencies, most often post-secondary institutions, to deliver training that is aligned with CF needs and embeds CF support as part of the overall program. These arrangements serve to improve the overall end product by minimizing delta training and by including the provision of a military context during the training process.

- **Optimize Methods and Instructional Strategies**: This approach involves the implementation of methods which shift in-service IT&E delivery beyond traditional techniques by situating more learning in the workplace as well as within a workplace context. This shift includes assessing current instructional tactics and implementing distributed methods as well as encouraging on-job performance support systems and structured workplace experience. The options also involve providing more learning experiences online and the use of blended learning which combines learning at a distance with a centralized delivery model. Finally, the approach encourages the use of performance based simulation systems, devices and other technologies which can situate learning in multiple conditions and accelerate the transfer of learning to the job context.

The options to satisfy CF requirements continue to evolve. Some are more appropriate than others and it is not a one size fits all scenario. A CF training requirement is the basis for what is to be learned and this begins with having a clearly defined operational need. Training requirements go through a formal review process, more broadly referred to as instructional design, which is intended to define an optimal strategy to satisfy the need. The alternative approaches will require greater consideration during the CF's formal review process in order for the CF IT&E system to move beyond the reliance on the traditional in-service delivery model. The full details on the processes are outlined in a series of publications that provide guidance supporting the CF IT&E system.[9]

As the alternative approaches for CF IT&E take hold it is essential that they are reviewed and the effectiveness is confirmed. Validation is a quality control activity within the system supporting CF IT&E. Validation closes the loop on the initial analysis, design and delivery of IT&E. It is the mechanism to confirm if a training need has been satisfied through a particular strategy. Many of the alternative strategies will lead to the CF having less direct control over how IT&E is delivered and how CF training requirements are satisfied. As a result validation becomes an even more essential mechanism to confirm CF needs are being met through a particular strategy.

The Imperatives and the Barriers

The imperative for seeking alternative IT&E approaches remains rooted in very diverse needs which evolve and change with time. At the tactical level, the concerns tend to be focus on delivering courses to meet the assigned near-term personnel production targets. Changes to course delivery at the tactical level is often executed as the need arises and on a case by case basis. Over the past decade the challenge at the tactical level was primarily fuelled by force expansion and in some situations there were issues with the language of instruction and being capable of offering training in both official languages.

At the strategic level the focus is longer term. The focus is towards a personnel production model that is agile and responsive, capable of anticipating and responding to the shifting conditions. The challenge is effectively generating personnel amidst potentially turbulent funding levels while also rationalizing the commitment to infrastructure, personnel and the other resources necessary to sustain the IT&E system. There are other pressures which impact personnel production planning and this includes attrition levels and demographic trends.

Reconciling the imperatives and achieving institutional alignment from the strategic through to the tactical level can be challenged by contradictions in intent, presumed threats as well as the long-term and near-term personnel production needs. The most significant strategic level force driving change is likely to be determining how best to employ uniformed personnel as part of a modernized CFIT&E system. These are the forces that took root during CF Transformation and are likely to be revisited as new capabilities are introduced to the CF and the demand to employ uniformed personnel outside the IT&E system increases.

The CF's default IT&E strategy remains, for the most part, a resident instructional paradigm which is mainly centred around uniformed subject-matter-experts delivering instruction within largely occupation centric Training Establishments. The current governance structure within the CF IT&E system and the practices supporting how IT&E strategies are identified and defined tend to reinforce the *status quo* when it comes to IT&E delivery. This approach remains ensconced given it is quite often the best strategy to use and often it is the only strategy that is appropriate.

Most CF Training Establishments have environmental links as well as CF Branch/ Corps affiliations. In some cases these links influence the creation of very strong CF sub-cultures and they can also have a profound impact fostering *esprit de corps* and shaping allegiances. The Training Establishment is more than just a place to develop and refine skills, frequently it is considered the home for a particular CF Branch/Corps. Making changes to this model can be met with considerable resistance, given the strong ties to defining culture. It is also the model that many of today's leaders are most comfortable with given they are a product of it. A study by the National Defence Research Institute recounts the resistance to change as part of an examination of the feasibility of using civilian institutions to provide initial skills training (IST) for US armed forces personnel. They reported:

> In addition to the difficult choices associated with developing and using civilian-provided IST programs, we believe that the military's

inclination to embrace widespread use of civilian institutions is in doubt and is a cause for concern in future attempts at implementing civilian training programs. Furthermore, military resistance to civilian-provided training is not likely to be overcome simply with positive results from a demonstration project. It seems clear that without appropriate incentives, the propensity of the services will be to shy away from civilian-provided IST.[10]

Governance can play an important role influencing change within the CF IT&E system. The current management configuration for the CF IT&E system has clearly assigned responsibilities; however, the structure appears to lack a command and control authority to effect system wide change. CF IT&E responsibilities are defined within a management framework which allocates functions primarily along environmental lines to the Royal Canadian Navy, Canadian Army and the Royal Canadian Air Force. The requirements supporting common IT&E, including professional military education as well as the needs of the occupations which are common across the environments, are assigned to the Canadian Defence Academy.[11] Contributing to this framework are additional training authorities that have a more narrowly focused, designated, IT&E management role. There are also other stakeholders, including Occupation Authorities, who are relied upon to identify and assist with defining IT&E requirements. The Occupation Authorities drive the need for IT&E and can significantly influence the length of time it takes to achieve employment ready status; however, they are not necessarily accountable for the resources required to achieve the prescribed performance levels. The increasingly decentralized IT&E structure leans more towards a shared governance framework. This is a management framework that has evolved over the years from an approach that was previously predicated on a strong central authority with an associated command structure.

CF IT&E is an important component supporting personnel production and part of the broader CF personnel system. In 2006, the OAG noted that the broader system had lacked a recognized authority with clear accountability.[12] Subsequently, it was affirmed that the Chief of Military Personnel is the departmental authority; however, the OAG had observed that this was primarily viewed as an advisory, vice authoritative, position by the Environmental Commands. The Chief of Military Personnel has subsequently devolved departmental authority for CF IT&E to the Canadian Defence Academy. For institutional change to be achieved the linkage with the departmental authority needs to be reinforced in order to ensure the strategic intent is understood and there is a unified effort throughout the IT&E management framework. Within the present construct direction that may be promulgated by the departmental authority regarding CF IT&E plans often have little impact or influence at the tactical level. The departmental level planning guidance is rarely integrated into the planning instructions promulgated by each of the respective training authorities and the associated Environmental Commands that control most of the tactical level IT&E units across the CF.

The fundamental operating principles and effects to be achieved as part of sustaining the CF IT&E system remain sound and a committee structure ensures there is effective coordination for routine affairs. The processes supporting quality control within the CF IT&E system are also well defined and, for the most part, respected. Some of the existing quality control processes tend to lead decisions towards the default in-service IT&E delivery solution and this serves as a significant barrier to innovation and change. It should be noted that there are several examples where alternative approaches for CF IT&E have been successfully integrated and this includes adapting new technologies to the traditional learning environment, introducing learning at a distance as well as increasing the use of simulation. Some CF IT&E delivery is being completed in community colleges as well as through partnerships formed with industry and robust foreign military cooperatives. These approaches have typically been driven by necessity, as opposed to being conscious decisions made during the more routine processes supporting CF IT&E instructional design. Delivering IT&E through in-service Training Establishments tends to remain the default option selected during the routine instructional design activity undertaken within the CF.

A Training Plan Writing Board (TPWB) is the forum most often used to formulate instructional strategies to address specific CF training requirements. The TPWB supports the Design Phase of the CF IT&E Quality Control System and it follows steps that are consistent with traditional models for Instructional Systems Design (ISD).[13] The CF training requirement is analyzed as part of the instructional design process by subject-matter experts and the requirements are converted into learning outcomes. The learning outcomes become the basis for an instructional strategy that is determined to be the best fit for the content, the context, and the CF learners. This process has proven to be effective within the CF and it is consistent with those of other nations and civilian practice. A criticism that is often levelled at the traditional models for ISD is that the resulting instructional strategy tends to default to the classroom paradigm.[14] The same is often the case within the CF training design context. Explicit direction, prior to convening a TPWB, is essential if there is an intent to explore and utilize the alternative IT&E delivery options.

At the tactical level, when it becomes clear that the demand for in-service IT&E exceeds the resident capability to deliver the necessary courses, alternatives approaches are sought. When the shortfall involves the capabilities of the resident instructor cadre the initial solutions often centre on augmenting the cadre through incremental staff from within the CF. When incremental staff is not an option, arrangements are often made with outside service providers to provide contracted instructor services. In some situations the tactical level limitations are that of physical infrastructure, support and possibly equipment; however, more often it is a shortfall in personnel. Augmenting with contractors sustains the reliance on the in-service IT&E delivery model; it remains intact because there is great comfort in its tradition as well as its effectiveness. The existing structures and support processes for the CF IT&E system, which lead to the design of the IT&E solutions, also tend to reinforce it. Here in lies the structural dichotomy which often opposes changes to the delivery of CF IT&E.

The strategic level efforts to exploit alternative approaches for occupation specific CF IT&E are generally met with scepticism, especially when the proposals involve shifting delivery outside the traditional tactical level context. Change is often stymied by deep rooted institutional and cultural barriers and other opposing forces which may not be cognizant of the broader strategic pressures or intent. The implementation of alternative approaches are often stalled and delayed long enough for the momentum to shift. Change proposals are often subjected to extensive review often as a matter of course for managing risks but more often it is a tactic leading to delays. Time generally becomes the instrument to sustain the *status quo*. Without a threat to achieving the near-term personnel production targets there is indifference and a lack of urgency to adopt change at the tactical level. In short, "if it's not broke, why fix it."

The CF IT&E system, while resilient and principally sound, is not impervious to a periodic azimuth adjustment. The one aspect that has been proven over time, and is confirmed in the previous studies, is that the fundamentals of the system are working and that the system is adaptable. Experiences over the past decade in Afghanistan as well as during other operational missions appear to verify that CF personnel have acquired both the professional and occupation related skills sets essential for mission success. The more recent questions that have been asked, and which now serve as an imperative for change, relate to the sustainability of the current approach, the affordability of the system as well as the alignment with the refocused organizational mission for the CF. This situation is not unique to the CF, it is echoed in the formal review of other armed forces which have similar IT&E systems facing competing demands.[15]

Rationalizing fiscal expenditures while also sustaining an operational focus and a general push to improve have resulted in significant changes in CF capabilities. The pressure for change has not concentrated exclusively on the CF IT&E system. Examples of significant shifts include CF healthcare, which now relies on referring CF members to local medical specialists who primarily support the broader public healthcare system as opposed to referrals to medical specialists who primarily worked out of the National Defence Medical Centre. Outsourcing has also occurred within the CF supply system which resulted with the introduction of the clothing online procurement system and a points model which replaced the clothing up keep allowance. Other, more gradual, changes occurred in the Royal Canadian Air Force where for many years the CF sustained a unique air and ground transport capability which moved personnel across Canada and to Europe on a regular schedule. The recurring need to deploy CF aircraft on higher priority operations was, in part, responsible for the eventual shift away from a domestic air service to an approach that relies almost exclusively on commercial air carriers for routine transportation. Initially, the transition involved using a contracted air charter to provide exclusive services to CF personnel. This was later replaced by pre-purchased, reserved seats on specific commercial flight routes. Today, the routine domestic and international air travel is reliant on the same pay per use commercial flight air service used by the Canadian public while the CF's air assets are now focused almost exclusively towards operations.

Prior studies of the CF IT&E system outline the intent to pursue alternative approaches. In many respects CF Training Establishments deliver IT&E because they can, but does that mean they should? Here in lies the strategic case for change that was put forward in 2006 by General Rick Hillier, during his period as the CDS, as part of the CF Transformation agenda:

> …we [as Canadians] spend hundreds of billions of dollars a year for education across our country and I don't feel obligated to repeat all the same thing inside the Canadian Forces when it can do it for us as easily with an agreement that we would have.[16]

At the Conference of Defence Associations, General Hillier outlined his intent for the CF to explore an overarching IT&E strategy which would shift further away from the reliance on an in-service solution as the default IT&E option. His focus appeared to be on the greater use of post-secondary institutions to address CF occupation related IT&E requirements. This push followed the publication of a report by CDS Action Team 4 (CAT 4) in July 2005 which explored issues regarding institutional alignment as part of CF Transformation.[17] The final CAT 4 report was influenced by previous efforts supporting the Human Resources System Transformation (HRST) Project. The final CAT 4 report contained several options to consider such as improvements to CF IT&E governance and the use of alternative approaches for generating trained personnel, including a greater reliance on community colleges. At a subsequent General Office/Flag Officer Seminar, General Hillier challenged the senior leaders present to determine, "To what extent can the CF further utilize the full range of Canadian learning institutions to meet our training and education needs?"[18]

While the strategic intent appears clear the subsequent execution appeared to stall. This can be tied back to the challenge regarding CF IT&E system governance highlighted by the OAG and detailed earlier in this chapter. More than eighteen months after General Hillier put forward a strategic case for change, Armed Forces Council did revisit this issue. As the senior council for the CF, AFC subsequently directed that the CF will make, "use of CF training resources [for IT&E delivery] where essential, and maximize use of civilian educational resources otherwise."[19] The CMP followed up with guidance on this issue; however, leveraging the Canadian education system did not appear to resonate through to the tactical levels and there was little follow up with AFC to confirm progress had been made.[20]

Force expansion was the catalyst to increase the productive capacity of the CF IT&E system. Direction developed within the Environmental Commands addressed the need to enhance capacity; however, the guidance was not congruent with that which was eventually provided by the Chief Military Personnel. A scan of strategic level reports did reveal that the Environmental Commands were, for the most part, exploring other options. In the 2006-2007 Departmental Performance Report to Parliament, the Royal Canadian Air Force outlined their progress regarding the Aircraft Technician Training Renewal program and efforts to increase system productivity and ensure the in-service capacity matches the demand.[21] This included enhancing their in-service capability through modeling and simulation to improve the efficiency. A year later temporary

infrastructure was erected and instructor services were subsequently contracted to support the expansion of the in-service capacity. In the Departmental Performance Report for 2007-2008, the Army outlined the Training Capacity
Enhancement Program and the Individual Training Capacity Backfill initiative.[22]
Among the outcomes was the intent to reduce the requirement to augment the
in-service training institutions with field-force. A combination of contractors and
Reserve Force personnel were called upon to free up Regular Force personnel for
operations and expand training capacity.

During the period of force expansion, the Royal Canadian Navy was facing the
added challenge of attrition. Despite having exceptional training capabilities,
and the necessary capacity, the Navy needed to take a far more aggressive approach to personnel production. Among the areas of greatest need was the
shortfall of technical trades. The fleet was facing a dire shortage of qualified
technicians and the prolonged shortage was becoming a threat to operational
capability.[23] Initially, the recruiting efforts were unable to achieve the planned
intake of unskilled applicants for the Navy's priority occupations. The Navy aggressively embraced outsourcing and sought to increase the level of initial occupation training in Canadian colleges. As colleges across Canada became engaged, the awareness of naval career opportunities among the broader college
student population increased. The shift of initial occupation training to colleges
across Canada greatly accelerated the recovery of the Navy's ability to produce
trained personnel.

Force expansion and transformation became driving forces to reinvigorate the
use of alternative IT&E approaches within the CF. As the CF personnel manning
levels achieve the intended force expansion targets the strategic needs are likely to shift once again. The next imperative for change from the strategic level
will likely stem from sustaining operations and the introduction of new equipment and added operational capabilities as part of the Canada First Defence
Strategy.[24] There are challenges ahead regarding the allocation of the existing Regular Force positions to support this new equipment and these new
capabilities. This may turn out to be at the root of the future pressures to free up
uniformed personnel working within the CF IT&E system.

The Community College Option

Canadian community colleges were created by provincial governments beginning in the 1960s in recognition that they would serve as an economic engine

through the development of human capital. There are now nearly 150 publically funded colleges in Canada with campuses situated in more than 1000 urban and rural communities. In the Province of Quebec, where tuition remains virtually free, a "College of General and Vocational Education," is better know as a Cégep, the *Collège d'enseignement général et professionnel*. The Association of Canadian Community Colleges estimates that there are more than 1.5 million learners annually enrolled in college programs with more than 500,000 entering on a full time basis each year.[25] The college system employs more than 65,000 educators and the institutions play a pivotal role in ensuring that Canada's labour force remains robust, competent and competitive.

Community colleges are a critical enabler for economic prosperity and growth through the development of a technically-skilled and well-educated work force.[26] The fit with the CF is straightforward. Delivering technical, vocational and occupational training is the core business of Canadian community colleges. Colleges exist to prepare individuals for employment in very diverse industry sectors, including health services, information technology, motive power and aviation. The CF requires personnel with similar skill sets in some of the very same sectors already being serviced by colleges. Delivering training; however, is not at the core of the CF mission but it is done in order to generate a modern, effective and professional fighting force. The past reviews of the CF IT&E system have consistently proposed that it may be better to shift CF IT&E delivery to the institutions which have this at the core of their existence. The result is that highly valued CF personnel can be dedicated to tasks which are more closely aligned with the CF's core mission.

The CF has built a remarkable and envied capability to train and educate military personnel. The question that is often asked is, do we still require the IT&E delivery capability for some areas where there is an overlap with other publically funded institutions? The potential for using community colleges to address CF IT&E needs has been reviewed as part of several studies. A synopsis of this previous work is provided here and this is extracted from a more recent study of Alternative Training Delivery within the CF:[27]

- Project CAN-TECH was initiated in 1985 with the intent to investigate the potential and capabilities of industry and civilian educational institutions to respond to CF training requirements. This was followed in 1989 with the *Total Community 89* project.[28] This project was led by

Major-General (Retired) J.P.R. Larose and was commissioned to determine what individual training could be transferred to Canada's community colleges. It was concluded that out of the 101 military occupations reviewed, 60 were aligned with complementary college programs that could meet CF requirements. The study also confirmed that community colleges had shown a strong desire to engage in collaborative initiatives with the CF. The study further concluded that the transfer of CF individual training requirements to community colleges supported the Total Force concept and provided significant capacity to tap into in case of mobilization.

- In July 1990, the *Alternate Approaches to Training and Education* report was published. The report reviewed the responsiveness, accountability and innovation within the CF's training system. The report was focused on change during a time marked by decreased funding. The study concluded that there was a need to enhance communications with civilian training agencies and that, "it is often possible to obtain high quality instruction through a community college more economically than could be arranged in-house."[29]

- In 1998, the Defence Management Committee, through the auspices of the Vice Chief of the Defence Staff, initiated a further review of the CF training system. The focus of this study was the identification of Alternate Service Delivery/Re-Engineering options and opportunities. This study was contracted to ADGA Group Consultants. The ADGA Senior Consultant Team supporting this study consisted of: Lieutenant-General (Retired) Robert Morton and Major-General (Retired) Ray Desloges. In their findings, the study team identified 37 CF occupations out of 113 (33%) that had parallel training readily available in community colleges and they concluded:

> Canada has a world class national training and educational network which is comprised of a community college network, university systems and private sector training capacity. DND requirements for IT&E can be partially met through this network, and using this network would provide DND with ready access to quality IT&E while converting fixed infrastructure costs to variable costs. The synergy that would result from the

integration of military requirements into the rest of the national IT&E network would also serve broader national goals as espoused by the federal government. In addition, it could contribute to enhancing the image of the CF nationally.[30]

- In 2005, the merits of the community college system were further commented on in a report produced by the Chief Review Services (CRS) entitled, Evaluation of Military Individual Training and Education. The report noted that contracting out with civilian institutions is limited. "Our assessment is that significant opportunities exist in Canadian community colleges for contracting out many IT&E programs."[31]

The benefits of working with colleges, as part of initial occupation training delivery, have been documented by other armed forces.[32] The college partnerships have become entrenched in some armed force including the Australian Defence Force which, in 1999, stopped delivering initial in-service training for the cook and steward trades. Training for their Health Services personnel is delivered by a variety of post-secondary institutions and the Royal Australian Navy has also integrated colleges as part of the initial and advanced occupation training continuum for their electronic systems technicians. Defense Scientists from the US Department of Defense offer this perspective, "while there is a myriad of possible training options to choose from, some simply make better sense than others....[a] potentially controversial set of alternatives that we have suggested includes turning over curriculum control to civilian institutions."[33]

So while it appears that college delivered programs offer considerable promise for addressing military IT&E requirements, and strategic reviews consistently endorse such a shift, there often remains reticence to the idea. Concerns often centre around three areas: quality, cost, and the implications for the CF culture; the latter is often framed in terms of risk to the development of military ethos.

In terms of quality, colleges have become ensconced as the source for the skilled labour that supports many of the sectors that form Canada's economic base, this includes aviation, automotive, health services and broader science and technology sectors/fields. Many of these sectors align, to varying degrees, with CF needs. The challenge, when looking at college programs, is to identify the areas of difference with CF IT&E and refocus the CF's IT&E system towards the requirements that remain. This provides the opportunity to emphasize the requirements addressing contemporary and future operations. Considerable time is spent within the CF's IT&E system developing fairly generic artisan and craftsman skill sets. These are skill sets that often become refined through experience. Developing the initial skills is the essence of the existence for Canada's college system. This is not new, for many years the CF has enrolled semi-skilled applicants and already recognized the skills and knowledge acquired through institutions outside the CF IT&E system. Arguably, it may be the time to shift the model and have external institutions become even more of the source for trained personnel as opposed to a being the source for only a few.

This decision to shift to an alternative IT&E strategy often comes down to cost and the willingness to pay to achieve specific effects, such as free up more experienced uniformed personnel for other tasks. Attempting to determine the cost effectiveness of a particular IT&E strategy can be a time consuming and laborious exercise. Avoiding this activity is often all the motivation necessary to sustain the *status quo*. Complex costing exercises can also create enough of a delay that the momentum for change stalls just long enough to have the focus and attention shift to other issues. There are other challenges that can make the costing exercise difficult. The challenges include the debates encountered when attempting to account for cost drivers associated with systemic issues such as the institutional delays that lead to personnel awaiting training. Other costing challenges included accounting for the sunk cost associated with the cancellation of IT&E serials. It is also difficult to accurately account for the recruiting effect generated from having CF personnel on a college campus. CF personnel on a campus can generate an awareness of a CF career option, this is something that many college students may not have otherwise been exposed to.

The cost of college program options will vary significantly. Customized programs come with a premium but this ensures the services provided are aligned more precisely with the CF requirements. Enrolling in standard tuition programs comes with a significant cost advantage, especially relative to in-service options given the institutions are subsidized by each provincial government. This advantage may be lost in some situations given that custom college programs tend to be shorter in duration than the regular college programs. Ironically, much of what causes college programs to run longer than in-service occupation training are the mandated, broad-based, liberal arts courses which publically funded colleges are mandated to incorporate in their programs. Many of these courses may be considered relevant to developing the foundation for CF

members within the profession of arms.[34] Be that as it may, the additional courses increase the length of college programs and this causes costs to increase.

Instructor and student wages are among the largest cost drivers for most of the
CF's technical, vocational and occupational IT&E requirements. The longer an individual spends in the IT&E environment, be it a college program or an in-service
qualification course, the greater the cost that is attributed to that particular strategy. In making a conscious decision to shift to a college tuition option, there are
opportunities to make some changes that will result with the college option
being the more cost effective choice, and this can be demonstrated without
complex calculations.

When it comes to initial CF IT&E requirements the assumption is that the CF
entrant is subsidized for the entire duration of a college program, given most
applicants generally enter the CF untrained. Breaking free from this paradigm,
the alternative is to shift enrolment to the point in time during the college program at which it clearly becomes cost effective to do so. As an example, a Naval
Weapons Technician requires approximately 280 days of academic instruction
as part of their initial occupation qualification training. This works out to slightly
over 400 calendar days. The 280 days of initial in-service IT&E is waived for a
graduate of a college program which has been reviewed and is considered to
be aligned with the Navy's requirement. Recruiting a college student entering
the second year of their college program provides a far more cost effective option given a significant cost driver (wages) has now been marginalized. This is
achieved without factoring in savings concerning infrastructure, support costs,
instructor wages or overhead.

The CF is a very attractive career choice for college students as they move into
the final year of their academic program. It is attractive to a college student
given their education will be subsidized, while earning an initial salary, and upon
graduation they will commence a career in an occupation related to their program. The challenge will be engaging college students and generating awareness of the CF as a career option. Attracting and enrolling individuals entering
into their second year of college minimizes the risk of academic attrition and, if
properly synchronized, can leverage the break between the academic years of a
college program to complete the recruit phase.

Often the final, and most passionate, argument against shifting away from the
in-service IT&E delivery model is the risk this interruption would pose to the

process of military socialization and the subsequent shaping of the Canadian military ethos. Early in a career is often viewed to be the point at which military ethos is developing and therefore most vulnerable. Military ethos is integral to performing duty with honour and it forms the basis of military professionalism. *Duty with Honour: The Profession of Arms in Canada* provides one of the best frame of reference for examining military ethos and it begins with an explanation of what it is:

> The military ethos embodies the spirit that binds the profession together. It clarifies how members view their responsibilities, apply their expertise and express their unique military identity. It identifies and explains military values and defines the subordination of the armed forces to civilian control and the rule of law.[35]

Duty with Honour goes on to explore the three components to sustaining military ethos and the shaping of military professionalism, this is illustrated in Figure 20.2.[36]

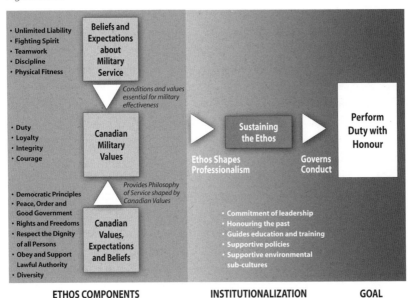

Figure 20.2: The Military Ethos

Defence Scientist Justin Wright has neatly consolidated this and the following serves as a point of reference when examining the potential risks involved with completing initial occupation training in colleges:

Beliefs and Expectations about Military Service: Including accepting Unlimited Liability; internalizing the Fighting Spirit; maintaining Discipline, which among professionals means primarily self-discipline; and fostering Teamwork.

Canadian Values: The CF is sworn to uphold the values and democratic principles that are fundamental to Canadian society, such as peace, order and good government, and those articulated in the *Charter of Rights and Freedoms* and the *Constitution Act of 1982*.

Core Canadian Military Values: Duty, Loyalty, Integrity and Courage.[37]

Military ethos and the link to socialization is a complex issue; however, this should not become the basis for sustaining the in-service IT&E delivery model. These concerns are an excellent starting point for better understanding the issue and formulating strategies that ensures any risk to military ethos is appropriately managed and any new opportunities for developing desired traits is fully leveraged. Military socialization begins as a very formalized and structured process, an integral step in the transition from civilian life to a military career.

Basic training starts the socialization process and it begins with distancing recruits from current social networks and attempts to reorient an individual's established self-identity. Strategies to accomplish this tend to fall under the overarching concepts of power, control and custom. Recruits begin basic training as strangers and live in isolation from the influences of the broader civilian society. The rituals of the socialization experience are intended to create a strong normative group bond. Removing any alternative sources of meaning, the military becomes the normative frame of reference with which the group identifies. While this apparent transformational experience bolsters the behavioural elements and leads in part to conformity, all of which is easily observed, it is a matter of debate if social isolation and the related strategies that are used actually shape the values that influence professional conduct and the components that define military ethos when extended over a long periods. Defence Scientists Dr. Phyllis Browne and Justin Wright highlight the apparent moral and ethical dilemmas in their review of the formal socialization efforts for officer cadets at the Royal Military College of Canada, especially as this relates to personal and professional values as well as the development of sub-cultures. As cadets neared graduation, following four years of intensive socialization, they generally endorsed the values promoted at RMCC; however, Browne and Wright found that the majority (65%) of the 23 participants in their longitudinal study felt that breaking the rules and trying not to get caught was acceptable behaviour.[38]

Returning to the capstone document defining the Profession of Arms in Canada, *Duty with Honour*, it becomes clear that ethos is sustained and shaped over a career. Ethos is influenced by personal experience and significantly by the leadership, structures and, as documented by military historian David Bercuson, the culture at the subsequent units of employment.[39] Phillip Zimbardo, a former president of the American Psychological Association, reinforces this in his examination of the torture and abuses in Iraq at the Abu Ghraib prison.[40] The situation Zimbardo examined mirrored his earlier research findings involving human subjects in a prison simulation at Stanford University.[41] The failures in ethical and moral behaviour highlighted by Zimbardo can also be extended to partially explain the failures involving the death of Shidane Arone during Op DELIVERANCE in Somalia in 1993. All of these situations highlighted a lack of leadership, failed organizational structure as well as the influence of rogue sub-cultures and the subsequent impact on shaping ethos. As noted in *Duty with Honour*, "the Canadian military ethos is neither static nor fixed but maintained and sustained by the accumulated actions of individuals and groups, shaping it over time and ensuring that it remains relevant."[42]

Appreciating the dynamic nature of ethos and the importance of socialization, Wright has subsequently posed, "To what extent does the socializing experience of the occupational training period provide an essential foundation upon which the leadership and culture of the unit can continue to develop the military ethos of new members?"[43] The rituals associated with the initial transition from civilian life to military service establish the basis of self-categorization as a member of the profession of arms. It forms the basis for the beliefs and expectations about military service and ensures there is congruence between the individual and the institution. The transition occurs primarily in social isolation. Building upon these initial steps through occupation training in a alternative environment, such as a community college, now provides an opportunity to generate a deeper appreciation of the components that define military ethos, especially as it relates to Canadian values.

Changing how initial occupation skill sets are acquired by CF personnel may also better position the CF following the Cold War as a postmodern military.[44] The CF's traditional approach to developing occupational competence is often insular and remains predicated on a conditioned response to fairly predictable situations. This may not be the best approach for the future. Expanding on this model through a greater reliance on community colleges may serve to strengthen the professional warrior construct and better equip the CF with the professional fighting force required for the uncertainties of modern operations and the predictability of a Cold War context. As mentioned previously, publically funded colleges have liberal arts courses as part of the curriculum. In some institutions the courses are clearly specified and can include ethics, psychology, philosophy and an understanding of government. At Centennial College in Toronto, where there is significant cultural and ethnic diversity on campus, the college mandates that all diploma students complete a course in *Global Citizenship: Social Analysis to Social Action* as part of the learning experience. In addition to serving as an ideal source for potential applicants to address the CF's shortfall in the area of visible minorities and aboriginals, the college is mandating a course which targets a component of CF ethos, specifically Canadian values, expectations and beliefs.

Many military professionals, as well as scholars of military analysis believe that there is now an expectation that, along with performing traditional combat roles, CF personnel are also required to be diplomats, humanitarians and technical experts. Is the CF's Professional Development System for Non-Commissioned Members doing enough to achieve this? Having CF members develop initial occupation and vocational skills in a college context may actually be beneficial, as opposed to a risk, to shaping military ethos. A college context fosters both social and cognitive agility. CF members in college programs are self-directed and require personal discipline to be successful. College students are often required to work in teams in order to achieve success. Once again this aligns with values essential for military effectiveness. Tolerance and respect for diversity including visible minorities is a hallmark of the college learning environment. In his 2005 review of army climate and culture, Colonel Michael Capstick and his research team remarked that, "Although soldiers are generally accepting of diversity, acceptance is neither strong nor universal."[45] Completing initial occupation training within an alternative environment has potential effects that may better prepare the modern warrior. Such an approach may also serve to further entrench the connection with the next generation of Canadian citizenry who are also progressing through the college system.

Concerns for "living the chain of command" are often part of the rational for ensuring a formalized and structured military socialization process is embedded in the initial occupation IT&E continuum following the recruit training phase. Strong and passionate arguments are made that this is the time tested traditional approach and how military personnel are normally indoctrinated. Interestingly, the debate regarding military ethos is not raised as an issue for the CF's Reserve Force component which regularly transitions between periodic military service and a career as well as life in the civilian environment. It appears clear that the success in current operations would have been near impossible to achieve without augmenting deployed forces with Reserve Force personnel. Also lost in this discussion are the CF officers that enter under the Regular Officer Training Plan and complete an undergraduate degree at a civilian university. Clearly there is a distinctive break in the developmental continuum when a Officer Cadet completes basic training and then returns to a civilian academic environment over the next four years of military service.

The issue of socialization and ethos can be avoided in its entirety by having new entrants complete the initial recruit qualification following the college program. This would be consistent with the approach taken with semi-skilled and skilled entrants that currently join the CF. By focusing recruiting efforts towards individuals in their final year of a suitable college program the recruit qualification could commence upon college graduation and well within the first year of service. The result is there would be no break in the post recruit training continuum. An individual would complete college, commence the recruit phase followed by an initial phase of occupation related delta training and any other required environmental training.

Summary

The CF IT&E system has relied heavily upon uniformed personnel to delivery the instruction that satisfies initial occupation training requirements. Several studies of the CF IT&E system have encouraged an expansion of alternative approaches and encourage a shift from the centralized in-service model used to satisfy CF IT&E requirements. The use of alternative approaches is consistently supported and driven from the highest levels within the CF.

Moving forward with alternative IT&E approaches requires a clear need to drive change. There are pressures at the strategic and tactical level that have provided the impetus. The pressure to adapt, adopt, and implement alternative IT&E approaches is likely to continue into the future as the CF IT&E system is scrutinized for economic advantages and greater efficiencies. The tactical level pressures are more often driven by capacity concerns stemming from the near-term person-nel production targets. The strategic level issues involve the pressure to reduce the reliance on a uniformed instructor cadre and the push to rationalize the commitment to infrastructure and the other resources necessary to sustain the IT&E system, especially amidst turbulent funding levels.

There are many options available to satisfy CF IT&E requirements and it is unlikely that one specific approach will become the default or preferred global strategy for the CF. Each alternative approach comes with benefits, costs and risks and these factors need to be assessed when exploring options for each unique train-ing requirement. The current institutional processes that support the design and delivery of CF IT&E programs tend to gravitate towards relying on the traditional in-service instructional paradigm; this can make change and the assessment of alternatives difficult. It will take change in the formalized process for developing IT&E strategies in order for alternatives approaches to be given proper consider-ation. The change begins with the introduction of a clear Commander's Intent at the outset, each time a training requirement is reviewed, along with improved decision support tools to facilitate the process so as to avoid positioning the existing in-service approach as the default option.

Within the CF IT&E system having the tools and a need may not be enough to bring about institutional change. There can be obstacles to be overcome when the time arrives for implementing alternatives within the CF IT&E system. The current governance structure, while effective for sustaining the existing system, doesn't appear to have the necessary mechanisms for moving forward and co-ordinating broad institutional change. A sustained impetus from the strategic level, complete with clear and coordinated direction as well as a complemen-tary performance reporting framework, will be essential to bring about account-ability and to ensure institutional alignment. When alternative approaches are introduced it would be prudent to make the new training strategies the focus of review in order to assess their effectiveness. It is here that the CF IT&E validation process should be focused.

Canada's network of community colleges is a sophisticated and comprehensive education and training capability. A greater reliance upon community colleges for technical and vocational requirements is often proposed as a viable and cost-effective option for CF IT&E delivery. Making this shift has the potential to complement CF preparedness. Operations have evolved significantly since the end of the Cold War. Focusing in-service IT&E towards the essentials for success in modern operations, while seeking alternatives for the fairly generic artisan and craftsman skill sets commonly developed within the college system, appears to be a logical option.

The willingness to pay to access the college system is most certainly appealing given this provides the CF with the opportunity to focus personnel and other resources towards the core CF mission. Colleges also offer the benefit of sustaining the connection with Canadians and generating the awareness of CF career opportunities within a highly valued, multi-culturally diverse, demographic. College programs often contain additional elements within their academic programs which develop a broader intellectual capacity and this appears to align with the objectives for fostering the CF profession of arms. Ultimately, having CF personnel learn within a college context fosters social, cultural and cognitive agility.

The arguments opposing the outsourcing of CF IT&E to colleges have been examined on the basis of cost, quality and in terms of the implications for the CF ethos. The arguments appear to fall short and in some situations they actually support the greater collaboration with colleges. The risk to CF ethos is often the area of greatest concern when outsourcing is considered. The CF's formal socialization practices are critical to the indoctrination of new entrants to the CF. The initial transition phase serves to correct inappropriate attitudes and it refocuses individuals in line with the reality of the military professional ideology, identity and ethos. CF ethos is subsequently sustained and shaped over a career and at a certain point there may be diminishing returns using formal socialization techniques. It appears that culture, along with the leadership and associated structures at the unit of employment, have a far more significant influence and impact on sustaining professionalism and fostering ethos.

Delivering CF IT&E in-service with military instructors is in many situations essential. There are; however, many other situations where IT&E delivery is done in-service simply because it can. The institutionalized traditions are well rooted. The quality of what is now available and the potential cost avoidance that results will continue to sustain the pressure for changing how CF IT&E is delivered. This shift may well be essential in the future as new operational capabilities are introduced into the CF and personnel are needed to support them.

1   Department of National Defence, *Training: Preparation for the Future – Alternative Approaches to Training and Education.* (Ottawa, ON: Chief of Defence Staff, July 1990).

2   ADGA Group Consultants Inc., *Analysis of DND/CF Individual Training and Education.* (Ottawa: July, 1998); Chief of Review Services, *Evaluation of Military Individual Training and Education* (Ottawa, ON: National Defence and Canadian Forces, 2005); Colonel Gerry Gillis and Major Mark R. Russell. *A Study of Alternative Training Delivery in the Canadian Forces.* (Kingston, ON: Canadian Defence Academy, June 2009).

3   Department of National Defence, *Departmental Performance Report 2005-2006.* (Ottawa, ON: Minister of National Defence, 2006), 26, 30; Department of National Defence. *Reports on Plans and Priorities 2006-2007.* (Ottawa, ON: Minister of National Defence, 2006), 13; Department of National Defence. Reports on Plans and Priorities 2007-2008. (Ottawa, ON: Minister of National Defence, 2007), 21, 23, 27-30.

4   Auditor General of Canada, *Report of the Auditor General of Canada to the House of Commons – Chapter 5 National Defence – Recruitment and Retention of Military Personnel* (Ottawa, ON; Office of the Auditor General of Canada, 2002), 11, retrieved on 15 Jan 2012 from <http://www.oag-bvg.gc.ca/internet/docs/0205ce.pdf>.

5   Auditor General of Canada, *A Status Report of the Auditor General of Canada to the House of Commons – Chapter 2 National Defence – Military Recruiting and Retention* (Ottawa, ON: Office of the Auditor General of Canada, 2006), 63, retrieved on 15 Jan 2012 from <http://www.oag-bvg.gc.ca/internet/docs/20060502ce.pdf>.

6   Department of National Defence, *National Defence 2008-09 Estimates Part III – Departmental Performance Report* (2009), 36-37, retrieved on 10 Nov 2011 from <http://www.tbs-sct.gc.ca/dpr-rmr/2008-2009/inst/dnd/dnd-eng.pdf>.

7   Colonel Gerry Gillis and Major Mark R. Russell, *A Study of Alternative Training Delivery in the Canadian Forces* (Kingston, ON: Canadian Defence Academy: June 2009).

8   Gillis and Russell, 9.

9   Department of National Defence, *Canadian Forces Individual Training & Education System, Manual of Individual Training and Education (Volume 1) Interim Guidance - Introduction/ Description, A-P9-050-000/PT-001* (Kingston, ON: Canadian Defence Academy, Director Training and Education, 2007).

10   Lawrence M. Hanser, Joyce N. Davidson and Cathleen Stasz, W*ho Should Train? Substituting Civilian-Provided Training for Military Training* (Santa Monica, CA: RAND National Defence Research Institute, 1991), 76.

11   Department of National Defence, *Defence Administrative Orders and Directives 5031-2, Individual Training and Education Strategic Framework,* retrieved on 10 November 2011 from <http://www.admfincs.forces.gc.ca/dao-doa/5000/5031-2-eng.asp>.

12   Auditor General of Canada (2006), 66-68.

13   Department of National Defence, *Canadian Forces Individual Training & Education System, Manual of Individual Training and Education* (Volume 4) Design of Instructional Programmes, A-P9-050-000/PT-004 (Kingston, ON: Canadian Defence Academy, Director Training and Education, 1999).

14   Kent L. Gustafson and Robert Maribe Branch, "Revisioning Models of Instructional Development", *Educational Technology Research and Development*, Vol. 45, No. 3 (1997), 73-89, retrieved on 10 Nov 2011 from <http://www.quasar.ualberta.ca/edpy597mappin/readings/m12_
Gustafson.htm>.

15   Ministry of Defence (New Zealand). *Review of Army Individual Training, Report No. 9*
(2009), 14; *United States Air Force. On Learning: The Future of Air Force Education and Training.
Air Education and Training Command*, 30 January 2008 (Randolph, TX: Air Education and Training
Command - AFB HQ AETC/A5/8/9, 2008), retrieved on 10 Nov 2011 from <http://www.aetc.af.mil/
shared/media/document/AFD-080130-066.pdf >.

16   General Rick Hiller, "Thinking Outside the Box", *Frontline Magazine* (Mar/Apr 2006), 13.

17   Department of National Defence. *Enabling Transformation – Canadian Forces Transformation: Institutional Alignment* (Ottawa, ON: CDS Action Team 4 Report, 6 July 2005).

18   Department of National Defence, *General Office/Flag Officer Seminar III – Personnel Generation*, 16-18 May 06, Record of Discussion dated June 2006 (DRAFT), (Ottawa, ON: Chief of Defence Staff).

19   Department of National Defence, *Armed Forces Council Meeting 12/07– Record of Decisions. 1180-1* (D NDHQ Sec) held on 3-4 December 2007, (Ottawa, ON: Chief of Defence Staff, 14
December 2007), 2.

20   Department of National Defence, *Military Personnel Management Functional Planning
Guidance FY 10/11* (Ottawa, ON: Chief Military Personnel, 19 July 2009), 11.

21   Department of National Defence, *National Defence Performance Report for the Period
Ending March 31, 2007*, 26, retrieved on 10 Nov 2011 from <http://www.tbs-sct.gc.ca/dpr-
rmr/2006-2007/inst/dnd/dnd-eng.pdf>.

22   Department of National Defence, *Departmental Performance Report for the Fiscal Year
Ending March 31, 200*8, 19, retrieved on 10 Nov 2011 from <http://www.tbs-sct.gc.ca/dpr-
rmr/2007-2008/inst/dnd/dnd-eng.pdf>.

23   Auditor General of Canada (2002), 5.

24   Department of National Defence, *Canada First Defence Strategy*, retrieved on 10 Nov 2011
from <http://www.forces.gc.ca/site/pri/first-premier/June18_0910_CFDS_english_low-res.pdf>.

25   Statistics Canada and Council of Ministers of Education, *Education indicators in Canada:
Report of the Pan-Canadian Education Indicators Program, Catalogue no. 81-582-XIE* (Ottawa,
ON: 2007), retrieved on 10 Nov 2011 from <http://www.statcan.gc.ca/pub/81-582-x/2007001/
excel/chapd1-en.xls>.

26   Paul Gallagher and John D. Dennison, "Canada's Community College Systems: A Study in
Diversity", *Community College Journal of Research and Practice*, Vol. 19, No. 5 (1995), 383.

27   Gillis and Russell, 69-88.

28   Robert J.P. Larose, *Study Report on "Total Community 89"* (Toronto, ON: Canadian Forces
College, 1989).

29   Department of National Defence, *Training: Preparation for the Future – Alternative Approaches to Training and Education* (Ottawa, ON: Chief of Defence Staff, July 1990).

30   ADGA Group Consultants Inc., *Analysis of DND/CF Individual Training and Education* (Ottawa, ON: ADGA Group, July 1998), 48.

31   Chief of Review Services, *Evaluation of Military Individual Training and Education* (Ottawa, ON: National Defence and Canadian Forces, 2005).

32   Peggy A. Golfin and Lisa A. Curtin, CDR, USN, *Partnerships with Community Colleges: Vehicles to Benefit Navy Training and Recruiting* (Alexandra, VI: Center for Naval Analyses, 1998); Peggy A. Golfin, John D. White and Lisa A. Curtin, CDR, USN., A Role for Community Colleges in Navy Training (Alexandra, VI: Center for Naval Analyses, 1998); Hanser, Davidson and Stasz.

33   Hanser, Davidson and Stasz, 72.

34   Lieutenant-Colonel Lorne W. Bentley, *Professional Ideology and the Profession of Arms in Canada.* (Kingston, ON: Brown Book Company and the Strategic Institute of Strategic Studies, 2005), 38.

35   Canada, *Duty with Honour: The Profession of Arms in Canada* (Kingston, ON: Canadian Defence Academy – Canadian Forces Leadership Institute, 2003), 21.

36   *Duty with Honour*, 36.

37   Justin Wright, *Alternative Training Delivery and the Early Socialization of Non-Commissioned Members – CFLI Technical Memorandum 2008-01* (Kingston, ON: Canadian Forces Leadership Institute, 2008).

38   Phyllis Browne and Justin Wright, *Tradition and Change: The Socialization of Officer Cadets at the Royal Military College of Canada – Final Report on the Interview Protocol – CFLI Technical Memorandum 2007-03* (Kingston, ON: Canadian Forces Leadership Institute, 2007), 17-19.

39   David Bercuson, *Significant Incident: Canada's Army, the Airbourne, and the Murder in Somalia* (Toronto, ON: McClelland and Stewart, 1996).

40   Philip Zimbardo, *The Lucifer Effect: Understanding How Good People Turn Evil* (New York, NY: Random House, 2007).

41   Craig Haney, Curtis W. Banks and Philip Zimbardo, "Study of Prisoners and Guards in a Simulated Prison", *Naval Research Review*, Vol. 9 (1973), 1-17.

42   Department of National Defence, *Duty with Honour: The Profession of Arms in Canada.* (Kingston, ON: Canadian Defence Academy – Canadian Forces Leadership Institute, 2003), 33.

43   Wright, 9-10.

44   Charles Moskos, John Williams and David Segal, "Armed Forces after the Cold War", in Charles Moskos, John Williams and David Segal, eds., *The Post-Modern Military: Armed Forces After the Cold War* (New York, NY: Oxford University Press, 2000), 1-13.

45   Colonel Mike Capstick, Lieutenant-Colonel Kelly Farley, Lieutenant-Colonel Bill Wild (Retired) and Lieutenant-Commander Mike Parkes. *Canada's Soldiers: Military Ethos and Canadian Values in the 21st Century* (Ottawa, ON: Director General Land Capability Development, 2005).

CHAPTER 21

TECHNOLOGICAL CHANGE AND ITS IMPACT

Regan Reshke

**Innumerable confusions and a profound feeling of despair invariably
emerge in periods of great technological and cultural transitions.
Our "Age of Anxiety" is, in great part, the result of trying to do today's job
with yesterday's tools—with yesterday's concepts.**[1]

Advances in science and technology affect our lives in important and profound ways, influencing our choices in everything from food to smartphones to medicine.[2] Within modern societies and their militaries, technology is ubiquitous, and indeed both military and societal strength are built upon a foundation of science, technology and engineering. Unfortunately, despite its pervasiveness, there is a tendency today to view technology very narrowly; believing that it only pertains to computers, electronics, and the internet. In its broadest sense, however, technology is the process by which humans modify nature to meet their needs and desires. Thus, technology is more than just products and artifacts; it is also the knowledge and processes necessary to create and operate those products, such as engineering know-how and design, manufacturing expertise, and various technical skills.[3]

In fact, the use of technology in the execution of warfare is as old as human society itself. Certainly the intimate relationship between technology and warfare has been well documented throughout humanity's historical record. Moreover, there is ample empirical evidence to demonstrate the central role that innovative technologies play with regard to shaping the types of warfare that are even possible. Clearly, many types of modern warfare would be impossible without scientific, technological, and engineering innovations. A wide variety of examples are available, including: air warfare; submarine warfare; naval warfare; mechanized warfare; chemical warfare; biological warfare; space warfare; nuclear warfare; and cyber warfare.

As such, technological change is, and will continue to be, the most dynamic factor influencing the future security environment.[4] The synergistic forces of globalization and commercialization of science and technology are providing current and future adversaries with ready access to advanced technologies and also the knowledge needed to exploit them in disruptive ways. A multitude of rapidly evolving technologies exist, driven by the global commercial scientific, technical and engineering communities. Although several lists can be found which point to the high-impact technologies that are expected to advance swiftly in the coming years, virtually every list contains some permutation of information and communications technologies, biotechnologies, nanotechnologies, neuroscience and robotics. These domains promise to not only provide the foundational building blocks for solving humanity's greatest challenges,[5] but paradoxically, they enable the creation of militarily relevant capabilities, by both friendly forces and adversaries alike, with sufficient destructive potential to threaten the very survival of humankind.[6]

Overcoming the harmful aspects of Science and Technology (S&T) advances will not be an easy undertaking if for no other reason than the fact that technological systems tend to introduce a multitude of interdependencies such as those upon electricity, communication and data networks, and security systems. Consequently, societal complexity is amplified due to broad institutional commitments and obligations to guarantee the continuous operation of these systems – systems that have become *de facto* essential services within modern societies. And moreover, long-term loss of any one of these interdependent systems would undoubtedly lead to cascading failures throughout much of modern society's technological infrastructure. Acknowledging the inseparability of technology and society, it is logical to conclude that widespread technological infrastructure failures would be followed by societal stress and deterioration. It is contingent upon policy makers, therefore, to make the assurance of socio-technological resilience foremost amongst their priorities.

Shaping policies that will ensure societal resilience while leveraging the benefits of S&T developments will require a cooperative, collaborative, and global outlook. This remains a daunting challenge today because although human creativity, interests, values, and decisions ultimately determine the trajectory that S&T innovations take, there are no unifying regulations, strategies or policies that guide global S&T progress. And despite efforts by the constructive technology assessment community to anticipate effects or impacts of new technologies or new projects with a strong technological component, global S&T innovation and development is so widespread as to make this impractical for anything beyond localized regions. There are in fact a multitude of contrasting and heterogeneous factors that shape S&T trajectories on a global scale. Competing human and societal interests coupled with an ongoing global diffusion of S&T expertise and governance driven by substantial investment in broad S&T domains by both developed and emerging nations will conspire to make hegemonic control and influence of S&T policy and regulation practically impossible. Such is the nature of the complexity within our contemporary global system. Flexibility, adaptability, and resilience must therefore become the cornerstone characteristics of modern societies amongst the growing complexity, uncertainty, and pace of change of the 21st century.

In this regard, the well recognized economic benefits of S&T innovation coupled with the eternally present "security dilemma",[7] will continue to provide ample incentive for diverse societies to invest in ever more S&T development. So, while no single entity is in control of global S&T progress, and although humans do indeed exercise their right to choose specific S&T areas in which to invest, there is mounting evidence that the aggregation of these choices throughout humanity's complex global socio-technological system ultimately leads to exponential technological growth. One of the first to study and theorize about this apparent emergent property of modern global society is internationally acclaimed innovator and futurist, Ray Kurzweil. In a series of best selling books,[8] Kurzweil describes at great length a litany of S&T domains that have undergone exponential growth since their inception. He has also developed a general theory to explain exponential technological growth which he calls the law of accelerating returns.[9] More recently, Kurzweil has been appointed as the Chancellor of the Singularity University,[10] a revolutionary new interdisciplinary university whose mission is to assemble, educate and inspire a cadre of leaders who strive to understand and facilitate the development of exponentially advancing technologies, and apply, focus and guide these tools to address humanity's grand challenges. For the Canadian Forces, vital long-term strategic value would result from incorporating a similar, though suitably adapted curriculum within a defence and security context.

Given the acknowledged significant contribution that technological advances make towards enabling superior military capabilities, the defence community cannot ignore the importance and impact of technological change. Thus, within the CF's leadership and professional development programs, a focus on understanding and harnessing exponential technological change would represent a significant educational shift that would enable members of the CF to better leverage and adapt to the changes that will be wrought by accelerating technological change.

Without doubt, monitoring rapidly changing technological developments and anticipating their impact upon ongoing military capability development, training, and education requirements has become critical. Ignorance of the trends will undoubtedly lead to surprises and perhaps strategic shock, particularly given mounting evidence that an increasing number of (S&T) fields are experiencing exponential growth resulting in an increasing number of innovations maturing at unprecedented rates. Equally important is a requirement to actively shape technological advances for maximum benefit and effect while minimizing potential adverse consequences – objectives that can best be met within a defence community that is educated in technological assessment and strategic foresight.[11] Indeed, in a compelling presentation,[12] Dr. John Moravec demonstrates the importance of technological literacy within today's society and suggests that the accelerating change in modern society – resulting from exponentially improving technologies – has a direct impact on the half-life of knowledge. In other words, if the amount of information available doubles at an increasing rate,[13] then the half-life of knowledge is decreasing exponentially. It is no wonder that all major human resource departments are proponents of lifelong learning. Incorporating technology literacy and foresight into CF education programs is necessary to address the rising tide of data and information that surrounds us. The complex interaction of people and technology and their impact on society is becoming increasingly important in today's world.

Indeed, it is becoming increasingly apparent that those societies that choose to ignore technological exponential growth trends do so at their own peril. Human nature and the rapid growth in world population can be expected to inevitably lead to conflict due to competition for dwindling non-renewable resources, economic dislocation and natural disasters exacerbated by climate change. Conflict resolution under these circumstances will likely require military intervention; hence capabilities will need to be in place and operative. We can also anticipate a requirement for the continuous evolution of military capabilities given that friend and foe alike are perpetually seeking capability overmatch – because whoever stops developing, loses. In other words, the only losing strategy in such an evolutionary environment is choosing to not participate.[14] In a well-argued paper,[15] US Republican presidential candidate, Newt Gingrich, describes this situation rather bluntly – adapt or die.

As a result of the intertwined nature of socio-technological change, the shape that future societies assume due to their adaptation to emergent and continuous exponential technological growth trends remains the source of much speculation and uncertainty. Science fiction writers often paint alarmingly dystopian views of future technology-enabled societies. Interestingly, despite the often dark and dystopian warnings of much historical science fiction, modern societies seem to create and implement, with surprising consistency, the very technologies that they have been cautioned against. Few better examples exist than the modern surveillance societies that have emerged despite George Orwell's classic cautionary tale, *1984*. Today's technological developments, the result of converging exponential growth trends across broad S&T domains, undoubtedly surprise those unfamiliar with the trends. Indeed, much that has been achieved recently remained firmly within the realm of science fiction just a few short years ago. Whether societies will succeed in shaping their socio-technological futures in positive ways, thereby ensuring the long-term survival of the species while avoiding catastrophic collapse, remains an open and worrisome question.

In this regard, technological foresight and organizational speed will become increasingly important enablers of institutional resilience. Foresight techniques will be needed to help acquire an understanding of the nature and significance of possible events before they occur in order to mitigate potential risks to Canadian defence and security. This will require active scanning for new technologies and early signals of new usages of existing technologies. Experience tells us that robust and sustained strategic and technological forecasting is worth the effort.

After all, the ambiguity concerning the nature of future innovations and the pace of change will prove challenging for current capability development efforts because procurement speed is, more than ever, an important factor. But cost also matters. These two factors will need to be carefully balanced. In times of such rapid change the organization that emerges successfully will be the one most able to adapt to the change. Capability development efforts will need to focus on optimizing capabilities in some key emerging strategic technology areas. These may not centre on traditional military weapons, equipment or vehicles, though these, as well, will benefit from new technological advances.

The technological trends towards convergence, miniaturization, integration and digitization all suggest that threats will manifest themselves in smaller and smaller packages with more capability than before. A genetically engineered virus, for example, represents both an instrument of power and a threat that is available in a microscopic package. Sophisticated intelligent software agents roaming cyberspace are also anticipated. Already, the Stuxnet Computer Virus that attacked Iran's Bushehr Nuclear Plant[16] demonstrates the reality that adversaries can, and will, develop sophisticated tools aimed at crippling military and civilian infrastructures and networks. The projection of power, therefore, has become possible with the use of information and not just through the movement of military forces. Small, highly networked and collaborative entities will likely be capable of defeating larger and more powerful organizations.

History is replete with examples revealing that military technological superiority is a tenuous state. Challengers will always find a way to copy or adapt low-cost, mass-produced technology and employ new tactics that will offset any disadvantage in military capability. For example, Al-Qaeda has adopted readily available 21st century technology – the internet (for global collaboration); digital cameras (for information gathering); cell phones (for tactical communications); and, satellite television (for global information warfare) – to facilitate their global insurgency. Combined with largely unsophisticated improvised explosive devices, this insurgency has proven remarkably resilient in the face of far superior military capabilities.

Undisputedly, the world is in the midst of an unprecedented global technology revolution across the converging domains of nanotechnology and materials technology, biotechnology and genetics, information and communications technology, and neuroscience. The result of this convergence will be the emergence of novel capabilities that have heretofore existed only in human imagination. It is probable that these converging technologies will be aimed in two principal directions. First, they will be directed inward – at understanding and improving the human mind and body. Second, they will be focused on autonomous robotic technologies, or more generically, toward intelligent automation of the environment. These two emerging areas will see new capabilities surface and exponential growth take place in a range of adjacent disciplines that will bring about radical and unpredictable changes in all dimensions of life. Social, economic and military systems will be greatly affected. It is important to consider the trajectories that these converging disciplines may take.

Significant advances in these shrinking technologies will be driven largely by commercial demand on a global scale rather than military-specific investment. This implies the need for a strong technology warning community focused on understanding and anticipating technology trends. This should be coupled with a force founded upon principles of institutional agility and adaptability that is able to effect change in its technological foundation in a timely manner. Institutional flexibility, resiliency and relevance ultimately depends on striking the right balance between effectiveness and efficiency in national capability development.

Overcoming the challenges posed by technology will require deliberate efforts including institutional recognition of the importance and critical nature of smart acquisition practices. There should be a move away from the current approach to project management in favour of spiral development or planned technology insertion points where each development block is based on proven technology rather than anticipated technology. Current methods drive up costs, delay project delivery and compromise capability objectives.

To many, technology is a sign of progress. Others see the proliferation of 21st century technologies as a source of societal destabilization, depriving people of dignity and autonomy. The reality is that technology raises important questions about the balance between promise and peril – with the same knowledge and tools often capable of being readily adapted for either benevolent or malicious purposes. The shift of the sources of advanced technology from primarily military and government to commercial and public, due in part to the globalization of science and technology, is contributing to the exponentially accelerating pace of technological development, which in turn threatens this precarious balance. Confounding this situation is the often unexpected and non-linear nature of scientific and technological advance – making the degree and implications of technological convergence difficult to predict. These developments are often disruptive, provoking revolutionary changes in how humans adapt, manipulate, and control their environments. In this context the experience with and impact of the internet in the course of only ten years is both characteristic and informative.

It is likely, however, that as information technologies continue to undergo exponential performance growth and thorough integration across all aspects of society, warfare will gradually shift from the physical domain to the informational and moral. For example, imagine the damage adversaries could inflict by immobilizing critical components of civilian or military computer networks for extended periods using nothing more than focused computer network attacks. Within this context, crashing stock markets and global trade disruptions are as possible as the ability to disrupt advanced network-enabled weapons systems. When this shift will occur is not certain, however, an agile and adaptable force and force structure will facilitate the transition needed while mitigating the risks inherent in this transition period.

Preparing for future risks of radically disruptive adversarial capabilities brought about by exponential technological advance and convergence, must be balanced against the demands for ongoing support to current operations. Excessive focus on present problems risks a myopic treatment of evolving threats and ultimately contributes to conservative capability development and incremental change. In an era of exponential growth trends, incremental change is a clear path to irrelevance. The CF and its ongoing capability development must therefore be innovative. Prudent military capability development will continue to require coverage of a broad spectrum of technical capabilities and a technologically literate CF. This will be realized through a culture of innovation fostered by lifelong learning educational programs with appropriate technological emphasis.

However, institutional inertia and resource constraints will in all likelihood prevent the development of a full complement of CF capabilities that exceeds those of well-funded adversaries, intent on focusing only on a few niche areas. The CF must remain aware of technological trends across the spectrum, in particular those that are likely to lead to disruptions. The need for adaptability and agility will be paramount in this era of change; however, this environment of near continuous change will place great stress on the human resources of the CF – requiring careful consideration and management of the human dimension if indeed the potential for technological progress is to be realized.

---

1   Marshall McLuhan, Quentin Fiore and Jerome Agel. *The Medium is the Massage: An Inventory of Effects* (New York, NY: Bantam Books, 1967), 8-9.

2   Elizabeth Dowdeswell, "Council of Canadian Academies. President's Message", *Council E-News, June 2011, The Art of Science Communication*, retrieved on 15 January 2012 from <http://www.scienceadvice.ca/uploads/eng/council%20news/june2011.html>.

3   Committee on Technological Literacy, National Academy of Engineering, National Research Council, Greg Pearson and A. Thomas Young, eds, *Technically Speaking: Why All Americans Need to Know More About Technology* (Washington, DC: National Academy Press, 2002).

4   The use of mobile devices and social networking tools to accelerate the 2011 uprising in Egypt during the so-called Arab Spring illustrates this point. See: <http://www.fastcompany.com/1722492/how-social-media-accelerated-the-uprising-in-egypt>.

5   Although there are numerous domain specific grand challenges, the World Federation of UN Associations Millennium Project maintains a list of 15 global challenges for humanity. Retrieved on 25 April 2008 from <http://www.millennium-project.org/millennium/challeng.html>.

6   The Institute for Ethics and Emerging Technologies (see: <http://ieet.org/index.php/tpwiki/Existential_risks>) is one of many technology foresight groups that acknowledges the seemingly utopian promise and inseparable existential peril of rapidly advancing technologies.

7   Robert Jervis, "Was the Cold War a Security Dilemma?", *Journal of Cold War Studies*, Vol. 3, No. 1, (Winter 2001), 36-60, retrieved on 15 January 2012 from <http://www.ou.edu/uschina/SASD/SASD2006/Jervis2001CWSecDil.pdf>.

8   Ray Kurzweil's books include: Ray Kurzweil, *The Singularity is Near: When Humans Transcend Biology*, (New York, NY: Penguin Group, 2005); Ray Kurzweil and Terry Grossman, *Fantastic Voyage: Live Long Enough to Live Forever* (Emmaus, PE: Rodale Books, 2004); Ray Kurzweil, *The Age of Spiritual Machines: When Computers Exceed Human Intelligence* (New York, NY: Penguin Paperbacks, 2000); Ray Kurzweil and Terry Grossman, *Transcend: Nine Steps to Living Well Forever* (Emmaus, PE: Rodale Books, 2010); and, Ray Kurzweil, *The Age of Intelligent Machines* (Cambridge, MA: The MIT Press, 1992).

9   Ray Kurzweil, *The Singularity is Near: When Humans Transcend Biology* (New York, NY: Penguin Books, 2005), 7-14.

10   See: Singularity University, retrieved on 15 January 2012 from <http://singularityu.org/>.

11   Foresight Canada (see: <http://www.foresightcanada.ca/> retrieved on 15 January 2012) defines strategic foresight as an integrated, reflexive and conscious human capacity to see, think through and do what needs to be done NOW in light of the trajectory-altering implications of the signals of contextual change, while there is still time to act creatively and proactively – before hidden opportunities are lost and unseen threats have become crises.

12   John Moravec, *Toward Society 3.0: New Futures for Human Capital Development* (University of Minnesota, Presentation, 2008), 44.

13   Senior University of California at Berkeley researchers, Peter Lyman and Hal Varian measured the total production of all information channels in the world for two different years, 2000 and 2003. Their study estimated that the total production of new information in 2000 reached 1.5 exabytes, which they explain is about 37,000 times as much information as is contained in the entire holdings of the Library of Congress. In 2003, the estimated annual total of new information reached 3.5 exabytes. Lyman and Varian concluded that the amount of new information stored on paper, film, magnetic, and optical media had doubled in the three year period of the study. An executive summary of this study is available online: <http://www2.sims.berkeley.edu/research/projects/how-much-info-2003/execsum.htm>.

14   DSAB Report 1002/3, *Enhancement, Augmentation and Automation – Improved Human Effectiveness* (Ottawa, ON: Department of National Defence, 2011), 4, retrieved on 15 January 2012

from <http://cfd.mil.ca/documents/DSAB/DSAB%20Reports/DSAB_report_1002-03_Enhancement_Augmentation_and_Automation_Improved_Human_effectiveness_15Nov11-u.doc>.

15   Newt Gingrich and Ronald E. Weisbrook. "Adapt or Die", *Strategic Studies Quarterly*, Vol. 1, No. 2 (2007), 18-34.

16   Tabassum Zakaria, "First Came Stuxnet Computer Virus: Now there's Duqu", *Reuters*, retrieved on 15 January 2012 from <http://www.reuters.com/article/2011/10/18/us-usa-cyber-duqu-idUSTRE79H8CU20111018>.

CONTRIBUTORS

Wendy H. Appelbaum is working within the ADM (HR-Civ) organization (as part of DG Workforce Development) with a Special Assignment in the ADM (Mat) Group. She is currently responsible for managing a Learning Office within the Material Management Group supporting this group in exercising their Functional Authority over Material Acquisition and Support training. She received her Masters Degree in Educational Technology in 1995 and has been involved in the learning and development field for the past 15 years. She began her career in the private sector developing computer-based training, educational learning products and corporate e-learning solutions. She transitioned into the Government of Canada, specifically the Department of National Defence where she worked as a Learning and Development Consultant in delivering corporate HR solutions as well as Government Consulting Services where she provided consulting services in the area of learning policy and evaluation.

Dr. Bill Bentley is a retired Lieutenant-Colonel who served over 30 years in the Canadian infantry. During his career Dr. Bentley had extensive experience with both the United Nations and NATO. He served as a Professor of Military Science at the US Army Command and Staff College and a three year secondment with the Department of Foreign Affairs. Dr. Bentley has been with the CF Leadership Institute since its creation in 2001. He received the DM/CDS Innovation Award for writing *Duty With Honour: The Profession of Arms in Canada* and the Meritorious Service Medal for his contribution to the reform of the CF Professional Development System.

Major Frédéric Brulier is the Canadian Defence Academy Staff Officer for Officer Professional Development for Major, Lieutenant-Colonel, Colonel and General/Flag Officers. He is the policy development coordinator for Officer Developmental Periods 3 to 5. Major Brulier joined the CF in 1983 as an Air Weapons Controller 22nd NORAD Region, North Bay, ON. In 1988 he was transferred to the Region Software Support Facility (now SSF) Tyndall AFB, Florida. In 1992 He was transferred to the 12 Rdr Sqn Bagotville Quebec, as a Tactical Fighter Controller in charge of TPS-70 Mobile Rdr Deployments and Standards. In 1995 and 1996 he was deployed to NATO Ops in Italy in support of Deny Flight and Joint Guardian Ops in the Balkans. In 1996 he was transferred to Fighter Group Headquarters Plans Office. That same year he was appointed EA to Fighter Group Commander. In 1999, was assigned to the

CONTRIBUTORS

NAEWF Geillenkirchen Germany as a Passive Detection Controller on NATO E3A AWACS. During his tour in Germany Major Brulier flew in support of NATO Ops in the Balkans and in the US after 9/11 Ops Eagle Assist. In 2004 he was assigned to the NSSF/SFF as the Deputy Director and was responsible for the operations of the SSF.

Dr. Howard G. Coombs retired from active duty with the Canadian Forces in 2003. He is a graduate of the Canadian Forces Staff School, Canadian Land Force Command and Staff College, United States Army Command and General Staff College, and the US Army School of Advanced Military Studies, which awarded his Masters degree. Dr. Coombs received his PhD in military history from Queen's University in Kingston, Ontario and is currently an Assistant Professor of the Department of Defence Studies, Royal Military College of Canada. He is also a part-time reserve officer affiliated with 33 Canadian Brigade Group, head quartered in Ottawa. His latest book is *The Report of the Officer Development Board: Maj-Gen Roger Rowley and Education for Canada's Officer Corps*, co-edited with Dr. Randy Wakelam, and published by Wilfrid Laurier University Press. Dr. Coombs was deployed with Joint Task Force Afghanistan from September 2010 to July 2011 as a civilian advisor to the Task Force Commander.

Karen D. Davis, CD, is a defence scientist currently assigned to the Canadian Forces Leadership Institute. She holds a Master of Arts in Sociology from McGill University and is a PhD candidate at the Royal Military College of Canada. She has conducted research on a range of military topics related to gender, leadership, and cultural diversity. Her most recent publications include contributing writer and the editor of *Women and Leadership in the Canadian Forces: Perspectives and Experience* (2007), *Cultural Intelligence and Leadership: An Introduction for Canadian Forces Leaders* (2009); and contributing writer and co-editor of *Transforming Traditions: Women, Leadership & the Canadian Navy, 1942-2010* (2010).

Dr. Beverlie Dietze has an educational background in early childhood education, adult education and theory and policy in higher education. She has held faculty and administrative positions in the Ontario College system, including Director of Teaching and Learning and has been a facilitator of adult education courses with Brock University before accepting a position with Mount Saint Vincent University. Her latest book, *Playing and Learning in Early Childhood Education* has just been released with Pearson Canada.

Lieutenant-Colonel Dennis G. Hartnett joined the Regular Force in 1974 and was commissioned as an officer in the Artillery in 1976 following completion of an Arts degree from Queen's University. He has served in a variety of appointments in airborne, light and mechanized artillery units in Second and Third Regiments Royal Canadian Horse Artillery in Petawawa, Ontario and Shilo, Manitoba respectively. He has served in staff positions in the 4th Canadian Mechanized Brigade Group Headquarters in Lahr, Germany, 1st Canadian Division Headquarters in Kingston and Land Force Command Headquarters in St-Hubert, Quebec. He also served as the Firepower Section Head in the Directorate of Army Doctrine and as a member of the directing staff and later deputy commandant of the Canadian Land Force Command and Staff College. Lieutenant-Colonel Hartnett is currently employed as the Senior Staff Officer Professional Development at the Canadian Defence Academy in Kingston.

Colonel Bernd Horn, OMM, MSM, CD, PhD, is an experienced infantry officer who has commanded at the unit and sub-unit level. He has filled key command appointments such as the Deputy Commander Canadian Special Operations Forces Command, Commanding Officer of the 1st Battalion, The Royal Canadian Regiment and Officer Commanding 3 Commando, the Canadian Airborne Regiment. Dr. Horn has a PhD from the Royal Military College of Canada where he is also an Adjunct Professor of History. He has authored, co-authored, edited and co-edited in 32 books and over 100 chapters and articles on military history and military affairs.

Dr. Molly McCarthy-Senebald is a Training and Education Specialist with more than thirty years experience in adult education and leadership development. She holds a Masters in Adult Education from St. Francis Xavier University and a Doctorate in Educational Technology from the University of Calgary. Recently retired from the Canadian Forces, she has held various leadership positions including that of Commandant of the CF Training Development Centre, Chief Standards for the Canadian Defence Academy, CF Support Training Group, the CF Experimentation Centre and two naval schools. She has also been employed as a senior policy officer for training and education at National Defence Headquarters and the Canadian Defence Academy. In 2009, she served with the Joint Task Force Headquarters in Kandahar as Officer in Charge of Lessons Learned. She is currently engaged delivering Defence Educator Programs with the NATO Partnership for Peace Consortium, and undertakes independent and sponsored research projects.

CONTRIBUTORS

Danielle McMullen-Dubé was the former Team Leader, Performance Measurement and Learning Support in the Assistant Deputy Minister Human Resources Civilian – ADM (HR Civ) Branch of the Department of National Defence and is currently a manager at the Public Service Commission. She completed her Master of Distance Education at Athabasca University. She began her career as a classroom teacher and has spent the majority of her time in the Public Service dedicated to working in the Learning and Professional Development field.

Dr. Richard (Rick) D. Monaghan is the Senior Staff Officer for CF Language Programs Planning and Policy at the Canadian Defence Academy Headquarters in Kingston, Ontario. He has been a member of the Defence Team since 2003. Dr. Monaghan is a professional educator who has taught college and university courses in language and linguistics for thirty years, has managed large scale assessment projects for the Ministry of Education in Québec, chaired a college faculty, served on the Board of Governors and Executive Committee of Dawson College in Montréal, and on boards of companies engaged in educational development. He holds a Masters degree in Language and Literature from Simon Fraser University and a doctorate from the Université de Montréal, and has been a Canada Council Fellow. He has taught in Québec, British Columbia, Ontario, and in England, and has extensive experience in language assessment and instructional technology. Dr. Monaghan is currently Chair of the Bureau for International Language Co-ordination (BILC), NATO's advisory body on language issues, appended to Joint Force Trainer at SACT HQ.

Lieutenant-Commander (Retired) Randy Purse served as a MARS Officer for 18 years serving in a variety of positions aboard ship as well as in a US Navy Exchange position, a UN military observer position and several operational and personnel staff positions. After his transfer to the Training Development Branch, he served as a Training Advisor within the CF Naval Operations School and then assumed the position of Senior Instructor for the Training Development Officer Basic Qualification Course at the Canadian Forces Training Development Centre. He finished off his military career at the Canadian Defence Academy in Kingston, first as the Staff Officer IT&E Modernization and then as the Special Assistant to the Commander CDA. During his career he completed both his undergraduate degree and a Masters of Education (Information Technology) and is in the process of pursuing his PhD. He has continued his career of service as a civilian at the Communications Security Establishment Canada (CSEC) where he is the

Learning Advisor for Information Technology Security, serves as a key advisor on strategic learning and development issues and represents CSEC at the Government of Canada Heads of Learning forum.

Regan Reshke enrolled in the Canadian Forces in June 1980 and graduated in 1985 from the Royal Military College (RMC) of Kingston with a Bachelor of Engineering Degree in Civil Engineering. Following a 21-year career as a Military Construction Engineer and Military Mapper, during which he completed an Undergraduate Degree in Civil Engineering, a Graduate Diploma in Mapping, Charting and Geodesy, and a Masters Degree in Structural Engineering, he joined Defence Research and Development Canada in April of 2002 where he is currently Director Science & Technology Land 7, serving as Scientific Advisor to Director Land Concepts and Designs in Kingston. In this capacity he researches and advises on science and technology (S&T) trends and their implications for Army Capability Development initiatives. Additionally, he provides a liaison function between the Army's Capability Development staffs and the Science and Technology community – seeking to inform Capability Developers on what the S&T community can provide, and in turn advising the S&T community on what the Capability Developers require.

Major Mark Russell joined the Canadian Forces in May 1983 as a Training Development Officer. He is currently the Staff Officer responsible for Alternative Training Delivery and manages the Canadian Forces College Opportunities Program within the Canadian Defence Academy. Major Russell completed his undergraduate studies at the University of Manitoba and this included a Technical/Vocational Training diploma earned through Red River College. Major Russell completed his Masters in Education at the University of Toronto in 2001. In 2003 he was deployed as the Deputy Commanding Officer for Task Force Freetown in Sierra Leone, West Africa.

Natacha Saintonge is the Manager, Learning Strategies and Policies in the Assistant Deputy Minister Human Resources Civilian – ADM (HR Civ) Branch of the Department of National Defence. She received her Masters of Education at Ottawa University. Most of her career has been spent in a Human Resources policy analyst role with a particular focus on Official Languages policies, and Learning and Professional Development policies.

CONTRIBUTORS

Dr. Grazia Scoppio is an Associate Professor at the Canadian Forces Leadership Institute, a Department of the Canadian Defence Academy. She is cross-appointed at the Royal Military College where she has been teaching various courses including an on-line course – Leading and Working in a Diverse Environment. She holds a PhD from the Ontario Institute for Studies in Education of the University of Toronto (OISE/UT). Her multi-disciplinary research interests include: diversity in organizations, multiculturalism, migration, comparative education, and program evaluation. She has co-authored several technical reports on education and training in the Canadian Forces. She has published in the *Canadian Military Journal, UNESCO-UNEVOC International Handbook of Technical and Vocational Education and Training*, the *International Journal of Diversity in Organizations, Communities and Nations, Connections, Quarterly Journal of the Partnership for Peace Consortium, Current Issues in Comparative Education (CICE),* Columbia University, and *Refuge,* Centre for Refugee Studies, York University, Toronto. She has presented at several national and international conferences. She has served for over ten years in various roles on the Executive Committee of the Comparative and International Education Society of Canada.

Dr. Norm D. Vaughan is an educator and researcher with interests in blended learning, faculty development and K to 12 schooling, Dr. Norm Vaughan is an Associate Professor in the Department of Education, Faculty of Teaching and Learning at Mount Royal University in Calgary, Alberta. He recently co-authored the book *Blended Learning in Higher Education* (Jossey-Bass, 2008) and has published a series of articles on blended learning and faculty development. Norm is the Co-founder of the Blended Online Design Network (BOLD), a member of the Community of Inquiry Research Group, the Associate Editor of the *International Journal of Mobile and Blended Learning* and he is on the Editorial Boards of the *International Journal of Excellence in e-Learning, Canadian Journal of Learning and Technology,* the *Journal of Distance Education,* the *Journal on Centres for Teaching & Learning, Learning Communities Journal,* and the *Journal of Information Fluency.*

Dr. Randall Wakelam has a PhD from Wilfrid Laurier and teaches history and leadership at the Royal Military College of Canada. Previously, Colonel (retired) Wakelam had an extensive military career which began in 1969 as a Reserve musician in Ottawa. After graduating from the Royal Military College in 1975 he flew helicopters for the Army, serving in three different squadrons before commanding 408 Squadron in Edmonton from 1991 to 1993. Subsequently he was a member of faculty at the Canadian Forces College in Toronto, the military's professional graduate school, and a senior administrator at the Canadian Defence Academy in Kingston, the military's "ministry of education". Dr. Wakelam is a faculty associate at the Laurier Centre for Military Strategic and Disarmament Studies and serves on a number of editorial boards. In 2009 he published *The Science of Bombing: Operational Research in RAF Bomber Command* and in 2010 co-edited *The Report of the Officer Development Board: Maj-Gen Roger Rowley and the Education of the Canadian Forces. Cold War Fighters,* which deals with fighter aircraft procurement in Canada in the decade before the AVRO Arrow saga, was published in 2011. He is currently preparing a biography of Wilfred Curtis who was Canada's Chief of the Air Staff from 1947 to 1953 before going on to help establish York University. After living in all regions of Canada, Dr. Wakelam and his family have been in Kingston since 2002.

GLOSSARY

3D+C	Defence, Diplomacy, Development and Commerce
4GW	Fourth Generation Warfare
9/11	Terrorist attack on the Twin Towers of the World Trade Center on 11 September 2001
ACA	Air Command Academy
ADM (HR-Civ)	Assistant Deputy Minister, Human Resources
AFC	Armed Forces Council
ALOY	Aboriginal Opportunity Year
ALP	Advanced Leadership Program
AMOR	Annual Military Occupation Review
AMSC	Advanced Military Studies Course
AMSP	Advanced Military Studies Program
ATD	Alternate Training Delivery
BILC	Bureau for International Language Coordination
BMOQ	Basic Military Officer Qualification
BMQ	Basic Military Qualification
BTL	Basic Training List
BU	Bilingual Unit
CAS	Chief of the Air Staff
CAS	Complex Adaptive Systems
CASC	Canadian Army Staff College
CAT 4	CDS Action Team 4
CBM	Competency-Based Management
CBRN	Chemical, Biological, Radiological and Nuclear
CDA	Canadian Defence Academy
CDEC	Canadian Defence Education Centre
CDS	Chief of the Defence Staff
CF	Canadian Forces
CFC	Canadian Forces College
CFDS	*Canada First* Defence Strategy
CFFS (E)	Canadian Forces Fleet School Esquimalt
CFITES	Canadian Forces Individual Training and Education System

GLOSSARY

CFLI	Canadian Forces Leadership Institute
CFLRS	Canadian Forces Leadership and Recruit School
CFLS	Canadian Forces Language School
CFNA	Canadian Forces Northern Area
CFNOS	Canadian Forces Naval Operations School
CFPDS	Canadian Forces Professional Development System
CLFCSC	Canadian Land Force Command and Staff College
CLS	Chief of the Land Staff
CMP	Chief of Military Personnel
CMRSJ	Collège militaire royal de St-Jean
CMS	Chief of the Maritime Staff
COE	Contemporary Operating Environment
Comd	Commander
COS	Chief of Staff
CPPR	Civilian Performance Planning and Review
CQ	Cultural Intelligence
CRB	Curriculum Review Board
CRS	Chief Review Services
CSC	Command and Staff Course
CSM	Company Sergeant-Major
CSPS	Canada School of Public Service
CWO	Chief Warrant Officer
DAOD	Defence Administrative Order and Directive
DDC	Defence Diversity Council
DDSM	Directorate of Defence Strategic Management
DDWB	Director of Diversity and Well-Being
DGIFD	Canadian Forces Integrated Force Development
DGMC	Director General Military Careers
DGMP	Director General Military Personnel
DGMPR	Director General Military Personnel Requirements
DGRET	Director General Recruiting, Education and Training
DHRD	Directorate of Human Rights and Diversity
DL	Distance Learning
DL	Distributed Learning
DLC	Defence Leadership Curriculum
DM	Deputy Minister
DMilC	Director Military Careers

DMTCP	Director of the Military Training Cooperation Program
DND	Department of National Defence
DOL	Director Official Languages
DP	Developmental Period
DPR	Departmental Performance Report
DS	Directing Staff
DTA	Designated Training Authority
EC	Environmental Command
EDP	Executive Development Program
EE	Employment Equity
EEA	*Employment Equity Act*
ELP	Executive Leaders' Program
ER	Education Reimbursement
EU	English-speaking Units
EX	Executive
FA	Functional Authority
FAA	*Financial Administration Act*
FL	Foreign Language
FOL	First Official Language
FU	French-speaking Units
GO/Col	General Officer/Colonel
GO/FO	General Officer/Flag Officer
GS	General Specification
GSoWC	General System of War and Conflict
HQ	Headquarters
HR	Human Resource
HRST	Human Resources System Transformation
IED	Improvised Explosive Device
ILP	Intermediate Leadership Program
ISAF	International Security Assistance Force
ISD	Instructional Systems Design
IST	Initial Skills Training
IT&E	Individual Training and Education

GLOSSARY

JCSP	Joint Command and Staff Program
JCSP DL	Joint Command and Staff Program Distance Learning
JCSP RESID	Joint Command and Staff Program Residential
JIMP	Joint, inter-agency, multi-national, and public
KLC	Key Leadership Competencies
KMS	Knowledge Management System
KSA	Knowledge, Skills and Attributes
LCCN	Learning and Career Centre Network
LDF	Leader Development Framework
LFC St-Jean	L'École des langues de Forces canadiennes de St-Jean
LFDTS	Land Forces Doctrine and Training System
LMS	Learning Management System
LPD	Language Program Delivery
LPD	Learning and Professional Development
LPP	Language Planning and Policy
MAF	Management Accountability Framework
MDS	Master's of Defence Studies
MES	Military Employment Structure
MIT	Massachusetts Institute of Technology
MND	Minister of National Defence
MPRR	Member's Personnel Record Resume
MRI	Magnetic resonance imaging
MRRS	Management, Resources and Results Structures
MSLTP	Military Second Language Training Program
NASA	National Aeronautics and Space Administration
NATO	North Atlantic Treaty Organization
NCM	Non-Commissioned Member
NCMPDC	Non-Commissioned Member Professional Development Centre
NCMGS	Non-Commissioned Member General Specifications
NCMPDS	Non-Commissioned Member Professional Development System
NCO	Non-Commissioned Officer
NCR	National Capital Region
NDC	National Defence College
NDHQ	National Defence Headquarters
NGO	Non-Governmental Organization

NORAD	North American Aerospace Defence Command
NSP	National Security Program
NSSC	National Security Studies Course
NSSP	National Strategic Studies Program
OAG	Office of the Auditor
OECD	Organization for Economic Co-operation and Development
OGD	Other Government Department
OGS	Officer General Specifications
OJT	On the Job Training
OL	Official Language
OLA	*Official Languages Act*
OLPTM	Official Languages Program Transformation Model
OPDS	Officer Professional Development System
OPI	Officer of Primary Interest
OPME	Officer Professional Military Education Program
OPP	Operational Planning Process
PAA	Program Activity Architecture
PBK	Professional Body of Knowledge
PD	Professional Development
PDC	Professional Development Council
PDF	Professional Development Framework
PDS	Professional Development System
PER	Personnel Evaluation Report
PL	Proficiency Levels
PLP	Personal Learning Plan
PLQ	Primary Leadership Qualification
PME	Professional Military Education
PMF	Performance Management Framework
PO2/Sgt	Petty Officer Second Class/Sergeant
PSC	Public Service Commission
PSE	Public Service Evaluation
QS	Qualification Standard
RCAF	Royal Canadian Air Force
RCN	Royal Canadian Navy
RD	Root Definition

GLOSSARY

RMCC	Royal Military College of Canada
ROE	Return on Expectation
ROI	Return on Investment
RPP	Report on Plans and Priorities
RT	Required Training
S&T	Science and Technology
SAP	Senior Appointments Program
SHARP	Standard for Harassment and Racism Prevention
SLE	Second Language Education
SLP	Senior Leadership Program
SLT	Second Language Training
SME	Subject Matter Expert
SOLET	Second Official Language Education and Training
SOPs	Standing Operating Procedures
SPECT/PET	Single Proton/Positron emission computed tomography
SSM	Soft Systems Methodology
SSPC	Senior Officer Second Language Selection Planning Committee
STEP	Strategic Training and Education Programs
SWE	Salary Wage Envelope
T&E	Training and Education
TAD	Tutorat-à-distance
TB	Treasury Board
TBS	Treasury Board Secretariat
TEs	Training Establishment
TEL	Technology Enabled Learning
TP	Training Plan
TPWB	Training Plan Writing Board
TRADOC	Training and Doctrine Command
UN	United Nations
US	United States
VCDS	Vice Chief of the Defence Staff

INDEX

INDEX

INDEX

INDEX